# Understanding Second Language Acquisition

Published in this series

# Understanding Second Language Acquisition

*Second Edition*

ROD ELLIS

OXFORD
UNIVERSITY PRESS

## OXFORD
UNIVERSITY PRESS

Great Clarendon Street, Oxford, OX2 6DP, United Kingdom

Oxford University Press is a department of the University of Oxford.
It furthers the University's objective of excellence in research, scholarship,
and education by publishing worldwide. Oxford is a registered trade
mark of Oxford University Press in the UK and in certain other countries

First published in 2015
2019 2018 2017
10 9 8 7 6 5 4 3

ISBN: 978 0 19 442204 8

Printed in Great Britain by Ashford Colour Press Ltd, Gosport, Hampshire

This book is printed on paper from certified and well-managed sources

ACKNOWLEDGEMENTS

*The authors and publisher are grateful to those who have given permission to reproduce
the following extracts and adaptations of copyright material*: p.98 Figure from "On
the Variability of Interlanguage Systems" by Elaine Tarone, *Applied Linguistics*,
Vol. 4 (2), 1983. Reproduced by permission of Oxford University Press. p.107
Figure adapted from "A Dynamic Look at L2 Phonological Learning: Seeking
Processing Explanations for Implicational Phenomena" by Pavel Trofimovich,
Elizabeth Gatbonton and Norman Segalowitz, *Studies in Second Language
Acquisition*, Indiana University Linguistics Club. Reproduced by permission
of Cambridge University Press. p.122 Table from *The Study of Second Language
Acquisition* by Rod Ellis (Oxford University Press, 2008), adapted from *The Sounds
of English and Spanish* by Robert P Stockwell and J Donald Bowen (University
of Chicago Press, 1965). Reproduced by permission of Oxford University
Press and University of Chicago Press. p.125 Extract from "Markedness and
the Contrastive Analysis Hypothesis" by Fred R. Eckman, *Language Learning*,
Vol. 27 (2), 1977. © 1977 Language Learning Research Club, University
of Michigan. Reproduced by permission of John Wiley and Sons. p.187
Table from *Input Processing and Grammar Instruction* by Bill VanPatten (Ablex
Publishing Company, 1996). Reproduced by permission. p.242 Table from
*Investigations in Instructed Second Language Acquisition* by Alex Housen and Michel
Pierrard, (De Gruyter, 2004). Reproduced by permission of De Gruyter.

Although every effort has been made to trace and contact copyright holders
before publication, this has not been possible in some cases. We apologize for
any apparent infringement of copyright and if notified, the publisher will be
pleased to rectify any errors or omissions at the earliest opportunity.

*To my children – Lwindi, Emma, Anne, and James – for their forbearance*

# Contents

ground for theories of grammar. My decision was based partly on what I considered to be of relevance to the primary readers of this book—language teachers or students training to become teachers—and partly on my own conviction that purely linguistic theories, especially those that assume a separate language faculty, cannot provide an adequate account of how second languages are learned. SLA, of course, does have a role to play in linguistics, but that would need a very different kind of book to this one.

Two entirely new chapters (Chapters 8 and 9) address respectively the cognitive and social aspects of second language acquisition, two of the more recent major developments in SLA. They outline the key theoretical constructs and discuss different theoretical positions, replacing the chapter in the 1985 edition called 'Theories of Second Language Acquisition'. Increasingly, researchers have turned to research in cognitive psychology to explain the mechanisms responsible for processing input and output and the role these play in learners' developing second-language systems. More recently, however, some researchers have challenged the view that acquisition is just a cognitive phenomenon and argued that it is just as much, if not more so, social in nature. Social theories view second language learning as inextricably connected with learners' social identities and the social communities they belong to. They also see acquisition as taking place not in the learner's mind but within the social interactions in which they participate.

In the first edition, I included a single chapter on **form-focused instruction**. In this book, there are two separate chapters addressing instruction and second language acquisition. Chapter 10 examines different types of **explicit instruction** (i.e. instruction directed at **intentional learning** of specific linguistic features). Chapter 11 considers **implicit instruction** (i.e. instruction catering to the incidental acquisition of specific linguistic forms). In both cases, I consider these two types of instruction and the research that has investigated them in relation to theoretical positions introduced in earlier chapters.

Much of the earlier research focused on the acquisition of grammar. This led to the criticism that SLA was overly narrow in scope as it paid scant **attention** to phonology and vocabulary and ignored almost completely the acquisition of macro-aspects of language such as pragmatic features and interactional routines. I have tried to address this imbalance in the new book by including reference to research on all the micro-aspects of language and also on some of the macro-aspects. However, the book continues to reflect the continuing importance of grammar in SLA.

The intended readers of this book are the same as those of the first edition: undergraduate students taking an initial course in SLA who want more than a bare-bones account of the field; graduate students enrolled in applied linguistics or language teaching programmes; and teachers who want to improve their understanding of how second languages are learned both in naturalistic and instructed contexts.

their first language, followed a similar order and sequence when learning the grammar of a second language. This led Corder (1967) to propose that 'at least some of the strategies adopted by the learner of a second language are substantially the same as those by which a first language is acquired' (p. 164). Corder suggested that second language learners, like first language learners have a 'built-in syllabus' that directs when the grammar of a second language is acquired. Selinker (1972) subsequently gave the name that has become the standard term for referring to the mental grammar that a learner constructs and reconstructs—**interlanguage**.

The analogy with first language acquisition, however, only worked so far. There was one obvious difference. All normal children are successful in acquiring their mother tongue. There may be differences in the rate of acquisition and also in children's ability to make use of their first language, but they all succeed in acquiring the grammar of their first language. In contrast, most L2 learners do not achieve full grammatical competence. Selinker (1972) coined the term **fossilization** to refer to the fact that learners stop learning even though their interlanguage does not fully conform to the target language system. However, as we will see later, the extent to which fossilization actually occurs is controversial.

The research investigating the order and sequence of L2 acquisition can be thought of as the starting point for SLA. Numerous studies appeared in the 1960s and 1970s and continue up to today although they are no longer as common as they once were. Whereas the early work was essentially descriptive in nature—i.e. it involved collecting and analysing samples of learner language—later work has been more theoretically driven, aimed at investigating specific hypotheses regarding why one grammatical feature is acquired earlier than another (see, for example, Pienemann 1998).

More recently, however, the existence of a fixed order and sequence of acquisition has been challenged by some researchers (for example, Tarone and Liu 1995), who claim that what learners acquire and the order they acquire it in depends not on their so-called built-in syllabus, but on the **social context** in which they are learning the second language. This is a point I will return to later in this chapter.

The early influence of L1 acquisition research in SLA is also evident in the attention that L2 researchers paid to **formulaic sequences**. A formulaic sequence is a ready-made chunk of language that is accessed as a whole rather than generated by combining its individual elements. We will see later that formulaic sequences are not just important for language use, but also play a role in language acquisition. Learners gradually identify the type of elements that comprise a sequence. For example, they discover that words like 'book', 'pencil', and 'ruler' can all be used to complete the 'Can I have a ___?' chunk and thus come to recognize that these words all belong to the same grammatical category.

The research that has investigated the order and sequence of acquisition and formulaic sequences is considered in Chapter 4.

## Variability in learner language

At any stage of development, learners will manifest variability in their use of the second language. Sometimes they will make errors and at other times they will use the target language form. In part, this can be explained by the fact that learners will sometimes draw on well-formed formulaic chunks (for example, 'I don't like') and at other times construct utterances on the basis of their current interlanguage rules (for example, 'I no like'). Variability also occurs because learners do not abandon old forms when they acquire new ones. For example, learners initially produce questions without inversion:

Where the book is?

and then later begin to use subject-verb inversion:

Where is the book?

However, learners do not instantly switch from the earlier to the later construction. Rather, they alternate between the two **constructions** and only gradually abandon the non-target form.

Researchers such as Tarone (1983) and R. Ellis (1985) sought explanations for this variability. Tarone claimed that, by and large, variability is systematic. She argued that learners are responsive to the situational context and make use of their linguistic resources accordingly. In situations where they do not need to attend carefully to their choice of L2 forms, they employ a **vernacular style** (i.e. the style of speech associated with every-day, informal use of language) while in those contexts that call for close attention to speech, they make use of their **careful style** (i.e. the style of speech associated with formal situations). In particular, learners are responsive to their addressee. For example, a learner might say 'Where the book is?' when addressing another learner of equal status but say 'Where is the book?' when directing the question at a teacher. Another source of systematic variability is the linguistic context. For example, learners might use the target language third-person *-s* form when the verb follows a pronoun (for example, 'She lives in London') but use the uninflected interlanguage form when the verb follows a noun (for example, 'My mother live in London').

R. Ellis (1985) argued that not all variability is systematic in the way Tarone (1983) described. He proposed that when a new linguistic form first enters the learner's interlanguage, it is likely to be used interchangeably with an old form: in other words, for a while learners alternate freely between 'Where…is?' and 'Where is…?' Later on, however, they seek to use their linguistic resources systematically in accordance with the social context.

The importance of variability in understanding L2 acquisition is reflected in Widdowson's (1979) comment: '…change is only the temporal consequence of current variation' (p. 196). This is evident in a number of ways. **Free variation** gives way to **systematic variation**. Forms that are initially only part of the learner's careful style, over time, enter the vernacular style. Forms that figure initially only in easy linguistic contexts will gradually become available for use in more difficult linguistic contexts. The study of variability in learner language has continued over the years, drawing on increasingly sophisticated sociolinguistic models (for example, Preston 1996) and theories that emphasize the dynamic nature of second language systems (for example, de Bot, Lowie, and Verspoor 2007).

Variability in learner language is examined in Chapter 5.

## Rethinking the role of the first language

For a long time, there was a general assumption that the difficulties facing the L2 learner were largely due to 'interference' from the first language. It was thought that learning a second language involved overcoming the effects of negative **language transfer**. Where the L1 and the L2 were similar, **positive transfer** assisted learning, but where the two languages differed there would be **negative transfer** and learning would be impeded. This was a view reinforced by proposals for language teaching at this time, which encouraged teachers to focus on the areas of difficulty created by negative transfer through intensive drilling to ensure correct L2 'habits'. This view of L2 learning and teaching was challenged by the research showing that learners follow a similar order and sequence of acquisition irrespective of their first language.

The initial response was to downplay the effect of the first language. Some researchers (for example, Burt 1975) argued that negative transfer played a relatively minor role in L2 acquisition, accounting for only five per cent of the errors that learners made. However, other researchers continued to acknowledge that it played a significant role. Selinker (1972) saw it as one of the five 'central processes' in interlanguage development. Language transfer began to be seen as just one of several factors that contributed to L2 acquisition, rather than as the single, all-important factor.

The research that followed was directed at identifying the conditions that governed when transfer occurred and when it did not. As Kellerman (1983) put it 'now you see it, now you don't'. Kellerman proposed a number of factors that could explain when transfer was likely to manifest itself. One of these was **language distance**: learners whose first language was very similar to the second language—for example, Dutch learners of English—were more likely to draw on their L1 than learners whose language was very different—for example, Chinese learners of English. But language distance was not the only factor. Learners also had an inbuilt capacity to assess which features were likely to be transferable. Researchers also recognized that first language transfer did not just manifest itself in learner errors but exerted its influence in other ways—for example, in **avoidance** of structures that differed from the first language. Other researchers (for example, Ringbom 1987) emphasized the role of positive transfer, especially in the acquisition of vocabulary.

Researchers have continued to show a strong interest in language transfer right up to today. The focus of this research has broadened, however. It is not focused so exclusively on pronunciation, vocabulary, and grammar but also addresses how the first language influences the expression of politeness, discourse conventions, and even gesture. There is now wide acceptance that the L1 plays a significant role in L2 acquisition, but that to understand this role it is necessary to examine how language transfer functions as a cognitive process alongside other cognitive processes. The study of language transfer has also broadened its scope to consider **conceptual transfer** (i.e. how the concepts associated with one language affect the linguistic choices made in another language). Language transfer is examined in detail in Chapter 6 and again in Chapter 8.

## Input and interaction

The recognition that second language learners manifest a definite developmental route—as shown by the existence of order and sequences of L2 acquisition—together with the rejection of L1 **interference** as the sole factor influencing L2 acquisition led researchers to look for an alternative explanation of L2 acquisition. One possibility they examined was the role of input and interaction. The term 'input' refers to the samples of the oral or written language a learner is exposed to. This constitutes the 'data' that learners have to work with to construct their interlanguage. The term 'interaction' refers to the oral exchanges a learner participates in—with native speakers or with other learners—which provide both 'input' and opportunities for 'output' (i.e. use of the L2 in production).

Early research on input focused on **foreigner talk**. This is the special register that native speakers adopt when talking to non-native speakers. It is characterized by a number of 'modifications' to the normal talk that native speakers use when communicating with each other—i.e. when native speakers address learners they typically speak more slowly; pause more; use simpler high-frequency vocabulary; use full forms rather than contractions (for example, 'She is coming' rather than 'She's coming'); move topics to the front of a sentence (for example, 'John, I like him'); and avoid complex subordinate constructions. Researchers like Hatch (1983) suggested that such modifications might help to make grammatical features more salient and thus help learning. Krashen (1985) argued that input modifications make input 'comprehensible' for learners and, more controversially, that **comprehensible input** is all that was needed to activate the learner's built-in syllabus.

One possibility that researchers considered was whether the frequency of different forms in the input learners were exposed to matched the order of acquisition. However, the results were somewhat disappointing as the correlation was not a close one. Nevertheless, input frequency has continued to be viewed as one of the main factors that determine acquisition. N. Ellis (2002), for example, claimed that it was 'an all-pervasive causal factor' (p. 179) although he also acknowledged that 'there are many other determinants of acquisition' (p. 178). In fact, 'frequency' is not a straightforward concept. For a start, it is necessary to distinguish **token frequency** and **type frequency**. The former refers to the number of times a specific linguistic form occurs in the input. The latter refers to the nature of the linguistic forms that can occur in a particular slot in a construction. For example, verbs like 'know', 'understand', and 'like' occur frequently in the construction 'I don't ___'. The early research investigated token frequency, but it is now thought that it is type frequency that is important as it helps learners to develop more abstract categories.

Humans have an innate desire to communicate with each other—what Lee, Mikesell, Joaquin, Mates, and Schumann (2009) called their 'interactional instinct'. Learners learn a language in order to interact and also they learn language through interacting. In the case of SLA, however, this fundamental truism took a while to take hold. Hatch (1978) advanced what, at that time, was a radical idea: she suggested that learners do not first learn syntactical features and then try to use them in interaction, but rather syntax emerges as a result of the kinds of interaction they typically engage in. Drawing on the methods employed in discourse analysis, she described the interactions involving both child and adult second language learners and illustrated how syntax grew out of their attempts to communicate. This idea was then developed by Long (1983b) who proposed that when there was a communication problem which speakers attempt to resolve, **negotiation of meaning** takes place which both helps learners to comprehend and directs their attention to specific linguistic features.

Long's proposal, which was eventually formalized as the **Interaction Hypothesis**, has proven enormously influential, leading to numerous studies investigating whether the interactional modifications that occurred in the negotiation of meaning assisted comprehension and whether they helped learners to progress along a sequence of acquisition (for example, Mackey 1999). However, the initial formulation of this hypothesis was limited as it saw negotiation only as a source of comprehensible input and allowed no role for learner output.

The role of output in L2 acquisition proved a controversial issue. Krashen's (1985) **Input Hypothesis** claimed that L2 acquisition is entirely input-driven; that is, output (speaking or writing) plays no role in acquisition. However, drawing on research that showed that immersion language learners (i.e. learners who received all their school subjects through the medium of the second language) still failed to acquire a target-like grammar even though they had experienced ample comprehensible input, Swain (1985) advanced the **Comprehensible Output Hypothesis**. This proposed that, as well as comprehensible input, learners needed opportunities to produce 'pushed output' (i.e. output where they struggled to make themselves comprehensible). She pointed out that it is possible for learners to comprehend input without having to process it linguistically (for example, they could use context to guess its meaning), but that to produce concise and comprehensible output they had to engage in syntactical processing.

It is now generally acknowledged that both comprehensible input and comprehensible output are needed if learners are to achieve high levels of linguistic **accuracy** in a second language. Long (1996) revised the Interaction Hypothesis to take account of this. He now proposed that the negotiation of meaning facilitated acquisition in three major ways: (1) by providing the learner with comprehensible input; (2) through feedback that showed the learner when an error had been made; and (3) by prompting **monitoring**—i.e. encouraging the learner to make changes to the utterance that had triggered negotiation. Subsequent research has focused on (2) and (3). In particular, there are an increasing number of studies investigating **corrective feedback** (i.e. the effect that different ways of correcting learners' errors has on acquisition).

The Input Hypothesis, the Comprehensible Output Hypothesis, and the Interaction Hypothesis have had an enormous influence on SLA. They have spawned countless studies investigating how input is made comprehensible, the role of production in L2 acquisition, and the role played by interaction in facilitating acquisition. While the Input Hypothesis has not changed since its initial formulation, both the Comprehensible Output Hypothesis and the Interaction Hypothesis have evolved over time, in particular as a result of the importance that researchers began to attach to the role of consciousness in language learning.

The roles of input, interaction, and output are examined in Chapter 7.

## Consciousness and L2 acquisition

It was at this point that SLA researchers turned to cognitive psychology to explain how input was processed by learners and thus how acquisition—viewed as an internal, mental phenomenon—took place. What motivated this development in SLA was a rather unique case study of an individual learner. Schmidt and Frota (1986) investigated the first author's acquisition of Portuguese during a five-month stay in Brazil. Schmidt kept a diary of his observations and experiences and his interactions with native speakers were audio recorded. One of the main findings was that he only learned what he had first noticed in the input. Schmidt 'subjectively felt...that conscious awareness of what was present in the input was causal' (p. 281). He also reported **noticing-the-gap** when he compared a non-target form he had produced with the target form that appeared in the input. This often occurred when Schmidt received corrective feedback on his own utterances.

Schmidt's claims about the role of 'noticing' and 'noticing-the-gap' concern the role that attention plays in acquisition. In subsequent publications (for example, Schmidt 1994; 2001), he developed what has become known as the **Noticing Hypothesis**. The crucial question for Schmidt was 'Can there be learning without attention?' The conclusion he reached was that while some learning might be possible without conscious attention (i.e. noticing), the more that learners noticed, the more they learned. However, Schmidt was careful to point out that noticing did not imply intentionality on the part of learners; it could occur incidentally while they were primarily concerned with comprehending input. He also emphasized that learners did not notice 'higher-level categories' but rather exemplars of them. For example, they might notice the /s/ sound on 'boys' and also consciously register that it signalled 'more than one'. But this did not constitute conscious awareness of the rule for making nouns plural.

Schmidt's claims about the importance of conscious noticing are controversial, however. Krashen's Input Hypothesis is based on the assumption that L2 acquisition is a subconscious process; that is, he claimed that learners automatically acquire new L2 features simply as a result of comprehending the input they were exposed to. Some studies have shown learners are able to pick up some L2 features without any conscious awareness. We will consider this possibility more closely in the next section. In general, however, SLA has accepted that noticing is facilitative of acquisition. Both Long's (1996) revised Interaction Hypothesis and Swain's (1995) later account of the Comprehensible Output Hypothesis have incorporated the idea of **noticing**. Conscious attention is seen as the key mechanism that connects input to acquisition.

Schmidt's Noticing Hypothesis has informed an increasing number of studies investigating whether (1) learners do notice linguistic forms in the input, and under what conditions, and (2) whether this results in learning. For example, researchers have experimented with various ways of highlighting problematic features in the input that learners are exposed to (for example, by putting them in bold type in a reading passage) to see if this results in their acquisition. These studies have shown that learners tend to notice some features (for example, lexis and word order) but are less likely to notice others (for example, morphological features such as third-person -s). This can explain one of the central puzzles of L2 acquisition—why learners often fail to fully acquire some grammatical features even though these occur with high frequency in the input. Features such as third-person -s (for example, 'comes') are not noticed because they are semantically redundant (i.e. they are not necessary for understanding the meaning of an utterance) and not very salient (i.e. they can easily be overlooked) and, as a result, they are not acquired. Left to their own devices, learners are much more likely to notice those features that are meaning-bearing—individual words or grammatical structures like plural -s.

## Implicit and explicit learning

The influence of cognitive psychology on SLA is perhaps most evident in the research and theorizing related to the distinction between **implicit** and **explicit learning**. N. Ellis (1994) defined **implicit learning** as 'acquisition of knowledge about the underlying structure of a complex stimulus environment by a process which takes place naturally, simply and without conscious operations' (p. 1). Explicit learning is a 'more conscious operation where the individual makes and tests hypotheses in search of structure' (p. 1). As defined, implicit learning is incidental (i.e. there is no intention to learn), whereas explicit learning is intentional (i.e. the learner makes deliberate attempts to learn an L2 feature). This distinction, then, echoes the earlier one that Krashen (1981) made between 'acquisition' and 'learning'.

Theories differ in how they conceptualize the **implicit knowledge** that results from implicit learning. Symbolic theories adhere to the idea that implicit knowledge consists of 'rules' (i.e. abstract representations of the features and patterns that underlie the actual use of the second language). This is probably how most people conceptualize 'knowing a second language' and also constitutes Krashen's view of implicit knowledge. N. Ellis (1996), however, drew on a radically different theory of implicit knowledge. **Connectionist theories** claim that although learners may appear to behave in a rule-like way, they do not acquire rules but rather construct a web of connections in the neural structure of the brain. Implicit learning is an associative process whereby combinations of sounds, words, and larger units of language are internalized in accordance with the frequency with which these combinations occur in the input. For example, through exposure, learners perceive that the sounds /s/, /t/, and /r/ constitute a chunk that occurs in words like 'strong' or that the chunk 'I don't' can co-occur with words like 'know', 'understand', and 'like' or that a larger chunk such as 'I don't know' can combine with another chunk such as 'where is it?' to construct what is traditionally called a complex sentence ('I don't know where it is'). Learning a language according to connectionist theories is not a matter of learning rules, but of learning the possible associations between chunks of varying sizes that occur in the input. Knowing a language, then, is a matter of gradually building an elaborate network of such associations through the implicit registration of their occurrence in the input. It is a slow, organic process that requires exposure to massive amounts of input.

On the face of it, a connectionist view of learning contradicts the Noticing Hypothesis as it assumes that an associative network is constructed without consciousness. However, N. Ellis (2005) acknowledged that the initial registration of a linguistic feature might occur consciously but 'thereafter there is scope for its implicit learning on every subsequent occasion of use' (p. 321). In other words, explicit learning serves as a foundation for implicit learning. Thus, although—like Krashen—N. Ellis saw implicit and explicit learning as distinct, involving separate neurological mechanisms, he did not see them as entirely unconnected. R. Ellis (1994) suggested ways in which the **explicit knowledge** resulting from explicit learning can assist the processes involved in implicit learning. He suggested that if learners have explicit knowledge of a grammatical rule, they are more likely to pay attention (i.e. 'notice') exemplars of this rule in the input they are exposed to and—through noticing—fine-tune their developing, implicit knowledge-system. Explicit knowledge of rules could also prime 'noticing-the-gap'. Furthermore, learners could use their explicit knowledge to construct sentences in the L2, which then served as 'auto-input' that fed into the mechanisms responsible for implicit learning. Thus, whereas Krashen saw little value in explicit knowledge, both N. Ellis and R. Ellis argued that learners could utilize their conscious understanding of underlying rules in ways that facilitate implicit learning.

The distinction between implicit and explicit learning is important for understanding the role played by form-focused instruction in L2 acquisition. A key question is whether teaching learners 'rules' can assist the development of learners' implicit knowledge, or whether it simply results in explicit knowledge. Another key question is what type of instruction is needed to facilitate implicit learning.

## Dual-mode system

It should be clear from the foregoing explanation that the learner's second language knowledge can be both explicit and rule based or implicit and exemplar based—i.e. consists of ready-made stored chunks. In other words, learners may possess a **dual-mode system**. For example, the utterance 'I don't know' can be processed as a single chunk or can be computed on the basis of the learner's knowledge of the rules for negation in English. Skehan (1998) claimed 'two systems co-exist, the rule-based analytic, on the one hand, and the formulaic, exemplar-based on the other' (p. 54).

There is a good reason for a dual-mode system. As Skehan pointed out, memory is organized for convenience of use and to take account of the fact that learners' capacity for processing information is limited. When they need to communicate rapidly and fluently, learners will draw substantially on the **exemplar-based system** which is capacious and easily accessed. However, when they need to communicate complex ideas concisely and accurately, they will resort to the **rule-based system**. Skehan argued that L2 learners need to build both systems and proposed that this could be achieved by manipulating the conditions under which they were required to use the L2. For example, if learners are given time to plan before they perform a task, they will be able to draw on their rule-based knowledge but if they have to perform the task straight off they will more likely draw on their exemplar-based knowledge.

## L2 acquisition as skill-learning

**Skill-learning theory** also originated in cognitive psychology. It draws on a similar distinction to the implicit/explicit distinction but proposes a very different relationship between them. Anderson's (1993) ACT theory distinguishes **declarative knowledge** (i.e. the representation of facts) and **procedural knowledge** (i.e. the representation of actions in particular situations). The theory proposes that declarative knowledge can be transformed into proceduralized knowledge through practice (DeKeyser 1998). Applied to language learning, this process involves (1) developing an explicit representation of a linguistic feature; (2) practising the use of the feature using the explicit representation as an aid to performance; and (3) proceduralizing the feature and automatizing its use. Thus there is a progression from conscious, controlled processing to unconscious, automatic use. To give a simple example, learners might first learn a rule for plural -*s* (declarative knowledge) and construct an 'if-then procedure' i.e. 'if the noun refers to more than one, add -*s*' (procedural knowledge), and then automatize the use of this procedure (automatic knowledge). At this point, there is no longer any need for the declarative rule which consequently might be forgotten through disuse.

The transformation from declarative to proceduralized/automatic knowledge of a linguistic feature requires practice. DeKeyser (2007) defined 'practice' broadly as 'specific activities in the second language, engaged in systematically, deliberately, with the goal of developing knowledge of and skills in the second language' (p. 1). He argued that 'good practice needs to involve real operating conditions as soon as possible, which means comprehending and expressing real thoughts, and this necessarily involves a variety of structures, some of which will be much further along the declarative-procedural-automatic path than others' (p. 292). DeKeyser also claimed that the development of procedural knowledge was more likely to occur when the cognitive operations involved in the practice activity matched those in a natural communicative context.

Thus, an integral premise of skill-acquisition theory is the importance of **transfer appropriate processing.** DeKeyser (2007) noted that practice leads to qualitative changes in the learner's knowledge system over time but only 'in the basic cognitive mechanisms used to execute the same task' (p. 99): in other words, learning would be restricted to the situations and conditions of use that mirrored the operating conditions which figured in the practice provided. Two key points follow from this. First, for a feature to become automatic for use in natural communication learners need to experience practising it under communicative conditions; controlled, mechanical practice will not suffice. Second, acquisition is domain-specific and thus proceeds separately for comprehension and production; learning to process a feature receptively will not enable the learner to use it in production and vice versa.

Skill-learning theory differs from theories based on the distinction between implicit and explicit knowledge, in particular with regard to the nature of the interface between the two types of knowledge. Skill-learning theory assumes a more or less direct interface between the two types of knowledge (i.e. declarative knowledge can transform into procedural knowledge providing there is sufficient practice of the right kind). In contrast, implicit/explicit theories see the two types of knowledge as disassociated and only indirectly related (i.e. explicit knowledge does not transform into implicit knowledge, but can facilitate the processes involved in implicit learning).

Skill-learning theory may account for the main way in which adult learners learn an L2. However, it is difficult to accept that the acquisition of *all* L2 features—even by adults—begins with declarative knowledge. There would appear to be little room for any implicit learning in skill-learning theory. However, the theory has proved influential in language pedagogy as it supports the idea that language can be taught by systematically presenting and practising discrete linguistic features.

In Chapter 8, we will examine the various constructs and theories borrowed from cognitive psychology.

## The social turn in L2 acquisition

SLA, as I have described it so far, was primarily cognitive-interactionist in orientation: that is to say, the underlying view was that learning takes place inside the learner's head as a result of processing input and output through interaction. Block (2003) noted 'until the mid-1990s explicit calls for an interdisciplinary, socially informed SLA were notable by their absence' (p. 3). Although this was not entirely true, Block was correct in pointing to the relative neglect of the social context in SLA.

In fact, the earliest attempt to theorize the role of social factors (apart from the work on variability in learner language) was Schumann's (1978a) **Acculturation Model**. Schumann proposed that factors governing the **social distance** between the L2 learner and the target-language community influenced the likelihood of the learner acculturating (i.e. becoming a member of the target-language community) and thus the speed at which learning takes place. For example, if the L2 learner was a member of a relatively large and self-contained community of learners speaking the same first language, the learner would be likely to experience limited contact with L2 speakers and so learning would be slow. Schumann's view of how social factors affect L2 acquisition was deterministic in nature. In the Acculturation Model, social factors were simply grafted on to the underlying cognitive-interactionist model of learning.

The case for including a fuller social perspective was convincingly made by Firth and Wagner (1997), who proposed what is known as **social-interactionist SLA**. They argued that cognitive accounts of L2 acquisition were 'individualistic and mechanistic' and that to achieve a better balance it was necessary to consider the contextual dimensions of language use. They were especially critical of the way in which SLA researchers characterized the subject of their enquiry as a 'learner' or a 'non-native speaker', ignoring the host of other social identities (for example, 'parent', 'worker', 'husband', 'friend') which might influence the use and acquisition of an L2. They argued, too, that mainstream SLA had largely focused on classroom settings and on interactions between learners and native speakers whereas many learning contexts were multilingual in nature in which learners were more likely to interact with other learners than with native speakers. They pointed out the importance of people's local agendas and the social and institutional factors that were instantiated in the interactions they participated in. Thus, in Firth and Wagner's **social-interactionist SLA**, learners were not just subject to social factors, as in Schumann's Acculturation Theory, but could also influence the social world they inhabited.

The importance of **social identity** in shaping learners' opportunities for learning is most fully argued in Norton's (2000) **Social Identity Theory**. This is concerned with the relationship between power, identity, and language learning. Norton saw social identity as multiple, contradictory, and dynamic. To obtain the 'right to speak' learners need to be able to see themselves as legitimate speakers of the L2, not as defective communicators. They have to be prepared to challenge the subservient social identity that native speakers often thrust upon them and assert the right to communicate. Norton illustrated her theory in research on adult female immigrants to Canada. In some cases, these women were successful in establishing a social identity that afforded them opportunities to speak on equal terms; in other cases they were not successful and withdrew from contact with native speakers.

However, missing from both of these social accounts is any explanation of how social context and identity influences L2 acquisition. Firth and Wagner focused on L2 use as manifested in the social interactions that learners participate in. Norton focused on social identity. In both cases, the emphasis is on the opportunities for learning but not on learning itself. The theories explain how 'affordances' for learning are created, but they offer no explanation of how these affordances lead to actual learning. This led Long (1997) to insist that critics of cognitive SLA should offer some evidence to show that social identity and a broader view of social context make a difference to how an L2 is acquired. Revisiting their 1997 paper, Firth and Wagner (2007) acknowledged the need for this and there has been some headway made in achieving it, especially in research in **sociocultural SLA**.

## Sociocultural SLA

Sociocultural accounts of L2 acquisition had been around for some time but made little impact on SLA until the 1990s. A special issue of *The Modern Language Journal* published in 1994 was devoted to sociocultural studies of L2 learners. This served as the impetus for a steady growth of interest in sociocultural theory in SLA, which shows no signs of diminishing today.

Sociocultural SLA draws on the work of the Russian psychologist, Lev Vygotsky (1986), who argued that learning arises when an expert (for example, a teacher) interacts with a novice (i.e. a learner) to enable the novice to learn a new concept. When this happens, the expert and the novice jointly construct a **zone of proximal development (ZPD)**. For example, a learner may be incapable of independently producing a target-like negative construction (for example, 'Marcelle did not come') resorting instead to a developmentally simpler negative form ('Marcelle no coming'). But the help provided by a skilled interlocutor can enable the learner to produce the target construction:

A   Marcelle no coming.
B   He didn't come yesterday?
A   Yeah, he didn't come.

On the face of it, this looks like an example of the negotiation of meaning but sociocultural theory views what is going on in such interactions very differently from the Interaction Hypothesis. Whereas the Interaction Hypothesis sees such exchanges as providing learners with 'data'—which they then process internally—sociocultural theory sees them as examples of 'learning' taking place 'in flight'. That is, learning is initially accomplished socially *in* (not through) interaction. Later, 'development' takes place when the learner internalizes the new form. At this time, **self-regulation** has been achieved and the learner is now capable of producing the form without any external assistance.

Central to sociocultural SLA, is the idea of **mediation** (Lantolf 2000). In cognitive SLA, to show that learning has occurred it is necessary to show that the learner is able to produce a structure like 'Marcelle did not come' independently. In sociocultural theory, however, learning is also evident when it can be shown that the extent of the mediation needed to construct a ZPD reduces from one time to another. In this example:

A   Marcelle no coming.
B   Yesterday?
A   Yeah, he didn't come.

the learner is now able to self-correct without the other speaker providing the target form. As in the first example, a ZPD is created but in this case it requires less assistance. Sociocultural theory, then, is premised on a very different view of what language learning entails.

Sociocultural theory has informed the work of a number of researchers in recent years. Much of the research, however, is somewhat limited as it has tended to simply describe the various types of mediation that arise in social interactions with learners without demonstrating that either 'learning' (i.e. the initial production of a target feature) or 'development' (i.e. movement towards self-regulation) has taken place. An exception, however, is the work of Swain. Swain and her co-researchers (for example, Swain and Lapkin 1995) asked learners to participate collaboratively in performing various kinds of tasks. Their interactions were recorded, transcribed, and **language-related episodes** identified. These were sequences of interaction where the learners explicitly discussed some language point that they found problematic. Swain then examined whether the collaborative work undertaken when performing the initial task enabled the learners to use those forms that had figured in the language-related episodes independently in a later, new task. Later, Swain (2006) referred to the talk-about-language in these language-related episodes as **languaging**. Her research suggests that this assists both learning (i.e. initial use) and development (i.e.

internalization)—at least in the case of adult learners who have already acquired some proficiency in the L2.

Social aspects of L2 acquisition, including sociocultural theory, are discussed in Chapter 9.

## Emergentism

**Emergentism** constitutes an appropriate way of rounding up this brief history of SLA because it is an all-embracing theory, incorporating both cognitive and social dimensions of learning. According to N. Ellis (1998), there is no need to posit a **language acquisition device** to explain how language acquisition (first or second) takes place as claimed by Chomsky. Like Skill-Learning Theory, emergentism assumes that learning a language is like learning any other skill and that all that is needed to explain it is a simple learning mechanism that can handle the information available from a massively complex environment.

Emergentism informs a number of theories of L2 acquisition. One of these is **Complexity Theory**:

> Complexity theory seeks to explain complex, dynamic, open, adaptive, self-organizing, non-linear systems...It sees complex behavior as arising from interactions among many components – a bottom-up process based on the contributions of each, which are subject to change over time.
> (Larsen-Freeman 2011: 52).

By 'complex', Larsen-Freeman refers to the fact that an L2 system is influenced by a range of different factors—both social and cognitive in nature—which affect learning in different ways and at different times. A complex system is 'dynamic' and 'open' in the sense that it is constantly changing. Complexity Theory rejects the notion of a 'final state' in any language system (including the native speaker's) and, in accordance with connectionist views of language, claims that small changes are forever ongoing. A system is always in movement and never reaches complete equilibrium although there may be periods of relative stability. From the perspective of Complexity Theory, then, there is no such thing as fossilization. A complex system is 'adaptive' because it is responsive to the linguistic environment; grammar is 'a by-product of communication'. By 'self-organizing', Larsen-Freeman was referring to the fact that change in one part of the system can trigger changes in other parts. Finally, a language system does not develop in linear ways; different parts of the system develop at different rates. However, while it is not possible to predict the precise pattern of development of a complex system, stable patterns do emerge from time to time. There are **attractor states**—regions of the system that achieve prominence at one time or another. The transitional stages evident in sequences of acquisition that we considered earlier can be viewed as attractor states emerging in the process of acquisition. The theory also emphasizes the active role played by the learner. As Larsen-Freeman put it 'intentionality and agency are important' (p. 58). Complexity Theory, then, incorporates many of the proposals of both cognitive SLA and social SLA. Learners have choices. Interaction is central, but learners can shape the interactions they participate in and what they consciously choose to learn. Complexity Theory is considered in Chapter 8.

## Summary

In this historical survey of SLA, we can see a number of ways in which the field has developed. Much of the early research was descriptive in nature, focusing on identifying the key features of learner language and how these change over time. This led to a re-evaluation of the role of the L1 in L2 acquisition and also to an interest in the linguistic environment (i.e. input and interaction) and how this influenced learning. Increasingly, descriptive research gave way to theoretically driven research based on a cognitive-interactionist view of L2 acquisition. This served as a basis for investigating specific hypotheses relating to such constructs as the negotiation of meaning, noticing, implicit/explicit learning, the dual-mode system, and skill-learning. At this point, acquisition was viewed as something that took place inside the learner's head and social factors were only of interest in terms of the 'data' they made available for 'input crunching'. In the 1990s, however, a reaction set in and the case for a constitutive role for social factors in L2 acquisition was advanced. Learners were not just to be seen as defective communicators and they had agency. According to sociocultural SLA, learning takes place externally in the social interactions that learners participate in. Finally theories began to appear that sought to integrate cognitive and social perspectives on L2 acquisition.

SLA had now reached a point where there was no clear consensus about how L2 acquisition took place. There are competing theories giving rise to a large body of empirical research that have often produced conflicting results. The complexity of SLA as a field of enquiry was mirrored in the aptly named Complexity Theory—an all-encompassing theory that insisted there were no simple answers to the key question 'How do learners acquire a second language?' Readers of this book, therefore, must be prepared to grapple with this complexity. They should look for 'insights' rather than definite 'answers' and then come to their own informed conclusions about how a second language is acquired.

This historical introduction to SLA has neglected two important areas of enquiry: the role of age in L2 acquisition and the role of individual learner factors such as language aptitude and motivation. We will remedy these lacunae in Chapters 2 and 3. This chapter has not considered the role of instruction either, an area which has received considerable attention in SLA— not only because investigating how instruction affects learning serves as a means of testing the claims of different theories—but also because SLA has, from the start, been concerned with how it can contribute to effective language pedagogy. The significance of the role of instruction is considered in Chapters 10 and 11.

## Notes

1 This definition of L2 acquisition excludes children who are acquiring two languages as their mother tongues. This situation is referred to as 'simultaneous bilingual acquisition'.

2 Some researchers prefer the term 'additional language acquisition' to second language acquisition' because it avoids the potentially negative connotation of 'second'. For some learners—such as those who leave their own country and migrate to a country where the L2 is widely used—the language that they learned 'second' can become their 'first'—i.e. primary—language.

3 Ortega (2012) argued that the 'human language faculty is potentially by default bi/multilingual' and that 'the possibility of bi/multilingualism remains true all along the life span, from birth across all ages' (p. 17).

# 2

# Age and second language acquisition

## Introduction

A main aim of SLA is to identify those aspects of L2 acquisition that are universal. This is entirely justified as human beings share a common propensity to learn language so that we can expect them to grapple with the cognitive and social issues involved in acquisition in much the same way. However, learners also differ in a number of ways and these differences impact on the rate of acquisition, ultimate success, and—potentially—on the processes involved in acquiring a language. Thus—before embarking on the detailed study of the various dimensions of acquisition introduced in Chapter 1—in this, and in the following chapter, I will focus on the learner, pointing out some of the ways in which learners differ from each other and how these differences impact on learning.

One of the most obvious ways in which second language learners differ is in terms of their starting age. Some learners start learning a second language in early childhood while many others have to wait till they go to school (often secondary school). The study of the influence that learners' starting age has on L2 acquisition is motivated by both theoretical and practical considerations. It is a source of empirical evidence about the nature of human beings' language learning capability and how this may change as they grow older. It also provides educational policy makers with information that they can use to decide when to introduce the teaching of a foreign language into the school system and also what instructional approach might be best suited to learners of different ages.

A common assumption is that children are better language learners than adults and that, therefore, learners will be more successful if they start learning a second language when they are young. However—while there is some truth in this assumption—the research evidence shows that the effects of age on L2 acquisition are complex. For a start, it is necessary to distinguish the effect of age on ultimate attainment, the rate of acquisition, and the route of acquisition. I will begin by examining age in relationship to ultimate attainment as this is the most controversial and theoretically inter-esting issue. I will then consider its effect on the rate and route of acquisition. This section will conclude with a consideration of educational policy regarding the best age to start foreign language instruction.

Many of the studies I will consider in this chapter are correlational in nature. That is, they obtained measures of two different variables (for example, starting age and L2 proficiency) and then calculated the strength of the relationship between them statistically. A perfect correlation—never attested—is represented arithmetically as 1.0. A strong correlation is one that is close to the perfect correlation (for example, 0.85) while a weak correlation is one that is close to zero (for example, 0.15). Correlations can be positive (i.e. the stronger the learners' motivation, the stronger their L2 scores) or nega-tive (i.e. the older the learners' starting age, the weaker their L2 scores).

## Age and ultimate attainment

To address the relationship between starting age and ultimate attainment, two separate questions need to be investigated:

1 Can adult learners of a second language acquire native-like proficiency in a second language?
2 Do learners who start learning a second language in childhood acquire higher levels of L2 proficiency than learners who start as adults?

To answer these questions, it is necessary to define the variables involved. What is meant by an 'adult learner' and by a 'child' learner? What is 'language proficiency'? In fact, these constructs are not easy to define. Some researchers (for example, Snow and Hoefnagel-Höhle 1978) have distinguished pre-puberty learners, adolescents, and adults (i.e. post-puberty learners). However, this constitutes a somewhat crude way of characterizing 'age'; there is a big difference, for example, between a four-year-old and a ten-year-old child and perhaps an even bigger one between a 17-year-old and a 50-year-old adult learner. Researchers have investigated 'proficiency' primarily in terms of pro-nunciation (for example, the learner's accent) and grammar, but there are other important aspects of proficiency that need to be considered—for example, lexical knowledge (including formulaic sequences) and the pragmatic ability needed to use language in sociolinguistically appropriate ways—which have been little investigated. A further issue is whether proficiency is to be conceptualized as **implicit knowledge** (i.e. the kind of knowledge needed to engage in fluent, spontaneous language use) or **explicit knowledge** (i.e. the kind of knowledge that many traditional language tests tap).

## Critical Period Hypothesis

The first of the above questions is the most important one from a theoretical standpoint. It concerns the **Critical Period Hypothesis (CPH),** first proposed by Penfield and Roberts (1959). The hypothesis states that there is a period (typically defined as the period up to the onset of puberty) during which learners can acquire a second language easily and implicitly and achieve native-speaker competence, but after which L2 acquisition becomes more difficult and is rarely entirely successful.

Evidence in support of the hypothesis initially came from outside SLA. Lenneberg (1967) reported research which showed that when children suffered injuries to the right hemisphere they experienced language problems, but adults did not. Conversely, when adults underwent surgery to the left hemisphere almost total loss of language occurred whereas this did not occur with children. Adults showed permanent language impairment after such operations, but children rapidly recovered total language control. Lenneberg concluded that the biological basis of language in children and adults differs.

Further evidence for this conclusion came from cases of unfortunate children who were deprived of opportunities to hear and speak a language during childhood. Curtiss (1977) reported a study of Genie, who was kept in virtual isolation for most of her life. When discovered at the age of 13, she had no language. Genie was subsequently successful in learning English to some extent, especially vocabulary, but failed to achieve full grammatical competence. She also had problems in engaging in normal social interaction. Curtiss suggested that her limited grammatical development was because she had passed the critical period for language acquisition. Rymer (1993) pointed out, however, that the root cause may have been the emotional disturbance that Genie had experienced as a child and continued to manifest as an adult. This could explain her problems with social interaction which in turn may have limited the development of her grammatical competence.

There is no clear consensus on when the critical period for language learning ends. Singleton (2005) in a survey of the literature that addressed this issue reported claims ranging from near birth to late adolescence. Also, it has become clear that—if there is a critical period—this varies depending on the aspect of language under examination. Granena and Long (2012), for example, provided evidence to suggest that the window of opportunity closes first for L2 phonology (perhaps as early as four-years-old), then for lexis and collocation, and finally (in the mid-teens) for grammar.

## Theoretical importance of the CPH

The theoretical importance of the CPH lies in the fact that it supports Chomsky's (1965) view of language. Chomsky argued that children are equipped with a **language acquisition device**—an innate, biologically-given capacity for learning language that is distinct from other cognitive abilities. This device—according to Chomsky—contains knowledge of the linguistic universals that underlie the grammatical rules of every language and—because children have access to these universals—they are able to master the grammar of their mother tongue. This nativist account of language learning, which downplays the role of the linguistic environment, was prominent in the early period of SLA when **behaviourist learning theory** with the emphasis on habit-formation was called into question (see Chapter 6). It provided a psycholinguistic rationale for the CPH. Children acquire full grammatical competence because they have access to the language acquisition device. Adults, however, lose access to it and therefore are forced to rely on general cognitive abilities such as those associated with the formal operational stage of development (Piaget 1973), which begins at the onset of puberty. At this point, people develop the capacity for logical thought, deductive reasoning, and systematic planning. Such abilities suffice to enable people to learn a language to a certain extent but do not totally compensate for the loss of the language acquisition device. As a result, older learners fail to acquire all of the grammatical features of the L2.

## Investigating the CPH

The CPH has been subjected to empirical study in two main ways. One way involves comparing groups of learners who commenced learning as children with other groups who started post puberty. The second way involves investigating whether learners who started learning post puberty were successful in achieving full competence in the second language (i.e. had become totally native-like). These two approaches reflect somewhat different versions of the hypothesis. One version is that the end of the critical period signals the point at which decline in the ability to learn a second language begins. This can be considered the weak version of the hypothesis. The strong version of the hypothesis is that once past the critical age, natural acquisition is blocked irrespective of whether learners are just past it or many years past it. What both conceptualizations have in common, however, is the notion of a discontinuity in learning; that is, after a certain age, the pattern of learning changes.

One of the most commonly cited studies is Johnson and Newport (1989). They studied 46 native Koreans and Chinese who had arrived in the United States between the ages of three and 39, half before the age of 15 and half after 17. The learners were asked to judge the grammaticality of 276 spoken sentences, about half of which were grammatical. Overall the correlation between age at arrival and correct judgement scores was –0.77 (i.e. the older the learners were at arrival, the lower their scores). In contrast, neither the number of years of exposure to English beyond five nor the amount of classroom instruction they had received was related to their grammaticality judgement scores. Also, although an effect for 'identification with American culture' was found, this was much weaker than that for age. Johnson and Newport interpreted the results of their study as evidence for the strong version of the CPH as they argued that there was a sharp discontinuity in the effects evident for age after the critical period. In the case of the early starters, there was a gradual decline in performance according to age. However, in the case of the late starters, the relationship between age and performance was essentially random. However, this claim was subsequently disputed. Bialystok and Hakuta (1999) reanalysed Johnson and Newport's data and concluded that there was no evidence of a clear discontinuity[1].

Turning now to the second approach to investigating the CPH, I will focus first on two studies that, like Johnson and Newport, measured achievement by means of **grammaticality judgement tests** (i.e. tests that present learners with a set of sentences and ask them to judge whether they are grammatical or not). I will then consider a number of other studies of post-puberty L2 learners that examined attainment in ways that some researchers (including me) consider more valid.

Coppetiers (1987) compared the performance of 20 native speakers and 21 highly proficient learners of French on a grammaticality judgement test. All the learners had begun learning as adults and they all appeared native-like in their spoken French. The results showed clear differences between the two groups. Coppetiers concluded that the grammatical competence of the L2 learners differed from that of native speakers. However, Birdsong (1992) replicated this study and reported very different results. He administered a grammaticality judgement test to 20 English-speaking learners of L2 French who were native-like in their oral ability and to 20 native speakers of French. Birdsong found no evidence of any dramatic differences in the judgements of the two groups. A number of the non-native speakers performed in the same range as the native speakers. This study, then, suggests that at least some learners who start learning a second language after puberty can achieve a level of competence indistinguishable from that of native speakers.

Other studies carried out in-depth investigations of individual learners. Table 2.1 summarizes two such studies. Ioup, Boustagui, El Tigi, and Moselle (1994) studied a highly successful learner (Julie) who did not start learning her L2 (Arabic) until she was 21 years. Lardiere (2007) studied a learner (Patty) who had had almost no contact with the L2 (English) until she was 18 years old but subsequently—like Julie—was immersed in the L2 environment. Both learners had been learning their L2 for more than 20 years and both—especially Julie—demonstrated a high level of grammatical proficiency. However, arguably neither of them achieved totally native-like ability. Julie, for example, did make some mistakes in a translation test and did not perform exactly like native speakers in a grammaticality judgement test. Patty continued to make morphological errors in features such as subject-verb agreement and plural -$s$[2]. These studies, then, lend support to the CPH.

However, other studies suggest that L2 learners who started learning post-puberty were able to achieve native proficiency. Bongaerts (1999), for example, used native-speaker ratings to investigate whether nine post-adolescent Dutch learners of L2 French had attained a native-level accent. Recordings of their speech were mixed in with recordings of 18 lower-level Dutch learners of French and nine native speakers. Three of the advanced learners passed for native speakers. Bongaerts argued that high motivation combined with pronunciation training enabled these talented learners to achieve native level.

| | Ioup et al. (1994) | Lardiere (2007) |
|---|---|---|
| Learner | Julie was an L1 speaker of British English. When she married an Egyptian she moved to Cairo at the age of 21. She reported that Arabic became her dominant language after her third year of residence in Cairo. She had been living in Egypt for 26 years at the time of data collection. She was entirely a naturalistic learner (i.e. she never received any formal instruction in Arabic). | Patty was Chinese. She was born in Indonesia in 1953 but left for China in 1969 and lived there for two years before moving to Hong Kong. After finishing high school, she worked in an import-export company in Hong Kong, rarely speaking English. She arrived in the United States in 1976 at the age of 22. She lived with her Vietnamese fiancé's family and began college-level study and, a little later, took a waitressing job. In 1985, she separated from her husband and in 1989 married a native English speaker. |
| Target language | Arabic | English |
| Data collection | Data collected from both native speakers of Egyptian Arabic, Julie and other L2 learners:<br>1 Oral recordings of their explanations of their favourite recipes.<br>2 A test of their ability to distinguish different Arabic accents. | Oral recording (1) was made in 1986 when Patty had been living in the United States for about 10 years. Recordings (2) and (3) were made two months apart in 1995. Written samples, mainly from email messages, were also collected. |
| Measures of proficiency | Native-speaker ratings of all the participants' accents; Julie's ability to distinguish different Arabic accents; a translation task (English into Arabic); a grammaticality judgement test (GJT); a test of ability to process complex syntactic structure (anaphora). | Lardiere investigated a number of grammatical features in Patty's English speech and writing, including tense, aspect, and agreement, English question formation, and possessive pronouns and plural marking. |
| Results | Seven of the 13 judges rated Julie's accent as native. Julie was able to successfully distinguish Arabic accents. She made very few mistakes in the translation test. Her judgements differed from those of native speakers on only five out of 37 sentences. Her ability to process complex syntactic structure was comparable to the native speakers'. | Patty had not achieved a native-like grammar by the end of the study. She was able to employ English syntactical constructions correctly, but continued to make errors in morphological features (for example, frequent omission or overuse of inflectional markers on verbs and nouns). Patty's written English was more accurate than her spoken English. |

*Table 2.1 Summary of two studies of advanced adult L2 learners*

To counter Bongaert's claim, it is necessary to show that there are at least some differences between very successful late-starting learners and native speakers. Abrahamsson and Hyltenstam (2009) found evidence of this. Using ten measures of pronunciation, vocabulary, and grammar, they reported that none of the late-starting native-like learners in their study scored in the same range as native speakers on *all* of the measures although they did on some. In contrast, some of the early-starters (younger than 12) did succeed in performing identically to the native speakers. Hyltenstam and Abrahamsson (2003) argued that the subtle differences between near-native and native proficiency, which they found evidence of, give support to the CPH, but they also noted that these differences 'are probably highly insignificant in all aspects of the second language speaker's life' (p. 580).

## Reaching a conclusion about the CPH

On balance, the research suggests that it is unlikely that post-puberty L2 learners are capable of achieving completely native levels of proficiency—at least when highly sensitive measures of L2 proficiency are examined. However, to claim that there is a critical period for learning a second language, it is necessary to demonstrate that there is a clear discontinuity between a period when full competence is possible and a period when it is not possible. Birdsong (2006) concluded that there is no such discontinuity. He undertook an analysis of data from a wide range of studies and commented 'in all analyses of pooled data from the early and late arrivals, age effects persist indefinitely across the span of surveyed age of arrival' (p. 14). In other words, age does have an effect, but it is continuous in nature (i.e. there is no clearly defined 'window of opportunity' for learning a second language). In contrast, other researchers (for example, Granena and Long 2012) claimed that there are clear discontinuities according to age in the acquisition of different L2 systems.

There is, however, another reason for circumspection about the CPH. Birdsong (2006), drawing on Cook's (1991) idea of **multicompetence,** pointed out that 'it is more reasonable to argue that minor quantitative departures from monolingual values are artefacts of the nature of bilingualism, wherein each language affects the other and neither is identical to that of the monolingual' (p. 22). Such a view is clearly compatible with a connectionist account of language and learning (see Chapter 1). L2 acquisition does not just entail the development of a completely new and separate neural network, but an elaboration of an established network. That is, the neural networks of the two languages become interwoven. Thus, when someone learns another language, they do not become a native speaker of their first language and a non-native speaker of the second language but a multicompetent speaker of two languages. From this perspective, the CPH is perhaps conceptually misguided.

## The ultimate attainment of child and adult L2 learners

We turn now to briefly examine the comparison that Singleton (2003) considered to be the only appropriate one—i.e. 'between post-pubertal L2 beginners and those who begin to acquire an L2 in childhood' (p. 10). In order to make a valid comparison, of course, it is necessary to ensure that both groups of learners had experienced a similar learning context and to take account of any difference in the number of years of exposure to the second language. There are a number of studies that satisfy these conditions.

Research shows that naturalistic learners who start as children achieve a more native-like accent than those who start as adolescents or adults. Oyama (1976) investigated 60 male immigrants who had entered the United States at ages ranging from six to 20 years and had been resident there for between five and 18 years. She asked two adult native speakers to judge the learners' accents in two 45-second extracts taken from performance on a reading-aloud task and a free-speech task. Oyama reported a very strong effect for 'age of arrival' but almost no effect for 'number of years' in the United States.

Similar results have been obtained for the acquisition of grammar. Patkowski (1980) investigated 67 educated immigrants to the United States. He found that those learners who had entered the United States before the age of 15 were rated as more syntactically proficient than learners who had entered after 15. Furthermore, there was a marked difference in the distribution of the scores (based on native speakers' ratings on a five-point scale) for the two groups. The adult group's scores were evenly distributed, with the majority at midpoint on the rating scale. The child group's scores clustered at the high end of the rating scale, with 29 out of 33 achieving a rating of four-plus or five. Patkowski also investigated the effects of the number of years spent in the United States, the amount of informal exposure to English, and the amount of formal instruction. Only the amount of informal exposure had any significant effect, and even this was negligible in comparison with the age factor.

Singleton (1989) concluded his review of studies that compared groups of learners starting as children and as adults in this way:

> Concerning the hypothesis that those who begin learning a second language in childhood in the long run generally achieve higher levels of proficiency than those who begin in later life, one can say that there is some good supportive evidence and that there is no actual counter evidence.
> (Singleton 1989: 137)

In fact, Singleton felt this was one of the few definite conclusions he was able to reach in his comprehensive survey of age-related research.

## Age and rate of acquisition

In general, older learners learn more rapidly than child learners at first except possibly in pronunciation. On the face of it, this contradicts the conclusion reached in the previous section but, in fact, it is compatible with it. Older learners only have an initial advantage but, over time, child learners catch up and surpass them.

The most cited study addressing age and the rate of acquisition is Snow and Hoefnagel-Höhle (1978). This study investigated the naturalistic acquisition of Dutch by eight- to ten-year-old English-speaking children, 12- to 15-year-old adolescents, and adults over a ten-month period. The learners' proficiency was measured on three separate occasions (after three months, after six months, and at the end of the study). With regard to morphology and syntax the adolescents did best, followed by the adults, with the children last. However, there were only small differences in pronunciation, and the grammar differences diminished over time as the children began to catch up.

Experimental research also indicates that in formal learning situations adults seem to do better than children—even in pronunciation—the area of learning that most favours children. For example, Cochrane (1980) investigated the ability of 54 Japanese children and 24 adults to discriminate English /r/ and /l/. The average length of naturalistic exposure was calculated as 245 hours for the adults and 193 for the children (i.e. relatively little). Before the instruction, the children outperformed the adults. However, when the two groups were taught the phonemic distinction, the adults benefited while the children did not.

Older learners also outperform younger learners in vocabulary development (Singleton 1999). No matter whether the context is a naturalistic one, a short-term instructional one, or a long-term instructional one, older children outperform younger children and adult/adolescent learners progress more rapidly than child learners.

Overall, then, older learners have an initial advantage over younger learners, especially in grammar and vocabulary. This can be explained by the more advanced abilities that come with the formal operations stage of cognitive development; older learners are better equipped to make use of conscious **learning strategies**. Children, however, have an advantage in **implicit learning** and over time this enables them to catch up and overtake older learners.

## Age and the route of L2 acquisition

In Chapter 1, we saw that L2 learners manifest relatively fixed orders and sequences of acquisition. Thus, the final question we can ask is whether child and adult learners follow the same route in acquiring the grammar of a second language. In the first edition of this book, I concluded that the available evidence indicated that age did not affect the route of L2 acquisition. I cited studies that have reported the same **order of acquisition** of grammatical morphemes for adults and children (Dulay and Burt 1973; Bailey, Madden, and Krashen 1974). Similarly, Cancino, Rosansky, and Schumann's (1978) study, which included child, adolescent, and adult learners found the same **sequence of acquisition** for English negatives and interrogatives. I concluded that learners process linguistic data in the same way, irrespective of how old they are.

This conclusion has received support from later research. Harley (1986), for example, compared early and later French immersion students. She found that the older starters demonstrated greater attainment of the French verb system than the younger ones, but that there was no difference in the order in which they acquired different verb forms. Alvarez (2006) compared the developmental sequence evident in child and adult learners' performance of an oral narrative. As in previous studies, the adults demonstrated more rapid progress through the transitional stages of the sequences and had already reached a relatively advanced stage at the beginning of the study. However, Alvarez reported that from that stage onwards, the developmental pattern for the two groups of learners coincided closely.

However, it may be premature to dismiss the possibility that age affects the process of acquisition. Child learners are likely to rely on **implicit learning** while older learners are more likely to make use of **explicit learning**. It is reasonable to suppose that the more analytical approach of older learners will have some impact on the route of acquisition. A recent study provides evidence of this. Dimroth (2008) examined two untutored Russian beginners (aged eight and 14) of L2 German under similar conditions. She focused on the acquisition of negation and verb tense markings. The 14-year-old displayed a similar developmental pattern to that reported for adults. However, the eight-year-old child manifested a different order of acquisition (for example, tense was marked on lexical verbs before auxiliaries). Dimroth concluded that the older learner was dependent on a step-wise path to the target system while the younger learner was able to adopt target patterns immediately without going through analytical steps. She concluded that the process of L2 acquisition and not just the end product is influenced by age[3].

## Educational policy

Finally, we will briefly consider educational policy regarding the best age to introduce instruction in a foreign language in school systems. Recent years have witnessed a change in policy. In many countries, language instruction traditionally began in secondary school (i.e. around the onset of puberty), but increasingly countries are opting to start at the elementary-school level. This has been motivated by the belief that younger learners are better equipped to learn a second language than older learners. However, as we have seen, this is not quite correct as older learners develop more rapidly than younger ones and the advantage that child learners hold in terms of ultimate attainment only emerges after massive amounts of exposure to the second language. Provision for language instruction in most school systems is insufficient to enable the potential advantage that young starters hold to manifest itself. In other words, from the perspective of the research we reviewed above, it is unlikely that starting foreign language instruction early will confer any real benefit.

Studies comparing the proficiency of learners who started at the elementary- and secondary-school levels support this claim. The Barcelona Age Factor Project (Muñoz 2006), for example, examined the acquisition of English by classroom learners of English in Catalonia (Spain), comparing students who began their study at the age of eight, 11, and 14 and controlling for exposure to English outside the classroom. Data from a battery of tests were collected on three occasions—after 200 hundred hours of instruction, 416 hours, and 726 hours. The main finding was that the older learners progressed faster than the younger learners, who failed to catch up over time. The advantage for the older learners was strong and durable on measures of grammar, but was less evident on measures of speech perception, listening comprehension, and oral fluency. Larson-Hall (2008) in a study of Japanese college students—some of whom had started between the ages of three and 12 and others at 12 or 13— also found no advantage for the early starters in grammar, but did find they were better able to distinguish the sounds /l/ and /w/.

The research on age and L2 acquisition and especially these studies of school learners suggests that policy makers would do well to consider carefully before introducing L2 instruction at the elementary-school level to avoid false expectations. At best, it might assist the development of a more native-like pronunciation, but there is no clear evidence that it holds any advantage for other aspects of L2 acquisition.

## Summing up

1 While learners who start learning as adults can achieve high levels of L2 proficiency, there is growing evidence that they fall short of total native-like competence. However, this may simply reflect the fact a bilingual's 'multi-competence' is qualitatively different from a monolingual's competence.
2 Controversy exists as to whether there is a critical period for language acquisition. However, even if there are no well-defined age limits for achieving native ability in a second language, starting age has been shown to correlate with ultimate achievement. To avoid the problem of whether or not there are clear discontinuities before and after a critical age, some researchers have opted to talk about a 'sensitive period' rather than a 'critical period'.
3 Critical (or sensitive) periods have been found for different aspects of language—the period ends first for phonology, then for lexis and collocation, and finally for grammar.
4 The advantage of starting young for ultimate attainment only arises if learners have ample exposure to the target language. For this reason, doubts exist about the value of starting to learn a foreign language in a classroom at an early age.
5 Older learners acquire a second language more rapidly than younger learners in the initial stages, except in the case of pronunciation. This may reflect

the fact that older learners make fuller use of conscious learning strategies while children rely more on implicit learning.

6 Whether age has an effect on the process of L2 acquisition is uncertain. Some research shows that starting age has no effect on the order and sequence of acquisition, but other research suggests that the analytical skills of older learners have an impact on how they acquire specific grammatical features.

## Concluding comment

From a theoretical perspective, the key question is *why* young learners are capable of higher levels of attainment than older learners (after controlling for the number of years of exposure to the second language). One possibility is that younger learners are better equipped to engage in implicit learning and older learners rely more on explicit learning. Implicit learning is a slow process that requires massive exposure to the second language so no immediate advantage is apparent for younger learners. In fact, explicit learning may lead to more immediate success. However, over time, implicit learning wins out because it is more likely to enable learners to develop high levels of L2 proficiency.

## Notes

1 This critique of Johnson and Newport's (1989) study was itself critiqued by DeKeyser (2000). The debate testifies to the difficulty of drawing firm conclusions about the CPH.

2 Julie was clearly more native-like than Patty. A likely explanation for this is the language distance between these learners' first and second languages. Arguably, the distance between Chinese and English is greater than that between English and Arabic. The role of **language distance** in L2 acquisition is considered in Chapter 6.

3 Further evidence that age affects the process of L2 acquisition can be found in Dijk, Verspoor, and Lowie (2011). They reanalysed the data in Cancino et al.'s (1978) study and concluded that the learning trajectory of the children in this study differed from that of the adolescents and adults. See Chapter 5.

# 3

# Psychological factors and second language acquisition

## Introduction

Psychological factors are traditionally divided into three principal types: cognitive, conative, and affective. Cognitive factors are those that influence the processing, storing, and retrieval of information. The cognitive factor that has attracted the most attention in SLA is **language aptitude**. Conative factors influence the learner's ability to establish a goal and maintain effort to achieve it. In SLA, the key conative factor is **motivation**. Affective factors determine whether people respond positively or negatively to specific situations. For example, learners may vary in the extent to which they experience language anxiety. These psychological factors have been of interest to researchers because they help to explain differences in individual learners' rate and success in learning a second language.

There is both an advantage and a danger of isolating specific factors for study. The advantage lies in the possibility of the in-depth investigation of a single factor and how it affects language learning. The main danger is that investigating individual factors will result in losing sight of the 'whole' learner. This is a point I will return to in the concluding section of this chapter.

## Key psychological factors

Table 3.1 presents a brief description of the main factors that have been investigated in SLA in terms of these three dimensions. However, I will make no attempt to survey the research on all these factors but instead focus on three key factors generally considered to be representative of the three dimensions—language aptitude, motivation, and language anxiety. This is justified as the research has shown that these are the factors that impact most strongly on L2 learning[1]. There is a scarcity of research that has investigated the direct influence of the other factors on the processes involved in language learning.

| Factors | Definition and commentary |
| --- | --- |
| **Cognitive factors** | |
| *Intelligence* | Intelligence is 'a general sort of aptitude that is not limited to a specific performance area but is transferable to many sorts of performance' (Dörnyei 2005: 32). Intelligence has often been treated as a general ability but H. Gardner (1993) proposed that there are multiple intelligences (for example, mathematical intelligence, spatial intelligence, and linguistic intelligence). |
| *Language aptitude* | Language aptitude is the special ability for learning a second language. It is considered to be at least partly separate from general intelligence. Language aptitude has been theorized as involving a number of distinct abilities—phonemic coding ability, grammatical sensitivity, inductive language-learning ability, and rote-learning ability (Carroll 1965). |
| *Learner beliefs* | Learners form 'mini theories' consisting of the beliefs that they hold about language learning. Beliefs can be classified in terms of whether they reflect an experiential or analytic approach to learning. Learners also hold beliefs about their own self-efficacy as language learners. |
| **Conative factors** | |
| *Motivation* | Motivation is a complex construct that involves the reasons or goals learners have for learning a second language, the effort they put into learning, and the attributes they form as a result of their attempts to learn. Various theories of the role played by motivation in L2 learning have been proposed. Early theories distinguished 'instrumental' and 'integrative' motivation and 'extrinsic' and 'intrinsic' motivation. Theories of motivation have continued to develop and currently emphasize its dynamic nature and the importance of context. |
| *Willingness to communicate* | Willingness to communicate is defined as 'the intention to initiate communication, given a choice' by MacIntyre, Baker, Clement, and Conrad (2001: 369). It is viewed as influenced by a number of other factors and as the immediate antecedent of communication behaviour. |
| **Affective factors** | |
| *Language anxiety* | Different types of anxiety have been identified: (1) trait anxiety (a characteristic of a learner's personality), (2) state anxiety (apprehension that is experienced at a particular moment in response to a definite situation), and (3) situation-specific anxiety (the anxiety aroused by a particular type of situation). Language anxiety is seen as a specific type of situation-specific anxiety. It can be facilitating (i.e. have a positive effect on L2 acquisition) but is generally seen as debilitating (i.e. have a negative effect). |

| Mixed factors | |
|---|---|
| *Personality* | Personality is generally conceived of as being composed of a series of traits such as extraversion/introversion and neuroticism/stability. An array of different personality characteristics such as self-esteem, openness to experience, and risk-taking have been claimed to be significant in language learning. |
| *Learning style* | Learning style refers to the preferred way in which a person sets about learning in general. It reflects 'the totality of psychological functioning' (Willing 1987: 6) involving affective as well as cognitive activity. A variety of learning styles have been considered relevant to language learning (for example, sensory preferences, inductive vs deductive, synthetic vs analytic). |

*Table 3.1  Key individual difference factors in language learning*

## Language aptitude

Language aptitude is traditionally viewed as a 'special talent' for language learning. However, it is perhaps better defined as a conglomerate of abilities that interact dynamically with the situation in which learning takes place (Kormos 2013). Learners who possess these abilities, who are able to use them appropriately in the learning situations they find themselves, and who are motivated to do so are likely to achieve a high level of proficiency in a second language.

Language aptitude is not the same as **intelligence.** Sasaki (1996) conducted a study with Japanese learners of English and concluded that although the two constructs were related they were also in part distinct. Intelligence was found to be related to one aspect of language aptitude in particular—**language analytical ability**—but not to other aspects. Language aptitude is best seen as a complex construct involving a number of distinct abilities. We will now examine what these abilities are, starting with the early work by Carroll (1965) and then taking a closer look at more recent models of language aptitude.

## Carroll's model of language aptitude

Carroll saw language aptitude as determining 'the amount of time a student needs to learn a given task, unit of instruction, or curriculum to an acceptable criterion of mastery under optimal conditions of instruction and student motivation' (Carroll 1990: 26). His research in the 1950s was directed at designing tests that would indicate which learners were likely to be successful in terms of how rapidly they could learn a second language. His method of enquiry was to develop a series of tests and then select those tests that correlated most strongly with measures of L2 proficiency. He ended up with the

| Ability | Definition |
|---|---|
| Phonemic coding ability | The ability to code unfamiliar sounds in a way that they can be remembered later. |
| Grammatical sensitivity | The ability to recognize the grammatical functions of words in sentences. |
| Inductive language-learning ability | The ability to identify patterns of correspondence and relationships between form and meaning. |
| Rote-learning ability | The ability to form and remember associations between L1 and L2 vocabulary items. |

*Table 3.2  Carroll's model of language aptitude[2]*

five tests comprising the **Modern Language Aptitude Test (MLAT)** (Carroll and Sapon 1959). These tests measured the four abilities shown in Table 3.2.

The MLAT was designed to predict which learners would be successful when taught by the pattern-drilling method of language teaching popular at that time. Later, researchers asked whether a new model of language aptitude and a different battery of tests were needed to account for the abilities required by more communicative approaches to teaching and for learning in natural-istic contexts. Krashen (1981), for example, argued that language aptitude only predicted 'learning', not 'acquisition' (see Chapter 1). Carroll (1990), however, remained 'somewhat sceptical about the possibilities for greatly improving foreign language aptitude predictions beyond their present levels' (p. 27). By and large, his scepticism has been shown to be well founded, as tests developed later (for example, Grigorenko, Sternberg, and Ehrman 2000; Kiss and Nikolov 2005) have not been found to be notably more effective.

In fact, the MLAT has proven to be a robust and useful instrument and sur-vives as the most popular measure of language aptitude today. Carroll (1981) pointed out that the studies he carried out with the MLAT produced correlations between .40 and .60 with measures of L2 achievement—correlations that are stronger than those reported for any other individual factor other than possibly motivation. Gardner and MacIntyre (1992) commented: 'in the long run lan-guage aptitude is probably the single best predictor of achievement in a second language' (p. 215). It has also become clear that it is not just a predictor of per-formance on traditional language tests and formal classroom learning. It also predicts success in more communicative tests and in naturalistic, 'acquisition-rich' contexts. However, as we will see later, there are some learning conditions where it does not seem to play a significant role.

Carroll's model of language aptitude has led to a number of questions being raised. It was used to characterize learners as having 'high' or 'low' language aptitude, but researchers have increasingly recognized the need to differentiate learners according to the specific cognitive abilities they possessed. Carroll's claim that language aptitude was largely stable and not amenable to training was also challenged. It was questioned whether language aptitude played any role in how children learned a second language. Finally—and most importantly perhaps—researchers began to question whether the four abilities that the MLAT measured constituted a valid conceptualization of language aptitude. I will turn now to a consideration of these various issues.

## Differentiating types of learners

The MLAT (and other tests of language aptitude) provide measures of different abilities. One possibility, then, is that learners may be strong in some of these abilities, but weak in others. In other words, there may be more than one route to success. Wesche (1981) used language-aptitude test scores to distinguish those learners who were strong in language analytical abilities and those strong in memory. She conducted an experimental study to investigate whether learners benefitted most if they were matched to a type of instruction that she hypothesized would suit their aptitude type. The results provided support for this hypothesis. Skehan (1986) conducted a study of learners studying Arabic in the Army School of Languages in Britain. His analysis of the results of aptitude tests indicated that some of the learners demonstrated strength in grammatical sensitivity whereas others were strong in memory and 'chunk-learning' (i.e. learning **formulaic sequences**). He proposed that learners could be distinguished in terms of whether they were analytic or memory-oriented and showed that both types were successful.

## Stable or trainable?

Carroll (1990) considered that language aptitude was a fixed ability that was not influenced by training. However, other researchers have taken a different view. Grigorenko et al. (2000), for example, claimed that 'language aptitude is a form of developing expertise rather than a fixed entity at birth' (p. 401). The test of these rival views of aptitude is whether it changes as a result of experience of learning languages or as a result of attempts to train the abilities involved. Nation and McLaughlin (1986) provided evidence that expert learners (i.e. learners with experience of learning several L2s) were superior to novice learners (i.e. learners with experience of learning just one language) in **implicit learning**. They suggested that this was because expert learners made more efficient use of **learning strategies,** but it is also possible that their superiority was due to their enhanced language aptitude. However, Harley and Hart (1997) did not find that learners in an early **immersion programme** with 12 years of experience demonstrated higher levels of aptitude than late immersion learners with only four years' experience. They suggested language aptitude may function differently for young and older learners (see next section).

Skehan's (2002) evaluation of the research relevant to this issue was that 'for now, following Carroll, we will assume that aptitude does not change with the seasons' (p. 79). One possibility, however, is that some of the abilities involved in language aptitude are amenable to experience and training while others are not. Kormos and Sáfár (2006) reported that intensive experience of language learning by a group of immersion Hungarian learners of English resulted in a significant increase in their phonological sensitivity. This is clearly an area in need of further research.

## Language aptitude and age

In the last chapter, we saw that learners' age has an impact on the rate, ultimate attainment, and (possibly) the process of L2 acquisition and that this may reflect the different approaches to learning employed by young as opposed to adolescent/adult learners; older learners, for example, may make use of their greater analytical skills. This suggests that the role of language aptitude varies according to the age of the learner.

DeKeyser (2000) investigated the hypothesis that language analytical ability contributes to the success of learners who start learning as adults, but not for those who start as children. He investigated 57 adult Hungarian-speaking immigrants to the United States, some of whom had arrived as children and others as adults. He found that language analytical ability was not a significant predictor of the childhood arrivals' performance on a **grammaticality judgement test**, but that it was for the adult arrivals. Only those adult arrivals with high analytical ability scored in the same range as the young arrivals. In other words, analytical ability made a difference, but only for those learners who started to learn as adults. If it is assumed that child learners rely primarily on implicit learning while adults are engaged in explicit learning, this study suggests that the relevance of language analytical ability depends on the type of learning involved.

It is important to note, however, that DeKeyser's study only investigated one aspect of language aptitude—language analytical ability. It is possible that other abilities (for example, phonemic coding ability and memory) are just as important for children as for adults. Harley and Hart's (1997) study of French immersion learners in Canada supports this hypothesis. They reported a positive correlation between memory ability and L2 proficiency in the early starters, but between language analytical ability and proficiency in the learners who began in grade seven. However, Harley and Hart pointed out-that this result could also be explained by the kind of instructional approach that the two groups had experienced. That is, the instruction for the early-starters emphasized memory-related activities whereas the instruction received by the late-starters was more demanding of analytical skills.

## Aptitude and type of learning

Both DeKeyser's (2000) and Harley and Hart's (1997) studies suggest that the importance of language aptitude depends on the type of learning. But we have also seen that this is a controversial issue. Now we will consider two studies that investigated the role of language aptitude in implicit and explicit learning.

De Graaff (1997) investigated the relationship between two measures of language aptitude (grammatical sensitivity and memory) and the learning of simple and complex grammatical structures by adult learners, some of whom received **explicit instruction**—where the rules were explained—and others **implicit instruction**—where there was no rule explanation. Language aptitude correlated with the test scores of both groups of learners for both grammatical structures and there was no difference between the two groups. In other words, language aptitude proved to be an explanatory factor irrespective of the type of instruction.

Robinson (1996) also reported a study that showed language analytical ability correlated with measures of learning resulting from (1) an explicit condition where learners were given an explanation of the grammatical rules; (2) a rule-search condition where they were asked to search for the rules in sets of sentences that exemplified them; and (3) an implicit condition where they were asked to simply read and memorize sets of sentences. Language aptitude was implicated in the learning resulting from all three conditions. However, there was no relationship between analytical ability and learning in (4) an **incidental learning** condition where learners completed a meaning-focused task that simply involved exposure to the target structures. Arguably, it is this condition that corresponds most closely to the kind of implicit learning that takes place in a real-world context. Thus, this study can be interpreted as showing that a key component of language aptitude is a factor in explicit and memory-based learning but not in implicit learning.

Some studies (for example, Erlam 2005), however, suggest that aptitude may not necessarily play a role even in explicit learning. There are two possible hypotheses regarding the relationship between aptitude and explicit instruction. One is that learners with greater aptitude (especially language analytical ability) will be better equipped to handle instruction involving rule explanation. The other hypothesis is that careful rule explanation can compensate for differences in aptitude. It is not yet possible to determine which of these hypotheses is correct. Overall, no clear conclusion can be reached about the role of language aptitude in different types of learning. It would seem likely, however, that some abilities (for example, phonological ability and memory) are important in both implicit and explicit learning.

## Reconceptualizing language aptitude

The developments that we will now consider were of two main kinds. The first involved an attempt to relate language aptitude to concepts as **noticing**, **noticing-the-gap**, and **pushed output** (see Chapter 1). In other words, language aptitude was now examined in relation to the *process* of acquisition and not just to its *product*. The second approach entailed attempts to develop

| Stage | Processes involved | Aptitude components |
|---|---|---|
| 1 Noticing | Learner directs attention at some specific feature in the input. | auditory segmentation; attention management; working memory; phonemic coding |
| 2 Patterning | Learner constructs a hypothesis (implicitly or explicitly) about the feature, subsequently extends the domain of the hypothesis before recognizing its limitations and restructuring it and integrating the new representation into the interlanguage system. | working memory; grammatical sensitivity; inductive language learning ability; restructuring capacity |
| 3 Controlling | Learner is able to use the integrated feature with increasing ease and accuracy. | automatization; proceduralization; retrieval processes |
| 4 Lexicalizing | Learner is now able to produce the feature as a 'lexicalized element' (i.e. it is accessed as a whole rather than by applying a rule). | integrative memory; chunking; retrieval processes |

*Table 3.3  Skehan's (2002) model of language aptitude and L2 acquisition*

new ways of measuring aptitude, in particular, by incorporating **working memory** into the model.

Skehan (2002) proposed a model of language aptitude that links different components to four macro stages in the process of language acquisition: (1) noticing, (2) patterning, (3) controlling, and (4) lexicalizing (see Table 3.3). In the case of (1) the relevant abilities are those involved in processing input; (2) involves analytic ability; (3) involves those abilities associated with controlling existing L2 knowledge whilst; (4) involves the memory abilities associated with converting rule-based knowledge into ready-made chunks that facilitate easy communication (a process Skehan called 'lexicalizing').

Skehan's model expands on the traditional model by identifying a whole range of micro-abilities associated with specific acquisition processes. Robinson (2002) further developed this approach by attempting to show how what he termed 'basic cognitive abilities' (for example, 'pattern recognition' and 'rote memory') contributed to what he called 'aptitude complexes'—such as 'noticing-the-gap'—which are associated with specific 'task aptitudes'—such as whether a communicative task calls for one-way or two-way communication. In this way, Robinson sought to identify the different abilities required to benefit from **Task-based Language Teaching** (see Chapter 11). These new models are clearly programmatic. The constructs they propose are in need of tighter definition, but they enrich our understanding of language aptitude and also afford specific hypotheses about how language aptitude relates to L2 acquisition.

A feature of these models is the importance they attach to working memory. Working memory is generally conceived as a multi-component memory system. Baddeley (2003) distinguished four sub-components: (1) the central executive that controls attention; (2) the visuospatial sketchpad that stores and rehearses visual information; (3) the phonological loop that stores and rehearses oral information; and (4) the episodic buffer that combines information from different sources. The two components that have received the greatest attention are the phonological loop and the central executive. The phonological loop holds phonological information for short periods of time and is also able to silently rehearse the information to reactive fading memory traces. It constitutes a limited-capacity component. The central executive is a supervisory system that controls complex operations such as focusing attention and regulating the flow of information between short-term and long-term memory. It is also seen as a limited-capacity system.

It is not difficult to see why learners' working memory capacity is so important for language learning. Learners with a larger capacity will be able to store more linguistic data, rehearse it more fully, and make links with information stored in long-term memory. Working memory is hypothesized to be especially important in implicit learning when learners are primarily focused on meaning. J. Williams (2005), for example, provided evidence to show that differences in **phonological short-term memory** (i.e. the ability to store auditory traces) predicted differences in learners' ability to learn certain grammatical features such as gender agreement in Spanish implicitly.

However, the results of working memory research in SLA to date have not always produced easily interpretable results. As Ortega (2009) noted, research has only begun to 'scratch the surface' of the relationship between working memory and L2 learning. Nevertheless, there are strong theoretical reasons, supported by some research findings, to indicate that working memory is an important component of language aptitude. In particular, short-term phonological memory appears to play a significant role. Working memory is considered further in Chapters 7 and 8.

## Summing up

1 Early work in language aptitude centred around the development of tests— such as Carroll and Sapon's (1959) Modern language Aptitude Test (MLAT)—that were used to predict how easily learners would learn a second language.

2 The MLAT is a robust and useful instrument and continues to be used in research today. It has been shown to predict success in learning in both naturalistic and instructed contexts.

3 As language aptitude is comprised of a number of distinct abilities, it is possible that learners differ in the abilities they are strong in. Skehan (1986) proposed a distinction between analytic-oriented and memory-oriented learners, both of whom can achieve success.

4 Language aptitude was initially seen as a stable, trait-like construct, but this view was subsequently challenged. There is evidence to suggest that abilities change as a result of learning experience and therefore may be trainable.

5 There is a relationship between language aptitude and age. A high level of language analytical ability may be required to enable adult learners to achieve high levels of L2 proficiency (DeKeyser 2000). This ability, however, appears to be of less importance for child learners.

6 The abilities required for implicit and explicit learning may also differ. For example, phonological coding ability is more important for implicit learning while language analytical ability is more important for explicit learning.

7 The original conceptualization of language aptitude has changed. New models (Skehan 2002; Robinson 2002) have been developed that link specific abilities to stages in the process of L2 acquisition and to the requirements of different instructional tasks. Central to these new models is working memory, which is now seen as a key component of language aptitude.

## Motivation

Like language aptitude, motivation is a complex construct. It involves:

1 The reasons a learner has for needing or wanting to learn an L2 (i.e. motivational orientation).

2 The effort a learner makes to learn the L2, the learner's persistence with the learning task, and the impact immediate context has on these (i.e. behavioural motivation).

3 The effect that the learner's evaluation of his/her progress has on subsequent learning behaviour (i.e. attributional motivation).

Like language aptitude, motivation is primarily seen as affecting the rate of learning and ultimate achievement. However, there have been only limited attempts to link the study of motivation to mainstream work in SLA by demonstrating how it is related to the processes responsible for acquisition. But see Tseng and Schmitt (2008) for an attempt to do this for vocabulary learning.

Following Dörnyei (2005), I will adopt a historical approach by outlining how the study of motivation has evolved over the last 50 or so years. I will then focus on a recent theory of motivation and the research it has generated.

## The social-psychological period (1959–1990)

This period was dominated by the work of Canadian social psychologists, who were interested in the role that motivation played in language learning in a society that was divided into Anglophone and Francophone communities. The starting point was the recognition that learners' motivation depended on their attitudes towards the other community and to the target language, and that these were socially determined.

Gardner and Lambert (1972) distinguished two broad orientations: an **integrative orientation** entails a desire to identify with the target-language culture and its speakers; an **instrumental orientation** arises when learners wish to learn a second language for functional purposes (for example, to pass an examination or obtain a job). However, initially, **instrumental motivation** was not fully theorized as they saw the integrative orientation as central in the Canadian context. Later, however, Gardner (2001) came to recognize that 'there can be other supports for motivation not directly associated with **integrative motivation**' (p. 7).

Motivation, however, comprises more than the learner's orientation. It is also influenced by the learner's attitudes towards the learning situation (for example, attitudes towards the teacher and the instruction) and the actual effort that the learner puts into learning a second language. 'Motivation', then, is a composite construct involving orientation, attitudes, and effort. Gardner's (1985) **Socio-educational Model** also emphasized the importance of the social and cultural milieu in which learning took place. This determined the cultural beliefs learners held, which in turn influenced their orientation and attitudes to the learning situation. Gardner also acknowledged the role played by language aptitude in determining learning outcomes, but saw it as only relevant in formal learning contexts.

The theory was enormously influential. Dörnyei (2005) commented that it was the dominant theory for three decades. It generated a large number of correlational studies. These made use of the instrument that Gardner developed to measure motivation—the Attitude Motivation Test Battery (AMTB) (1985), which included questions relating to motivational orientation, attitudes, and effort. The main findings of this research can be summarized as follows:

1 Integrative motivation is positively correlated with various measures of L2 achievement. Gardner (2005) reported a median correlation of 0.37 in a survey of studies of learners of L2 French conducted in seven different geographical areas in Canada.

2 Learners' integrative motivation was also found to be related to the teacher's and students' classroom behaviours (for example, students' voluntary responses to teacher questions).

3 Learners with an integrative motivation were less likely to abandon learning a second language (Ramage 1990).

4 In some contexts, however, integrative motivation was found to be negatively associated with achievement and that other motivations could be important: for example, Oller, Baca, and Vigil (1977) reported that Hispanic learners of English in California were more motivated by a 'Machiavellian motivation' (i.e. a desire to manipulate and overcome speakers of the target language).

5 Overall, instrumental motivation is a much weaker predictor of L2 achievement than integrative motivation (Masgoret and Gardner 2003).

6 However, instrumental motivation can play a bigger role in foreign language contexts where learners have little interest in the target language culture. Gardner and Lambert (1972) reported that this was the case with Tagalog learners of L2 English in the Philippines.

7 The benefits of an instrumental motivation are likely to wear off once the instrumental objective has been achieved as learners cease making any effort to learn. This is especially likely to occur in some foreign language contexts.

Gardner's Socio-educational Model has been subjected to considerable criticism. It took no account of the impact that success in learning can have on a learner's motivation. Gardner (1985) claimed that motivation was a causative variable, but this ignores the fact that learners can derive motivation from their actual or perceived success in learning a second language. Gardner's theory paid scant regard to the fact that a learner's motivation is not static but dynamic, continuously responsive to the learning conditions. Perhaps the most serious limitation, however, lies in how the role of social milieu was conceived. The key notion of integrativeness is of obvious relevance to a socio-cultural context such as Canada where there are clear L1 and L2 communities, but is less clearly relevant to many contexts where the notion of the 'target language community' is highly problematic (for example, monolingual contexts such as Japan, or the complex multilingual and multicultural contexts found in the USA). Also, in Gardner's model, the social milieu is seen as determining the motivational disposition of the learner and no recognition was given of the fact that learners have agency and that local social contexts are actively and continuously constructed by learners (Pavlenko 2002). In other words the 'social' component of the theory was under-theorized. See Chapter 9 for further comments on this limitation.

The Socio-educational Model was not the only socio-psychological theory of this period. Clement (1986) failed to find any relationship between integrativeness and English language ability in Francophone students studying at the University Ottowa. However, the learners' self-confidence (i.e. the extent they believed in their own ability to learn a second language successfully) proved a strong predictor. Self-confidence constituted a social-psychological variable as it originated in the quality and quantity of the contact between members of the target and L2 communities. Clement argued that 'frequency of contact and the concomitant self-confidence might be more important in determining second language proficiency than socio-contextual or affective factors' (p. 287).

## The cognitive-situated period

In this period, responding to criticisms levelled at the social-psychological approach, researchers turned to mainstream theories of motivation in cognitive psychology. In so doing, they broadened the scope of enquiry into the motivation for second lanaguage learning by examining factors that aroused intrinsic interest in learners and learners' perceptions of the reasons for their success or failure.

### Self-determination Theory

**Self-determination Theory** (Deci and Ryan 1985) was built around the common-sense notion that people are motivated by both external factors such as rewards, grades, or the opinions of others and by internal ones such as personal interests, curiosity, or experiencing an activity as fun. The theory was applied to L2 motivation by Noels, Pelletier, Clement, and Vallerand (2000), who developed a model based on the distinction between **intrinsic motivation** and **extrinsic motivation**. They defined extrinsically motivated behaviours as 'those actions carried out to achieve some instrumental end' and intrinsic motivation as 'motivation to engage in an activity because it is enjoyable and satisfying to do so' (p. 61). Various sub-categories of each type were distinguished. For example, intrinsic motivation could be derived from (1) knowledge (i.e. the motivation derived from exploring new ideas and knowledge), (2) accomplishment (i.e. the pleasant sensations aroused by trying to achieve a task or goal), and (3) stimulation (i.e. the fun and excitement generated by actually performing a task). Noels et al. also included amotivation (i.e. the absence of any motivation to learn) in their model. In a study of Anglophone learners of L2 French, they found both extrinsic and especially intrinsic motivation were positively related to measures of perceived competence and intention to continue study while amotivation was negatively correlated with these measures. Noels et al. concluded that the more self-determined learners' motivation, the greater their achievement.

The concept of intrinsic motivation accords more closely with how teachers conceive of students' motivation. Crookes and Schmidt (1991) observed that 'it is probably fair to say that teachers would describe a student as motivated if s/he becomes productively engaged in learning tasks, and sustains that engagement, without the need for continual encouragement or direction' (p. 480). They also recognized that teachers see it as their responsibility to help generate intrinsic motivation in their students.

### Attribution Theory

**Attribution Theory** (Weiner 1992) views motivation as deriving from the explanations that learners give for their progress in learning a second language. As Dörnyei (2005) put it 'the subjective reasons to which we attribute our past successes and failures considerably shape our motivational disposition underlying future action' (p. 79). There are three main types of attributions. First, they can be internal (i.e. learners explain their performance in terms of their own ability or lack of it) or external (i.e. learners place the blame for learning problems on external factors). Second, learners can perceive the outcome of their learning efforts as stable or unstable. In the case of the former, learners may be less inclined to make any further effort as they believe it will make no difference, but in the case of the latter, they may try harder. The third set of attributions concerns whether the factors influencing success or failure are seen as controllable or uncontrollable. Learners will be more motivated to improve if they perceive the cause of their difficulties lies within themselves rather than in other people (for example, a poor teacher).

In one of the few L2 studies based on attribution theory, Williams and Burden (1999) reported that British secondary school students tended to explain how well they were performing in terms of external factors. They attributed success to their own aptitude and the efforts of others and failure to the difficulty of the tasks they were assigned or poor teaching. In another study, Ushioda (2001) conducted interviews with adult Irish learners of French to investigate what factors enabled these learners to maintain a positive self-concept and belief in their capacity to learn French. She identified two attributional patterns that contributed to this: (1) attributing positive L2 outcomes to personal ability and/or effort and (2) attributing negative L2 outcomes to temporary shortcomings, such as lack of effort or inadequate opportunity to learn, which could be overcome.

Both self-determination theory and attribution theory recognized the importance of situation-specific factors. These theories also recognize the dynamic nature of motivation as motivation is not fixed, but rises and falls according to the situational conditions and the attributions learners form. However, neither theory fully captures the ebb and flow of motivation over time or within a single lesson.

## The process-oriented period

During this period, researchers turned their attention to examining the dynamic character of motivation and the temporal variation that can occur both over the lifetime of a learner and within a single lesson. This phase in motivational research was associated with a number of important developments in the modelling of motivation:

1 the identification of phases of motivation, involving the reasons for learning a second language, deciding to do something, and sustaining the effort over time (Williams and Burden 1997)

2 the influence of group dynamics on learners' motivation
3 the role of self-regulation in helping learners to maintain their motivation when faced with challenges
4 the motivational forces that arise as a product of interacting with others in the second language.

## The Process Model of L2 Motivation

The **Process Model of L2 Motivation** (Dörnyei and Otto 1998) constitutes the fullest attempt to represent the complex, dynamic nature of motivation. It proposes three phases:

1 *Pre-actional phase.* This involves goal-setting and the formation of an action plan. Motivational influences in this stage include 'attitudes towards the L2 and its speakers', as in Gardner's model, but also a range of other factors (for example, 'expectancy of success' and 'perceived coping potential'). Dörnyei and Otto refer to this stage as 'choice motivation'.
2 *Actional stage.* This is when learners begin to implement their action plan. It involves 'executive motivation'. Three basic processes come into play in this stage: implementation of the sub-tasks in the action plan; ongoing appraisal of the extent to which the goals of the sub-tasks have been achieved; and action control involving the use of self-regulatory strategies such as motivational maintenance strategies and language-learning strategies.
3 *Post-actional phase.* This is when the learner evaluates the outcome of the actions undertaken and forms causal attributions about the reasons for the success or failure of the action plan. During this phase, the learner will also consider what changes need to be made to the choice of action-specific strategies to ensure a more successful outcome in the future.

The Process Model of L2 Motivation constitutes an attempt to build on previous L2 motivation research. The pre-actional phase draws on Gardner's social-psychological perspective although it includes a much wider range of factors influencing choice motivation. The actional stage draws on the importance that self-determination theory attaches to the intrinsic motivation derived from performing learning tasks. The post-actional stage incorporates attribution theory.

The model is an impressive attempt to construct a comprehensive theory of motivation that acknowledges its dynamic nature. Change can originate in any of the three phases of the model. However—as Dörnyei (2005) acknowledged—it has its limitations. As the labels of the different stages suggest, it reflects a linear view of motivation, whereas motivation must involve parallel action processes. Learners are involved in making choices, deciding on and implementing action, and evaluating outcomes concurrently in what Dörnyei calls a 'motivational complex'. The model is useful, however, because it provides a basis for identifying specific strategies that teachers can employ to help motivate learners (see Dörnyei 2001).

## Group dynamics and motivation

The second major development during this period centred on the powerful motivating force of group dynamics. As Dörnyei and Murphey (2003) noted, 'groups have been found to have a 'life of their own'—that is, individuals in groups behave differently from the way they do outside the group' (p. 3). In other words, while motivation is a construct that relates to the individual learner, it will be influenced by the other members of the group that the learner is part of. A good example of this can be found in Dörnyei's (2002) study of the motivational forces at work when learners performed a communicative task in pairs. He obtained measures of the motivation of Hungarian second-ary-school learners' of L2 English and also their attitudes to task-based teaching. He then asked them to perform an argumentative task in pairs and obtained measures of the number of words and turns produced by each student. He found that the learners were strongly influenced by their partner's motivational disposition and this affected how they performed the task. He concluded that task-motivation is co-constructed (i.e. one learner's motivation affects the other's).

## Self-regulation and motivation

**Self-regulation,** broadly defined, refers to the actions people take to organize and manage their learning. It is relevant to all three phases of Dörnyei and Otto's Process Model but, arguably, is of central importance in the actional stage. Strong learning goals without effective self-regulation will have limited impact on learning.

Kormos and Csizér (2014) investigated the inter-relationships between motivation, self-regulatory strategies, and learner autonomy in 638 Hungarian learners of English. Using a questionnaire, they obtained separate measures of motivation (for example, the learners' attitudes to English as an international language and the instrumental value of learning English); self-regulation (for example, the learners' willingness to actively seek out opportunities for learning English and their ability to plan their study time efficiently); and autonomy (for example, their capacity to exert control over learning resources). The results suggested that the learners' motivation was a prerequisite for effective use of regulatory strategies, which in turn influence their level of autonomy.

## Motivation as an act of communication

Finally, motivation can be seen as constructed in and through interaction. As McNamara (1973) noted long ago, 'the really important part of motivation lies in the act of communication itself' (p. 252). This perspective affords the most dynamic view of motivation.

The theoretical basis for this approach was spelled out by Ushioda (2009). She proposed what she called a 'person-in-context relational view of motivation' (p. 220). Rejecting the dualism of 'context' and 'learner' inherent in earlier models of motivation, she argued that the learner is part of the context, both influenced by it, but also able to influence and shape it. Ushioda went on to suggest that questionnaires were not the best way to investigate learners' motivation and that instead researchers should focus on the discourse that learners participate in. Drawing on Richards' (2006) study of the different identities that teachers and students can enact in a classroom and how these affect the interactions they participate in, she noted that what Richards called 'transportable identities' (i.e. the identities that the classroom participants possess as individuals and can bring into the classroom) have a powerful motivational impact on the nature of classroom talk. However, very little is currently known about how interactional practices constitute social displays of motivation or how motivation arises or is lost in the interactions that learners participate in.

The recognition that motivation is displayed in and developed through interaction potentially brings motivation research closer to one of the main branches of SLA we noted in Chapter 1—the role of interaction in L2 learning. Does the **negotiation of meaning** foster motivation or—as Aston (1986) noted—can it sometimes frustrate? There has been little attempt to relate models of motivation to the **information-processing model** that informs much of SLA research. Krashen (1981) saw motivation as an 'affective filter' that influences how much comprehensible input a learner processes. Schmidt (2010) proposed that more motivated learners notice more and also develop higher levels of awareness. However, there is currently little research to support either of these propositions.

## Dörnyei's L2 Motivational Self System

Drawing on the insights from the range of theories considered in the previous sections, Dörnyei (2009) proposed a new theory of L2 motivation. The underlying principle of this theory is that motivation does not arise when learners identify with other speakers of the language (as in Gardner's socio-educational model), but with future versions of their own selves. Dörnyei argued that learners have ideas of what they might become—their 'possible selves'—and that these function as 'future self-guides' which set the standards the learner hopes to achieve. He proposed that a learner's self-image as a second language speaker is partly based on actual experiences of the second language community and partly on imagination. The theory also recognized the impact that environmental conditions can have on motivation.

There are three components to the **L2 Motivational Self System**:

1 *Ideal L2 Self*. 'If the person we would like to become speaks an L2, the '*ideal L2 self*' is a powerful motivator to learn the L2 because of the desire to reduce the discrepancy between our actual and ideal selves' (Dörnyei 2009: 29)[3]. This component incorporates both integrative and instrumental aspirations relating to a desired end state, such as a better job. The ideal self also facilitates the self-regulation needed to succeed.

2  *Ought-to Self*. This 'concerns the attributes that one believes one ought
   to possess to meet expectations and to avoid possible negative outcomes'
   (p. 29). Instrumentality is involved here but is preventive—directed at
   preventing negative outcomes (for example, performing poorly in an
   examination).

3  *L2 Learning Experience*. This refers to the 'executive motives related to the
   immediate learning environment and experience' (p. 29). Important factors
   here are the impact of the teacher, the curriculum, the peer group, and the
   experience of success. This component, therefore, incorporates insights
   from self-determination and attribution theories.

Dörnyei (2009) claimed that the results of a number of early studies provided
'solid confirmation' of the L2 Motivational Self System. He noted that the
Ideal L2 Self was closely related to integrativeness, but that it explained a
higher percentage of variance in measures of learners' intended effort. The
Ideal L2 Self also correlated with measures of promotional instrumentality
while the Ought-to Self correlated with measures of preventive instrumentality, as predicted by the theory.

Later studies, however, have not always supported the important role the
theory attaches to the Ideal L2 Self. Lamb (2012) investigated the motivation
of adolescent Indonesian learners in three contexts—a metropolitan city, a
provincial city, and a rural district in Indonesia. Using a questionnaire based
on Dörnyei's own research, he was unable to obtain a satisfactory measure of
the Ought-to Self. Of the other two components, it was L2 Learning Experience rather than the Ideal L2 Self that was found to be of greater importance
in motivating the learners. Interestingly, the Ideal L2 Self was found to contribute significantly to learning in the metropolitan context (but less so than
L2 Learning Experience), but did not contribute at all in the provincial and
rural contexts.

The **L2 Motivational Self System** has been shown to work well with learners in Hungary and in a number of other foreign language contexts (for
example, Japan and Chile), but Lamb's study suggests that the theory does
not apply to all learning contexts. Perhaps the drive to develop a theory of L2
motivation that is applicable to every context is mistaken as separate theories
may be needed to take account of contextual differences.

Another limitation of Dörnyei's theory is that it does not really account for
the dynamic nature of motivation, a point acknowledged by Dörnyei. Like so
many of the other theories, it has been investigated by means of a questionnaire that taps the general factors that shape learners' motivation and assumes
these to be stable. There is clearly a need for more qualitative studies of the
kind Ushioda (2009) argued for. A final limitation is that, like all the other
theories we have examined, no attempt has been made to relate motivational
constructs to the underlying cognitive processes involved in second language
learning.

## Summing up

Over the years, thinking about motivation has evolved and complexified. The following is a summary of the main dimensions of motivation that have been identified:

1 The Socio-educational Model emphasized the role of integrativeness in L2 achievement. In some contexts, such as bilingual Canada, learners who have a desire to identify with the target-language culture and its speakers achieve more than those who lack this desire.
2 Learners' self-confidence also plays a role in second language learning.
3 Situation-specific factors are influential in facilitating learners' intrinsic motivation, which is likely to be more powerful than extrinsic motivation in promoting learning.
4 Learners form attributions about their success and failure and their subsequent motivation will depend on these attributions.
5 Motivation should ultimately be seen as a 'process' rather than a 'state'. Dörnyei and Otto proposed a model of motivation-as-process by distinguishing the factors involved in choice, executive, and retrospective motivation.
6 Motivated learners are self-regulated (i.e. they plan, monitor, and evaluate their attempts to learn).
7 A learner's motivation is influenced by other learners; the dynamics of a classroom or of a learning group affect the extent to which individual learners are motivated, both overall and when performing specific tasks.
8 In part at least, motivation is an interactional phenomenon as it is generated and maintained in and through the social interactions a learner participates in.
9 Dörnyei's L2 Motivational Self System constitutes an attempt to construct a composite theory of L2 motivation by distinguishing three components— the Ideal L2 Self, the Ought-to Self, and the L2 Learning Experience.

Ultimately, motivation is a highly situated phenomenon; the factors that shape it will vary according to the macro- and micro-settings learners find themselves in and will change dynamically in both the short and long term. For this reason, qualitative case studies of individual learners may prove a more effective way of investigating motivation than quantitative, survey-based methods.

## Language anxiety

I turn now to consider briefly one of the key affective factors that has been shown to impact on L2 learning. **Language anxiety** is the anxiety that results from learners' emotional responses to the learning conditions they experience in a specific situation. It differs from, but is related to, trait anxiety (i.e. the learner's overall tendency to be anxious as a result of their personality). It has been investigated primarily in classroom learners by means of both quantitative and qualitative research methods.

Much of the research has focused on the sources of language anxiety. Bailey (1983) analysed the diaries of 11 learners and found that they tended to become anxious when they compared themselves with other learners in the class and found themselves less proficient. Other sources of anxiety include being asked to communicate spontaneously in the second language, fear of negative evaluation, and tests. Horwitz, Horwitz, and Cope (1986) developed a questionnaire that has been widely used by researchers—the Foreign Language Classroom Anxiety Scale—based on these three major sources. Learners, however, differ in what they find anxiety-provoking. Horwitz (2001) noted that 'in almost all cases, any task that was judged "comfortable" by some learners was also judged "stressful" by others' (p. 118).

Researchers disagree about how anxiety affects language learning although the prevailing view is that high levels of anxiety impede learning. MacIntyre and Gardner (1991a), in a comprehensive review of the research, concluded:

> Covering several measures of proficiency, in several different samples, and even in somewhat different conceptual frameworks, it has been shown that anxiety negatively affects performance in the second language. In some cases, anxiety provides some of the highest simple correlations of attitudes with achievement.
>
> (MacIntyre and Gardner 1991a: 103)

However, as with motivation, anxiety can be both the result as well as the cause of poor achievement. Sparks, Ganschow, and Javorsky's (2000) **Linguistic Coding Difference Hypothesis** claims that success in foreign language learning is primarily dependent on language aptitude and that students' anxiety about learning an L2 is a consequence of the learning difficulties they experience because of deficits in their aptitude.

As with language aptitude, attempts have been made to relate language anxiety to the process of learning. MacIntyre and Gardner (1991b) proposed that learners generally experience little anxiety initially, so there is no immediate effect on learning. Subsequently, language anxiety develops if learners have bad learning experiences (such as those documented in Bailey's diary studies). These have a debilitative effect on learning. Their model also recognizes that poor performance can be the cause as well as the result of anxiety. MacIntyre and Gardner (1991b) hypothesized that anxiety can affect the different stages of the learning process: the input stage (i.e. when learners encounter material for the first time); the processing stage (i.e. when they make connections between the new information and existing knowledge); and the output stage (i.e. when they demonstrate the new knowledge). Sheen (2008) showed that anxiety can affect the learners' ability to process input. She found that the low-anxiety learners were much more likely to **repair** their errors following **recasts** and consequently learn from them. High anxiety, then, can impede learning because it interferes with the learners' ability to process input in their working memory.

Anxiety can be seen as an aspect of motivation as it impacts negatively on learners' motivation to learn. It can also be seen as a personality variable. However, it would be a mistake to see low anxiety as a <u>necessary</u> condition for successful second language learning. In some cases, anxiety can be facilitative, driving learners to make more effort.

## Learning strategies

Oxford (1989) defined **learning strategies** as 'behaviors or actions which learners use to make language learning more successful, self-directed and enjoyable' (p. 235). There are, however considerable problems in deciding exactly what constitutes a '**learning strategy**'. Researchers differ in whether they should be restricted to strategies directed at attempts to learn or should also include communication strategies (i.e. strategies such as 'requesting clarification' used to resolve a communication problem). They also differ in whether they see them as involving conscious application on the part of the learner or as performed automatically without consciousness. One possibility—compatible with **Skill-learning Theory** (see Chapter 1)—is that they start out as conscious but subsequently, as a result of continuous use, become automatic and unconscious.

## Typologies of learning strategies

A further problem is that there is no agreed typology of learning strategies. Different typologies appear with regularity. Some of the typologies (for example, Cohen and Chi 2001) distinguish the strategies associated with different language skills (for example, strategies for speaking, listening, reading, and writing). Others, such as O'Malley and Chamot (1990), list and classify the strategies believed to contribute to general language proficiency. Their typology has proven one of the most popular. It distinguishes three basic categories of strategies:

1  Metacognitive strategies, for example 'selective attention' (deciding in advance to attend to specific aspects of language input).
2  Cognitive strategies, for example 'inferencing' (using available information to guess meanings of new items, predict outcomes, or fill in missing information).
3  Social/affective strategies, for example 'question for clarification' (asking a teacher or another native speaker for repetition, paraphrasing, explanation).

## Correlational studies

Much of the learning-strategy research has used questionnaires (for example, Oxford's, 1990, Strategy Inventory for Language Learning). These ask learners to self-report which specific strategies they use or how frequently they use them. Quantitative scores derived from these questionnaires are then correlated with measures of L2 achievement/proficiency. Studies that have employed such an approach (for example, Wharton 2000) generally report that higher-proficiency learners use more strategies than lower proficiency learners. Such studies are inherently problematic, however, as it is impossible to tell whether it is strategy use that causes learning or whether the ability to use particular strategies is dependent on proficiency. For example, more advanced learners have been found to make greater use of **metacognitive strategies** (Macaro 2006), but this might simply be because their greater language proficiency gives them access to these strategies

## Effects of strategy instruction

More interesting is the research that has investigated the effects of **strategy instruction** on learning. Given the uncertainty about which strategies are important for learning, perhaps not much should be expected of such studies. Another reason for being doubtful is the lack of standardization in both the instructional packages and the manner in which learning was assessed (Macaro 2006). However, there is evidence that strategy instruction is effective.

Hassan et al. (2005) carried out a review of 25 strategy training studies and concluded that 17 reported positive results, five mixed results, and only two negative results. However, the effectiveness of the training varied according to the different language skills, with the most robust effect in reading comprehension and writing skills. It was not possible to determine which types of strategy training or which particular training techniques were effective. The studies investigated mainly non-school populations so Hassan et al. did not comment on the effectiveness of strategy training with school-based learners. Nor were they able to determine whether the learners' stage of development was a significant factor influencing the success of training.

A more comprehensive, meta-analytic review of strategy instruction studies (Plonsky 2011) provides a clearer endorsement of strategy training. Plonsky's **meta-analysis** included 61 studies involving 6,791 learners in his meta-analysis. He calculated the average 'effect size' of the strategy instruction in all the studies and also investigated how moderating variables such as the age of the learners, the kind of the strategy instruction, and the type of learning outcome impacted on the overall effect. The overall effect size was 'small to medium'. He argued that this compared favourably with the effect sizes reported in meta-analyses of strategy training studies in general education, but was modest compared to meta-analyses of other types of L2 instruction (see Chapter 10). He found that instruction directed at cognitive strategies was more effective than instruction directed at metacognitive strategies. This casts some doubt on the emphasis that other researchers have placed on metacognitive strategies. The effects of the strategy instruction were clearly evident in the case of reading, writing, speaking, vocabulary, and pronunciation, but weak or not evident at all in listening, grammar, or general proficiency.

There are some major theoretical problems with learning strategy research. Dörnyei (2005) noted that whereas research on learning strategies was popular in general educational research in the 1980s, it declined dramatically in the 1990s, and that language learning strategies should be re-conceptualized and investigated in terms of **self-regulation**. Tseng, Dörnyei, and Schmitt (2006) argued that an approach based on self-regulation provides a more satisfactory way of empowering learners than traditional strategy training as the real goal should be that of assisting learners to achieve self-regulation, not to use specific strategies. They developed an instrument to measure self-regulatory capacity for vocabulary learning.

Another rather surprising limitation is the failure of research on learning strategies to relate strategies to the processes that SLA researchers have proposed are important for learning. An exception is Purpura (1999). Purpura distinguished strategies in terms of whether they related to comprehending processes, storing/memory processes, or using/retrieval processes. The advantage of such an approach is that it aligns the study of learning strategies with mainstream thinking about the nature of language learning and would provide learning strategy research with a stronger theoretical base. It might be possible to identify not just which specific strategies are important for learning, but also when, and in what way.

## Age and psychological factors

It is interesting to consider whether the impact of the psychological factors we have considered in this chapter depends on the age of the learners. In the case of language aptitude, there is clear evidence that it does. Whereas short-term phonological memory may be of special importance for young learners, language analytical ability appears to be more important for older learners. Granena and Long (2012) showed that language aptitude mitigates the negative effects that increasing age has on the acquisition of lexical knowledge.

Age and motivation are also related. Kormos and Csizér (2008) investigated Hungarian school pupils, university students, and adult language learners and found that there were differences in what motivated these three groups. The school learners were primarily motivated by interest in English-language cultural products whereas the two older groups were more influenced by their attitudes to English in the globalized world. Relationships have also been found between age and language anxiety, with older learners tending to be more anxious than younger learners (for example, Onwuegbuzie, Bailey, and Daley 1999). Not surprisingly, given their mediating role, the learning strategies that learners prefer vary with age. Age differences in the speed of learning and ultimate attainment that we noted in the previous chapter may be—in part at least—traceable to the part played by key psychological factors.

## Conclusion

I have elected to examine the different psychological factors separately, reflecting the general approach adopted by researchers. However, the danger of such an approach is that it loses sight of the 'whole' learner. As Tudor (2001) pointed out, learners are 'complex human beings who bring with them to the classroom their own individual personality' (p. 14). Dörnyei (2010), too, is now critical of a modular approach to investigating individual differences on the grounds that the factors exert a cumulative effect that is not simply the sum of their individual effects and also they are continuously fluctuating in nature.

There is an interesting branch of early research into individual differences that I did not consider in this chapter, but that can be seen as addressing the 'whole' learner. The **'good language learner'** studies (for example, Naiman, Fröhlich, Stern, and Todesco 1978) sought to identify the characteristics of successful learners mainly in terms of the learning strategies that they reported using. These indicated five major aspects of successful learners: (1) a concern for language form; (2) a concern for communication; (3) an active task approach; (4) awareness of the learning process; and (5) flexible use of learning strategies. These studies, however, took little account of the role of language aptitude, motivation, or language anxiety. A more complete picture of the efficacious learner could perhaps incorporate the insights provided by research into these three areas.

One way of viewing how the 'parts' make up the 'whole' might be to consider what constitutes self-efficacy. The construct of the 'ideal language self' can also be seen as a composite construct that involves more than just motivation. Dörnyei (2010) argued that 'the effective functioning of the ideal L2 self is dependent on the operation of several underlying cognitive components, most notably on the learners' self-appraisal of their capabilities and evaluation of the affordances of their personal circumstances in order to anchor their vision in a sense of realistic expectations' (pp. 257–8). In other words, there is a cognitive and emotional dimension to this construct.

I have also not considered how motivation is treated in **neuropsychological SLA** which seeks to relate the mental processes involved in language learning to brain activity. Interestingly, this approach also points to the need to recognize the interconnections between emotion and cognition. Schumann's (1997, 2004b) neurobiological theory is built around the twin notions of 'stimulus appraisal' and 'mental foraging'. Learners appraise the stimuli they are exposed to in terms of their novelty, pleasantness, goal/need significance, coping potential (i.e. whether they feel able to cope), and self-social image (i.e. whether the stimuli conforms to the individual's sense of social and personal values). The appraisals they form are stored in memory. Mental foraging is the search for knowledge, which Schumann suggests involves the same neural mechanisms as foraging for food or for a mate. Learners are more inclined to engage in mental foraging if the appraisals they have stored provide them with an incentive for doing so. Learner differences arise as a result of differences in stored stimuli-appraisals and in the learners' preparedness for mental foraging. From the perspective of the brain, then, no clear distinction can be made between cognitive and affective memories and the actions of learners. This again points to the need to examine differences in terms of the whole learner.

The challenge facing researchers who wish to investigate the 'whole' learner is to determine how this can be undertaken. It is clearly much easier to investigate the effect of specific factors such as language aptitude, motivation, and language anxiety as there are instruments available to measure each. Dörnyei (2010) proposed applying **Dynamic Systems Theory** to the study of individual differences. This involves investigating the interactive effect of different factors and how this effect changes over time. Clearly, this is a challenging undertaking. Dynamic Systems Theory is considered further in Chapters 5 and 9.

## Notes

1 Dörnyei and Skehan (2003), in their review of psychological factors in SLA, considered that only two factors—language aptitude and motivation—have the 'capacity to generate research programs' (p. 622). I have included language anxiety as a separate factor as research has consistently shown it is also an influential factor.

2 Pimsleur (1966) produced a rival language aptitude test—the Pimsleur Language Aptitude Battery (PLAB). This was designed for use with younger learners and emphasized auditory ability more. It also included a test of inductive language learning ability, which was missing from the MLAT.

3 A very similar construct to Dörnyei's (2009) Ideal L2 Self is Yashima's (2002) **international posture**. This was defined as 'a general attitude towards the international community that influences English learning and communication among Japanese learners' (pp. 62–3). The Ideal L2 Self construct is, however, broader—international posture being just one 'possible self' that may motivate a learner.

# 4

# The development of a second language

## Introduction

In Chapter 1, I introduced the term **interlanguage** to refer to the mental system of a second language (L2) that a learner constructs and that is different from the target language system. We can talk about 'an interlanguage' to refer to the system that a learner has constructed at a particular point of time; we can also talk about the interlanguage continuum to refer to the series of systems that the learner constructs over time. Our concern in this chapter is with the interlanguage continuum—that is, with how the interlanguage system is constructed and reconstructed as acquisition takes place. By and large, the research that has investigated this has focused on how learners acquire the grammar of a second language, but there have also been studies of the acquisition of pronunciation, vocabulary, and pragmatic features (for example, requests and apologies).

I will begin by considering the methods researchers have used to investigate interlanguage development and then go on to examine what the research has shown about the nature of L2 development. A key issue in this chapter is whether it is possible to identify a 'natural route' that is common to all learners of a second language.

## Order of acquisition, sequence of acquisition, and usage-based accounts of L2 development

When we talk about interlanguage development we are necessarily concerned with 'change' (i.e. how a learner's interlanguage is modified over time). A key issue, however, is how this 'change' is conceptualized. We will consider three ways of looking at this—in terms of the 'order of acquisition', 'sequence of acquisition', and the more recent usage-based accounts of 'learning trajectory'.

## Order of acquisition

To determine the **order of acquisition** it is necessary to investigate when learners achieve mastery of different linguistic or pragmatic features. Mastery is defined in terms of the learner's ability to produce specific grammatical forms accurately (i.e. in accordance with target language norms). As native speakers do not typically achieve 100% accuracy all the time, especially when speaking, researchers have taken the 80% or 90% criterion level as indicating mastery (i.e. if learners use a specific feature accurately at least 80% of the time they are considered to have mastered it).

The ideal way to investigate order of acquisition is in longitudinal studies which show when learners reach the 80% criterion level for different linguistic features. However, many studies have been cross-sectional (i.e. they collect samples of learner language at just one time) and determine the order of acquisition by equating it with the **accuracy order**: they assume that if one feature has reached the criterion before another it must have been acquired earlier. However, as we will see, there are reasons for believing that accuracy order may not be a valid way of investigating acquisition order.

To determine the level of accuracy of different grammatical features researchers make use of **obligatory occasion analysis**. This involves identifying contexts that require the use of a specific linguistic feature (for example, English plural -*s*) and then establishing whether learners supply this feature in these contexts[1]. For example, if a learner says '*My father *live* in London', an obligatory occasion has been created for use of third-person -*s*—but in this case, it has not been supplied. But if a learner says 'My father lives in London', it has been correctly supplied.

This approach to investigating interlanguage development falls foul of the **comparative fallacy**. Bley-Vroman (1983) argued that interlanguages are unique systems and should not be investigated in terms of whether learners have achieved native-like mastery. Other researchers (for example, Seidlhofer 2001) have been even more critical of treating L2 systems as failed approximations of native language systems. They point out that in multilingual situations in particular, learners are more likely to be concerned with acquiring the diverse linguistic resources needed to function effectively in their speech community rather than with trying to speak like a native speaker. However, despite these objections, much of the SLA research—both old and more recent—has investigated interlanguage development in terms of **accuracy**.

## Sequence of acquisition

An alternative is to investigate the **sequence of acquisition**. Both syntactic features (for example, negation) and morphological features (for example, English regular past tense) are acquired gradually, with learners passing through a number of stages of development. Thus, development is determined not in terms of target-like accuracy, but in terms of whether there is evidence of the learner progressing from an early stage to a later one.

This requires undertaking a **frequency analysis**. Ellis and Barkhuizen (2005) provide a detailed account of this type of analysis. It involves selecting a specific linguistic feature for study (for example, negatives) and then identifying occasions when learners attempt to use this feature and documenting the various linguistic devices they employ and how these change over time. Such analyses can show how learners shift from the predominant use of one device at one time (for example, negative + verb as in '\*No coming today') to the use of another at another time (for example, 'don't' + verb as in '\*I don't coming today'). The advantage of investigating sequence of acquisition is that it can show that development is taking place even if the learner has not achieved target-like use.

## Usage-based accounts of learning

Frequency analysis figured in much of the early research (for example, Cancino, Rosansky, and Schumann 1978). However, it is not without problems. One is the well-attested phenomenon of formulaic speech. Learner language, especially in the early stages, is characterized by the use of **formulaic sequences** such as 'I don't understand' and 'I don't know'. Such chunks appear to show that the learner has reached a relatively late stage in the development of negation, but in fact they show nothing of the kind because the learner has simply learned some fixed lexical units. For this reason, researchers investigating the sequence of acquisition only examine learners' creative speech (i.e. utterances that have been constructed out of separate linguistic units). The problem here is that it is not always easy to tell whether an utterance constitutes a chunk or has been creatively constructed[2].

**Usage-based theories** of second (and first) language development (N. Ellis 2002) reject the view that chunks and creative constructions constitute a simple dichotomy. They claim that linguistic knowledge develops in response to the frequency of exposure to and use of exemplars of the language. Development involves a continuum from words and fixed expressions on the one hand to schematic templates that allow for utterances to be creatively constructed on the other. The continuum stretches from words and multiword chunks to partially analysed schemas or patterns and then on to increasingly more generalized schematic constructions. In all linguistic systems, these different representations co-exist so that an utterance such as 'I don't know' might be accessed as a whole or be partially or fully constructed.

A usage-based account of L2 development seeks to plot how learners gradually and dynamically move from chunks to constructions, but without claiming any fundamental distinction between the two. Thus, it avoids the idealized picture of L2 development inherent in the idea that a grammatical structure—such as negatives—involves a series of relatively distinct stages of development. It acknowledges the variability and non-linearity inherent in L2 development by plotting the messy 'trajectory of learning' that learners follow as they gradually unpack chunks and then repackage the parts into new chunks and constructions. It is compatible with Complexity Theory, which was introduced in Chapter 1 and is considered further in Chapter 8.

## Case studies of L2 learners

The case studies I will now consider all involved the analysis of oral data collected from learners over a lengthy period of time (more than a year). For each case study, I will provide background information about the learner(s) and the methods of data collection, summarize the main findings, and point out the key issues the studies raise.

### Schmidt's (1983) study of Wes

Wes was a 33-year-old Japanese learner of L2 English who left school at the age of fifteen and thus had had very little experience of formal instruction. He was a successful artist. He divided his time between living in Hawaii and Japan, spending increasing amounts of time in the former. He mixed predominantly with English speakers in Hawaii and thus experienced very little social distance from native speakers of English. Data were collected over a three year period mainly by means of one-hour tape-recorded monologues where Wes commented on his business, his daily activities, and his visits back to Japan. Schmidt also made recordings of informal conversations between Wes and native speakers.

The focus of Schmidt's study was the extent to which Wes's acculturation to American society could explain his development of **communicative competence**. Communicative competence was considered in terms of four components: (1) linguistic competence (i.e. the ability to use grammatical structures with target-like accuracy); (2) **sociolinguistic competence** (i.e. the ability to use language in socially appropriate ways); (3) **discourse competence** (i.e. the ability to participate in coherent and cohesive conversations); and (4) **strategic competence** (i.e. the ability to deal with communication breakdown) as in Canale (1983).

Schmidt's main finding was that development of these abilities proceeded separately. Wes's **linguistic competence** remained quite limited. His pronunciation was good (especially his intonation), but his grammar hardly developed over the three-year period. Of the nine grammatical morphemes Schmidt investigated, only three reached the 90 per cent criterion level of accuracy. There was greater evidence of development in his **sociolinguistic competence**. For example, initially Wes's directives relied extensively on formulaic expressions (for example, 'Can I have a ... ?'), but by the end of the three-year period, gross errors in his use of directives had been eliminated and his English utterances were largely socially appropriate although sometimes idiosyncratic. The aspect that showed the greatest development was

Wes's **discourse competence**. Wes also manifested considerable **strategic competence**. For example, he was able to repair communication breakdowns by making effective use of communication strategies such as paraphrase (for example, his use of 'money-girl' for 'prostitute'). However, he rarely bothered to repair his utterances when he received feedback and seemed to operate on the principle that it was the responsibility of native speakers to understand him rather than his responsibility to make himself understood. Overall, Wes proved to be an effective communicator but a poor learner in terms of linguistic development.

Schmidt's study was notable in two principal ways. First it showed the partial independence of grammatical competence from other aspects of communicative competence. Second, the lack of linguistic development could not be explained by Wes's failure to acculturate as in fact he became socially very integrated when he lived in Hawaii. One possible explanation is that, as a functionally-oriented learner Wes paid little attention to the input he was exposed to and also developed little metalinguistic awareness of English grammar.

## R. Ellis's (1984, 1992) study of two classroom learners

The next case study is my own. I investigated classroom rather than naturalistic L2 learners. There were three learners, all children aged ten to 13 years, and all complete beginners at the start of the study. They were learning English in a language centre in an outer suburb of London. The ten-year-old was Portuguese while the other two (a brother and sister) came from Pakistan. I collected data over a two-year period by sitting in their English classes and noting down all the utterances they produced together with contextual information relating to the function and audience of their utterances. I focused on their communicative speech rather than the language they produced in formal practice activities.

My initial purpose in conducting these case studies was to examine whether the pattern of development evident in these classroom learners was the same as or different from the pattern reported for naturalistic learners (for example, Cancino et al. 1978). In other words, I wanted to know whether the instructional setting influenced the way in which the children learned English.

In the 1984 publication, I focused on the learners' linguistic development. One of the main findings was that all three children made extensive use of **formulaic sequences** as a means of performing the communicative acts required of them in the classroom, where English served as the medium as well as the object of instruction. Over time, the learners were able to modify and extend these formulas. For example, for the 'I don't know' formula, they substituted other verbs (for example, 'I don't understand'), changed the subject (for example, 'You don't know') and added a constituent (for example, 'I don't know this one'). In other words, the learners were slowly unpacking the formulas, releasing their constituents for creative language use, as well as learning how to combine simple formulas into a more complex whole. Another feature of the three children's language was 'semantic simplification' (i.e. they omitted constituents that perform semantic roles that would normally be encoded by a native speaker). For example, one of the learners produced the utterance 'Sir, sir, pencil' after the teacher had taken his pencil, meaning 'You have taken my pencil'). Such utterances were readily understood because the missing constituents could easily be recovered with the help of contextual clues. Over time, such simplification diminished in the children's speech.

The study also investigated the **sequence of acquisition** for negatives and interrogatives. The developmental profiles for these structures of the three children were very similar to each other and showed a striking similarity to that reported for naturalistic learners. For example, they all began by producing verbless negatives such as 'No pencil' (i.e. 'I don't have a pencil'), before moving on to 'no' + verb negatives (for example, 'No looking my card') and then gradually introducing negatives with auxiliaries, first using 'don't (for example, 'Don't look my card') and then a wider range of auxiliary forms. After two years, however, these learners could still not consistently produce target-like negatives, although the Portuguese boy was clearly more advanced than the two Pakistani learners.

In the 1992 publication, I re-examined the same data to see what development took place in a pragmatic feature—which was requests. Over time, the range of request types expanded (for example, requests involving modal verbs such as 'could' began to appear) and requests that encoded the hearer's perspective (for example, 'Could you...') as opposed to the speaker's emerged. However, the learners' requests continued to be of the direct kind, more complex types of requests did not occur at all, and the range of formal devices for encoding requests remained limited. There was also no evidence of the learners systematically modifying their choice of request strategy according to addressee (i.e. when they addressed the teacher or another student in the class).

Three main conclusions emerged from my study. First, like Wes, these learners relied initially on formulaic chunks to express their communicative needs and gradually learned how to manipulate the linguistic elements in these chunks to produce more varied, novel utterances. Second, the general pattern of development was very similar to that reported for naturalistic learners, suggesting that the classroom setting did not have a major effect on how these learners' linguistic competence developed. Third, after two years, their development was still quite limited. They did not consistently produce target-like negatives and they still possessed only a limited range of requesting strategies. There are two mutually compatible explanations for these developmental limitations. The first is that the classroom setting did not afford the appropriate communicative conditions for acquisition. The other is that L2 development is inevitably a slow and gradual process and that full grammatical and pragmatic competence cannot be acquired even in a two-year period.

## Jia and Fuse's (2007) study of Chinese ESL learners

This was a five-year study that investigated the acquisition of a set of six English grammatical morphemes (regular and irregular past tense, third-person singular -*s*, verb + -*ing*, copula *be*, and auxiliary *do*). There were ten learners in this study—five girls and five boys who were aged between five and 16 years when they first arrived in the US. They all attended English-speaking schools where 70% of the students were native speakers of English. They all received focused ESL instruction for a period of time. Jia and Fuse divided the learners into two groups—six who were early arrivals and four who were late arrivals. The main aims were to investigate the acquisition trajectories of these features and whether there were any age-related differences.

Data were collected from the learners by means of language tasks involving story telling prompted by pictures and interviews about the learners' activities in their schools and at home and their language use in various situations. It took place regularly throughout the five years of the study. Obligatory occasions for the six morphemes were identified and the percentage correct calculated. A morpheme was considered to have been mastered if it achieved the 80% criterion level across three consecutive data collection sessions. **Order of acquisition** of the six morphemes was determined in two ways: by examining the number of learners who demonstrated mastery of each morpheme and by calculating the total percentage accuracy of each morpheme for all the learners.

The main findings were as follows. The age of arrival of the learners had no effect on the order of acquisition. The same structures fell into the low-, medium-, and high-accuracy levels for both the early and late arrival groups. The two easiest structures were progressive -*ing* and auxiliary 'do' and the two most difficult were regular past tense and third-person -*s*. However, there were some age-related effects. For example, at the end of the study, the early arrivals demonstrated greater accuracy than the late arrivals on the two most difficult morphemes. The acquisition trajectories of the morphemes differed markedly. Progressive -*ing* and plural -*s*, for example, showed accelerated learning initially and then levelled off. In contrast, third-person -*s* was acquired slowly but steadily with no plateauing, while regular past tense showed no significant growth over time, but with fluctuations from one point in time to the next.

Jia and Fuse discussed these results in terms of the factors that can account for the same order of acquisition manifested by the ten learners. They concluded that the most likely explanation lay in word frequency and salience; that is, learners learn those features that are more frequent and/or more salient earlier than those features that are less frequent and/or less salient. They also concluded that the results lent no support to the **Critical Period Hypothesis** as there was no evidence of any sharp discontinuity in the early and late arrivals' acquisition of English (see Chapter 2). They explained the advantage noted for the early arrivals in terms of the richer learning environment they experienced.

## Some general observations

These three case studies vary in the approach they adopted to investigating L2 development. Schmidt (1983) and Jia and Fuse (2007) used **obligatory occasion analysis** to determine the order of acquisition of grammatical morphemes. Ellis (1984, 1992) employed **frequency analysis** to identify the sequence of acquisition of grammatical structures. Ellis also investigated L2 pragmatic development and explored how his learners decomposed formulaic sequences.

The studies suggest a number of generalizations about how an L2 develops over time:

1 For some learners (for example, Wes), little grammatical development appears to take place. Such learners appear to be functionally-oriented and not motivated to acquire target-language norms.

2 L2 development is uneven. For Wes, development was evident in the sociolinguistic and discourse aspects of the L2 but not in grammar. Jia and Fuse showed that different grammatical features followed different trajectories, some developing steadily over time and others accelerating rapidly to begin with and then plateauing.

3 Grammatical development is not linear; there are notable fluctuations in the accuracy with which grammatical features are used from one time to another.

4 Learners' early attempts to use the L2 are characterized by **structural and semantic simplification**.

5 The studies reported that the learners made extensive use of formulaic expressions to communicate and that these were prevalent in the early stages. My own studies documented how the learners gradually unpacked the components of the formulas they had learned, constructing patterns that were less fixed and could be deployed more creatively.

6 Learners appear to acquire grammatical morphemes in a relatively fixed order irrespective of the age of the learners. Jia and Fuse suggested that morphemes that are salient and frequent are acquired earlier than those that are less salient and frequent.

7 There is also evidence of sequences of acquisition; grammatical features—such as negatives—and pragmatic features—such as requests—are acquired gradually in observable stages. This was evident in both the studies that investigated naturalistic acquisition (Jia and Fuse 2007) and the study that investigated classroom learners (Ellis 1984).

8 Considerable differences exist in the rate and success of acquisition by individual learners. Various factors can contribute to this—the learner's first language, the learner's age, and the richness of the learner's learning environment.

In the following sections, we will explore these generalizations in greater depth, beginning with research that has attempted to characterize the principles that underlie the development of **learner varieties** and then moving on to examine research that has focused on the acquisition of specific grammatical features.

## Learner varieties

Dimroth (2012) defined a learner variety as 'a coherent linguistic system produced by a language learner' and emphasized that it is to be seen as a language variety in the same way as a dialect. In other words, a learner variety constitutes an interlanguage.

The 'Second Language Acquisition of Adult Immigrants' project funded by the European Science Foundation (ESF) (Klein and Perdue 1997) involved a longitudinal study of the naturalistic acquisition of five European languages by 40 adult immigrants with different first languages, all of whom had only recently arrived in the target language country. Data consisted of free conversations and also oral production elicited by means of narrative and description tasks. The varieties were seen as manifesting particular **form-function mappings** and development as driven by the learners' need to communicate more effectively by means of increasingly complex language.

The initial variety is the pre-**basic variety**, which is characterized by nominal utterance organization (i.e. there were no verbs). At this stage, utterances are scaffolded (i.e. constructed over more than one turn) and context dependent. In time, this gives way to the **basic variety**. Utterances now include verbs, but these are non-finite (i.e. they are not inflected for tense or aspect). It constitutes a much more effective communicative tool than the pre-basic variety—in fact, it proved so effective for one third of the learners that they did not progress to the post-basic variety when finite verbal utterance organization finally occurs. Table 4.1 provides a more detailed description of the linguistic features that characterize each variety[3].

The ESF project found that development is similar for both learners of the same and for different second languages. All the learners showed the same progression through the learner varieties. However, the transition from one variety to the next is not sudden; rather, the utterance structure typical of one variety persists even when a learner has moved on to the next variety. Also, the source language of the learners was found to play a role. Klein and Perdue (1997) noted that when the target language offers alternative word orders (for example, Dutch and German allow both NP +V + NP and NP + NP + V word orders) the learners opted for the word order that corresponded most closely to their first language (for example, Turkish learners of these languages opted for verb-end in accordance with the word order in Turkish).

The project was directed at describing the path of development of adult, naturalistic learners. Klein and Perdue were careful to make no claims about instructed L2 acquisition. However, my own case study (Ellis 1984) suggests

| Learner variety | Linguistic features |
| --- | --- |
| Pre-basic variety—nominal utterance organization | Small vocabulary (around 50 words)<br>Two types of utterance structure:<br>1 NP + NP/adj/PP<br>e.g. 'girl hunger'; 'Marie old'; 'man in the street'.<br>2 NP + affirmative/negative particle<br>e.g. 'car no'; 'bicycle yes'.<br>A few adverbs and participles. |
| Basic variety—non-finite verb organization | Extended lexical repertoire<br>Three phrasal patterns:<br>1 NP1 + V + (NP2) + (NP2)<br>e.g. 'he come'; 'the man eat meal'; 'the man give girl a present'.<br>2 NP1 + copula + NP2/PP/adj<br>e.g. 'the man is doctor'; 'he is in the house'; 'he is tired'.<br>3 V + NP2<br>e.g. 'finish book'.<br>Verbs are not marked for tense or aspect.<br>Grammatical categories such as 'subject' and 'object' do not exist.<br>Rich repertoire of adverbs that can precede or follow all the patterns. |
| Post-basic variety—finite verb organization | Pronominal forms become productive.<br>Finite verb forms appear to mark grammatical agreement, tense and aspect.<br>Devices for encoding focus occur (e.g. 'It was the movie John liked best.'). |

*Table 4.1  Learner varieties*

that some classroom learners may manifest similar development. In Table 4.2, I provide examples of the utterances that one of the learners I investigated (the Portuguese boy) produced inside an ESL classroom. These utterances are listed chronologically the table. They show that he too seemed to proceed from the pre-basic, to the basic, and then to the post-basic variety in his communicative speech. It is possible, then, that irrespective of setting, learners follow a similar pattern of development when they attempt to use the L2 for communicative purposes.

What explanation is there for these learner varieties? Klein (1998) suggested that they reflect the nature of our innate capacity for learning a language. He argued that the basic variety cannot be explained by the surface properties of the input that the learners are exposed to and proposed instead that the constraints that govern it are part of our genetic endowment. This amounts to a nativist account of L2 acquisition, similar in some respects to that proposed by Chomsky (1986) for L1 acquisition. However, as we saw in

| Learner variety | Utterances of an L2 classroom learner |
|---|---|
| Pre-basic variety | 'Me no ruler.' (= I do not have a ruler.)<br>'Phoc no good.' (= Phoc is not a good boy.)<br>'We no school.' (= We don't come to school on Monday.)<br>'A door no downstairs.' (= There is no door in the downstairs part of the house.) |
| Basic variety | 'Mariana no coming.' (= Mariana is not coming to school today.)<br>'Drawing the picture?' (= Do I have to draw a picture?)<br>'Here writing Friday?' (= Do I have to write 'Friday' here?)<br>'Playing now bingo?' (= Are we going to play bingo now?)' |
| Post-basic variety | 'You did no read properly.' (criticizing another student)<br>'In this one the man is not shouting.' (describing a picture)<br>'This man can't read because the light is green.' (describing a picture) |

*Table 4.2  Examples of the learner varieties in the speech of an L2 classroom learner*

Chapter 1, the claim that the human capacity for language is biologically specified and distinct from other cognitive abilities is highly contentious. N. Ellis (2002), for example, argued that both L1 and L2 acquisition are driven by input frequency and general cognitive (rather than language-specific) strategies.

The research on learner varieties provides a general picture of how L2 development in naturalistic learners takes place. It was limited, however, in that it only looked at the relatively early stages of development and did not examine how specific grammatical features are acquired.

## Order of acquisition

Order of acquisition is determined by investigating either the accuracy of use of specific grammatical features by means of **obligatory occasion analysis** or the order of emergence of different features in learners' production. The studies that have investigated order of acquisition have been both cross sectional and longitudinal. The early studies conducted during the 1970s (and some later ones, such as Jia and Fuse 2007) examined a miscellaneous set of English morphemes (for example, verb + -*ing*, plural -*s*, articles, and regular and irregular past tense). Later studies focused on specific grammatical systems, such as verb tenses.

### The morpheme studies

The L2 **morpheme studies** borrowed the methodology used to study how children acquire the grammar of their first language. These studies showed that L1 acquisition involved a relatively clearly defined order of acquisition. Brown (1973), for example, reported a longitudinal study of three children learning English as their mother tongue. He showed that grammatical morphemes were mastered by all three children in the same fixed order. De Villiers and de Villiers (1973) found a very similar order for the same morphemes in a cross-sectional study of a large number of children. They examined the accuracy with which the children used the different morphemes at one time and then claimed that the **accuracy order** they found reflected the **order of acquisition**.

The key finding of the early L2 cross-sectional morpheme studies was that learners demonstrated a very similar accuracy order, irrespective of whether they were children or adults and irrespective of their first language. Dulay and Burt (1973, 1974) investigated Spanish and Chinese children learning L2 English. They found that the accuracy order for a mixed group of English morphemes was the same for both groups of learners. Bailey, Madden, and Krashen (1974) carried out a similar study on adults and reported that the order they found correlated significantly with that in Dulay and Burt. On the assumption that accuracy order reflects the acquisition order, it was proposed that there was a natural order of acquisition which all learners followed.

The existence of this 'natural order' has assumed an almost mythical status in SLA. It provided empirical support for Corder's (1967) claim that L2 learners, like children acquiring their first language, have a 'built-in syllabus'. There is, however, considerable evidence to suggest that the order is not as fixed as it was once assumed. Larsen-Freeman (1976), for example, found that different elicitation tasks produced somewhat different accuracy orders. In particular, she noted that some morphemes (for example, plural -*s* and third-person -*s*) were used more accurately in writing than in speech. Pica's (1983) study of naturalistic, instructed, and mixed learners of English found that although the accuracy orders in all three groups of learners were the same, there were differences among the groups in specific morphemes. The instructed group used plural -*s* more accurately than the naturalistic group, while the naturalistic group was more accurate than the instructed group in using verb + -*ing*, suggesting that the linguistic environment had some influence on how and when these features were acquired. Also, longitudinal studies of the same set of morphemes failed to find the same acquisition order as the accuracy order reported in the cross-sectional studies. Jia and Fuse's (2007) study did provide some support for the natural order. However, Hakuta's (1976) two-year longitudinal study of a five-year-old Japanese girl indicated that plural -*s*, which was 'acquired' early according to Dulay and Burt's accuracy order, was actually acquired much later. Hakuta suggested that this was because this morpheme had no equivalent in the learner's first language. Shin and Milroy's (1999) study of young Korean-American children's acquisition also suggested that the learners' first language influenced the order of acquisition. Thus, to some extent, both the learning environment and the learners' first language influence the order of acquisition.

Nevertheless, it is clear that some English grammatical morphemes are inherently more difficult for L2 learners to acquire than others. Larsen-Freeman and Long (1991) argued that 'there are ... too many studies ... showing sufficiently consistent general findings for the commonalities to be ignored' (p. 92). The question that arises, then, is how these commonalities can be explained. Goldschneider and DeKeyser (2001) examined some 20 morpheme studies in order to investigate whether a number of different factors could account for the order. They were able to show that the phonological salience of a morpheme, its syntactic category, and its frequency in input all had an influence on when a particular morpheme was acquired. They concluded that there was a single general factor that could explain the order of acquisition—'salience'. In other words, learners first learn those morphemes whose meanings are transparent and whose form is readily discernible in the input. For example, verb + -*ing* is more easily perceived in the input than third-person -*s* and is acquired earlier. Plural -*s* conveys a specific meaning ('more than one') and is acquired before third-person -*s* which is redundant.

Appealing to saliency as the explanation can also help to explain the differences in the morpheme order that some studies have reported. For example, it is reasonable to suppose that the learning environment and the learner's first language will have some impact on which features are salient to learners. Verb + -*ing* may be overused by classroom learners because of its high frequency in language instruction. Plural -*s* may lack saliency to Japanese learners because there is no equivalent feature in their first language.

There is, however, a more fundamental problem with the morpheme studies. They compare apples and oranges. Noun morphemes (for example, plural -*s* and possessive -*s*) constitute very different kinds of learning problems to verb morphemes (for example, irregular and regular past tense). Also, even those morphemes that belong to same sub-system (for example, verbs) may not be learned in the same way. Pinker (1999) claimed that irregular and regular morphemes involve different types of learning—item-based versus rule-based. Learners learn and store English irregular past tense forms as items, but learn a rule for the regular past tense. Kempe, Brooks, and Kharkhurin (2010) proposed that **rule-based learning** can override **item-based learning** when the input cues for the former are transparent and salient. This can lead to **overgeneralization** of a rule. A good example of this is when learners extend the rule for English regular past tense to irregular verbs. This results in the **U-shaped pattern of development** that has been observed for irregular past tense—i.e. learners initially say 'ate' only to later say 'eated' before reverting once more to the target language form. In fact, learners' use of grammatical morphemes manifests enormous variability from one time to the next (Huebner 1983).

Much of the later order-of-acquisition research avoided the rag-bag approach of the morpheme studies. It investigated particular grammatical sub-systems and also adopted a different way of determining whether a grammatical feature had been acquired—examining 'emergence' instead of 'accuracy'. We will briefly consider two examples of this research, one of which looked at word-order rules and the other at verb tenses.

## Order of acquisition of German word-order rules

Whereas the morpheme studies were carried out by US-based researchers, the study of the acquisition of word-order rules originated in the *Zweitspracher-werb Italienischer und Spanischer Arbeiter* (ZISA) project conducted by a group of German researchers (for example, Meisel, Clahsen, and Pienemann 1981). Initially, the research focused on German word-order rules, but was subsequently extended to the study of English word order in Johnston and Pienemann (1986) and other languages (Pienemann and Kessler 2011). It

| Stage | Name | Description | Examples |
|-------|------|-------------|----------|
| 1 | Canonical order | Romance learners begin with SVO as their initial hypothesis about German word order. Adverbials appear in sentence-final position | 'Die Kinder spielen mit Ball.' (= The children play with the ball.) |
| 2 | Adverb preposing | Learners able to move an adverbial to sentence-initial position, but do not yet invert subject and verb as required when a sentence begins with an adverbial. This is not acquired until stage 4. | 'Da Kinder spielen.' (= There children play.) |
| 3 | Verb separation | Learners move non-finite verbal elements into the required clause-final position. | 'Alle Kinder muss die Pause machen.' (= All the children must the pause make.) |
| 4 | Inversion | Learners learn that in certain contexts such as sentence-initial adverbials and interrogatives, the verb must precede the subject. | 'Dann hat sie wieder die Knocht gebringt.' (= Then has she again the bone bringed.) |
| 5 | Verb end | Learners learn that the finite verb in subordinate clauses goes in clause-final position. | 'Er sagte dass er nach Hause kommt.' (= He said that he to home comes.) |

*Table 4.3 Sequence of acquisition of German word-order rules (based on Pienemann, Johnston, and Brindley 1988)*

investigated learners with a variety of L1s and consisted of both cross-sectional and longitudinal studies.

Pienemann, Johnston, and Brindley (1988) claimed that the order of acquisition of German word-order rules shown in Table 4.3 is 'probably one of the most robust empirical findings in SLA research' (p. 222). A clear order emerged from the various studies. Learners began with a canonical word order (which varied according to the basic word order of the learner's L1) and then progressed through a series of other rules before arriving at the last acquired verb-end rule.

Initially, learners operate in accordance with a fixed word order which functions as a default processing strategy. Over time, they develop the ability to perform a series of increasingly complex processing operations that involve, in the first place, just adding a linguistic unit to the beginning or end of an utterance (as in adverb pre-posing) and then, incrementally, moving linguistic units from within an utterance to the beginning or end (as in verb separation), re-ordering the internal structure of linguistic units (as in inversion), and finally re-organizing the basic word order for subordinate constructions (as in verb end). These operations constitute ways of handling different word orders (for example, the question 'Is he coming?' involves a re-arrangement of elements from the default 'subject + verb' word order).

This account of L2 development was later incorporated into **Processability Theory** (Pienemann 1998). This claims that learners have to 'create language specific routines' (Pienemann 2011: 33)—which they do in stages—gradually extending their 'grammatical memory store' to enable them to handle the increasing complex ways in which grammatical information is exchanged across constituents. The details of this theory are presented in Chapter 8.

Although Pienemann considered the language-specific routines that underlie L2 acquisition to be universal, he also acknowledged that individual variation occurs. First, the emergence of a new structure may or may not guarantee its systematic use. Some learners continue to use it alongside an earlier acquired structure. For example, when learners of L2 English reach the inversion stage—and thus are capable of producing sentences like 'Have you seen him?'—they do not always do so consistently, sometimes producing forms belonging to an earlier period (for example, 'Have see him?' and 'You have seen him?'). Learners vary in how they apply a new processing operation. Some learners appear to move slowly, consolidating each new stage before they move on to the next, whereas others move on to a new stage very rapidly, not bothering if they have not achieved a high level of accuracy in the structures belonging to the prior stage. Other learners take time to acquire the rule in all its contexts before they progress to a new stage: many of the learners in the ZISA project failed to reach stages four and five. Finally, not all grammatical features are governed by these processing operations. Some features, such as copulas (for example, the verb 'be') appear to be 'variational'.

That is, they are not dependent on the processing routines that govern developmental features and thus can be acquired at any time[4].

## Acquisition of the tense-aspect system

Other researchers (for example, Dietrich, Klein, and Noyau 1995; Bardovi-Harlig 2000) have focused more narrowly on the emergence of verbal morphology. They adopted a different approach, focusing not just on the order in which verb forms emerged, but also on form-function mappings. The investigation of a number of different languages made it possible to arrive at cross-linguistic generalizations about the order of acquisition.

Dietrich et al.'s (1995) study was part of the ESF project we considered earlier. They investigated 23 learners of Dutch, French, German, Swedish, and English, identifying three broad stages in learners' expression of past time:

1 In the pre-basic variety, the learners relied entirely on pragmatic means. They produced utterances that contained no explicit marker of past time, but could be interpreted as such in the context of a previously produced utterance. They also relied on the situational context to make meanings clear. Other pragmatic strategies involved the use of contrasting events and chronological order. At this stage, in effect, the learners made no attempt to encode pastness linguistically.

2 In the **basic variety**, the learners used various lexical expressions (for example, locative adverbials such as 'in the morning' and 'yesterday' and connectives such as 'and' and 'then') to express pastness. Verbs were used either in the base form (for example, 'go' in English) or some idiosyncratic form (for example, 'going').

3 Finally, in the post-basic variety, morphological markers of pastness appeared. These were used non-systematically as the learners continued to also rely on pragmatic and lexical means to convey pastness. Over time, however, past-tense morphology stabilized with a corresponding decrease in the use of adverbials.

Bardovi-Harlig (2000) reported the following order for English verb tenses in her longitudinal study of 16 learners of L2 English from four different language backgrounds:

past > past progressive > present perfect > past perfect

Drawing together the results of a range of studies that had investigated the acquisition of verb morphology, she identified four general principles that govern the acquisition of verb morphology:

1 Acquisition is slow and gradual.

2 Form often precedes function. That is, when a given morpheme first appears it is overgeneralized and thus lacks a clear contrast with existing forms. Base forms tend to be used alongside other forms even at later stages of acquisition.

3 Irregular morphology precedes regular morphology, as illustrated by the prior acquisition of irregular past tense forms in English. This reflects the likelihood that irregular forms are acquired as distinct lexical items (i.e. through **item-based learning**).

4 When learners are acquiring compound verb tenses, such as the present/past progressive and the present/past perfect, they begin by using a verb with verbal suffix (for example, 'eating') and only subsequently produce verbs with auxiliaries (for example, 'is eating').

Bardovi-Harlig also noted that many of the learners she investigated had not acquired the full L2 tense-aspect system.

# Sequence of acquisition

Specific grammatical forms manifest their own sequence of development as learners gain gradual control over them and slowly fit them into their existing interlanguage system. Arguably, then, what is needed is an approach that acknowledges the fundamental organic nature of L2 development. In this section, we will explore research that has examined L2 negation—probably the most researched grammatical property. In so doing, I will illustrate the two different approaches I introduced in the opening section of the chapter—**frequency analysis** and **usage-based analysis**.

## Stages in the acquisition of L2 negation

The acquisition of L2 negation has attracted the attention of SLA researchers from early days. Studies by Ravem (1968), Cancino et al. (1978), and Wode (1976) examined how negation develops in Norwegian, Spanish, and German learners of English. Subsequently, researchers investigated other languages. De Swart (2006), for example, provided a composite account of how negation developed in all the languages investigated in the ESF project. These studies all involved naturalistic learners, but there were also longitudinal studies of tutored learners (for example, my own case study of three classroom learners). The research points to two general conclusions: there is surprising uniformity in how learners with different L1s acquire negation and this uniformity can be described in terms of a sequence of stages that learners pass through *en route* to the target structure.

In the following account of the different stages in the L2 acquisition of negation, I offer a composite picture derived from a number of studies. I will provide examples of typical learner utterances using both my own data and data from other sources. In these examples 'L' stands for 'learner' and 'S' for some other speaker, usually a native speaker.

The earliest negative utterances typically consist of just a lexical particle (for example, 'no') and express denial, refusal, rejection, or correction:

S   Mariana is Spanish.
L   No, Portuguese.

Early on, 'no' is combined with other non-verb elements (i.e. a noun or an adjective) with the negating particle appearing in either utterance-initial or final position:

L   Nee hier haus. ( = 'No here house.')
S   Il y a des taxis. (= 'There are some taxis.').
L   Non, taxi non. (= 'No, taxi no.').

These utterances correspond to the pre-basic variety. Verb negation does not appear until the **basic variety**. Here, the negative particle typically precedes the verb:

L   Mariana no coming. (= 'Mariana is not coming.')
L   Me no drawing in here. (= 'I won't draw here.')
L   Ils non comprehend. (= 'They don't understand.')

As learners enter the negative + verb stage, learners become responsive to the negative particles that occur in different sentence types (i.e. English 'no', 'not', and 'don't') and thus reduce their reliance on a single negative particle.

L   Not finished ('He has not finished his work.')
L   Nein spielen Katze (= 'No play cat.')
L   Don't look my card.

The last utterance seems target-like but, at this stage, 'don't' is morphologically unanalysed (i.e. it functions as a negative particle in its own right). The prevalence of negative + verb—irrespective of whether the source language is pre-verb-negating (like Spanish) or post-verb negating (like German)—suggests that it constitutes a basic option.

Post-verbal negation in L2 English typically appears first when learners begin to use modal verbs:

L   I can't play this one.
L   I won't go.

However, as with 'don't', it is likely that these negative forms are unanalysed initially. That is, they serve as alternatives as learners expand the lexical range of their negating words. Nevertheless, they constitute a stepping stone to the final stage which occurs when learners enter the post-basic variety when they are finally able to mark verbs for tense and aspect. In English, 'not' is now positioned between the auxiliary and main verb. At this stage the learner's negatives become more or less target-like:

L   He doesn't know anything.
L   He didn't said it.
L   She didn't believe me.

In L2 German, the negating particle is positioned after the verb in accordance with the target language:

L  Ich falle nicht runter. (= I fall not down)

Learners' development of negation, therefore, closely mirrors their progression through the **learner varieties**. As we noted earlier, however, this progression is not smooth. The stages—like the varieties—are not clearly defined, but overlap considerably. Development does not consist of sudden jumps, but of the gradual replacement of early patterns by later ones and not all learners reach the final stage. The learners' first language also has an effect (see Chapter 6). Similar stages of development have been observed in other grammatical structures—for example, in English interrogatives (Pienemann et al. 1988) and relative clauses (Schumann 1980; Mellow 2006). The acquisition of syntactical features—and also many morphological features—entails a stage-like progression towards the target structure.

## Formulaic sequences

A characteristic of learners' negative utterances, especially in the initial stages, is that they are often formulaic. However, in the studies of L2 negation we have just considered, formulaic chunks were discounted as the aim was to identify stages of acquisition in terms of learners' creative utterances. While researchers recognized that negative particles such as 'don't' were probably und units, they did not examine the possibility that such units were extracted from larger wholes such as 'I don't know'. We will now consider research that has looked at formulaic sequences in L2 acquisition and then consider how such sequences figure in the acquisition of negation.

Wray (2000) defines a **formulaic sequence** as:

'a sequence, continuous or discontinuous, of words or other meaning elements, which is, or appears to be, prefabricated; that is stored and retrieved whole from memory at the time of use, rather than being subject to generation or analysis by the language grammar' (Wray 2000: 465).

Formulaic sequences are of two kinds—routines which are totally unanalysed units and learned as wholes (for example, 'I don't know'), and patterns, which consist of a chunk with one or more open slots (for example, 'Can I have a … ?').

Myles, Hooper, and Mitchell (1998) proposed a number of criteria for determining whether an utterance is formulaic—it is:

1  at least two morphemes in length
2  phonologically coherent (i.e. fluently articulated, non-hesitant)
3  unrelated to productive patterns in the learner's speech
4  more complex in comparison with the learner's other output
5  used repeatedly in the same form
6  possibly inappropriate (syntactically, semantically, or pragmatically) or otherwise idiosyncratic

7 situationally dependent
8 community-wide in use.

Lin (2012) emphasized the second of these criteria. She proposed that formulaic expressions have distinctive prosodic qualities (for example, a fast speech rhythm). However, it is not easy to decide whether a given utterance is a fixed routine, a pattern, or a creative construction. Indeed, the usage-based account of negation we consider in the next section assumes that many learner utterances are indeterminate in nature.

Formulaic sequences are common in both adult and child L2 learners, especially in the early stages. Specific sequences emerge tied to the performance of specific language functions. For example, 'Can I have ...?' is used to perform a request, 'Why don't we ...?' to perform a suggestion, and 'I'm sorry' an apology. Both naturalistic and classroom learners rapidly acquire a repertoire of formulas which they use to perform the communicative functions important for them.

While there is wide acceptance that formulaic sequences play an important role in L2 use, there is less agreement about the role they play in L2 acquisition. Hakuta (1976) questioned whether routines and patterns facilitate or hinder the acquisition of grammar. Krashen and Scarcella (1978) argued that formulaic speech and rule-created speech are unrelated. The alternative position is that formulaic sequences constitute the building blocks for the construction of an L2 grammar. In a seminal article, Pawley and Syder (1983) argued that achieving native-like control of a language involves not only learning a rule system that will generate an infinite number of sentences, but also 'memorized sequences' and 'lexicalized sentence stems'. They saw the language learner's task as that of discovering precisely what permutations of a sentence stem are possible. It is this view of L2 learning that underlies the emergentist, **usage-based theories** of the kind promulgated by N. Ellis (2002) (see Chapter 1).

There is now ample evidence that learners are able to unpack the parts that comprise a sequence and, in this way, bootstrap their way to more creative constructions. Wong-Fillmore's (1976) longitudinal case study illustrated how this was done. For example, Nora, the fastest of the five child learners she investigated, used two formulas:

I wanna play wi' dese.
I don't wanna do dese.

She then discovered that the constituents following 'wanna' were interchangeable:

I don't wanna play dese.
I wanna do dese.

Wong-Fillmore commented that this 'formula-based analytical process ... was repeated in case after case' (p. 645). In my case study, I showed that the classroom learners I studied were able to extract the constituents from initial routines. For example, by analyzing the routines:

I don't know
I don't understand
I don't like

the learners arrived at the construction 'don't' + verb. Myles (2004) also argued that formulas constitute an important starting point. She found that those classroom learners who failed to acquire a set of formulas at the start showed very little subsequent development.

Individual learners vary in the extent to which they deconstruct formulaic sequences. Schmidt's (1983) case study of Wes showed that although Wes made advances in fluency by acquiring and using formulaic sequences, he made very little progress grammatically. Functionally-oriented learners like Wes may see no need to decompose chunks if their communicative needs are satisfied by their repertoire of formulaic sequences.

## A usage-based account of L2 negation

Eskildsen (2012) investigated the acquisition of L2 negation in a longitudinal study of two adult classroom learners (Carlos and Valerio). He had two aims. One was to explore what a usage-based account of the learners' utterances showed about their development of negation. The other was to investigate 'the situated nature' of these learners' 'emergent linguistic inventory' by examining the specific classroom interactions in which their negative utterances occurred.

Eskildsen showed how the learners' development started with recurring expressions and then evolved toward 'an increasingly, schematic, dynamic inventory of linguistic resources' (p. 363). Carlos, for example, demonstrated early use of the formulaic sequence 'I don't know' and then expanded this formula by employing an array of personal pronouns in the subject position. In so doing, he was able to overcome the entrenched 'no' + verb construction that also figured in his early utterances. Ultimately, he was also able to mark the auxiliary 'do' for tense. However, Eskildsen noted that Carlos's development was not linear and did not manifest the relatively discrete stages identified in the earlier studies of negation discussed above. He concluded 'the data ... showed no acquisitional stage-defining dominance' (p. 364). He also found differences in how Carlos and the other learner, Valerio, developed L2 negation.

Eskildsen illustrated how the interactions the learners participated in contributed to the development of L2 negation. For example, the sudden increase in Valerio's use of the subject + 'no' + verb pattern was traceable to a particular lesson where an exemplar of this pattern ('you no write') arose out of an interaction with another student and was used with the specific purpose of instructing the student about the task they had been given. Valerio went on to use this pattern eight more times on the same day.

Eskildsen's study is important for a number of reasons. First, it demonstrates the need to consider formulaic sequences when investigating developmental sequences. The 'I don't know' sequence served as an exemplar that sparked the learning of a pattern. Second, it suggests that there is variation in the learning trajectories of different negative patterns (for example, main verb negation as opposed to copula negation) and also differences in learners. Third, the study illustrates that 'interaction and learning ... cannot be kept apart' (p. 366).

An emergentist view of L2 development casts doubt on the existence of distinct developmental sequences, such as those reported for negation. It sees such sequences as idealized abstractions derived from the researchers' interpretations of learner language and their commitment to a view of interlanguage as a series of interlocking learner grammars. Instead, in an emergentist account development is seen as organic, dynamic, and variable with no clearly delineated stages. Development consists of a 'continuum of schematicity' ranging from concrete exemplars to 'generalizable schematic constructions'. (Eskildsen 2012: 33).

## Development of other linguistics systems

Much of the early work in SLA focused on grammatical development and, as we have seen, interest in this aspect has continued up to today. However, SLA researchers have also investigated how the learner's phonological and lexical systems evolve. We will briefly examine some of the key findings.

### Acquisition of L2 phonology

As with grammar, the acquisition of L2 phonology is a gradual, dynamic process but also displays some general tendencies:

1 Learners draw on the phonological features of their first language when speaking in the L2.
2 However, not all L1-target language phonological differences cause equal difficulty to learners. Some L2 features are 'marked' relative to the learner's first language and so will be difficult to acquire. For example, English learners of German have no problem devoicing 'd' in word final position (i.e. they pronounce 'und' correctly as 'unt') whereas German learners of English frequently substitute /t/ for /d/ in this position (i.e. they say 'bet' instead of 'bed'). The explanation according to Eckman (1977) is that the voiceless/voiced distinction in word final position in English is highly marked (i.e. it is only found in a few languages such as English). Thus, English learners of German have no problem with the unmarked devoicing in word final position whereas German learners of English find difficulty with the marked usage. See the discussion of **markedness** in Chapter 6.
3 Similarities between the first language and the target language do not always benefit the learner (Flege 1987). Beginner learners may incorporate an

L1 equivalent feature into their interlanguage but this may prevent them from establishing a completely new phonetic category for the target language and so slow down acquisition. In contrast, learners will need to set up new phonetic categories for those features they perceive as different from their first language and consequently progress more rapidly in acquiring them. In other words, dissimilar sounds can be easier to acquire than similar sounds.

4  Learners also manifest unique phonological forms in their production. That is, L2 phonological patterns that are independent of both the first language and the target language have been observed. In some cases, these patterns are the same as those found in L1 acquisition. Wode (1977), for instance, found that the German children he studied followed the same developmental sequence for /r/ as native English-speaking children.

5  In general, learners' ability to perceive sound contrasts that do not exist in their first language precedes their ability to produce the same contrasts[5]. Over time, as a result of exposure to the target language, learners acquire productive ability although their production of the sound contrasts may not be totally native-like (Hayes-Harb and Matsuda 2008).

To illustrate the dynamic and systematic nature of L2 phonological development we will consider Abrahamsson's (2003) study of three Chinese learners' acquisition of L2 Swedish syllable structure. This study, unlike many studies of L2 phonology, was longitudinal, covering a period of nearly two years. Syllables can be open or closed. An open syllable consists of an onset (one or more consonants) and a rhyme (a vowel) (for example, 'slow' in English). Closed syllables contain a coda (i.e. one or more final consonants) (for example, 'quick'). Swedish is predominantly a closed-syllable language whereas Chinese typically has open syllables. L2 learners of languages like Swedish frequently resort to simplification strategies when attempting to produce closed syllables. They may delete the final syllable, add a vowel (a process known as epenthesis) or devoice the final consonant. These processes can occur in all learners irrespective of the syllable structure of their first language, but they are especially prevalent in learners with an open-syllable first language.

Abrahamson identified an overall developmental profile in the three learners. Error frequencies were characterized by four phases: (1) an initial phase of relatively high error rates followed by a rapid decrease in error frequency; (2) a linear increase in error frequency; (3) a stable plateau of relatively high error frequencies; and (4) a final decrease in error rates. Thus—as has been observed in the acquisition of some grammatical features such as English irregular past tense—the learners manifested a **U-shaped pattern of development**. To explain this, Abrahamsson (2003) suggested that the learners initially focused on accurate production but then, as they paid more attention to fluency, their errors increased before decreasing when they had achieved sufficient fluency to pay attention to accuracy once again[6]. The nature of the learners' errors also changed over time. During the first year, deletion gradually gave way to epenthesis as a simplification strategy. In the second year, epenthesis also reduced. Abrahamsson proposed the following developmental sequence:

deletion > epenthesis > feature change (for example, devoicing) > target form

The acquisition of L2 phonology, then, is in many respects not dissimilar to the acquisition of L2 grammar. It is dynamic and complex, reflecting the variable impact of different factors (i.e. the learner's first language, the inherent difficulty of specific phonological forms, exposure to L2 input, and the linguistic and situational context). These factors affect performance at different times and in different ways with different learners. Within this complexity, however, as with grammar, it is possible to identify a general learning trajectory.

## Development of the L2 lexicon

Vocabulary development involves learning associations between lexemes (i.e. the phonological and graphological forms of words) and lemmas (i.e. the semantic-syntactic meanings of words). But it involves much more besides. For a start, as we have already noted, L2 learners acquire formulaic chunks (i.e. 'lexical phrases') as well as discrete words. Words and phrases are not stored as discrete items but in structured networks of semantic relations (Meara 2009). Individual words associate with other words paradigmatically (for example, 'war' associates with 'guns') and syntagmatically (for example, 'war' collocates with 'declare' in the phrase 'declare war'). Thus, to investigate how the L2 lexicon develops it is necessary to consider both the breadth (i.e. how many words the learner knows) and the depth (i.e. how words are interconnected) of the learner's lexicon and how both develop in the direction of the target-language lexicon.

There is now a large literature on L2 vocabulary learning (see, in particular, Nation 2001; Singleton 1999; Meara 2009). Here, I can only point to a number of generalizations that the research supports.

1 In general, receptive knowledge of individual words precedes productive knowledge. Meara (2009) argued that a word becomes available for productive use only when the learner has established connections with other words in the mental lexicon. In other words, productive ability is linked to depth of word learning.

2 Development involves not just knowing the meaning of a word and its connections to other words, but of being able to access this knowledge rapidly for both reception and production. Thus, learning vocabulary is not an instantaneous process and change is constant (Meara 2009). Also, words can fall in and out of prominence over time.

3 Words can be learned incidentally through exposure or intentionally, for example by memorizing lists of words. For **incidental learning** to take place

learners need to be able to infer the meaning of a new word from context. Nation (2001) pointed out that this becomes easier the more words the learner knows. Learners need to know 95% of the words in a written text to successfully guess the meanings of the other five per cent. In the case of learning from oral input, however, learners can make use of the situational context as well as the linguistic context. Multiple exposures to a new word in a variety of different contexts are needed for incidental learning to take place.

4 In general, lexical units (words or formulaic sequences) that occur frequently in the input will be acquired earlier than those that occur less frequently.

5 N. Ellis (1997) argued that lexical acquisition does not just involve the learning of individual lexemes, but can also take place by segmenting formulaic sequences. For example, by segmenting the formula 'I don't know', the learner discovers that 'I don't' and 'know' constitute separate lexical units which can then be combined with other words in the L2 lexicon. The process can also work the other way round. Learners can construct an utterance from their knowledge of individual words and then store the utterance as a chunk. In this respect, the processes involved in vocabulary and grammar acquisition cannot be easily distinguished.

6 Lexical development can also push grammatical development, providing further evidence of the interplay between the lexical and grammatical systems. As Bell (2009) put it, 'grammatical complexity can be fast forwarded by lexical formulae' (p. 126) as when the acquisition of the formula 'it seems that…' prompts the use of embedded clauses.

7 Learners draw on their first language in various ways. Initially, the link between an L2 lexical form and meaning may be indirect via the equivalent first language lexical form (L2 form → L1 form → meaning). Later a direct connection may be made (L2 → meaning) (see Jiang 2000). Learners also make use of cognates (i.e. words that are formally the same or similar in their first language and the target language) and sometimes establish false cognates.

It is clear that vocabulary acquisition is not a simple linear process of adding new words to an existing lexicon, but also of adding 'depth' to existing words and incorporating new words into a network of form—meaning connections that grow more complex over time. This process is intimately connected with the development of grammar.

In contrast to research on L2 grammar learning, there have been few longitudinal studies of vocabulary development in either naturalistic or instructed settings. Yoshida's (1978) longitudinal study of a young Japanese child's acquisition of L2 English reported that nouns were learned before verbs—a characteristic of the pre-basic variety. Wode et al.'s (1992) longitudinal study of four German children pointed to a number of differences between first language and second language vocabulary acquisition. For example, whereas vocabulary growth is slow in first language acquisition up to the first fifty words and then rapidly accelerates, it was initially much more rapid, but then decelerated in these children. Both of these studies investigated learners in a naturalistic setting. Palmberg (1987) reported a longitudinal study of vocabulary growth in Swedish learners of L2 English in a classroom setting. Unsurprisingly, most of the words the learners were able to produce were traceable to the textbook vocabulary. Laufer (1998) examined the development of passive and active vocabulary in adult foreign language learners over one year, reporting that their passive knowledge progressed considerably, but their controlled active knowledge much less so, and their free active vocabulary not at all.

These studies mainly focused on development in terms of vocabulary size. Schmitt (1998) in a longitudinal study of four advanced learners of L2 English investigated changes in depth of knowledge. He focused on four components of the learners' knowledge of 11 polysemous English words: form (i.e. spelling); association (i.e. the extent to which the learners' word associations corresponded to those of native speakers); grammatical characteristics (i.e. word class and word derivations); and meaning. The main finding of this study was that there was no evidence that these types of word knowledge were acquired in a sequence. Rather, development occurred in the different areas unevenly, but concurrently.

# L2 pragmatic development

Pragmatics is the study of how we put language to use in real-life contexts. That is, it is concerned with what we *do* with language in communication rather than what language *is*. It entails both how people use language to produce continuous discourse (for example, how they are able to stay on topic and manage the organization of conversations) and also how they perform specific speech acts—such as requests and apologies—in ways that are socially appropriate. For reasons of space, I will only consider how learners acquire the ability to perform speech acts.

Becoming pragmatically competent in a language is the process of developing sociopragmatic and pragmalinguistic competence. **Sociopragmatic competence** refers to the ability to adjust the way you speak to take account of the extent of the imposition on the other person, how familiar you are with that person and the person's social status. Thus, it concerns 'the social conditions placed on language in use' (Thomas 1983: 99). These conditions are cultural in nature and thus differences will be found in speakers of different languages. For example, Japanese people are likely to emphasize status differences over speaker familiarity, whereas Americans tend to do the opposite. **Pragmalinguistic competence** is knowledge of the linguistic forms required to encode specific sociopragmatic meanings. For example, making a polite request that places a high level of imposition on the addressee requires the use of complex request formulas such as 'I wonder if it would be possible for you to …'.

I will focus here on pragmalinguistic L2 development. This is investigated by identifying the linguistic strategies that a learner utilizes at particular stages of development. Drawing on a number of longitudinal studies of L2 requests, Kasper and Rose (2002) suggested that development involves five stages. Table 4.4 describes the stages and provides examples of the pragmalinguistic strategies found in each. The examples are taken from two different sources—from my case study summarized earlier in this chapter and Achiba's

| Stage | Description | Examples |
|---|---|---|
| 1 The pre-basic stage | Requests are context-dependent and lacking in verbs. | 'Sir, sir pencil.' (L asking for his pencil back). |
| 2 The formulaic stage | The learner relies on unanalysed formulaic sequences and imperatives. | 'Give me paper.' (L asking for a piece of paper) 'Can I have pen please?' (L asking for a pen) 'Have you got sellotape?' (L requesting another L to give him the sellotape). |
| 3 The unpacking stage | Formulaic sequences are analysed allowing for more productive use and the learner also relies less on very direct requesting strategies. | 'Can you pass on your paper?' (L telling another L to pass over her paper for collection) 'Can you make for me please?' (L asking T to staple his papers) |
| 4 The pragmatic expansion | The learners' pragmalinguistic repertoire is extended. They use a greater variety of strategies and make more attempts to mitigate the force of a request using more complex syntax. | 'Could you go over there? ' (L asking T to move away) 'Could you tell me how to play this?' (L to an family adult) 'I think you'd better put this…' (L to an adult family friend) |
| 5 The fine-tuning stage | Learners are able to fine-tune the force of their strengths to take account of participants, goals, and contexts. | 'Maybe we could paint it in this colour.' (L to an adult family friend) 'Don't eat too much because you might get tummy ache.' (L to another L) 'Maybe you could make it if you want to.' (L to another L) |

Key

L = Learner; T = Teacher

*Table 4.4  Stages in the pragmalinguistic development of requests (based on Kasper and Rose 2002)*

(2003) study of the acquisition of English requests by one seven-year-old Japanese girl living in Australia. What is interesting is that a very similar pattern of development was evident in the communicative speech of both the classroom and naturalistic learners.

A similar pattern of development is evident for other speech acts (for example, apologies and refusals). Three observations are in order. Not all learners reach the final, fine-tuning stage. The classroom learner in my study only reached stage four. There was no evidence of this learner modifying his requests to take account of different addressees, for example the teacher or other students. In contrast, Achiba's learner manifested a higher level of development and had clearly entered stage five, although she was still somewhat limited in her ability to mitigate the force of her requests at the end of the study. Both studies covered a similar period of time so the difference may reflect the different contexts in which the data were collected (i.e. the classroom versus play situations involving other children and adults). In both cases, development was quite slow.

The second observation is that the pattern of development reflects progression through the **learner varieties** described by Klein and Perdue (1997). Thus, requests in stage one are representative of the pre-basic variety, those in stages two of the basic variety, while those in stages four and five the post-basic variety. This raises the important question of the relationship between pragmalinguistic development and grammatical development. Do learners acquire grammar and then put this to use to convey pragmatic meanings or do they acquire pragmalinguistic devices and then derive grammar from them, or do pragmalinguistic and grammatical development feed off each other?

Schmidt's (1983) case study of Wes suggests that pragmatic and grammatical development proceed separately. Schmidt commented that Wes 'developed considerable control of the formulaic language that acts as social grease in interaction' (p. 154), but demonstrated little grammatical development. This study suggests that the early stage of acquisition is essentially pragmatic rather than grammatical. However, the development of more advanced stages of pragmalinguistic ability is only possible if learners have acquired the necessary grammatical resources. For example, Japanese university students' failure to make use of bi-clausal request formulas (Takahashi 1996) is best explained by the fact that they had not yet acquired bi-clausal constructions. The setting may also determine whether pragmatic need drives the acquisition of grammar or vice versa. Bardovi-Harlig and Dörnyei (1998), for example, found that—whereas ESL learners in the USA identified pragmatic errors more consistently than grammatical errors—the reverse was the case for EFL learners in Hungary.

The third observation is that the performance of speech acts like requests and apologies is clearly dependent on the use of formulas. Most of the examples in Table 4.4 are formulaic routines with a single open slot (for example, 'Give me...' and 'Can I have a...?'). Thus—to a considerable extent—the development of pragmatic competence rests on learners acquiring an increasing range of formulaic expressions. However, as Bardovi-Harlig (2006) pointed out—and as noted earlier in this chapter—formulas are themselves developmental. Thus, pragmatic development depends not just on learning new formulas but on the analysis of formulas already acquired. She proposed that formulas emerge in stages and illustrates this with data that show how a very simple formula ('yeah but' used as a marker of disagreement) evolved over time from an initial stage consisting of 'but ah…', through an interim stage involving the use of 'yeah so' and 'yeah no' to the final stage where the target formula ('yeah but') finally appears. As formulas develop, so pragmalinguistic ability also develops.

## Summing up

We have now considered a range of descriptive research about how learners' grammatical, phonological, and lexical systems develop and also how their L2 pragmalinguistic abilities evolve. This research has used a variety of methods: (1) case studies of individual learners, (2) descriptions of the learner varieties that evolve over time, (3) obligatory occasion analysis, (4) emergence, (5) frequency analysis, and (6) usage-based analyses. These different approaches are based on different theoretical assumptions about how L2 acquisition proceeds. For example: obligatory occasion analysis is predicated on the assumption that acquisition entails conformity to target-language norms; frequency analysis on the assumption that acquisition is a stage-like process involving **transitional constructions**; emergence on the assumption that the appearance of a new form demonstrates its acquisition; and usage-based analyses view acquisition as the unpacking of formulaic sequences.

These differences in research methods and their underlying assumptions make it difficult to arrive at a simple summing up of how L2 development takes place. However, I will attempt a number of generalizations about what the research shows about L2 development, reserving a consideration of how they can be explained for later chapters.

## The focus of the research has been on incidental acquisition

The bulk of the research reviewed in this chapter has investigated the communicative speech of learners in naturalistic settings. In effect, then, it has examined how languages are learned incidentally and how **implicit L2 knowledge** develops. Of course, learners can also learn intentionally through studying a language formally and, as a result, develop metalinguistic understanding of L2 features (i.e. explicit knowledge). However, there are limits on learners' ability to make use of their **explicit knowledge** in their communicative speech. Differences in the order of acquisition were only found when data were collected by means of tests or unspeeded writing tasks (Larsen-Freeman 1976), which allow time for learners to access their explicit knowledge. We have also seen that classroom learners manifest similar acquisitional tendencies to naturalistic learners when their communicative speech is examined (Ellis 1984; Eskildsen 2012).

## L2 development has been investigated primarily in terms of production

The regularities in L2 development that we have observed are regularities in the acquisition of productive abilities. However, a full account of how learners acquire an second language needs to account for their ability to process and comprehend the meaning of different grammatical forms in the input they are exposed to as well as their ability to produce them. Learning a morphological feature such as English plural -*s* does not commence with the production of this form, but with attending to it in the input and understanding the meaning it conveys. By and large, receptive knowledge precedes productive knowledge for grammar, just as it does for vocabulary.

## The interconnectedness of different L2 systems

In linguistics, grammar, phonology, lexis, and pragmatics are typically treated separately so it is no surprise that SLA researchers have generally adopted the same approach. However, it is clear that these different linguistic systems are interconnected in L2 development. Formulaic sequences are lexical, but they play an important role in the development of grammar (Eskildsen 2012). The acquisition of words necessarily includes acquisition of their grammatical properties (Meara 2009). The linguistic features of the pre-basic, basic, and post-basic varieties reflect the discourse strategies learners adopt (Klein and Perdue 1997). The development of syllable structure is dependent on the learners' general proficiency, which dictates the extent to which they can focus on producing the final consonant in closed syllables (Abrahamsson 2003). Pragmalinguistic development feeds into grammatical development but is also dependent on it. What drives the acquisition of form-meaning mappings is the learners' need to communicate more efficiently by utilizing a range of linguistic resources from all these systems. However, if communicative need can be satisfied through development of one particular system at the expense of others, as was the case with Wes, then development may be restricted.

## Development is gradual, dynamic, variable, and non-linear

All the research we have examined in this chapter points to the gradual, dynamic, variable, and non-linear nature of L2 development. Learners do not move suddenly from one learner variety to another. Mastery of grammatical morphemes is a slow process and different morphemes are acquired at different rates. Nor does the acquisition of individual morphemes proceed in a straightforward way. There are periods when development is rapid, followed by a plateau, and then further development (Jia and Fuse 2007). The acquisition of negatives may manifest distinct stages of development, but these stages overlap, resulting in highly variable use of the different negative devices available at any one stage (Cancino et al. 1978). Perhaps it is usage-based analyses—such as Eskildsen's (2012)—that most effectively capture the dynamic nature of development, as they show how forms and the uses they are put to evolve over time. They show the competition that exists between different forms and the meanings they realize, and how this is gradually sorted out.

## Development is characterized by a set of universal processes

There are differences in how individual learners' interlanguage develops. We have seen that the learner's first language influences development—for example, in the word order that figures in the basic variety (Klein and Perdue 1997) or in the acquisition of voicing in final consonants (Eckman 1977). L2 sociopragmatic competence is heavily influenced by the pragmatic norms of the first language. However, it is also possible to identify a set of processes that are common to all learners and that suggest that, to some extent at least, development is systematic and predictable. These include:

- *Analysis of formulaic sequences.* Throughout this chapter, we have pointed to the role that formulaic sequences play, not just in enhancing learners' communicative ability, but also in contributing to acquisition. Where once formulaic chunks were seen as separate from the rule-systems that learners draw on in their creative speech, they are now seen as feeding into grammatical development as learners discover how to segment and recombine the parts that comprise them.
- *Semantic and structural simplification* (i.e. the omission of content words and grammatical functors, as in 'no colour' (= 'I don't have a coloured pencil'). This is especially prevalent in the early stages of development (in the pre-basic variety), but is also likely to occur whenever learners are under pressure to communicate spontaneously and have had no opportunity to plan.
- *Overgeneralization* (i.e. the extension of a specific linguistic form to a context that does not require it in the target language, for example, 'eated'). Such forms do not occur in the input the learner is exposed to and thus must have been 'created' by the learner. In other cases, however, learners overgeneralize forms that do occur in the input, as when verb + *-ing* is overused to refer to habitual actions (for example, 'he coming every day').
- *Restructuring* (i.e. the process where the acquisition of a new linguistic feature leads to the reorganization of existing L2 knowledge). The change that takes place does not simply involve the addition of the new feature to the learner's interlanguage, but a qualitative re-organization of it. We saw examples of this in Eskildsen's (2012) study of L2 negation.
- *U-shaped behaviour* where a specific linguistic form is target-like initially, but is then replaced by an interlanguage form before the target form finally reappears (for example, ate → eated → ate). U-shaped behaviour has been observed in both the acquisition of grammatical and phonological L2 features.

## Conclusion

It is clear that there are regularities in the ways in which all learners approach the task of learning a second language and that these regularities are reflected in the general trajectory observed in L2 development. As VanPatten and Williams (2007) commented, 'learners' output (speech) often follows predictable paths with predictable stages in the acquisition of a particular structure' (p. 12). Ortega (2009) similarly concluded 'all L1 groups will traverse the same series of approximations to the target L2 systems' (p. 34). This chapter provides evidence to support these claims.

Some researchers, however, have questioned the existence of 'predictable paths'. They argue that the learner's L1 is much more influential than universalist accounts acknowledge. Larsen-Freeman (2010) wisely warned of the danger of treating all learners as behaving the same and noted that context can also affect development. More fundamentally, sociocultural theorists have queried whether acquisition orders and sequences have any validity at all. Lantolf (2005), for example, claimed that 'development is revolutionary and therefore unpredictable' and dismissed the view that developmental trajectories are 'impervious to instructional intervention' (p. 339). Johnson (2004) likewise argued that the adoption of Vygotskian sociocultural theory 'would require that we ... eradicate the assertion that L2 acquisition progresses a predetermined path' (p. 172).

However, there is far too much evidence of these developmental trajectories to dismiss them so lightly. It is, perhaps, not so much a question of *whether* they do emerge in learners' spontaneous communicative use, as examining *how* individual learner factors (such as the learner's first language) and context impact on them. It is necessary to reconcile the claim that there are universal tendencies in the way a second language is acquired with the variability that is evident in learners' use of a second language. We will consider this in the next chapter.

## Notes

1 Pica (1983) argued that in considering whether or not a feature has been mastered we need to consider not just whether learners can use it accurately in obligatory occasions, but also whether they overuse it—i.e. use it in contexts when it is not obligatory. An example of overuse of third-person -*s* is 'The children *goes* home at four o'clock'. She proposed a formula for investigating 'target-language use', which takes account of both suppliance in obligatory contexts and of overuse.

2 A similar problem arises with the use of emergence as the measure of acquisition. Pienemann (1984) defined emergence as the first occurrence of a specific grammatical feature in learners' creative speech. This method also requires a clear distinction to be made between formulaic sequences (which are discounted) and creative speech.

3 This description is based on Dimroth (2012). However, the English examples illustrating the different patterns have been constructed by me.

4 Variational features were identified in Meisel, Clahsen, and Pienemann (1981), but in subsequent publications have received little attention. It is not clear to me whether there is a theoretical basis for deciding whether a feature is variational or developmental or whether variational features can only be established empirically.

5 However, there is also evidence that production can sometimes precede speech perception (Sheldon and Strange 1982).

6 Abrahamsson's explanation supports Skehan's (1998) claim that learners will prioritize one aspect of L2 use (for example, fluency) over another (for example, accuracy). Abrahamsson's study indicated that the aspect learners prioritize is determined not just by the nature of the task they are asked to perform but also by their developmental stage.

# 5
# Variability in learner language

## Introduction

In the last chapter, we saw that learners' second language development is characterized by regularities that—to some extent at least—are universal. However, although it may be possible to identify stages in the development of specific linguistic features, there is variability within each stage. As Cancino, Rosansky, and Schumann (1978) noted in their study of the acquisition of negatives by Spanish learners of English:

> Our attempt to write rules for the negative proved fruitless. The
> constant development and concomitant variation in our subjects'
> speech at any one point made the task fruitless (p. 209)

Thus, while a specific negative device may be dominant at a given point of development (for example, 'no' + verb), other devices (for example, 'don't' + verb; auxiliary + negative + verb) also occur. Interlanguage systems are dynamic and, as a consequence, variability is endemic. This chapter will explore the nature of this variability and also examine its significance for identifying the factors that shape L2 development.

In this chapter, I will consider three approaches for investigating variability in learner language. The first draws on variationist sociolinguistics (Labov 1970; Tarone 1983), which accounts for variability in terms of **variable rules**. The second makes use of the **Dynamic Paradigm** (Bickerton 1975; Huebner 1983) to examine variability in terms of learner varieties. The third—**Dynamic Systems Theory** (Verspoor, de Bot, and Lowie 2011)—examines variability within a general theory of change and development. These three approaches differ in how they view variability. In the variationist sociolinguistic tradition, 'the concern is with discovering the underlying systematicity of variable learner production' (Bayley 2005: 2). The Dynamic Paradigm is used to account for learner varieties in terms of the evolving form-function systems that characterize interlanguage development. In Dynamic Systems Theory, however, change is viewed as constant and the concomitant variation as largely chaotic and unpredictable.

In this chapter, I will also explore two types of variation in learner language: type 1 variation is evident when learners vary between the use of a target and an interlanguage form; type 2 variation occurs when learners alternate between two or more target language forms although not necessarily in the same way as native speakers.

## Variationist sociolinguistics

L2 researchers in this tradition have drawn heavily on the work of Labov. I will briefly outline this approach before examining some of the SLA research that has been based on it. Two constructs are of particular importance in this paradigm; **speech styles** and **variable rules**. The paradigm also acknowledges that there are multiple factors that influence speakers' variable use of linguistic forms.

## Speech styles

Labov (1970) noted that 'there are no single style speakers' (p. 19) and that 'all speakers vary their language to some degree in accordance with the social context or topic'. He proposed that styles can be arranged along a single dimension, measured by the amount of attention paid to speech. In other words, language users vary in the degree to which they monitor their speech in different situations, with the least attention evident in the **vernacular style** (i.e. the style associated with informal, everyday speech) and the most in the **careful style** (i.e. the style associated with formal language use, as in a public speech). That is, speakers style shift in accordance with situational factors, in particular with how they perceive their relationship with the person they are addressing, which affects their choice of linguistic forms.

Drawing on Labov's work on style shifting, Tarone (1983) suggested that interlanguage is also characterized by a continuum of styles, each of which can be elicited by tasks varying in the extent to which they induce learners to attend to form (see Figure 5.1). An important implication of

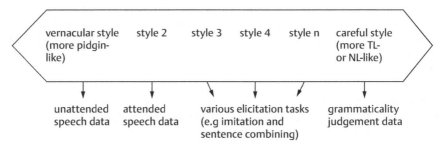

*Figure 5.1 Style-shifting in learner language (from Tarone 1983)—see Ellis (2008: 142)*

Tarone's model is that if we want to investigate learners' L2 competence (or 'capability' as she preferred to call it), we will need to use a variety of different tasks to collect data, as competence is heterogeneous, not homogeneous. Another implication, which—as we will later see—is only partly supported by research, is that learners are more likely to use target-language variants in the careful style and interlanguage variants in their vernacular style.

## Variable rules

A categorical rule states that a specific linguistic form occurs invariably in a specific context. For example, in standard varieties of English, verb + -s occurs after the pronouns 'he', 'she', and 'it' in the present simple tense. Even within a single variety, however, there are some linguistic features that are variable (i.e. they can be realized by two or more linguistic forms). For example, French negation can be realized by *ne* + verb + *pas* (for example, 'Je ne vais pas à Londres') or by verb + *pas* (for example, 'Je vais pas à Londres'). To capture such phenomena, a variable rule is needed. This states that a given variable (negation in French) is manifest as either one variant (*ne* + verb + *pas*) or another variant (verb + *pas*) with different levels of probability depending on the situational context. Ashby (1981), for example, reported that omission of *ne* occurred 61 per cent of the time in the informal speech of native speakers of French but only 40 per cent in their formal speech. However, more recent research (Armstrong 2002) showed that **style-shifting** in this feature is disappearing as many native French speakers now omit *ne* in both their vernacular and careful styles.

## Linguistic context

The choice of variant, however, is not influenced solely by the situational context. The linguistic context also plays a role. That is, the variant a speaker chooses is dependent in part on the words that precede and follow the variable being investigated. For example, Armstrong (2002) reported native French speakers were likely to delete *ne* following a pronoun, but retain it after a full noun phrase. Research indicates that—by and large—the linguistic context exerts a stronger effect on the choice of variant than the situational context.

## Multiple factors influencing variation

Romaine (2003) pointed out that 'variation is usually conditioned by multiple causes' (p. 431). Increasingly, researchers in the Labovian tradition have switched from investigating single factors to examining the multiple external (i.e. social) and internal (i.e. linguistic context) factors that influence the choice of variants. They have employed a statistical program called VARBRUL to determine the probabilistic weight of a whole range of factors on the operation of a variable rule. The aim is to account for the complexity and multidimensionality of speech variation. VARBRUL enables the researcher to investigate the different contributions of different factors to the choice of a specific variant (for example, omission of *ne* in French negatives). For those readers interested in the application of VARBRUL Young and Bayley (1996) provide a helpful account.

## SLA research in the Labovian paradigm

Much of the early work on variability in SLA utilized the methodology of variationist sociolinguistics to investigate the effects of the situational and linguistic context on L2 learners' choice of linguistic variants. More recent work has focused on identifying multiple influences using VARBRUL. For a comprehensive survey of this research see Howard, Mougeon, and Dewaele (2013). Here I will focus on a number of typical studies.

### Style shifting in learner language

One of the earliest studies was Dickerson's (1975) study of Japanese learners' use of /z/, as in 'boys'. Dickerson showed that the target language variant was used least frequently in free speech and most consistently when the learners read word lists aloud. Performance on a task that required learners to read dialogues aloud was intermediate. Using a similar methodology, Bayley (1996) found that native Mandarin learners of English who had lived in the United States for varying lengths of time were less likely to delete final *-t/-d* in consonant clusters in their careful style (i.e. when reading aloud) than in their casual style (i.e. in informal conversation). These studies provide evidence of the same kind of **style shifting** found in native-speaker speech. They suggest that the attention that L2 learners pay to their speech influences the extent to which they deploy the L2 variants when speaking.

Other studies, however, have reported that style shifting in learner language does not always occur, or is not always as regular as Dickerson (1975) and Bayley (1996) found. Sato (1985) collected data over a ten-month period by means of free conversation, oral reading of a continuous text, and elicited imitation of words and short phrases. She looked at target final consonants and consonant clusters. The accuracy ranking for target final consonants on the three tasks changed from one time to the next. Greater consistency, however, was evident for consonant clusters. Sato concluded that not all variables yield the same pattern of variation.

Form-function relations also need to be taken into account to provide a full explanation of style shifting. Tarone (1985) investigated three grammatical morphemes (third-person *-s*, the article, and plural *-s*) and one grammatical structure (direct object pronouns) using data collected from three tasks designed to elicit different degrees of attention to form. In the case of third-person *-s*, the results demonstrated the expected pattern of style shifting: that is, the learners were most accurate in a test and least accurate in an oral narrative. However, the pattern was reversed for the article and direct object pronouns—the learners were most accurate in the task that had been designed to require the least attention to form. Tarone explained these results by suggesting that the article and object pronouns served as important markers of discourse cohesiveness in the narrative task as this led the learners to attend to discourse cohesiveness to a greater extent than in the other two tasks[1].

Sometimes style shifting in learner language is influenced by learners' explicit knowledge of L2 rules. Regan (1996) investigated the style shifting in *ne* omission in the negative constructions of seven advanced learners of L2 French. She collected data before the learners spent time in France and after they returned. At time 1, the learners deleted *ne* more in their casual style than in their careful style. However, style made less of a difference at time 2 (one year later). This was because the learners now omitted it more regularly in their careful style. Regan suggests that this may have occurred because the learners believed that it was acceptable to delete *ne* and so extended this to their careful speech. By time 2—when their deletion rates were very close to those of native speakers—they appear to have abandoned this pedagogical rule. In other words, they had learned an explicit rule—'when you are being formal in French you retain *ne* but in casual speech you delete it'—but, as a result of exposure to French in France, rejected it.

Regan's (1996) study investigated advanced L2 learners. But do less-proficient learners style-shift? Dewaele (2004) drew on a study by Dewaele and Regan (2002) of a mixed proficiency group of Dutch learners of L2 French to suggest that there is a **U-shaped pattern of development** in the omission of *ne*. Beginner- and intermediate-level learners manifest a simplification strategy; they omit *ne* categorically in favour of the more salient *pas* in their negative utterances. Intermediate-level learners produce *ne* + verb + *pas* constructions categorically. Only very advanced learners demonstrate style-shifting, omitting *ne* in the casual style. In other words, omission of *ne* occurs regularly with beginner level learners, rarely with low-advanced learners, and then at a higher rate with very advanced learners. Thus, it seems that style-shifting only becomes apparent when learners have achieved sufficient proficiency.

These studies suggest that style shifting in learner language is a complex phenomenon. Sometimes the same pattern of style shifting as in native-speaker speech occurs. However, learners also sometimes style shift where native speakers do not, influenced perhaps by the explicit instruction they have received. Style shifting does not always occur when it might be expected. Sometimes it results in greater use of the target variant in careful than in casual speech. Also, native-like style shifting may only be possible when learners have attained knowledge of the variant forms and internalized the sociolinguistic rules that govern their use.

The situational context covers a whole host of factors (for example, time, topic, purpose, and tone). SLA research has examined only a few of these situational factors. Thus, although the studies I have considered were informed by a sociolinguistic model designed to account for how situational factors affect learners' language use, they have shed only limited light on this. The narrow focus on **stylistic** variation is also problematic for another reason. Style-shifting draws heavily on the notion of 'attention' which, arguably, is more of a psycholinguistic than a social phenomenon.

### The effects of linguistic context

There is much clearer evidence of the effect that linguistic context has on learners' use of variant forms. Preston (2002) observed 'linguistic influences are nearly always probabilistically heavier than sociocultural influences' (p. 146).

Dickerson's (1975) study mentioned above also investigated the effects of linguistic context on Japanese learners' production of English /z/. Dickerson examined four different phonological environments and found that in the dialogue reading task, the learners used the correct target-language form whenever /z/ was followed by a vowel, but were progressively less accurate in the other environments (for example, when /z/ was followed by consonants such as /m/ and /b/). Dickerson collected data at three different points in time and found that—although the learners improved in their ability to use target-language /z/ in the more difficult linguistic contexts over time—the environmental effects observed at time 1 were also evident at time 3. Dickerson's study suggests that the linguistic environment has a prevailing effect on learners' use of a target language phonological form.

The complex effect that the linguistic environment has on L2 phonological features is demonstrated in Bayley's (1996) study of /t/ and /d/ deletion at the end of English words by Chinese learners of English. Bayley found that the learners, like native speakers, were less likely to delete /t/ or /d/ following a liquid (for example, /l/) than an obstruent (for example, /s/) or a nasal (for example, /n/). However, unlike native speakers, the preceding phonological environment had no effect. The learners also differed from native speakers in another way. /t/ and /d/ deletion was affected by the grammatical category of a word: it was more likely in uninflected words like 'mist' than in regular past tense verbs such as 'missed'. Thus, both phonological and grammatical processes were involved interactively. Whereas semi-weak irregular verbs (for example, 'left') were subject to both processes, the past tense marking of strong verbs ('talked') was affected only by the grammatical process. Bayley concluded that 'Chinese-English interlanguage diverges from native-speaker English when competing rules are involved' (p. 116).

Hansen-Edwards (2011) reported similar results. She collected data from two conversational interviews with limited-proficiency Chinese learners of English conducted six months apart. She found that following linguistic constraints on /t/ and /d/ deletion were more powerful than preceding constraints. Overall, the learners displayed stable patterns of deletion with little change over. None of the learners had fully acquired target-like deletion patterns, but they did manifest native-like use of deletion with some patterns. Hansen-Edwards suggested that the reason for this may have been L1 transfer. She wondered whether L2 learners ever fully acquire native-like patterns, a point also raised in Chapter 2 when we looked at the role of age.

Other studies have shown that the linguistic context also affects grammatical variables. In Ellis (1988), I investigated the effects of linguistic context on copula -*s* in the English speech of three classroom learners (one Portuguese and two Punjabi-speaking) over a two-year period. The learners used three variants of copula -*s* (zero, full, and contracted). The target-language variants (full and contracted copula) were used more consistently when the preceding subject was a pronoun than when the preceding subject was a noun. Conversely, the interlanguage variant (zero copula) occurred more frequently when the subject was a noun. In other words, emergence of the target-language variants occurred initially in environments involving a closed class of items and then spread to those involving an open class. However, none of the learners achieved the same pattern of variability for copula use found in native-speaker speech even after two years. In other words, they did not acquire the target-language variable rule.

These studies indicate that learner language is influenced by the linguistic environment, sometimes in the same way as in native-speaker language use, but at other times in unique ways. They also show that, over time, learners approximate more closely to the pattern of variability evident in native speakers but that, even at very advanced levels, learners may not manifest exactly the same pattern of variability as native speakers. As Bayley noted in the conclusion to his study, 'even highly proficient learners...are unlikely to perform like native speakers' (1996: 116). The explanation for this may lie in the influence of the learners' first language, the inherent difficulty of some target forms, and the learner's starting age.

## Multiple influences on L2 variation

Bayley (2005) is critical of much of the research that has investigated interlanguage variation because it has sought a single, over-arching explanation. This is true of the studies we have considered above—they investigated either single factors affecting stylistic variation or the effects of a limited set of linguistic factors. It is clear, however, that interlanguage variation is subject to multiple influences and that variationist research ideally needs to adopt the 'principle of multiple causes' (Young and Bayley 1996: 3).

One of the earliest studies to adopt a multi-factor approach is Young's (1988) study of one linguistic variable—plural -*s*—in the speech of twelve Chinese learners of English. The learners were interviewed in English twice, once by a native English speaker and the second time by a fellow Chinese speaker. Data relating to four general factors were obtained: (1) the context of the situation (in particular the extent to which each learner converged with the interviewers in terms of social factors such as ethnicity, sex, education, and occupation); (2) the subjects' proficiency in English (whether 'high' or 'low'); (3) the linguistic context (whether the plural nouns were definite or animate, whether the noun phrase was definite or indefinite, and the phonological environment), and (4) redundancy in plural marking (whether plural -*s* was omitted because plurality was indicated by some other linguistic device, such as a numeral). Young found that all four general factors accounted for the variability present in the data. However, some specific factors (for example, the definiteness of a noun phrase and the following phonological segment) had no effect on plural -*s* marking, irrespective of the learners' proficiency. Also, there were differences between the high- and low-proficiency learners for some of the factors. For example, the preceding phonological segment influenced plural marking only for the low-proficiency learners whereas social convergence with an interlocutor was only a factor for the high-proficiency learners.

Dewaele (2004) reported a multi-factor study investigating L2 learners' and native speakers' deletion of *ne* in negative utterances. In this study, the learners took it in turns to interview each other and were also interviewed by a native speaker. Dewaele focused on exogeneous variables (i.e. age, gender, and frequency of speaking French) and an endogenous variable (i.e. whether the interlocutor was another learner or a native speaker). Out of a total of 991 negations, there were 331 cases of omission of *ne*. Neither the age nor the gender of the learners had an effect on omission. A personality variable—extraversion—had a marginal effect. The main factor was the frequency of speaking French. Those learners who reported using French more frequently outside of the classroom were much more likely to omit *ne*. Also, interestingly, omission rates were much lower in the interviews between learners than in the interviews with a native speaker[2].

Several studies have investigated the factors influencing tense marking on verbs in different languages. Low-proficiency learners commonly over-extend the present form of a verb in past-time contexts and—even when past-time forms begin to be used—they vary in non-target-like ways. Two factors that have been shown to be influential are the inherent lexical aspect of a verb and discourse grounding. The **Aspect Hypothesis** (Andersen 1991) predicts that past-tense marking depends on whether a verb refers to a state (for example, 'be' or 'like'), an activity (for example, 'play' or 'read'), an accomplishment (for example, 'paint a fence') or an achievement (for example, 'die' or 'close'). Learners have been found to mark achievement and accomplishment verbs for past-time more consistently than state or activity verbs. The **Discourse Hypothesis** claims that past-tense marking in narratives is more likely to occur when the event is foregrounded than when it is backgrounded. Again, several studies have demonstrated that this is the case. Most of the studies, however, have investigated the predictions of the Aspect and Discourse Hypotheses separately. Howard (2004) investigated both hypotheses by examining temporal marking on verbs by Irish learners of L2 French. He first confirmed the predictions of the two hypotheses and then examined whether the two factors 'joined forces'. The learners were more likely to employ perfective tense marking in contexts involving an achievement verb and a foregrounded event and least likely in contexts involving a state verb and a backgrounded event.

These studies testify to the importance of examining multiple factors affecting interlanguage variation. They demonstrate that interlanguage variation is multidimensional. It is the product of the complex interplay of a range of social, psychological, linguistic, and discourse factors, each of which contributes to the pattern of variability to a greater or lesser extent. Only by examining multiple factors is it possible to determine the constraints exerted by different factors, how the constraints interact, and whether they operate in the same way at different levels of second language proficiency.

## The Dynamic Paradigm

In the Dynamic Paradigm (Bickerton 1975), variation is accounted for in terms of the 'varieties' evident in different speech communities. Language variation arises as the result of the spread of a rule from one variety to another over time. A rule spreads through a given speech community in waves in two ways. First, the rule manifests itself in the variety of one group of speakers and then spreads to another group while—at the same time—the first group may have introduced a new rule which exists in competition with the first rule, resulting in variation. Second, the spread of a new rule is influenced by the linguistic environment, with some environments favouring the application of the new feature, and other environments continuing to favour the old feature. The Dynamic Paradigm, then, assumes that a language variety is systematic, but also dynamic and that variation is the precursor of change.

The Dynamic Paradigm evolved out of research investigating how creole languages develop over time. A creole has several varieties (or 'lects' as Bickerton 1975, called them). The lects can be arranged on a continuum from the basilect (the simplest, most basic variety) to the acrolect (the most complex variety) with the mesolect intermediate. A creole grammar is polylectal as it manifests features from different lects.

Bickerton was interested in the group varieties of creole speakers, but the Dynamic Paradigm can also account for variation in individual L2 learners—whose linguistic systems are more open to rapid change than the lects that comprise the creole continuum—and, thus, more likely to display variation. The Dynamic Paradigm also allows for the possibility of **free variation** (i.e. the non-systematic use of two or more variants) as it acknowledges that—for a short period of time when a learner acquires a new feature—this is likely to exist alongside a previously learned feature.

Whereas the Labovian approach employed variables rules to account for the factors that systematically induce variability, research based on the Dynamic Paradigm makes use of implicational scaling. This plots the variation that occurs at any one time (i.e. in cross-sectional data) to order the varieties of different learners according to how complex they are. It assumes that simpler varieties are developmentally prior to more complex varieties. Thus implicational scaling relates **horizontal variability** (i.e. the variability evident at a particular time) to **vertical variability** (i.e. stages of L2 development). An example of vertical scaling is provided below.

The Dynamic Paradigm also affords a way of investigating variability in form-function systems. In any language variety, specific linguistic forms are used to realize specific functions. For example, in standard English verb + -*ing* can be used to refer to an ongoing action (for example, 'I'm eating at the moment') or to planned future action (for example, 'I'm flying to London tomorrow'). Learning a second language therefore involves learning the particular form-function mappings that characterize the variety the learner is targeting. Learners, however, develop their own unique form-function systems. The Dynamic paradigm offers a way of exploring how changes in form-function mappings occur over time.

## SLA research based on the Dynamic Paradigm

We will examine two strands of research that have drawn on the Dynamic Paradigm. The first is a direct application of the Dynamic Paradigm using the same methodology as in the creole studies. The second involves the study of learners' evolving form-function systems.

### Gradual Diffusion Model

Gatbonton's (1978) **Gradual Diffusion Model** proposes two broad stages of L2 development. In the 'acquisition stage', the learner begins by using a single form in all situations and contexts, and then subsequently introduces another form which is used alongside the first in all contexts (i.e. it is in free variation). In the 'replacement phase', each form is restricted to specific contexts of use as learners gradually and systematically eliminate competing forms from these contexts. Gatbonton developed this model to account for the patterns of variation, which she found in the production of three phonological features (/θ/, /ð/, and /h/) in the speech of 27 French-Canadian learners of English, elicited by means of reading-aloud and spontaneous-speaking tasks. Gatbonton found that in learners in the 'acquisition stage', a single variant or free variation was evident, whereas in the 'replacement phase', systematic variation in accordance with linguistic context occurred.

In a follow-up study, Trofimovich, Gatbonton, and Segalowitz (2007) collected data from 40 adult francophone speakers of L2 English. They reported that their production of /ð/ followed the dynamic and implicational pattern predicted by Gatbonton's Gradual Diffusion Model. That is, target renditions of /ð/ replaced variable and non-target ones systematically, beginning in easy contexts and then spreading to difficult ones. This is shown in the implicational scaling in Figure 5.2. Trofimovich et al. found that the learners could be ordered in terms of the contexts in which they produced /ð/. Thus, the learners at stage one failed to produce it in any context; those at stage two produced it variably in one or more contexts; those at stage three began to produce it categorically in some contexts; and those at stage four were producing is categorically in all the contexts.

| Learners | Phonetic context | | | | | | Stage |
|---|---|---|---|---|---|---|---|
| | Initial | Vowel | Liquid | Nasal | Vd stop | Vl stop | |
| 31 | 0 | 0 | 0 | 0 | 0 | 0 | 1 |
| 18 | 0 | 0 | 0 | 0 | 0 | 0 | 1 |
| 29 | 0 | 0 | 0 | 0 | 0 | 0 | 1 |
| 10 | 01 | 0 | 0 | 0 | 0 | 0 | 2 |
| 7 | 01 | 01 | 0 | 0 | 0 | 0 | 2 |
| 38 | 01 | 01 | 01 | 01 | 01 | 01 | 2 |
| 28 | 1 | 01 | 01 | 01 | 01 | 01 | 3 |
| 25 | 1 | 1 | 1 | 1 | 01 | 1* | 3 |
| 17 | 1 | 1 | 1 | 1 | 1 | 1 | 4 |
| 9 | 1 | 1 | 1 | 1 | 1 | 1 | 4 |

Key

0 = /ð/ not supplied; 01 = /ð/ supplied variably; 1 = /ð/ supplied;
* = cell not conforming to implicational pattern

*Figure 5.2  Implication scaling of /ð/ according to linguistic context (simplified from Trofimovich et al. 2007)*

Trofimovich et al. also investigated two factors that determined the likelihood of learners supplying /ð/ in the different contexts—input frequency and cross-language similarity. They were more likely to supply it in a context where /ð/ occurred frequently in the input and where /ð/ was perceived as dissimilar to an L1 consonant. They were less likely to do so in a context where /ð/ occurred less frequently in the input and where /ð/ was perceived as similar to an L1 consonant. This study, then, indicates that input frequency and the learners' perceptions of L1–L2 differences determined the likelihood of a phonological feature being supplied in different contexts.

### Form-function studies

Before we examine examples of longitudinal studies that have investigated **form-function mapping,** a word on the meaning of 'function' is needed. Tarone (1988) noted that this term covers 'pragmatic function' (for example, requests and denials), 'discourse function' (for example, topic, and cohesion), 'semantic function' (for example, specific and non-specific reference), and 'grammatical function' (for example, subject and object). Tarone argued that studying form-function mappings in learners' interlanguage 'can reveal the linguistic system hidden in a learner's apparently unsystematic use' (1988: 54).

A good example of a form-function study is Huebner's (1979, 1983) longitudinal study of Ge, a Hmong refugee acquiring English naturalistically in the United States. Huebner was able to show that although Ge's form-function mappings were not the same as those in the target language (English), they were systematic and they changed over time. Huebner focused on Ge's use of articles (*da* and zero). He based his analysis on Bickerton's (1981) Semantic

Wheel. This distinguishes two binary categories of the semantic function of noun phrases:

+/- information assumed to be known by the hearer (HK)
+/- specific referent (SR)

When combined, these yield four types of noun phrases, as shown in Table 5.1.

| Type | Standard English forms | Examples |
|---|---|---|
| 1 - SR/+ HK | 'the', 'a', or zero | 'Lions are beautiful.' |
| 2 + SR/+ HK | 'the' | 'Ask the man over there.' |
| 3 + SR/- HK | 'a' or zero | 'She gave me a present.' |
| 4 - SR/- HK | 'a' or zero | 'He's a nice man.' |

*Table 5.1   Noun phrase types*

Initially, Ge used *da* mainly for (2) (i.e. to mark nouns as specific and known to the hearer). This resulted in apparent target-like accuracy although not completely; when the noun phrase in question functioned as a topic of the sentence Ge used the zero article. A month and a half later he used *da* for all four types of noun phrase. This constituted a stage where Ge overgeneralized *da*. Huebner described this stage as 'flooding'. Five months into the study, he began to eliminate the use of *da* first from type (4) contexts and at 7 months from type (3) contexts. By the end of the study, Ge was using *da* at an 80 to 90 per cent level of accuracy. Huebner's main point is that what would be seen as random use of articles in an obligatory occasion analysis turns out to be largely systematic in a form-function analysis.

However, Huebner's study also suggests that learners pass through a stage of development where the linguistic forms at their disposal are used in free variation (i.e. randomly). In the 'flooding' stage, Ge's use of *da* was not categorical. That is, he did not invariably use it with nouns. During this stage of the learner's development, *da* appeared to be used randomly and randomly omitted. Huebner also acknowledged that even at the end of his one-year study, there was an unexplained residue of between ten and 20 per cent of non-target use. It is possible of course that there were other factors that constrained the use of *da* in a systematic way at this time but—to some extent at least—*da* was used randomly. I will return to the whole issue of whether variability in learner language is systematic or—in part—random later in this chapter.

Schachter (1986) also used a form-function analysis to re-examine the data for one of Cancino et al.'s (1978) learners (Jorge). She investigated whether his use of negative forms was as random as the original authors suggested. She argued that the variability was not explicable in terms of different situational requirements, as the data collection took place on a regular basis with the same situational constraints throughout. However, she found evidence of 'a rich system, complex from the very beginning, which became even more so as time progressed' (1986: 123–4). Schachter identified seven functions performed by Jorge's productive negative utterances and found surprising regularity in his pairing of forms and functions. For example, the formula 'I don't know' was always used to perform the same function of 'no information' (i.e. to indicate that the speaker is not in a position to confirm or deny whether something is the case), while 'no' + verb carried the 'denial' function (i.e. to assert that an actual, supposed, or proposed state of affairs does not hold for the speaker).

### Some conclusions

In some respects, the Dynamic Paradigm provides a more insightful account of interlanguage variability than the Labovian paradigm as it demonstrates more clearly how horizontal variability relates to L2 development. The following are the main conclusions that can be drawn from the research:

1 When a linguistic form emerges in a learner's interlanguage, it appears first in one linguistic context and then spreads systematically to other contexts.
2 The diffusion of a new form is also governed by both input frequency and the learner's first language.
3 Learners construct form-function systems in the process of learning and using a second language. These systems are likely to differ from the form-function systems found in the target language.
4 The learner's form-function systems evolve over time. Thus, at any stage of development, different form-function systems are likely to be observed.
5 Learners manifest free variation in the use of the linguistic forms at their disposal at some points in their development.

Point 5, however, is controversial as it runs contrary to the underlying assumption of the Labovian paradigm (i.e. that all variability is systematic). However, it is supported by the final approach we will now examine.

# Dynamic Systems Theory

**Dynamic Systems Theory** (DST), like the other approaches to investigating variability, views variation as inherent in language systems but—unlike the other approaches—it does not seek to identify the specific social and linguistic factors that predict variation. Rather, it examines how the interaction of a whole range of external and internal forces contributes to L2 development in individual learners. As de Bot and Larsen-Freeman (2011) put it 'instead of investigating single variables, we study patterns that emerge from interactions' (p. 21). DST claims that 'any account that focuses on one aspect only cannot but provide a gross oversimplification of reality' (de Bot, Lowie, and Verspoor 2007: 18)[3].

DST views the L2 learner as a complex system involving complete interconnectedness: that is, 'all variables are interrelated and therefore changes in one variable will have an impact on all other variables that are part of the system' (de Bot, Lowie, and Verspoor 2007: 8). Two points follow: (1) systems are inherently dynamic (i.e. constantly changing); (2) it is not possible to predict the outcome of development over time. Another key tenet of the theory is that L2 development is 'embodied' (i.e. cognition is not bounded within the individual but is socially constructed) and 'situated' (i.e. cognitive functions can only be understood in terms of the particular setting in which they were carried out). In these respects, DST is very similar to Complexity Theory (see Chapter 1).

I will focus on two assumptions of DST that are of special relevance to interlanguage variation: (1) variation is chaotic; (2) although change is constant, systems may temporarily settle into 'attractor' states that are relatively stable. These two characteristics are helpful for understanding two key aspects of interlanguage variation—free variation and systematic variation. Chaotic variation (i.e. variation that is impossible to predict) 'may be caused by a range of factors, such as physical fatigue, memory overload, or temporary disfunctioning of a part of the brain' (de Bot and Larsen-Freeman 2011: 15). It is an inevitable product of the system's flexibility and adaptability to the environment. Chaotic variation, therefore, should not be seen as 'noise' (as it is in variational sociolinguistics), but as evidence of ongoing change.

However, at times, a system evolves into a more settled form. An **attractor state** is defined as 'the state the system prefers to be in over other states at a particular point in time' (de Bot and Larsen-Freeman 2011: 14). Such states are not permanent, but—depending on the strength of the attraction—may resist change for a period of time. In terms of L2 development, attractor states might be understood as stages where variability in some aspect of the system becomes temporarily more systematic. In an attractor state, specific linguistic forms that have already emerged in the learner's system are now organized in such a way that they distinguish the different functions that are communicatively important to a learner. They are supplied more regularly in accordance with constraints that are both inherent in the system and social—as was seen in Ge's progression from a 'flooding stage' to more systematic use of *da*. Thus, from the perspective of DST, L2 development is a continuous process that involves both free and systematic variation, both of which are found in different parts of the overall system at different times.

Dijk, Verspoor, and Lowie (2011) point out the essential difference between how variability is viewed in traditional sociolinguistic approaches and in DST. The former 'have been mainly interested in discovering external causes of variability' whereas 'a DST approach is interested in variability to discover when and how changes take place in the process of development, how different subsystems develop and interact, and how different learners may have different developmental patterns' (p. 60–1). They point out that learners do not learn all the subsystems of language at one time and that chaotic variation is not therefore a characteristic of the complete system, but only of some parts of it. For example, at the very beginning stage of L2 acquisition, variation of any kind is largely absent, but once the learner has learned how to construct short, simple sentences, they may switch attention to verb forms and begin to manifest a high level of free variation in the use of these. After some time, attractor states will emerge in the learner's verb system, creating conditions for the development of some other system—such as complex sentences— which initially will display free variation. The aim of DST research, then, is to investigate how chaotic variation in a system can evolve into a stable 'attractor' state.

To illustrate this approach, Dijk et al. reanalysed the data from Cancino et al.[4]. This analysis revealed the following:

- The developmental curves for the individual learners investigated are quite different from the averaged curve for the whole group: in other words, inter-learner differences are pronounced.
- Two of the learners investigated in detail displayed equal levels of variability, but—whereas in one of the learners the variability was essentially random—in the other, a significant 'peak' was evident at a given stage of development, suggesting that this learner had settled into an attractor state.

Dijk et al. concluded that it is misleading to average data for a group of learners and then to claim that there is a common sequence of acquisition. Their re-analysis of the data challenges Cancino et al.'s claim that there was a distinct sequence in the acquisition of English negation. It also suggests that different variability patterns reveal different kinds of development. Free variation occurs when no or very little development is taking place, whereas the presence of a significant peak in a learner's use of a specific grammatical feature signals that the learner is ready to accommodate new constructions. They also noted that the patterns of variability of the six learners differed according to their age, with the children taking longer to produce peaks in the use of non-target forms than the teenagers, and the adults failing to show peaks to the same extent as the teenagers.

Research based on DST is still in its infancy. It faces several challenges. As de Bot and Larsen-Freeman (2011) noted, it is not clear whether it is valid to study any one linguistic feature (for example, L2 negation) separately from other linguistic features. The theory claims that the development of one subsystem of language interacts with the development of other sub-systems. Thus, how individual learners develop English negation is inextricably linked to the development of their general fluency, accuracy, and complexity in the use of English as a whole. It is difficult to see, then, how Dynamic Systems Theory can ever provide a full account of variability. That said, the theory affords some important insights; in particular, it challenges the assumption of variationist sociolinguistics that free variation is just uninteresting 'noise'.

## Conclusion

In this chapter, we have examined a number of studies that show how social and linguistic factors influence learners' choice of L2 forms. We have seen that 'change is only the temporal consequence of current variation' (Widdowson 1979: 195). This is evident in a number of ways:

- Linguistic forms may appear initially in one style (for example, the careful style) and then subsequently spread to another style (for example, the vernacular style).
- Linguistic forms may only be supplied in one linguistic context initially, but then spread to other linguistic contexts over time.
- Patterns of variability change as learners construct and then reconstruct their form-function systems as new forms enter their repertoire.
- Chaotic variation can give way to more systematic variation as learners enter an attractor state, which may in turn constitute a transitional point allowing for further development.

These generalizations, however, are not supported by all the theories of variation we have examined in this chapter. In particular, there is disagreement about both the existence and role of free variation in L2 development and of whether there are universal trends.

## The significance of free variation

Variational sociolinguists are generally dismissive of free variation. Preston (1996), for example commented 'I am suspicious that language variation which is influenced by nothing at all is a chimera' (p. 25). For Preston, free variation is only apparent because of researchers' failure to identify the sources of systematicity. He was critical of my own early claims about the role of free variation in L2 development (see Ellis 1985). In contrast, both the **Dynamic Paradigm** and **Dynamic Systems Theory** (especially the latter) view free variation as an inherent feature of interlanguage systems and of significance for understanding how linguistic systems are developed.

In Ellis (1999), I drew on Towell, Hawkins, and Bazergui (1996) to propose a general model of how learners acquire specific linguistic forms (see Table 5.2). Free variation occurs in stage three and functions as the precursor of systematic variation in stage four. The model is not intended as a model of interlanguage development as—clearly—learners' entire interlanguage systems do not progress neatly from one stage to another. Rather, stage-like progress is evident only in specific features. Thus, an individual learner may have reached a different stage for different linguistic features. The model inevitably constitutes an idealization: development is much more uneven and messy than the model suggests, given that sub-linguistic systems interact and affect each other, as proposed by DST. Nevertheless, I would claim that the model captures the way in which linguistic forms enter and then develop in the sub-systems that comprise interlanguage.

## Sequences of acquisition revisited

In Chapter 4, we considered evidence suggesting that the acquisition of grammatical sub-systems—such as negatives— characterized by relatively well-defined

| Stage | Description |
| --- | --- |
| 1 Non-linguistic | Learners operate in accordance with an 'accept what I am offered' strategy. During this stage they have no awareness of form-meaning mapping. |
| 2 Acquisition | Learners operate an overgeneralization strategy, selecting one form and using it in contexts that in target-language use would require two forms. |
| 3 Replacement | Learners allow an alternate form into their interlanguage but are unable to determine the functional differences between the two forms. This phase is characterized by free variation. |
| 4 Interlanguage | Learners now begin to use the two forms systematically, but in accordance with interlanguage rather than target language norms. This stage may be characterized by categorical use or systematic variation. |
| 5 Completion | Learners use the two forms in accordance with target language norms, which may be categorical or variable. |

*Table 5.2 Stages in the development of a grammatical sub-subsystem (based on Towell et al. 1996)*

stages, and that sequences of acquisition are universal. To what extent is this finding compatible with what we have discovered about the nature of variability in learner language?

Variationist research based on the Labovian and the Dynamic Paradigms does not challenge the existence of developmental sequences. Rather, it affords a more elaborate account of how one variable stage evolves into another variable stage. Stage-like development is not just a matter of learners acquiring a new linguistic form, or of making one form the dominant choice, but of gradually extending (or restricting) the use of the forms at their disposal in accordance with the social, linguistic, and functional norms of the variety the learner is targeting. Stage-like development, then, is reflected in variability within a stage and in shifting patterns of variability from one stage to the next. Table 5.2 is an attempt to capture this as a set of general stages that characterize the acquisition of specific grammatical features.

But do all learners manifest the same developmental sequence? How universal are the stages of development proposed in Table 5.2? The assumption of researchers in the Labovian and Dynamic Paradigms is that the constraints on the use of linguistics forms, the implicational hierarchies evident in the spread of forms from one variety to another, and the way in which form-function systems are re-organized apply to all learners. It is this assumption that Dynamic Systems Theory questions. Dijk et al. (2011) concluded that 'no individual behaves as the average person and that all individuals have their own patterns' (p. 83). From this theoretical perspective, then, we 'would expect different kinds of variability to show different kinds of development' (p. 84). In other words, there are no universal sequences of acquisition.

It is not easy to reconcile these different positions. They are based on different theoretical assumptions and have been researched using different methodological procedures. However, I find it difficult to accept that there are not major commonalities in the way in which all learners acquire a second language. Individual differences in acquisition sequences certainly do occur—in particular due to the influence of the learner's first language (see Chapter 6)—but the claim that there are universal paths in L2 acquisition constitutes a useful idealization.

## Sociolinguistic competence

In this chapter, we have examined both learners' variable use of interlanguage and target-language forms (i.e. Type 1 variation) and their variable use of target-language variants (Type 2 variation). The studies of Type 2 variation are of special value because they remind us that target languages are themselves variable and that—if the learner's goal is to attain target-language norms—this requires not just the ability to use target language forms correctly, but to use them in sociolinguistically appropriate ways. The study of variability in learner language, therefore, affords insights as to how learners develop **sociolinguistic competence**. The studies we have considered indicate that even very advanced L2 learners (especially those who started post-puberty or who were dependent on classroom instruction for L2 input) often fail to achieve full mastery of the sociolinguistic norms of the target language[5].

## Sources of variation

In this chapter, I have focused on the social and linguistic factors that can account for interlanguage variation. There is, of course, much more to the study of variability. In particular, psycholinguistic factors related to whether learners have the opportunity to plan before or as they speak will impact on their choice of linguistic forms. Another psycholinguistic factor that has been shown to result in variability in learner language is **monitoring** (i.e. the use of explicit knowledge to edit output). I will consider planning and monitoring more fully in later chapters.

## Notes

1 Tarone and Parrish (1988) provide a further, in-depth analysis of the same data. They showed that the discourse mode (narrative or interview) also influenced the learners' use of the definite article. Target-like accuracy was more evident in the former than the latter.

2 The greater likelihood of the learners omitting *ne* with the native speaker interlocutors than with other learners can be explained by Speech Accommodation Theory (Giles and Coupland 1991), which claims that speakers will generally converge on the norms of their interlocutors.

3 It can be argued that research that has investigated multiple influences on variability in the Labovian Paradigm also examined the interaction of external and internal factors. However, this research sought to predict variation in specific linguistic variables. Researchers drawing on Dynamic Systems Theory do not examine specific variables and reject the possibility of *a priori* predictions.

4 Dijk, Verspoor, and Lowie (2011) were not the only ones to re-analyse Cancino et al.'s (1978) data. Earlier in this chapter, we considered Schachter's (1986) form-function analysis of the data. Berdan (1996) also re-examined the data for one of the learners (Alberto) and found evidence of both linguistic context and style predicting his choice of 'don't' + verb. Berdan also reported that if Alberto used 'don't' + verb in one utterance, he was likely to also use it in the subsequent utterance. Although this study demonstrated that the variability was systematic, there was still a proportion of variation that could not be accounted for.

5 In some cases, L2 learners have full knowledge of the target forms but may elect not to use them if they do not fit with the self they wish to project. For example, Japanese L2 learners may have learned the different uses of *tu* and *vous* in French, but resist using the familiar *tu* with someone they would be deferential to in their L1 culture.

# 6

# The role of the first language

## Introduction

The role of the learners' native language in the acquisition of a second language, arguably, has received more sustained attention than any other area of SLA. Jarvis and Pavlenko (2008) list 17 full-length books devoted to it and there have been more since. This intensity of attention is testimony to the prevalence of the influence of the L1, its importance for understanding L2 acquisition, and the complexity of transfer phenomena.

Initially, this thinking was informed by behaviourist learning theory, which was dominant until researchers began to conduct empirical studies of second language learning. Behaviourist psychologists—such as Skinner (1957)—sought to account for language learning in terms of 'behaviour', rejecting any role for internal mental processes. Behaviour consisted of 'habits' which were formed when specific environmental stimuli were automatically associated with specific responses. This association arose through imitation (i.e. the learner copies the stimulus behaviour sufficiently often for the response to become habitual) and reinforcement (i.e. the feedback following a response that either 'rewards' or 'corrects' the learner). The theory claimed that old habits proactively inhibit the development of new habits. Thus—in the case of second language learning—the theory predicts that the habits of the L1 interfere with the development of L2 habits. This led to the **Contrastive Analysis Hypothesis** (Lado 1957). The strong form of this hypothesis claimed that all L2 errors can be <u>predicted</u> by identifying differences between the target language and the learner's first language, while the weak form more conservatively proposed that contrastive analysis served to <u>identify</u> which errors were the result of interference (Wardhaugh 1970).

It soon became clear, however, that many of the errors learners made could be neither predicted nor explained by L1 interference. Dulay and Burt (1974), for example, calculated the frequency of the grammatical errors made by Spanish-speaking children learning English. They classified the errors as (1) interference errors; (2) developmental errors (i.e. L2 errors that were the same as the errors observed in L1 acquisition); (3) ambiguous errors (i.e. those that could not categorized as either interference or developmental); and (4) unique errors (i.e. those that did not reflect the first language and were also not observed in first **language acquisition**). They reported that 85 per cent of the errors were developmental and only three per cent were interference errors, concluding that L1 interference played only a minor role in the learning of L2 grammar.

Such studies led to the recognition that behaviourist accounts of L2 learning were inadequate and that it was necessary to take account of the internal mental processing that learners engage in. In other words, learners do not acquire habits through imitation and reinforcement, but rather creatively construct their L2 systems. However, it soon became clear that Dulay and Burt had underestimated the extent of interference. A number of other studies (for example, Tran-Chi-Chau 1975) reported much higher levels of interference errors in the learner language samples they investigated. In short, Dulay and Burt's minimalist account of first language interference was rejected and, from the 1980s onwards, there was a re-appraisal of the role played by the first language directed at identifying the factors that governed both negative transfer effects (i.e. 'interference') and positive transfer (i.e. the role the L1 plays in facilitating L2 learning).

Currently, there is no theory of L2 learning that does not acknowledge the importance of the first language. However, current theories reject both the maximalist view of interference of behaviourists—such as Lado (1957)—and the minimalist view of researchers—such as Dulay and Burt (1974). They acknowledge that differences between the native and target languages do not always lead to learning difficulties. They emphasize the need to view the first language as one of many factors that shape L2 development and seek to explain how the learner's first language knowledge interacts with other external and internal factors. Thus, the role of the first language has been re-evaluated in terms of the cognitive processes involved in second language learning. The notion of 'interference' has given way to that of 'transfer'. Thus a good starting point is to consider exactly what is meant by the term 'language transfer'.

## Defining 'language transfer'

Language transfer is said to occur when there is evidence that the linguistic features of one language influence those of another language. This simple definition, however, requires elucidation.

### What constitutes 'evidence' of language transfer?

The most obvious kind of evidence is to be found in the errors that can be traced to another language. But there are other kinds of evidence. Knowledge of one language may facilitate the learning of another as, for example, when the two languages share cognates (for example, 'cosmopolitan' in English and 'cosmopolita' in Spanish). Also, the influence may be manifest in the overuse or avoidance of some linguistic feature rather than in actual errors. For example, Japanese and Korean learners of L2 English have been shown to avoid the use of relative clauses because of differences in the structure of relative clauses in these learners' L1s and English (Schachter 1974). Finally—as Ringbom (1992) pointed out—transfer is just as evident in reception as in production. Differences and similarities in the two languages can impede or facilitate the comprehension of both oral and written input. Japanese learners of Chinese, for example, have a huge advantage over English learners in learning to read Chinese because the two languages share a common set of written symbols.

**What linguistic features are subject to transfer?**

Transfer is most clearly evident in pronunciation. When French people speak English, they are likely to sound French. In fact, however, cross-linguistic influence has been observed in every aspect of language—in pronunciation, orthography, vocabulary, grammar, semantics, pragmatics, and discourse. Examples of such transfer effects will be provided later in the chapter.

**In what ways can one language influence another?**

The most obvious way is when the learner's first language influences the learning and use of an interlanguage. However, a learner may have already acquired one L2 and this can impact on the learning and use of a third language (Cenoz, Hufeisen, and Jessner 2001). Moroccan learners of English, for example, will have acquired Arabic as the L1, but are likely to have also learned French at school. Thus both Arabic and French influences on this learner's L2 English are likely to occur. Also, the learning of a second language can have an impact on the learner's first language, leading in some cases to language attrition (i.e. loss of L1 knowledge).

It should be clear that language transfer is a highly complex phenomenon. It involves much more than 'interference'. Reflecting this complexity, Sharwood Smith, and Kellerman (1986) proposed that 'crosslinguistic influence' would be a more theory-neutral term to refer to the way one language interacts with another. In this chapter, however, our focus is limited to the role of the first language in second language learning and thus I will adhere to 'transfer' as the more commonly used term.

## Investigating language transfer

Some researchers have investigated the overall relationship between L1 and L2 proficiency. Bylund, Abrahamsson, and Hyltenstam (2012), for example, compared the native-like proficiency of Swedish-Spanish bilinguals, all of whom had learned the L2 (Swedish) as children and who had been resident in Sweden for an average of 24 years. They posited three possibilities: (1) there would be no relationship; (2) there would be a negative relationship; and (3) there would be a positive relationship. They reported that native-like proficiency in the two languages was positively correlated, indicating that for these learners, who commenced learning within the Critical Period, maintenance of their first language did not prevent their successful acquisition of a second language.

Most transfer research, however, has examined transfer in relation to specific linguistic features. In Ellis (2008), I distinguished five different ways in which transfer of specific linguistic features has been investigated. Here, I will consider the two ways that have figured most commonly in transfer research:

1  L2 errors are identified and the learner's L1 is then examined to determine if the error type corresponds to an L1 feature.
2  Differences are identified in the L2 of learners with different L1s (for example, Japanese and Arabic learners of L2 English). Transfer (both negative and positive) is held to exist if the differences in the learners' second languages can be shown to correspond to differences in their first languages.

The second way is clearly superior to the first. Consider, for example, Spanish learners of L2 English. These have been shown to pass through a stage of development consisting of 'no' + verb (see Chapter 4). Negation in Spanish involves 'no' + verb. Thus, in a study involving a Type 1 comparison, it could be concluded that the 'no' + verb construction in the learners' L2 English was the result of negative transfer. Now consider a study that compared Spanish and German learners' acquisition of English negation. German, unlike Spanish, has post-verbal negation (i.e. verb + 'nicht'). Strong evidence of negative transfer would require demonstrating that the 'no' + verb construction occurred in the Spanish learners, but not in the German learners. In fact, German learners have also been found to pass through a 'no' + verb stage (Wode 1981). Thus, it would seem that the 'no' + verb construction is a 'developmental' rather than a 'transfer' feature of L2 learning. However, as will see later, a case can still be made for a transfer effect in the Spanish learners. Clearly, though, there are dangers in assuming transfer is occurring simply on the basis of Type 1 comparisons.

A good example of a study that adopted a Type 2 approach is Eckman and Iverson's (2013) comparison of Japanese and Korean learners' acquisition of the English /s/ and /ʃ/ contrast (as in 'sip' and 'ship'). These sounds are phonemic in Japanese (i.e. they distinguish Japanese words as they do in English) but only allophonic in Korean (i.e. the two sounds exist but do not distinguish words in Korean). Eckman and Iverson were able to show that differences in the path of acquisition and error patterns of Japanese and Korean learners of L2 English stemmed from this apparently small difference in their native language phonologies.

A final methodological issue concerns the distinction between implicit and explicit L2 knowledge (see Chapter 1). Theoretically, a distinction can be drawn between the transfer of these two types of knowledge: that is, transfer may be evident when the L2 is elicited by means of instruments that tap into explicit knowledge, but may not occur in free L2 production, which is more likely to draw on implicit knowledge. Bylund, Abrahamsson, and Hyltenstam's (2012) study—referred to above—is illustrative of this problem. The instruments they employed were more likely to elicit explicit knowledge. Thus, their study does not tell us whether transfer effects were evident in the learners' implicit knowledge.

I will turn now to considering the factors that influence whether, and to what extent, transfer effects are found in L2 learning by drawing on studies that have investigated the role of the L1 in different levels of language; in particular pronunciation, vocabulary, and grammar[1]. Five general categories of factors can be identified:

1 Linguistic—i.e. factors relating to the linguistic properties of the native and target languages.
2 Psycholinguistic—i.e. factors relating to the learners' perceptions about the transferability of L1 features.
3 Contextual—i.e. factors relating to the nature of the learners' exposure to the target language.
4 Developmental—i.e. how universal tendencies in L2 acquisition interact with L1 transfer.
5 Individual—i.e. how individual differences in learners affect the probability of transfer occurring.

# Linguistic factors

I begin by examining a key claim of the Contrastive Analysis Hypothesis, namely that learning difficulty (and thus the errors learners make) depends on the degree of difference between the native and target languages. I then move on to consider the role of **language distance** before concluding this section with a discussion of how **linguistic markedness** affects transfer.

## Linguistic difference and learning difficulty

The key assumption of the Contrastive Analysis Hypothesis is that linguistic differences between the learner's native language and the target language can cause learning difficulty and thus will result in errors. However, contrastive analysts acknowledged that linguistic differences are of different kinds and that some differences were likely to cause greater difficulty than others. Based on a contrastive analysis of Spanish and English, Stockwell, Bowen, and Martin (1965) proposed the hierarchy of difficulty shown in Table 6.1[2].

Table 6.1 suggests that the influence of the L1 is strongest when the difference between the native and target language is greatest and weakest when the difference is least. However, this need not be the case. Learners have been shown to find it more difficult to acquire sounds that are similar (but not

| Type of difficulty | L1: English | L2: Spanish | Example |
|---|---|---|---|
| 1 Split | x | xy | 'for' is either 'por' or 'para' |
| 2 New | o | x | grammatical gender |
| 3 Absent | x | o | 'do' as a tense carrier |
| 4 Coalesced | x | x | 'his/her' is realized as a single form 'su' |
|  | y |  |  |
| 5 Correspondence | x | x | -ing, -ndo as the complement of verbs of perception, e.g.'I saw the men running'; 'vi a los hombres corriendo'. |

Key: x = feature present; o = feature not present; x/y = two equivalent features

*Table 6.1  Simplified version of the hierarchy of difficulty (based on information given in Stockwell, Bowen, and Martin 1965)*

exactly the same) to sounds in their native language than sounds that are dissimilar. In other words, 'correspondence' between the native and target languages does not guarantee ease of acquisition while entirely 'new' features do not always pose learning difficulty.

Major and Kim (1996) proposed the **Similarity Differential Rate Hypothesis**, according to which L2 sounds dissimilar to the L1 may be difficult to acquire initially, but—over time—improvement takes place more rapidly than with similar sounds. They commented 'gross differences are more often noticed, due to their perceptual saliency, whereas minimal differences are more likely to be overlooked and to result in confusion or nonlearning' (p. 367). Major and Kim's study of the rate of acquisition of /j/ and /z/ by ten adult Korean learners of English supported this hypothesis. They noted that—although all the evidence they cited concerned pronunciation—there was every reason to believe that the hypothesis would also apply to other aspects of language.

However, where grammar is concerned, there is clear evidence that linguistic difference affects learning difficulty in both the short term and in the later stages of L2 learning. The **Morphological Congruency Hypothesis** (Jiang, Novokshanova, Masuda, and Wang 2011)—as its name suggests—claims that, when a grammatical morpheme with the same function is present in both the native and target language, learning will be easier than when it is present in the target language, but not in the native language. Jiang et al. investigated this claim by comparing Russian and Japanese ESL learners' ultimate attainment of English plural *-s*. Whereas Russian marks nouns for plurality, Japanese typically does not. A feature of this study is that it sought to examine the effects of L1 transfer on implicit L2 knowledge by measuring learning in terms of the extent to which the two groups of learners noticed plural -*s* errors in a self-paced reading task[3]. The results showed that—whereas the Russian learners were generally sensitive to the plural errors—the Japanese learners showed very little sensitivity. As the learners in both groups were near-native, Jiang et al. concluded that the effects of L1 transfer were long-lasting and possibly non-remediable without formal instruction.

Nevertheless, it would be wrong to conclude that all grammatical differences between the native and target languages result in learning difficulty. There is, in fact, no simple correlation between linguistic difference and learning difficulty as claimed by the Contrastive Analysis Hypothesis. For example, differences in word order between the native and target language do not typically result in learning difficulty. Japanese is a verb final language whereas in English the verb typically follows the subject; however Japanese learners of English do not appear to transfer their L1 word order and, if they do so, only in the very initial stages of L2 acquisition. Odlin (1989) in his extensive survey of transfer studies admitted that—although there were cases of basic word order transfer in the literature—such cases were rare. The obvious explanation for this is the saliency of word order in the L2 input: whereas a morpheme, such as plural -*s,* is not easily noticed in the input learners are exposed to, the basic order in which words appear in the target language is.

## Language distance

Language distance also has more complex effects on language transfer than those predicted by the Contrastive Analysis Hypothesis. A common assumption is that if the native and target languages are proximate (for example, Dutch and English) learning will be easier and more rapid than if they are distant (for example, Chinese and English). However, the similarity of two languages can result in negative as well as positive transfer. Sjöholm (1976) compared the acquisition of English by Swedish-speaking and Finnish-speaking Finns. Whereas 93 per cent of the population speak Finnish as their mother tongue, a language distant from English, six to seven per cent speak Swedish, a language much closer to English. Sjöholm found that Swedish-speaking Finns enjoyed a substantial learning advantage over Finnish-speaking Finns—i.e. positive transfer occurred. However, the Swedish-speaking Finns also made more errors, i.e. they manifested more negative transfer. Ringbom (1978) reported that both the Swedish- and Finnish-speaking groups (both of whom were bilingual in the two languages) were much more likely to transfer word morphology from Swedish into English than from Finnish. Whereas the Finnish speakers avoided transferring elements from their L1, preferring instead to fall back on their first L2 (Swedish), the Swedish speakers readily transferred elements from their L1 but avoided doing so from their first L2 (Finnish). In other words, when the distance between source and target language is small, both positive and negative transfer are likely to occur. In general, however, the greater the language distance, the more difficult a language is to acquire.

## Markedness

Marked linguistic features are those that are 'special' in relation to others; unmarked features are those that are, in some sense, 'basic'. Markedness has been defined differently in different traditions in linguistics. Here, I will focus on how markedness has been handled in a functional-typological approach. This involves comparing different groups of languages in order to distinguish those properties that are universal or specific to particular languages. The general claim is that those features that are common in the world's languages are less marked than those features that are only found rarely in the world's language. For example, pied piping—i.e. the process by which one element in a clause drags other words along with it—as in 'To whom did you speak?'—is much more common that preposition stranding, where the *wh-* element and the preposition are not attached—as in 'Who did you speak to?' The former is considered unmarked in relation to the latter.

Two general hypotheses have been investigated: (1) learners will transfer unmarked forms when the corresponding target form is marked, and (2) learners will resist transferring marked forms, especially when the corresponding target language form is unmarked. As Hyltenstam (1984) put it:

> Unmarked categories from the native language are substituted for corresponding marked categories in the target language … Marked structures are seldom transferred, and if they are transferred, they are much more easily eradicated from the target language. (p. 43)

A general assumption is 'marked structures tend to require more attention, more mental effort, and time to be processed' (Callies 2013: 406) and thus learners resist transferring L1 marked structures.

Perhaps the most convincing evidence of markedness effects on transfer can be found in studies that have examined asymmetrical patterns (i.e. involving a kind of type 2 comparison). A straight contrastive analysis is unable to cope with evidence that shows that a given feature (Z) is transferred in one direction—i.e. transfer of Z occurs from language X to language Y—but not in the other—i.e. transfer of Z does not occur from language Y to language X. A theory of transfer that incorporates markedness, however, can provide an explanation for such phenomena.

The study that is most commonly cited to illustrate asymmetrical patterns is Eckman (1977). This provides support for both of Hyltenstam's hypotheses. Eckman investigated transfer in English learners of L2 German and German learners of L2 English, focusing on voice contrast in pairs of phonemes such as /t/ and /d/. In British English, this contrast exists word initially (for example, 'tin' versus 'din'), word medially (for example, 'betting' versus 'bedding'), and word finally (for example, 'wed' versus 'wet'). In German, however, the distinction is only found word initially and word medially; in word-final position, only voiceless stops occur. Both the German and the English L2 learners, therefore, are faced with learning to make a known distinction (i.e. voiced/ voiceless stops) in a new position. Eckman argued that typologically, voice contrast in word-final position is more marked than in the other two positions. That is, the markedness relationship was established on the basis of a cross-linguistic implicational generalization. He provided evidence to show that English learners have no difficulty in learning that German has no voicing in word-final stops, but that German learners experience considerable problems in learning that English does. In other words, no transfer effects are evident when the L1 position is marked and the L2 position unmarked, but they appear when the L1 position is unmarked and the L2 marked.

In order to explain how markedness affects transfer, Eckman advanced the **Markedness Differential Hypothesis (MDH)**:

> The areas of difficulty that a second language learner will have can be predicted on the basis of a systematic comparison of the grammars of the native language (NL), the target language (TL) and the markedness relations stated in universal grammar, such that:
>
> (a) Those areas of the TL which differ from the NL and are more marked than in the NL will be difficult;
>
> (b) The relative degree of difficulty of the areas of the TL which are more marked than in the NL will correspond to the relative degree of markedness;
>
> (c) Those areas of the TL which are different from the NL, but are not more marked than the NL, will not be difficult.
> (Eckman 1977: 321)

The Markedness Differential Hypothesis constituted an attempt to reformulate the Contrastive Analysis Hypothesis to take account of markedness factors by explaining when differences between the native and target languages do or do not result in difficulty.

However, learners have also been shown to transfer marked features from their first language even though the corresponding feature in the target language is unmarked. For example, English permits pied piping (which is typologically unmarked) and preposition stranding (which is typologically marked):

> To *whom* did you speak? (pied piping)
> The man *to whom* I spoke is now in hospital. (pied piping)
> *Who(m)* did you speak *to*? (preposition stranding)
> The man *who(m)* I spoke *to* is now in hospital. (preposition stranding).

Other languages, however—for example, Spanish and French—do not permit preposition stranding (i.e. pied piping is obligatory). In accordance with the markedness hypothesis, one might expect English learners of L2 French or Spanish to opt for unmarked pied piping (i.e. resist transferring the marked preposition stranding). However, Liceras (1985) reported that 43 per cent of the English-speaking beginner learners she investigated accepted stranding in Spanish sentences such as *Es la mujer que Pedro vive con* (= 'This is the woman that Pedro lives with') providing evidence of the transfer of the marked variant.

As Jarvis and Pavlenko (2008) concluded, 'there is ample evidence to show that transfer of both marked and unmarked syntactic structures is quite common' (p. 187). In general, though, L2 learners do seem more ready to transfer unmarked L1 features irrespective of whether the corresponding L2 feature is marked or unmarked. In other words, they act in accordance with the general principle 'If a feature is unmarked in the L1, transfer it.' Overall, then, although linguistic markedness has been shown to account for some instances of transfer, it has failed to provide a convincing explanation for many instances of L1 transfer.

## Problems with linguistic accounts of L1 transfer

The main problem with the difference = difficulty approach to investigating language transfer is that whereas 'difference' is a linguistic concept, 'difficulty' is a psychological concept. It cannot be assumed that what constitutes 'difficulty' according to a linguistic theory (and, in fact, this itself is problematic as there is no agreement among linguists about which theory to apply) will have any psychological significance for the learner. A similar problem exists with markedness accounts of transfer. Markedness is a purely linguistic concept and although—as we have seen—it does seem to have some kind of psychological reality for learners, this cannot explain what goes on in the learner's mind. Also—as Callies (2013) noted—there is no agreed way of determining which features are marked in relation to others. Eckman (1985) also pointed out that 'more research is needed in defining markedness relations' (p. 306).

One way of addressing both these problems is by examining 'native speakers' own perceptions of the structure of their language—for example, by asking native speakers whether they perceive specific features as 'infrequent, irregular, semantically or structurally opaque, or in any other way exceptional' (Kellerman 1983: 117). In the next section I turn to research that has adopted a psycholinguistic perspective on first language transfer.

## Psycholinguistic factors

### Prototypicality

Kellerman (1978) hypothesized that learners have intuitions about which features in their first lanaguage are potentially transferable or non-transferable. In his 'breken' study he first investigated Dutch L1 speakers' perceptions of the 'coreness' of seventeen sentences containing the verb 'breken'. He then asked 81 Dutch students of English in their first and third years at university to say which of the sentences containing 'breken' they would translate using the English verb 'break'. He reported clear differences in the percentage of students prepared to translate each sentence. For example, whereas 81 per cent considered 'hij brak zijn been' (= he broke his leg) translatable only 9 per cent identified 'sommige arbeiders hebben de staking gebroken' (= some workers have broken the strike) as translatable. Kellerman found that the students were much more likely to consider the core meanings of 'breken' translatable than the non-core meanings.

In another study, Kellerman (1979) examined whether learners' perceptions of transferability differed according to their L2 proficiency. He asked 291 learners of English, who ranged from 12-year-olds in their second year of English to third-year university students, to assess the translatability of nine of the 17 'breken' sentences. He found a high level of similarity in their responses and concluded that 'the effects of teaching, learning, and growing older do not significantly alter learners' beliefs about the *relative* transferability of the "brekens"' (1979: 52).

These studies suggest that L2 learners have an intuitive understanding of the prototypical meaning of a lexical item such as 'breken' and that this matched the primary meanings of the word found in a dictionary. In a later study, Kellerman (1989) extended the notion of **prototypicality** to grammar. He provided evidence to show that advanced Dutch learners of L2 English are likely to produce errors of this kind:

> *If it would rain, they would cancel the concert in Damrosch Park.
> ( = If it rained they would cancel the concert in Damrosch Park.)

despite the fact that Dutch makes use of equivalent verb forms to English in both main and subordinate clauses. He suggested that positive transfer does not occur because learners perceived it as more natural to say 'would rain' than 'rained' because the verb is explicitly marked for future time.

The key point emerging from these studies is that learners—irrespective of their L2 proficiency—have perceptions about what is transferable from their first language and act in accordance with these perceptions. They prize 'reasonableness in language' and 'attempt to keep their L2s transparent' (Kellerman 1983: 129). Thus, L1 features that they perceive to be working against this principle—such as idioms that are highly metaphorical or grammatical structures where meanings are not overtly encoded—are not transferred. This claim has been supported in a number of more recent studies (for example, Kato 2006).

## Psychotypology

We noted above that the distance between the native and target languages can influence the degree and nature of transfer. Distance, however, can be viewed as a psycholinguistic phenomenon as well as a linguistic phenomenon and, arguably, what matters most is not the actual linguistic differences between

two languages, but whether learners *think* they are different. Kellerman
(1979) used the term '**psychotypology**' to refer to learners' perceptions about
language distance. He claimed that the decisions that learners make about
whether or not to draw on their first langauge are based on their beliefs as to
whether the native and target languages are the 'same' or 'different'.

An extension of the 'breken' study (Kellerman1979) provides support for
the idea of psychotypology. Kellerman compared Dutch learners' judgements
regarding the translatability of the 'brekens' into L2 German (a language
close to Dutch) with their judgements regarding their translatability into L2
English (a language more distant from Dutch). The results showed that, in
general, whereas they accepted the sentences in German, they sometimes
rejected them in English. In other words, there was a clear effect for perceived
language distance.

Further evidence comes from Singleton's (1987) case study of Philip, an
English-speaking learner of French. Philip displayed a high level of communicative efficiency in French, despite the fact that he had minimal opportunities
to learn it. He demonstrated well-informed notions about which languages
would assist him most in learning French. He utilized his knowledge of
Romance languages (i.e. those that were close to French) and was often able
to attribute the forms he borrowed to a particular language. Clearly, learners
do have well-defined perceptions regarding the similarities and differences
between languages.

However, learners' psychotypology is not fixed. Rather, it is revised as they
obtain more information about the target language. Kellerman (1979)
showed that Dutch learners of German may start out with the assumption
that the target language is very similar to their mother tongue, but later on
come to adjust this perception as they recognize differences. According to
Kellerman, learners' psychotypologies interact with their intuitive feel for
prototypicality. Their intuitions about prototypicality determine what learners are prepared to risk transferring, while their developing **psychotypology**
determines what is actually transferred at any given moment.

## Contextual factors

The likelihood of transfer occurring also depends on the context of learning.
This influences the input the learner is exposed to and, crucially, the extent to
which transfer is manifest in L2 implicit or explicit knowledge. A distinction can
be made between the macro-contexts of learning (for example, classroom vs
naturalistic) and the micro-contexts (for example, the learner's interlocutor
or the specific task used to elicit samples of language use).

## Macro-contextual influences

There is abundant evidence that transfer effects occur in both informal (i.e.
natural) and formal (i.e. instructed) settings. However, the setting can

influence the likelihood and extent of the transfer effects. This influence is related to the extent to which the context caters to the development of implicit—as opposed to explicit—L2 knowledge and also the effect that the context has on the type of language use—i.e. whether it encourages monitoring, using explicit knowledge, or spontaneous communication, involving implicit knowledge.

Odlin (1989) suggested that negative transfer is less common in classroom settings than in natural settings because, in the former, learners are more likely to treat L1 forms as intrusive and even stigmatized. This can be explained by the fact that learners employ their explicit knowledge of L2 forms and rules to monitor their use of the L2 and thus to inhibit transfer of first language forms and rules. However, this is only likely to occur when the conditions of language use permit monitoring: that is when learners have explicit knowledge of the relevant feature, have time to monitor, and are focused on accuracy (Krashen 1981). When the conditions call for spontaneous, meaning-based production, monitoring will be difficult and, as a result, learners may not be able to use their explicit L2 knowledge to inhibit transfer.

The situation is more complicated in natural settings. In general, such settings cater to the acquisition and use of implicit knowledge, so negative transfer is likely. However, this will depend on whether the natural setting is of a 'focused' or 'unfocused' kind. A focused natural setting is one where the learners have a clear idea of what constitutes a language (i.e. they make a clear distinction between their first and second language). An unfocused setting is one where two (or more) languages are mixed without much concern for what is 'grammatical' or 'ungrammatical'. Negative transfer is more likely to occur in unfocused than focused natural contexts.

These macro-differences can explain the differences in the results obtained by Abdullah and Jackson (1998) on the one hand, and Sridhar and Sridhar (1986) on the other. The first of these studies examined a foreign language setting in Syria. Abdullah and Jackson reported that the learners were reluctant to transfer L1 idiomatic expressions. Sridhar and Sridhar, however, claimed that learners in India and Nigeria often create English idioms based on their L1. The formal foreign language setting inhibited negative transfer. The unfocused, natural setting promoted it.

Generalizations regarding the effect of macro contexts on L1 transfer are dangerous, however. First, they do not take account of forms of transfer other than negative transfer. Positive transfer is likely in both formal and informal settings, even though the nature of the input learners receive may differ. For example, in formal settings learners are likely to be exposed to substantial written input, making it easier to detect similarities between the source and target languages (for example, cognates). On the other hand, avoidance may be less likely to occur in informal settings than in formal settings where errors are more stigmatized. As Jarvis and Pavlenko (2008) concluded, 'the formality of the context does affect transfer, but it includes forces that both foster and constrain the occurrence of transfer' (p. 208).

For this reason, an examination of the effect of micro-contexts on L1 transfer is more revealing.

## Micro-contextual influences

In Chapter 5, we noted that variationist sociolinguists distinguish between careful and vernacular styles. Tarone (1982) argued that negative transfer is likely to be more evident in learners' careful style than in their vernacular style, on the grounds that when learners are paying greater attention to how they speak, they are more likely to make use of all their potential resources, including L1 knowledge. On the face of it, this contradicts the general claim that negative transfer effects are less likely to occur in formal, instructed contexts, which prioritize the careful style, than in natural contexts where the vernacular style is primary. Jarvis and Pavlenko (2008), however, suggested how these contradicting positions can be reconciled. They proposed that instructed L2 learners have two goals—(1) to avoid errors and (2) to make use of those linguistic forms that serve as markers of formality. If they prioritize (1), negative transfer is likely to be inhibited, but if they prioritize (2) they may elect to employ L1 features that are markers of formality (for example, they will draw on L1 pragmatic devices to appear polite). In other words, much depends on how they orientate to the use of the L2 and on their perception of the importance of social factors in whatever situation they find themselves.

Evidence for this comes from Beebe (1980). She showed that learners do not always manifest the target-language variant more in their careful style. Sometimes they transfer forms from their L1, if these forms have prestige value in their speech community. Beebe found that her subjects (adult Thai learners of English) produced fewer instances of the target sound, /r/, in formal language use than in informal language use. This was because they used a prestige Thai variant of /r/, which they associated with formal language use in their own language.

**Pragmatic transfer** of the kind Beebe investigated also depends on the specific situational context. Olshtain (1983) found that—in the case of an apology situation involving backing into someone's car and causing damage—English speakers of L2 Hebrew apologised in much the same way as in their L1. In contrast, in a situation where they had insulted someone at a meeting, they did not transfer their first language strategies, but behaved in a similar way to native Hebrew speakers. She concluded that in a situation that calls for careful face-work transfer was more likely to occur than in a situation where politeness was deemed as less crucial.

More generally, the nature of the task learners are asked to perform will affect whether or not transfer occurs. Translation tasks, for example, are more likely to elicit both more positive and more negative transfer than tasks that involve spontaneous production. Tasks that allow for learners' use of their explicit L2 knowledge are likely to inhibit L1 transfer; conversely when performing tasks that require spontaneous production learners are more likely to draw on all their linguistic resources, including their L1, and thus transfer effects will be stronger.

## Performance-related versus learning-related transfer

A key question regarding the effects of the macro- and micro-linguistic contextual factors on L1 transfer that we have considered in this section is whether the effects are just performance related, or also learning related—i.e. are the transfer effects simply a manifestation of performance conditions, or do they reflect the influence of the L1 on actual learning? Jarvis and Pavlenko (2008) argued that they are just performance related. However, the distinction between performance-related and learning-related effects is not easy to make, and may not be theoretically justified. I will discuss this point later in the chapter.

## Developmental factors

In Chapter 4, I examined research that showed there are universal tendencies in L2 acquisition. This research suggests that the learner's L1 plays only a minimal role and thus contradicts the research we have reviewed in the previous sections of this chapter. This contradiction, however, can be resolved if it can be shown that transfer works alongside other universal and developmental factors.

While simplification and overgeneralization are universal features, the L1 does affect the *extent* to which these occur. All learners, for example, omit prepositions in the early stages of L2 acquisition, but as Schumann (1986a) found, this happens much less frequently in the case of Spanish learners of English than in the case of Chinese and Japanese learners. Whereas Spanish has prepositions that are broadly equivalent in meaning to English, Chinese and Japanese do not. Arguably, overgeneralization and transfer are manifestations of the same underlying psychological process—that of prior learning facilitating new learning. Taylor (1975), for example, documented a transition from L1 transfer to overgeneralization. The elementary and intermediate learners in his study made similar *kinds* of errors, but whereas the elementary learners made more transfer errors, the intermediate learners made more overgeneralization errors. In other words, beginners rely on what they know (their L1) but intermediate learners draw on what they have already learned about the L2.

Some **morpheme studies** have provided evidence of L1 effects. Japanese learners of English, for example, have greater difficulty in acquiring plural -*s* than learners whose first language includes a plural marker. As we noted in Chapter 4, Hakuta (1976) found that a five-year-old Japanese girl acquired plural -*s* later than was predicted by the morpheme order reported in cross-sectional studies (for example, Dulay and Burt 1973). He attributed this to the lack of an equivalent morpheme in the learners' first language. Jiang et al.'s (2011) study, which we considered earlier in this chapter, also testifies to the difficulty that Japanese learners have with plural -*s* in comparison to Russian learners whose L1 includes plural markers. Clearly, then, the morpheme order is not entirely 'universal'. The 'natural' order of acquisition is disturbed in the case of grammatical morphemes that are meaning bearing in the L2, but have no equivalent in the L1. However, non-meaning bearing morphemes—such as English third-person singular—appear to be equally difficult for all learners.

The first language can also impact on the sequence of acquisition of specific target language features. However, its impact appears to be developmentally constrained: that is, it only occurs if and when learners have reached a stage of development which can provide a 'crucial similarity measure' (Wode 1976). In the case of negation, for instance, the German children that Wode studied began, like other learners, with pre-verbal negation (i.e. 'no' + verb). But later—after they had discovered the negative particle could follow the verb 'be' in English (for example, 'Maria is not well')—they began to produce post-verbal negation in L2 English, but extended this to main verb negation (for example, 'Mary comes not') as in German. In other words, once they obtained evidence to suggest that post-verbal negation was possible in English they transferred the German rule for negation.

Further evidence of developmental constraints on transfer comes from studies based on **Processability Theory** (see Chapters 4 and 9). According to this theory, the processing operations responsible for the sequence of acquisition apply to all learners. It would seem, then, that there is no place for language transfer in Processability Theory. In fact, Pienemann (2005) recognized that transfer does have a role, but one that it is developmentally moderated. The fact that the L2 has to be 'reconstructed'—i.e. learners need to master each processing operation from the beginning for each language they learn—can block transfer occurring. Thus, for example, Polish learners of L2 English hold no advantage over Vietnamese learners when it comes to subject-verb agreement marking, even though Polish has such marking and Vietnamese does not. This is because the processing procedure required for this grammatical feature is developed late and thus the presence of the same procedure in the first language confers no advantage. However, once a specific procedure has been developed for the L2, the L1 can come into play.

However, not all theories support Pienemann's contention that L1 transfer is constrained by the processability of grammatical structures in the L2. As we will see in Chapter 8, other theories propose that L2 learning is a continuous process of **restructuring**: initially, learners are strongly influenced by their L1 and only learn to attend to target language forms gradually, as a result of exposure to them. Taylor's (1975) study, mentioned above, lends support to such a position.

These different positions are reflected in two different principles that govern L1 transfer. Andersen (1983) formulated the **Transfer to Somewhere**

**Principle,** which proposes that some degree of congruity between the first language and the target language is needed for transfer to take place. The 'somewhere' concerns the learning that results from the application of universal developmental principles. Kellerman (1995), however, advanced the **Transfer to Nowhere Principle** to reflect the fact that 'there can be transfer which is not licensed by similarity to the L2, and where the way the L2 works may very largely go unheeded' (p. 137). In other words, transfer is not necessarily developmentally constrained. The evidence suggests that these two principles are best seen as complementary. L1 transfer can occur at any time, but in some cases, it will only be evident when the learner has reached the requisite stage of development.

Finally, it should be noted that the effects of transfer can be seen not just in the linguistic forms observed in interlanguage, but also in the rate of development and ultimate attainment. The L1 can speed up or retard the development of an L2. Where there is similarity between the source and target languages, positive transfer can occur and learners can make rapid progress. Conversely, where there is difference, acquisition can be slowed down. Spanish learners of English, for example, tend to spend longer on the early 'no' + verb stage when acquiring English negation than German learners. This can be explained by the fact that this early stage corresponds to the L1 negative construction in Spanish, but not in German. Similarly, learners whose L1 includes an article system—for example, Spanish learners of English—are more likely to achieve a high level of accuracy in this system than learners whose L1 lacks an article system—for example, Japanese learners of English.

## Individual factors

In Chapters 2 and 3, we saw that learners' starting age and various psychological factors—such as language aptitude and motivation—affect L2 learning, in particular the rate of learning and ultimate attainment. Here, we will consider whether these same factors moderate the nature and extent of transfer, focusing on age and language aptitude. There are almost no studies that have investigated motivation and transfer and those that have done so have reported no difference in transfer effects for more and less motivated learners.

## Age and L1 transfer

Learners who start learning an L2 at a young age generally achieve a more native-like accent than those who start later. Some child learners—especially those who start before the age of three—become totally native-like in their pronunciation of the L2. This can be accounted for—in part, at least—by the fact that younger learners rely less on their first language and exhibit less transfer than older learners. As Guion, Flege, Lieu, and Yeni-Komshian (2000) put it, 'the more established the L1 is at the time of L2 acquisition, the greater the influence it will have on the L2' (p. 206). All learners have two primary sources of information to draw on—their first language and the second language input they are exposed to. If the L1 is not yet firmly established, it is less available as a resource for learning so learners will need to depend more on L2 input. Thus, one explanation for why children starting before the age of three are able to develop a totally native-like pronunciation is that their acquisition of target language sounds is not blocked by their L1.

Transfer of L1 grammatical forms is also less likely in younger than in older learners. Older learners may have an advantage when the source and target forms are similar and positive transfer occurs. However, when they are different, it can impede acquisition. Czinglar (2012) reported an interesting longitudinal study of two untutored Russian learners of L2 German. One was aged seven and the other 14. She focused on the acquisition of German word order rules—see Chapter 4, Table 4.3. She found that the two learners differed in their acquisition of the difficult verb-end rule, which has no equivalent in Russian. The younger learner fully acquired this rule in nine months, but the older learner took much longer. Czinglar argued that this difference in the rate of learning could be explained by the fact that the younger learner did not form hypotheses about German verb placement on the basis of the L1 whereas the older learner did. Once again, then, age can be seen to influence the extent to which learners depend on the L1 or L2 input.

Older learners, however, may have an advantage where vocabulary is concerned especially if the source and target languages share a number of cognates. Older learners, with a richer L1 vocabulary, are better equipped to benefit from positive transfer.

## Language aptitude and L1 transfer

There are good reasons to believe that learners' aptitude for learning an L2 influences the transfer of L1 features. For example, those learners with strong phonetic coding ability and phonological memory may be better equipped to process L2 sounds in the input and so may rely less on their L1 sounds. Conversely, individuals with little aptitude for mimicry of L2 sentences may be more likely to rely on their L1 (Odlin 1989). Learners with strong language analytical abilities will be able to identify the similarities and differences between their L1 and L2 grammars which may facilitate positive transfer and prevent negative transfer. However, there have been few studies examining the role of aptitude in L1 transfer. Jarvis and Pavlenko (2008), in their overview of research investigating crosslinguistic influences, did not consider language aptitude at all.

Two studies, however, indicate that language aptitude does mediate transfer effects. Sparks, Patton, Ganschow, and Humbach (2009), drawing on the **Linguistic Coding Difference Hypothesis**—which claims that both first and second language learning depend on the same basic language-learning mechanisms—provided evidence to show that there is a long-term, cross-linguistic transfer of skills from L1 to L2 and that this transfer is mediated by language aptitude. Learners with lower levels of L1 skills have lower levels of L2 aptitude and correspondingly greater difficulty in learning an L2—at least in a classroom setting. In this case, then, language aptitude is seen as related to positive transfer of L1 skills.

Trude and Tokowicz (2011) investigated the role played by working memory—which can be viewed as a component of language aptitude (see Chapter 3)—and language transfer in native English speakers' learning of letter-sound correspondences in L2 Portuguese. They found that those individuals with higher working memory performed more accurately than those with lower working memory and suggested that this was because they were better able to inhibit their first language. In other words, where pronunciation is concerned, higher working memory can help learning because it enables learners to avoid negative transfer.

## Language transfer as a multifactorial phenomenon

Having examined some of the key factors that influence L1 transfer, it has become clear that transfer needs to be considered as a complex, multifactorial phenomenon. Table 6.2 summarizes the various influences we have considered. By and large, researchers have investigated the influence of each factor separately, so little is known about how the factors interact to cause or inhibit transfer.

## Conceptual transfer

So far, we have examined transfer in terms of the structural influences of the L1 on the L2. However, there is growing interest in how the concepts associated with one language affect the linguistic choices made in another language. This interest can be traced back to the Sapir-Whorf Hypothesis which, in its strong version, claims that the way we think is determined by how our language is structured and, in its weaker version, that linguistic differences in languages reflect differences in how we think.

Conceptual transfer is clearly two way: that is, the conceptual framework of the first language impacts on the use and learning of a second language, and vice versa—i.e. there can be transfer from the L2 to the L1. However, in accordance with the main goal of this chapter—to examine the role of the L1 in L2 learning—I will focus only on L1-to-L2 conceptual transfer.

Following Jarvis and Pavlenko (2008), I will distinguish **semantic transfer** and **conceptual transfer**. Semantic transfer involves the mapping of a concept shared by two languages onto a translation equivalent. For example, a Finnish learner of L2 English needs to map the concept TONGUE onto the English word 'tongue': when a Finnish learner says 'He bit himself in the *language*', the error arises simply because the Finnish word 'language' can refer to the concepts of both TONGUE and LANGUAGE. Thus, overcoming semantic transfer only involves learning the correct target language form; there is no need to modify the underlying concept.

Conceptual transfer occurs when the concept itself differs in the two languages. Jarvis and Pavlenko illustrated this with reference to how English and Russian conceptualize PAPER CUP. In English, this belongs to the general category of CUP as it has the same function as other types of cups. In Russian, however, it belongs to the category of GLASS as it has a similar shape to a glass. Thus, when an English learner of Russian refers to a paper cup as

| Factors | Commentary |
|---|---|
| **Linguistic factors** | |
| *linguistic differences* | The key prediction of the Contrastive Analysis Hypothesis, namely that L1/TL differences cause learning difficulty, is not fully supported. In some cases, similarities cause greater difficulty. Grammatical differences cause learning difficulty especially in cases where the target feature is not salient in the L2 input. |
| *language distance* | In cases where there the L1 and TL are more proximate, both greater positive and negative transfer can occur than in cases were the languages are distant. |
| *markedness* | There is a greater likelihood that learners will transfer unmarked than marked L1 features, especially when the equivalent TL feature is marked. However, learners also sometimes transfer marked features. |
| **Psycholinguistic factors** | |
| *prototypicality* | Learners have intuitions about the transferability of L1 features based on their assessment of whether a particular L1 feature is considered 'core' and 'transparent'. |
| *psychotypology* | Learners' perceptions of language distance (rather than actual language distance) influence transfer. Intuitions about prototypicality determine whether learners are prepared to transfer; their psychotypology determines what is actually transferred. |
| **Contextual factors** | |
| *macro-contextual factors* | In general, a formal classroom setting inhibits transfer. In natural settings, negative transfer is more likely to occur when learners do not make a clear distinction between their L1 and the L2 (i.e. in unfocused contexts). But the relationship between the formality of the context and transfer is not clear cut. |
| *micro-contextual factors* | These affect the extent to which learners pay conscious attention to form. This can sometimes lead to negative transfer (when learners elect to use their L1 resources) but this can also inhibit negative transfer (when learners are focused on using the L2 accurately). |

| Developmental factors | Transfer works alongside universal and developmental factors. |
|---|---|
| *overgeneralization* | Initially, learners are likely to draw on their L1 but later they rely more on what they have learned about the L2; transfer and overgeneralization can as seen as two manifestations of the same process—prior learning facilitates new learning. |
| *order of acquisition* | The 'natural' order is disturbed if a grammatical morpheme that is meaning bearing in the L2 has no equivalent in the L1. |
| *sequence of acquisition* | The effects of the L1 become evident when learners have reached a stage of 'natural' development that allows them to access an L1 form that is similar or equivalent to the TL stage. L1 transfer can both speed up and retard the natural sequence of acquisition. |
| **Individual factors** | |
| *age* | In general, L1 transfer occurs to a greater extent in older than in younger learners. This reflects differences in the extent to which younger and older learners depend on their L1 or on L2 input as a source of data for learning. |
| *language aptitude* | Learners with higher language aptitude appear better equipped to transfer L1 skills when learning an L2. Learners with higher working memory may be better able to inhibit their L1 and thus avoid negative transfer. |

*Table 6.2  Summary of the various factors influencing L1 transfer*

'chaska' (= cup) rather than 'stakanchik' (= little glass), conceptual transfer has occurred. Conceptual transfer, then, arises as a result of 'similarities and differences in conceptual categories corresponding to lexical and grammatical categories of the source and recipient languages' (Jarvis and Pavlenko 2008: 112). Overcoming linguistic errors that arise as a result of conceptual transfer involves not just learning the correct L2 linguistic form, but also developing new concepts or modifying existing concepts. It is for this reason that Jarvis and Pavlenko claimed that conceptual transfer is more persistent than semantic transfer. However, they also acknowledged that it can be overcome as we all have the capacity for conceptual development.

Jarvis and Pavlenko (2008) provided many examples of conceptual transfer. They emphasized that a full understanding of transfer involves not only a consideration of the cross-linguistic effects that arise because of structural differences between the source and target languages, but also from differences in 'language-mediated concepts and language specific patterns of framing and conceptualization' (p. 148). They argued that the way concepts are realized linguistically in one language sensitizes speakers to think in particular ways and that learning a new language involves learning to conceptualize the world in different ways.

In some cases, conceptual modification through L2 learning may not be desirable. It should not be assumed, for example, that L2 learners need to abandon their concept of what it means to be polite when they learn a new language. Japanese learners of English, for example, express politeness by apologizing to their hosts after an enjoyable meal, rather than by thanking them. In so doing, they are drawing on their L1-mediated notion of what constitutes politeness in this situation by acknowledging the inconvenience they have caused their hosts. Simply thanking them would not be sufficiently polite[4]. The failure to overcome conceptual transfer in such cases may not be because learners are unable to but because—in some fundamental way—they do not wish to. Overcoming structural transfer is non threatening, but overcoming conceptual transfer can challenge the learner's sense of personal or cultural identity. However, this is perhaps less likely with child than adult learners—yet another reason why starting young is more likely to lead to native-like competence in an L2.

## Transfer in communication and learning

It remains to address the important issue of whether transfer is just a communication phenomenon, or whether it is also a feature of the learning process itself. Do learners just make use of their L1 as a **communication strategy** to help them overcome temporary performance problems or—as Selinker (1972) originally proposed—is it one of the central processes involved in interlanguage development?

Jarvis and Pavlenko (2008) argued that transfer leads to both performance-related and learning-related effects; that these two types of transfer are distinct; and that, therefore, it is necessary to distinguish between the two 'in order to avoid erroneous interpretations concerning the mechanisms through which transfer operates and about its ultimate impact on our knowledge representations' (p. 210). For example, they suggested that the setting influences performance rather than learning-related transfer, while the effects of developmental and universal processes on transfer are 'fundamentally learning-related' (p. 193). The roles of explicit knowledge and conscious processes—such as monitoring in transfer—are seen as both performance- and learning-related.

The distinction between these two types of transfer is problematic, however. First, evidence for transfer requires examining some kind of performance by the learner—by eliciting learners' perceptions of transferability—as in Kellerman (1979)—by examining learners' ability to process input containing specific target language features—as in Jiang et al. (2011), or—most commonly—by analysing learners' L2 production. Thus, in a sense, all transfer effects are performance related, so distinguishing the two types of transfer in the way Jarvis and Pavlenko propose is methodologically problematic.

Second, there are strong theoretical grounds for claiming that transfer affects learning via performance. Many years ago, Corder (1983) rejected the idea that learners transfer directly from their L1 into their interlanguages. He saw transfer occurring initially in communication and only subsequently becoming part of the learner's L2 knowledge system:

> ... persistent communicatively successful borrowing (from the L1) works backwards, as it were, and the successfully borrowed forms are eventually incorporated into the interlanguage grammar, both the correct and the incorrect. (p. 94)

Ringbom (1992) also claimed a relationship between communication and learning transfer:

> Transfer in communication is motivated by the learner's desire to comprehend or produce messages, but it may also have an effect on the process of hypothesis construction and testing, which many scholars see as central to interlanguage development. In other words, transfer in communication may lead to transfer in learning. (p. 106)

Such a position is compatible with current usage-based theories of L2 acquisition (for example, Complexity Theory—see Chapter 1). These propose that any exposure to or use of a linguistic form will contribute to change in the underlying representation of this form in the mind of the learner.

For these reasons, it may not be helpful to maintain a clear-cut distinction between performance-based and learning-based transfer effects.

## Conclusion

This chapter has provided a partial account of the cross-linguistic effects that arise from the interface of two languages in language use and in the minds of learners. I have elected to focus on the effects that a source language (the learner's L1) has on the use and learning of a second language—i.e. forward transfer—and have paid scant attention to the effects that the learning and use of a second language can have on the learners' L1 (i.e. reverse transfer). This is not because the latter effects are not well documented, but because the purpose of this book is to examine the acquisition of a second language. Thus, I have tried to show what SLA researchers have discovered about the role of the first language in second language learning and have focused on identifying the factors that govern transferability: the main findings relating to this are summarized in Table 6.2.

The effects of L1 transfer on L2 learning are extensive, varied, and persistent. They are also illuminative of the cognitive processes involved in L2 use and acquisition: no theory of L2 use or acquisition can be complete without an account of L1 transfer. However—just as there is no single, universally acknowledged theory of L2 acquisition—neither is there a general theory of L1 transfer. Such a theory would need to account for:

- the relative strength of positive and negative transfer in learners with different source and target languages

- the differential effects of transfer in different aspects of language—for example, its prominence in L2 phonology
- why learners transfer some L1 features in a particular area of language and not others
- the extent to which transfer is a conscious or subconscious process (i.e. whether it involves explicit and/or implicit knowledge of the source and target languages)
- the general relationship between L1 and L2 proficiency
- how developing L2 proficiency influences what and how much is transferred from the L1
- how natural processes of L2 acquisition interact with L1 transfer
- how macro- and micro-contextual factors affect transfer
- the extent to which transfer differs among learners of the same L1 as a result of factors such as age and language aptitude
- how—and to what extent—learning an L2 involves learning L1-mediated concepts
- how performance-based transfer contributes to learning-based transfer.

While it is clear that transfer is influenced by a range of linguistic, psycholinguistic, psychological, and social factors, there is no explicit theory to explain the interaction of these factors.

I conclude with a brief account of a very different perspective on the relationship between languages in the bilingual/multilingual mind—one that disputes two basic premises of much of the research discussed in this chapter—namely, the separateness of the learner's first and second languages and the assumption that the study of transfer involves a comparison of the source and target languages. Cook (2000) proposed that people who know two languages are different from monolinguals, and so need to be considered in their own right. He coined the term **multicompetence** to refer to the knowledge of more than one language in the same mind. He emphasized that multicompetence is not restricted to people who are highly proficient in two languages (balanced bilinguals), but is applicable to all users of an L2, irrespective of their level of achievement. The study of multicompetence calls for a holistic account of what it means to know more than one language. As Cook (2003) put it, 'since the first language and the other language or languages are in the same mind, they must form a language super-system at some level rather than completely isolated systems'. Cook (2000) also said that he preferred to avoid using the word 'transfer'. From this perspective, then, the distinction between the L1 and L2 becomes blurred and what is required is a focus on bilingual/multilingual language use.

## Notes

1 Transfer effects are also clearly evident in the pragmatic and discourse levels of language. For example, learners commonly draw on their L1 when performing requests or apologies.

2 Stockwell and Bowen (1965) also identified a hierarchy of difficulty for phonological features based on whether a given sound was phonemic, allophonic, or absent.

3 In a self-paced reading task, participants are exposed to a computerized sentence one word at a time and are in control of when to move on to the next word. The time taken to move forward to the next word is automatically recorded. Jiang et al. (2011) argued that if an error in a word was attended to, it would result in longer being spent on that word—or possibly the following words—than if it were not attended to. In effect, then, a self-paced task allows for the investigation of transfer effects on receptive, rather than productive, knowledge.

4 This is an example of sociopragmatic transfer. This kind of transfer arises 'when the social perceptions underlying learners' interpretation and performance of linguistic action are influenced by their assessment of subjectively equivalent L1 contexts' (Kasper 1992: 209).

# 7

# Input and interaction: the cognitive-interactionist perspective

## Introduction

This chapter examines what Gass and Mackey (2007) called the **interaction approach**. Broadly defined, this concerns what happens 'when learners encounter input, are involved in interaction, receive feedback and produce output' (p. 176). In part, then, it is concerned with the nature of the external processes involved when learners engage in communication. However, the interaction approach also draws on various cognitive constructs—such as **noticing** and **attention**—to explain how these external processes connect with internal processes to result in acquisition. In this way, the approach provides a cognitive-interactionist account of L2 acquisition.

I will begin by focusing on the 'interactionist' aspects of the approach by defining the key constructs involved. This is followed by an introduction to two key cognitive processes that are activated through interaction—focus on form and incidental acquisition. The rest of the chapter reviews research that has investigated the interaction approach, introducing important theoretical constructs as the review progresses.

## Key interactionist constructs

The constructs to be considered are shown schematically in Figure 7.1. Each construct is discussed and illustrated below.

## Non-interactive input

Non-interactive input consists of oral or written samples of the target language that learners are exposed to, but do not respond to verbally. It can be unmodified or pre-modified. Example (1)—taken from Long and Ross (1993)—illustrates non-interactive written input. It consists of three texts, (a), (b) and (c.) Text (a) is 'baseline input': that is, it is unmodified, typical of

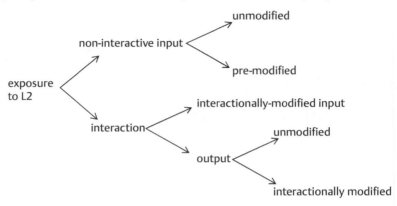

*Figure 7.1 Some key constructs*

the kind of input that occurs in communication between competent speakers of a language. It is characterized by lengthy sentences and dense propositional content. Texts (b) and (c) illustrate two ways of pre-modifying the input. In (b), the input is simplified by using short sentences and thinning-out the propositional content. In (c), modification takes the form of elaboration aimed at making the task of comprehending the input easier by structuring the propositional content more clearly. Elaborated input of this kind, however, is not necessarily more linguistically simple. Both (b) and (c) are examples of **pre-modified input**.

**Example (1)**

(a) Catfish have gills for use under water and lungs for use on land, where they can breathe for twelve hours or more. The hot daytime sun would dry them out, but they can slip out of their ponds at night and still stay cool while they hunt for food.

(b) Catfish have both gills and lungs. The gills are used for breathing under water. The lungs are for use on land. The fish can breathe on land for twelve hours or more. At night these fish can slip out of ponds. They move at night so they can stay cool. The hot sun would dry them out. They hunt at night too.

(c) Catfish have two systems for breathing: gills, like other fish, for use under water; and lungs, like people, for use on land, where they can breathe for twelve hours or more. Catfish would dry out and die from the heat of the sun, so they stay in water during the daytime. At night, on the other hand, they can slip out of their ponds and stay cool while they hunt for food.

(Long and Ross 1993: 51–2)

## Interactive input

Interactive input arises from the social interactions that a learner participates in with other people—either other learners or native speakers. Again, this input can be oral or written depending on whether the interaction occurs face to face or online in a chat room.

Interactive input is often simplified through the process of interaction; that is, when learners signal their failure to comprehend—for example, by requesting clarification—the input may be modified to accommodate them. Example (2) illustrates **interactionally modified input**. A native speaker (NS) is talking with a non-native speaker (NNS) (i.e. a learner) while performing an information-gap task involving describing the location of some objects. Initially, the NNS fails to understand 'mushroom' in the NS's instruction (turn 1) and requests clarification (turn 2). The NS responds by simplifying her initial instruction (turn 3), which enables the NNS to identify the source of her comprehension problem and request a definition of 'mushroom' (turn 4). The NS provides this (turn 5), and the NNS then seeks confirmation she has understood by offering a synonym (turn 6). The NS confirms and then provides further details (turn 7). This example illustrates how input that is initially not comprehensible to a learner is modified through interaction so that it becomes comprehensible.

**Example (2)**
1 **NS**   Place the mushroom with the four yellow dots underneath the two mushrooms that are already there.
2 **NNS**  Which one?
3 **NS**   OK? Place the *mushroom*.
4 **NNS**  What's a mushroom?
5 **NS**   It's another kind of plant.
6 **NNS**  A fungus.
7 **NS**   Yeah a fungus. It's a little brown thing... a little brown thing?
(Pica 1992: 211)

## Output

In interaction, learners have the opportunity to produce in the L2 (i.e. by speaking or writing). In other words, interaction affords not just input, but also output opportunities. Output is unmodified if the learner makes no attempt to modify an initial utterance. **Modified output** occurs when the learner attempts to reformulate an initial utterance. This can be self-initiated (i.e. the learner elects to try to modify the utterance without any external prompting). However, it often occurs following some kind of feedback from another speaker. If something the learner has said has not been understood and this is signalled to learner, this may result in the learner attempting to express the meaning more clearly and, perhaps, more linguistically accurately. Example (3) illustrates this. The NNS begins by seeking confirmation that she has identified the right objects (turn 1) and in the process commits an agreement error ('there is three...'). The NS responds with a clarification request (turn 2). This results in a repetition with the same error, but the learner then immediately self-corrects ('there are three...'). Self-correction is a form of modified output. It should be noted, however, that modified output does not always result in target-like language.

Example (3)
1 NNS  there is three buildings, right?
2 NS    Pardon?
3 NNS  there is three...there are three
4 NS    Right right I've described one so far.
(Pica 1992: 217)

## Focus on form and incidental learning

Both input and output can be meaning centred or form centred. Input is meaning centred when the learners' primary concern is to comprehend as, for example, in pleasure reading. Output is meaning centred if the goal is simply to communicate some message, as in normal conversation. Input is form centred when the learners' primary attention is directed at studying and learning the linguistic forms exemplified in the input. Output is form centred when the learner is primarily concerned with conforming to target language norms.

Related to this distinction are two different types of language learning: **incidental learning**—i.e. the picking up of new linguistic features while attention is focused on understanding the input—and **intentional learning**—i.e. the deliberate attempt to learn new linguistic forms. Input and output, however, can be both meaning- and form-centred when learners engage primarily in trying to understand, but also pay periodic attention to linguistic form when the need arises. Long (1991) coined the term **focus-on-form** to refer to the unplanned attention to form that can occur when learners are engaged in processing input and output for meaning.

The focus of this chapter is the incidental learning that takes place when meaning-centred input/interaction induces learners to focus on form. It is further considered in Chapter 11 when the role of implicit instruction in L2 acquisition is examined.

## Early research on input and interaction

Early research on input and interaction was descriptive in nature. That is, it focused on the special properties of input directed at L2 learners and the ways in which conversations with learners are structured.

## Simplified registers

We will briefly consider two types of simplified registers: **foreigner talk** and **teacher talk**. These share a number of features but also differ in some ways.

### Foreigner talk

In general, when NSs talk with learners they simplify their language although, as Gass (1997) showed, this does not always happen. NSs vary in their ability to engage in foreigner talk depending on their communicative skills and their prior experience of communicating with NNSs.

Sometimes simplification involves ungrammatical modifications. Ferguson (1975) suggested that ungrammaticality is evident in three ways: (1) omission of grammatical functors such as copula, articles, conjunctions, subject pronouns, and inflectional morphology; (2) expansion, as when 'you' is inserted before an imperative verb—for example, 'You give me money.'; (3) replacement/rearrangement, as when post-verbal negation is replaced by pre-verbal negation in English—for example, 'No want play'. Interestingly, the ungrammatical modifications evident in foreigner talk are very similar to the kinds of ungrammatical speech found in learner language (see Chapter 4).

In many situations, however, ungrammatical foreigner talk does not occur. Arthur, Weiner, Culver, Young, and Thomas (1980) recorded 60 telephone conversations between adult NNSs of English and NS airline ticket agents and reported no instance of ungrammatical input modifications. An obvious way in which input can be simplified grammatically is by adjusting speech rate and pausing more. Simplification can also be achieved by avoiding high-frequency words—for example, using 'flower' rather than 'tulip'—and by avoiding complex nominal phrases and subordinate constructions.

Grammatical foreigner talk does not always involve simplification. It can also entail regularization (i.e. the selection of forms that are in some way 'basic' or 'explicit'). Examples include the preference for full forms over contracted forms and the movement of topics to the front of sentences—for example, 'John, I like him.' Also, as we have already seen in example (1), input can be adjusted by making it more elaborate, for example, by lengthening sentences in an attempt to make the meaning clear or paraphrasing a low-frequency word—for example, saying 'hold on tightly' in place of 'cling'.

Why do native speakers engage in foreigner talk? Ungrammatical modifications can occur in 'talking down' situations—for example, when a NS in authority addresses foreign workers. But the main motivation is to promote communication. The fact that many of the formal characteristics of foreigner talk are very similar to those found in other simplified registers—such as child-directed speech and pidgins—suggests that universal processes of simplification are at work. Knowledge of how to modify the way we talk is part of our communicative competence.

## Teacher talk

**Teacher talk** shares many of the characteristics of grammatical foreigner talk. However, ungrammatical modifications are rare. One of the interesting research findings is that input modifications vary depending on the proficiency of the students. For example, Henzl's (1979) study of teacher talk in three different languages (Czech, English, and German) showed that the teachers adjusted their speech rate in accordance with the listeners' proficiency. This is an important finding as it shows that teacher talk is dynamically tailored to learners' needs, affording them increasingly richer input as they develop.

### Simplified registers and L2 acquisition

These studies of simplified registers did not investigate whether they assisted L2 acquisition. However, there are reasons for believing that they might do so. Krashen (1981) argued that they provide learners with **comprehensible input,** which he considered the primary source of data for acquisition. Chaudron (1983) claimed that modifications involving elaboration can help to make the message more 'cognitively simple'. Hatch (1983) suggested that regularization makes the meanings of utterances more transparent and enables learners to identify the constituent boundaries in utterances. One thing is clear: foreigner and teacher talk do not aim to teach the target language; if they help, they do so implicitly as the result of trying to communicate.

## Discourse management and repair

Just as input is modified, so too is the structure of conversations involving L2 learners. The interactional modifications that characterize these conversations are of two kinds—those relating to managing communication so as to avoid problems, and those that help to solve problems when they arise.

### Discourse management

When NSs converse with NNSs they use a variety of strategies to ensure that communication proceeds smoothly: they treat topics simply and briefly; they ask questions; they talk about the here and now; and they use comprehension checks:

- Arthur et al. (1980) compared the information airline agents included in their responses to telephone enquiries from NSs and NNSs ('What kind of plane is a ... ?'). They found there was no difference in the amount of simple information given to the NS and NNS callers, but there were significant differences in the amount of complex information, with the NNSs receiving far less.
- Asking questions serves as a way for native speakers to establish and control topics. Long (1991) suggested that questions compel answers, signal to the NNS that a turn is approaching, and lighten the learner's conversation burden because they encode part (and sometimes all) of the propositional content required to respond. Long also found differences in

the types of questions used. In conversations with the learners, the NSs made greater use of 'yes'/'no'- and 'or'-type questions. However, child NSs are less inclined to establish and develop topics through questioning with child L2 learners (Peck 1978).

- A here-and-now orientation allows learners to make use of the immediate context to interpret the meaning of utterances. It also leads to simpler verb forms. Long (1981) reported significantly more present-tense verbs in NS speech addressed to NNSs than in speech addressed to other NSs.
- Comprehension checks—for example, 'You understand?', 'Okay?'—have been found to occur more frequently in NS–NNS discourse than in NS–NS discourse (Long 1981). Teacher talk, in particular, seems to be rich in comprehension checks.

### Discourse repair

Two different kinds of problems can be identified—(1) communication problems, and (2) linguistic problems. In the case of the former, the repair involves the **negotiation of meaning**. Example (2) illustrated this. The NNS failed to understand what the NS had said and this led to an attempt to resolve the communication impasse. When the problem is purely linguistic, **negotiation of form** may take place. In Example (4), the student mispronounces 'patriot'. The teacher clearly understood what the learner meant, so there was no communication problem, but nevertheless negotiation ensued with the teacher's correction.

**Example (4)**
1 S Yeah, I'm a patriost.
2 T A patriot.
3 S Yeah.
(Ellis, Basturkmen, and Loewen 2001)

In natural conversation, negotiation of meaning is more likely to occur than negotiation of form as NSs do not typically bother to negotiate unless a communication problem occurs. In classroom interaction, however, negotiation of form is common. Negotiation of both meaning and form can also occur in conversations between learners.

Negotiation is accomplished by means of interactional strategies (see Table 7.1). These strategies are of two basic kinds. Output prompting strategies—for example, requests for clarification and elicitation—push learners to modify their problematic utterances. Input-providing strategies—for example, recasts and **explicit correction**—help to solve problems by supplying learners with the correct target language form. These strategies also differ in terms of how implicit—i.e. they are not overtly corrective—or explicit—i.e. they are more clearly corrective—they are. Context is important here, but, in general, clarification requests and recasts are implicit and elicitation and metalinguistic comments are explicit. Later, we will see that strong claims have been made regarding the facilitative role that these negotiation strategies play in acquisition.

| Negotiation strategy | Description | Example | Type |
|---|---|---|---|
| Request for clarification | an utterance that elicits clarification of the preceding utterance | NNS: When I get to Paris, I'm going to sleep for one whole day.<br>NNS: What?<br>(Varonis and Gass 1985) | implicit; output-prompting |
| Confirmation check | an utterance immediately following the previous speaker's utterance intended to confirm that the utterance was understood | NNS: Mexican food have a lot of ulcers.<br>NS: Mexicans have a lot of ulcers?<br>(Young and Doughty 1987). | implicit; input-providing |
| Recast | an utterance that rephrases the learner's utterance by changing one or more components (subject, verb, object) while still referring to its central meaning (Long 1996) | NNS: En las mesa hay una taza rojo.<br>NS: Um, hmm, una taza roja.<br>(Leeman 2003) | implicit; input-providing |
| Repetition | an utterance that repeats the learner's erroneous utterance highlighting the error | S: Le ... le girafe?<br>T: Le girafe?<br>(Lyster and Ranta 1997) | implicit; output-prompting |
| Metalinguistic feedback | an utterance that provides comments, information, or questions related to the well-formedness of the learner's utterance | S: Euhm, le, le éléphant, Le éléphant gronde.<br>T: Est-ce-qu'on dit le éléphant? | explicit; output-prompting |
| Elicitation | a question aimed at eliciting the correct form after a learner has produced an erroneous utterance | S: The chien peut court.<br>T: The chien peut court? Le chien peut ...<br>(Lyster and Ranta 1997) | explicit; output-prompting |
| Explicit correction | an utterance that provides the learner with the correct form while at the same time indicating an error was committed | S: La note pour le shot.<br>T: Oh, pour la, oh, pour ça. Tu veux dire pour la piqûre. Oui?<br>(Lyster and Ranta 1997) | explicit; output-prompting |

*Table 7.1  Strategies used in the negotiation of meaning and form (from Ellis 2008)*

# The Input and Noticing Hypotheses

We turn now to consider what kind of input is needed for acquisition to take place. We will start by examining two hypotheses that have been very influential in SLA.

Krashen's (1985) **Input Hypothesis** claims that 'if input is understood and there is enough of it, the necessary grammar is automatically provided' (p. 2). Krashen considered **comprehensible input** the essential environmental ingredient. He argued that simplified registers are beneficial for acquisition because they constitute one of the main ways of making input comprehensible. However, as Sharwood-Smith (1986) pointed out, there are two ways of processing input—for comprehension, and for acquisition. If learners use top-down strategies to process input (for example, by inferring the meaning from the situational or linguistic context) they will be able to comprehend without needing to process the input linguistically. For example, if learners hear this sentence:

Tomoko bought a new smart phone yesterday.

they can work out that the action occurred in the past without processing 'bought'. Linguistic-processing is important for acquisition.

The importance of conscious attention to linguistic forms in the input has been demonstrated most clearly in the work of Schmidt (1994, 2001). His **Noticing Hypothesis** claims that 'people learn about the things they attend to and do not learn much from the things they do not attend to' (2001: 30). We will take a closer look at the Noticing Hypothesis in Chapter 8, but we will draw extensively on the general idea of 'noticing' in this chapter.

# Pre-modified input and noticing

Given the importance of 'noticing', the key question becomes 'How can learners be helped to notice linguistic forms in the input?' One way is by pre-modifying the input to draw learners' attention to specific linguistic features. This can be achieved by input-enhancement either through (1) 'flooding' the input with exemplars of a specific feature, or (2) highlighting a specific form through intonation in oral input or by putting it in bold type, in italics, or paraphrasing in written input. In both cases, the aim is to induce selective attention to pre-determined linguistic forms.

Several studies have investigated the effect of input enhancement on noticing. A good example is Shook (1999). In this study, learners of L2 Spanish were exposed to written input under three conditions: (1) textually enhanced, (2) textually enhanced plus explicit instruction, and (3) textually unenhanced. The highlighted grammatical features were the Spanish present perfect verb tense and relative pronouns. The learners were then asked to write down what they could recall from reading the passages. The textually unenhanced input (3) resulted in more idea units being reported suggesting better

comprehension, whilst the textually enhanced model (1) led to greater noticing of the grammatical features, especially the more-meaningful present
perfect. This study therefore suggests a trade-off between comprehension and
noticing: if learners focus on the top-down processing required for effective
comprehension, less noticing occurs and the opposite is true if learners engage
in bottom-up processing and attend to the enhanced items in the text.

Not all enhanced grammatical forms are equally salient to learners. Some
forms are more likely to be attended to than others. Learners are likely to pay
greater attention to those enhanced linguistic features whose meanings are
more transparent. Also, learners are more likely to notice forms that they have
already partially acquired than those that are entirely new to them.

Overall, the research shows that text enhancement does facilitate noticing,
but it has only a limited effect (Lee and Huang 2008). To date, it is not possible
to comment on the relative effectiveness of different kinds of input enhancement (for example, input flooding versus highlighting). As Han, Park, and
Combs (2008: 600) noted, 'there are numerous methodological idiosyncrasies
characterizing the individual studies'—such as the number of times a specific
feature was highlighted, the number of texts involved, and whether learners
received explicit instruction on the targeted feature(s) prior to exposure to the
input.

## Interactionally-modified input and noticing

Interactionally modified input also provides opportunities for noticing—
arguably in ways more likely to be successful. A number of studies have used
a research technique called **stimulated recall** to investigate whether noticing
occurs as a result of the negotiation of meaning or form. This technique
involves replaying extracts of interactions involving negotiation and asking
learners to comment on their perceptions of what took place.

Egi (2007) is a good example of this kind of study. She investigated whether
learners paid attention to specific linguistic forms in the recasts they received
during negotiation. She distinguished (1) whether they showed awareness
that an error had been made, but no awareness of the target-like form in the
recast; (2) awareness of the target-like model, but no awareness that their
original utterance was problematic; and (3) awareness of an error, and also
that the target-like model had been provided. No noticing was reported most
of the time for morphosyntactical features. However, Egi reported that 18.7
per cent of the learners' comments demonstrated awareness in terms of (2)
and a further 26.05 per cent awareness in terms of (3).

This and other studies suggest that interaction induces noticing but variably
so. Morphosyntactical features are often not attended to probably because
learners are primarily focused on meaning and thus engaged in top-down
rather than bottom-up processing of the input. The extent to which noticing
occurs also depends on the nature of the negotiation (for example, whether a
recast is implicit or more explicit) and whether the learner is developmentally

ready to notice a feature. However, one thing is clear: noticing occurs more frequently in interactionally modified input than in interaction where there is no negotiation.

## Pre-modified input and acquisition

Noticing may be necessary for acquisition, but it does not guarantee it. Thus, it is important to ask whether the noticing of specific linguistic forms in the input leads to their acquisition. We will consider two ways in which researchers have investigated the effects of pre-modified input on acquisition—by simplifying the input to make it comprehensible, and by input enhancement.

### Comprehensible input and acquisition

In line with the Input Hypothesis, Krashen (1985) sought to demonstrate that acquisition takes place when the input is comprehensible. One way in which this can occur is through extensive reading involving graded readers. Rodrigo, Krashen, and Gibbons (2004) reported that a group of learners—taught by a Reading Method consisting of an extensive reading programme of graded books—and another group—taught by a Reading-Discussion Method where students read graded books and then participated in debates and discussions about them—outperformed a third group taught by a traditional Grammar and Composition Method in both vocabulary and grammar learning. There is now clear evidence that massive exposure to comprehensible input through extensive reading is beneficial for acquisition, especially where vocabulary is concerned. However, there are limits to how much can be acquired in this way. Low-ability readers may learn very few words incidentally.

### Text-enhancement and acquisition

Comprehensible input alone may not suffice for acquisition to take place unless learners also pay conscious attention to the words and grammatical features in the input—as claimed by the Noticing Hypothesis. Perhaps, then, just as enhanced input can induce noticing, it can also facilitate acquisition.

Lee and Huang (2008) examined 20 studies that had investigated the effects of typographical enhancement and input flooding on L2 acquisition. They reported an overall positive effect in tests administered shortly after the learners had completed reading the enhanced texts, but acknowledged that this was quite small. There were considerable differences in the results of individual studies. For example, in some of the studies there was no effect at all. Lee and Huang also reported that the benefits of the exposure wore off over time.

In the case of grammar acquisition, text enhancement is limited in another way. While it may help learners to see what is grammatically possible in the target language, it may not help them to eradicate an erroneous rule, especially if this rule corresponds to an L1 rule. In an interesting study, Trahey and

White (1993) investigated the effects of input-flooding on French-speaking learners' acquisition of adverb placement in English. English permits adverb placement between the subject and the verb—for example, 'Mary hurriedly hid her book'—but French does not; while English does not permit placement between the verb and object—for example, *Mary hid hurriedly her book'— and French does. Exposure to input containing adverbs was extensive in this study: one hour a day for ten days. The learners succeeded in learning the grammatical position for adverbs, but failed to 'unlearn' the ungrammatical position.

Sometimes text enhancement can lead to overuse of the target forms. Han et al. (2008) suggested that this may be due to over-enhancement—i.e. a combination of typographical enhancement and flooding. They cite studies where overuse occurred and where in each case there was double-enhancement. Han et al. concluded that for text enhancement to be effective there needs to be the right balance between frequency and saliency of target forms.

Overall, then, the evidence is quite mixed. Clearly, input enhancement does not always have an effect. As Lyddon (2011) pointed out, 'even the most deliberate attempts to modify a stimulus are no guarantee of its perception' (p. 116) and—even if noticing does occur—acquisition may not. At best, input enhancement only increases the likelihood of acquisition and—in the case of over-enhancement—it can have a deleterious effect.

## Interactionally-modified input and acquisition

Studies that have investigated the effects of interactionally-modified input on acquisition have drawn on Long's (1983b, 1996) **Interaction Hypothesis**. I will begin by explaining this hypothesis and then move on to consider studies based on it.

### The Interaction Hypothesis (IH)

There is an early and later version of the IH. In the early version, Long (1983) drew on the Input Hypothesis to suggest that the negotiation of meaning assists acquisition by making input comprehensible. Long (1983) was in agreement with Krashen (1981) that simplified input and context help to make input comprehensible. However, he argued that interactive input is more important because it supplies learners with information relating to those linguistic forms that are problematic for them. In the later version, Long (1996) incorporated Schmidt's (1994) views about the importance of noticing to claim that 'negotiation of meaning, and especially negotiation work that triggers interactional adjustments by the native speaker or more competent interlocutor, facilitates acquisition because it connects input, internal learner capacities, particularly selective attention, and output in productive ways' (pp. 451–52.). However, Long only claimed that negotiation *facilitates* acquisition—i.e. it makes it possible—not that it guarantees it.

Also, the IH does not claim that meaning negotiation is the *only* type of interaction that fosters learning; 'uninterrupted communication'—i.e. communication where there is no problem of understanding—can also contribute to acquisition.

The later version of the IH afforded a much richer view of how negotiation can assist language learning. It provides learners with **positive evidence** (i.e. 'models of what is grammatical and acceptable'); **negative evidence** (i.e. 'direct or indirect evidence of what is ungrammatical' (Long 1996: 413)); and opportunities for modified output. Pica (1992) suggested a fourth way. She proposed that interactional modifications can help learners to see how input is composed of constituent parts. For example, it can show learners how what they first perceive as a chunk can be broken down into separate words. Closely associated with the updated IH are Long's (1991) views about focus on form. As explained earlier, this refers to the incidental attention to linguistic form that arises when learners are primarily focused on meaning. Long viewed the negotiation of meaning as one of the main ways of achieving a focus on form and fostering acquisition. However, other researchers (e.g. Aston 1986) have questioned whether the negotiation of meaning does in fact play a major role in L2 acquisition, pointing out that learners may be resistant to nit-picking negotiation.

We will now turn to examine whether the research supports Long's claims about the importance of negotiation and focus on form. I will first focus on two of the benefits that Long proposed for negotiation—comprehensible input and the provision of positive evidence—reserving consideration of the third—modified output—till later when I discuss the role of output.

## Interactionally modified input and comprehension

Drawing on the earlier version of the IH, a number of studies investigated whether meaning negotiation assists comprehension by making input comprehensible. These studies compared the effects of three types of input on comprehension—baseline (unmodified) input, pre-modified input, and interactionally modified input.

Pica, Young, and Doughty (1987) used a task that required learners to listen to directions for choosing and placing objects on a small board illustrating an outdoor scene. The extent to which the participants were able to locate the objects correctly provided a measure of their comprehension. An analysis of the input in the three conditions showed that the interactionally-modified directions were longer and more redundant than the baseline directions with the premodified directions intermediate. The main finding was that interactionally modified input resulted in better comprehension than pre-modified input, which in turn was comprehended better than the baseline input. Other studies (for example, Loschky 1994) also found that interactionally-modified input leads to superior comprehension. These studies all involved adult learners. Young children, however, may be less ready to engage in negotiation of meaning although when they do so, their comprehension also benefits (Ellis and Heimbach 1997).

Overall, then, there is clear evidence that negotiation results in more input and more comprehensible input than unmodified input. However, it is not entirely clear whether it is the modifications themselves that facilitate comprehension or the additional time for processing input that results when negotiation occurs. Ellis and He (1999) found that when the amount of time allocated to the premodified and interactionally modified input was the same, no advantage for negotiation was seen.

## Negotiated interaction and L2 acquisition

As I noted earlier in the chapter, the processes involved in acquiring from input are not the same as those involved in comprehending input. Thus it does not follow that interactionally-modified input that assists comprehension also facilitates acquisition. Increasingly, then, researchers have turned their attention to examining whether and how interaction facilitates acquisition. This vein of research has proved one of the richest in SLA to date. Mackey (2007) identified more than 40 published studies that have investigated the relationship between interaction and L2 learning.

A number of these studies asked 'Do learners acquire those features that learners claim to have noticed?' In Mackey (2006), learners took part in a game show activity and received recasts or clarification requests when they made errors in questions, plurals, and past tense. Mackey found that the level of noticing varied according to target structure, with higher levels evident for questions forms, much lower levels for past tense, and intermediate levels for plurals. 83 per cent of the learners who reported noticing question forms also improved their ability to form questions. However, the relationship between noticing and the other two target features was not established. This study suggests that when learners do notice a grammatical form, acquisition occurs. However, as noted earlier, noticing itself depends on the grammatical feature.

Most studies have investigated the effects of interaction on acquisition without obtaining measures of noticing. Mackey and Goo (2007) conducted a meta-analysis of these studies. They found that interaction had a stronger effect on vocabulary than on grammar. This is not surprising as lexical problems are more likely to result in both negotiation and noticing. Just about all the studies that have investigated the impact of negotiated interaction on vocabulary have reported positive effects. Importantly, negotiation does not just benefit those learners who participate actively in it, but also learners who are auditors of negotiation involving others. This is more likely to occur if the task motivates them to attend to closely to the input as in Ellis, Tanaka, and Yamazaki (1994).

There is another reason why negotiated interaction is not always beneficial for grammar learning. As we saw in Chapter 4, learners do not acquire new grammatical features immediately, but pass through transitional stages on route to the target structure. If learners are not developmentally ready, the input they receive from negotiation may not connect with their internal processing mechanisms so acquisition does not take place. However—even if they do not master the target structure—negotiation may still help them progress to a more advanced transitional stage. Mackey's (1999) study set out to examine if this was the case. She found that only those learners who received interactionally modified input demonstrated clear evidence of having advanced along the developmental sequence for questions. That is, even if they did not reach the final target stage, the interaction helped them developmentally.

Another important question is whether the positive effects for negotiated interaction are durable or just short-lived. This can be addressed by comparing the results of post-tests administered shortly after the interactive activity has been completed with those of post-tests completed later. In fact, a number of studies have reported stronger effects in a delayed post-test. Ellis, Loewen, and Erlam (2006), for example, investigated the effects of two feedback strategies—recasts and metalinguistic comments—on learners' acquisition of regular English past tense. The effect was more clearly evident in the delayed test administered two weeks later. This might seem surprising, but can be explained by the fact that sometimes information is not immediately integrated into the learner's interlanguage, but is put into storage and only fully activated later—as proposed by Gass (1997).

Contextual factors have also been found to influence the effect that negotiated interaction has on acquisition. Many of the studies have been laboratory based. Mackey and Goo's (2007) meta-analysis included 18 laboratory-based studies and ten classroom-based studies. Also, the majority of the studies in this meta-analysis involved foreign as opposed to second language contexts. These contextual differences can affect the extent to which learners are predisposed to attend to the linguistic features that are negotiated. Many of the laboratory studies involved one-on-one interactions where the target features were likely to have been more salient to learners than in classrooms, where the teacher is interacting with the whole class. Also, foreign language learners are likely to be more form-conscious than second language learners. Negotiated interaction has been found to have a larger effect on acquisition in laboratory and foreign language settings than in classroom and second language settings.

Another contextual factor is whether the interaction takes place face to face or synchronously in a chat room. The fact that the online interaction is written allows more time for noticing. However, the absence of non-verbal cues may make the online input less comprehensible. Researchers have addressed two key questions: 'Does negotiation of meaning occur in synchronous computer-based interaction?' and, if so, 'Does it facilitate acquisition?' A number of studies (for example, de la Fuente 2003) found that negotiation is common when learners perform communicative tasks online and that—as in face-to-face negotiation—much of it is directed at lexical rather than grammatical problems. Ziegler (2015) reported a meta-analysis of studies that had compared the effects of negotiation on acquisition in face-to-face and synchronous computer-mediated communication. The main finding was that negotiation was beneficial in both modes and that overall there were no significant differences.

So far, we have considered the overall benefits of negotiated interaction. However, we also need to consider more precisely how negotiated interaction assists acquisition. In the next section, I focus on the role of output and then move on to examine the effects of different negotiation/feedback strategies.

## Modified output and acquisition

Long's revised Interaction Hypothesis drew in part on Swain's (1985, 1995) Output Hypothesis which proposed that language acquisition is not just driven by input but also by output, a view that is now widely accepted.

### The Output Hypothesis[1]

Swain (1985) proposed the Output Hypothesis as a complement to the Input Hypothesis. Her conviction that output plays an important role in L2 acquisition grew out of her experience of investigating immersion programmes in Canada. These programmes cater to incidental acquisition by teaching subject content in the L2—for example, maths or science. The Input Hypothesis provided a theoretical basis for such programmes as they afforded plentiful comprehensible input. However, Swain's evaluation of the immersion programmes showed that although learners developed considerable fluency in the L2, they did not achieve high levels of grammatical and sociolinguistic competence. This led her to conclude that comprehensible input was insufficient and that what was missing was the opportunity for students to engage in **pushed output**—i.e. output consisting of messages that were concise and socially appropriate. As Swain (1985) put it, 'learners ... can fake it, so to speak, in comprehension, but they cannot do so in the same way in production' (p. 127). As we have already seen, learners can comprehend input using top-down strategies. Production, however, requires learners to process bottom-up. Swain (1995) went on to suggest that production was important in three main ways: (1) it can trigger noticing when learners realize that something they said does not effectively communicate what they wanted to say; (2) it serves a hypothesis-testing function when learners try out a way of saying something and then receive feedback; and (3) it provides a basis for metalinguistic reflection when learners consciously think about what they have said or written.

### Modified output creates opportunities for learning

Interaction is not the only way in which learners can be 'pushed' to modify their output, but it is certainly one of the main ways[2]. Interaction involving feedback on learners' attempts to express their meaning often results in modified output, which constitutes one kind of pushed output. Example (5) below illustrates this. The problem arises when Learner 2 does not hear (or understand) the word 'nuclear' and signals a problem by means of a confirmation check (turn 2). Learner 1 responds by explicitly disconfirming Learner 2's hypothesis and repeating the key word ('nuclear') three times (turn 3). The modified output occurs in turn 4, where Learner 2 produces the correct word and also indicates her understanding ('Ah, I see.'). We do not know if this learner acquired 'nuclear', but it is clear that the negotiation helped the learner to both understand and pronounce the word correctly. Thus, there is potential for acquisition to have taken place.

**Example (5)[3]**
1 L1  Einstein's scientific work helped Americans make the nuclear bomb.
2 L2  Clear bomb?
3 L1  No nuclear, nuclear, nuclear bomb.
4 L2  *Nuclear bomb.* Ah, I see.
(Aubrey: unpublished data)

Example (5) shows how modified output can arise in negotiation, triggered by a learner's failure to comprehend another speaker's utterance. Example (6) illustrates how learners modify their own utterances when these cause a problem. The problem arises in turn 3. The NS responds with a confirmation request that corrects the learner's utterance (turn 4). The learner then modifies her initial utterance (turn 5). This example illustrates how negotiation can help learners to notice the gap between their own ill-formed utterance and the target-language version. Again, though, we cannot be sure that this has helped the learner to acquire the irregular verb 'came'. It is possible that the learner is just parroting the native speaker's correction. But it is also possible that genuine **intake** has occurred, establishing the potential for acquisition.

**Example (6)**
1 L   After that he was waiting for her every day.
2 NS  Waiting and waiting mhm.
3 L   But she was never come back.
4 NS  She never came back?
5 L   *Never came back,* he was very sad.
(McDonough 2007: 332)

In Example (6), the learner is provided with the correct form. In Example (7), however, the learner is pushed to reformulate the initial utterance, but without any positive evidence. This occurs when the negotiation sequence involves a prompt (in this case a clarification request). In turn 2, the teacher requests clarification which pushes the learner to produce the correct past tense form in turn 3. In this kind of negotiation sequence, however, a learner will only be able to modify her output if she already knows the correct form. Such sequences may still assist acquisition by enabling the learner to achieve fuller control over a partially acquired feature.

**Example (7)**
1 L   He pass his house.
2 T   Sorry?
3 L   He passed, he passed, ah, his sign.
(Nobuyoshi and Ellis 1993: 204)

In these examples, the learners succeeded in correcting their errors when they modified their output. In fact, this does not always happen. Sometimes, learners modify their output, but fail to produce the correct target form. However, Mackey (2007) argued that benefits can accrue even when the modified output is not target-like.

Finally, modified output does not only occur as a result of negotiation. Swain (1998) chose to investigate output in **language-related episodes (LREs)**, which she defined as 'any part of a dialogue in which students talk about the language they are producing, question their language use, or other- or self-correct' (p. 70). LREs include both negotiation of meaning and negotiation of form sequences, but they also include sequences where learners elect to focus pre-emptively on some linguistic object that they wish to use in production, as illustrated in Example (8). Pre-emptive attention to form often involves metalinguistic reflection—the third of the functions of output that Swain proposed in her Output Hypothesis.

**Example (8)**
1 L1   How can I say that? Ay. I don't remember, but I know the name.
       It's go whoo and you can make choice.
2 L2   Ah, blender?
(Swain 1998)

## Experimental studies of modified output and acquisition

As already noted, the fact that learners modify their output—often correcting their errors in the process—is not in itself evidence of acquisition. At best, it demonstrates that intake has occurred (i.e. learners have noticed their error and may have carried out a **cognitive comparison**). Experimental studies are needed to demonstrate that output modification leads to acquisition. In such studies, scores in a pre-test administered before the interaction took place are compared with scores in a post-test administered after the interaction is over. Recent years have seen a plethora of experimental studies investigating the effects of modified output on acquisition.

One of the earliest experimental studies was Nobuyoshi and Ellis (1993). Three learners performed an oral narrative and were pushed to modify their output through clarification requests whenever they made an error in the use of a regular past tense. Nobuyoshi and Ellis found that two of these learners responded by correcting their errors, but the other learner did not. Only the learners who self-corrected demonstrated gains in accuracy in the use of the past tense when they performed another oral narrative. Another group of learners who performed the same tasks—but without any negotiation—also failed to improve in accuracy. This study was small scale but it suggests that pushing learners to produce more target-like output has an effect on acquisition for some learners.

There is also some evidence that modified output works more effectively for acquisition than either pre-modified or interactionally-modified input. Both Ellis and He (1999) and de la Fuente (2002) reported that negotiated interaction that led to pushed output promoted productive acquisition of new words to a greater extent than either pre-modified input or negotiated interaction without pushed output. Izumi (2002) also found that groups of learners who performed a task where they had to produce the target structure (English relative clauses) outperformed those groups that just received pre-modified input. In line with Swain's Output Hypothesis, Izumi suggested that output was more effective because it induced a cognitive comparison.

A number of studies have looked at the effect of modified output in learner–learner interactions. Adams, Nuevo, and Egi (2011) reviewed the relevant studies. They noted that modified output occurs in negotiation sequences between learners but that 'learner–learner feedback may not always prompt modified output that can lead to learning gains' (p. 47). Their own study of adult ESL learners found that the production of modified output following recasts and explicit corrections was related to learning, but only in a delayed grammaticality judgement test, which they suggested afforded a measure of **explicit knowledge**. They reported no relationship when learning was measured by tests that were more likely to tap **implicit knowledge**.

Overall, modified output is more likely to occur in interactions with competent speakers of the language than with other learners. However, not all studies involving native speaker interlocutors have found that modified output following feedback aids acquisition. Mackey and Goo (2007) felt unable to come to any clear conclusion about the contribution that modified output makes to acquisition. One reason for this is that, in many instances, modified output may simply involve repeating or mimicking a recast. McDonough and Mackey (2006) reported a laboratory-based study, which showed that repeating or mimicking a recast was not beneficial for learning, whereas productive use of a form a short time after hearing it—suggestive of deeper processing—was.

## Corrective feedback and L2 acquisition

The studies we will now consider all involved **corrective feedback** strategies[4]. Earlier, I pointed out that these strategies can be input-providing or output-prompting and implicit or explicit (see Table 7.1). The question that researchers have addressed is 'Are some types of corrective feedback strategies more effective than others?'

## Input-providing vs. output-prompting strategies

The relative effectiveness of input-providing strategies—such as recasts[1] or confirmation checks (CF) which reformulate the learner's erroneous utterances—and prompts—such as requests for clarification which push learners to modify their output—has been a matter of debate. In part, this debate hangs on the importance that is attached to modified output. If acquisition is viewed as primarily input driven, then, clearly, whether or not learners repair their errors is of little importance. If, on the other hand, modified output is seen as assisting acquisition, as claimed by the Output Hypothesis, then negotiation that results in repair of errors is desirable. Long (2006) argued that it is recasts that are important for acquisition on the grounds that learners cannot acquire new target features unless they receive input. In contrast, Lyster (2004) has argued that output-prompting CF is more likely to facilitate acquisition because it helps learners to achieve greater control over those grammatical structures they have partially acquired. Lyster and Saito's (2010) meta-analysis of studies that had compared input-providing and output-prompting CF reported in favour of the latter.

However, a number of caveats are in order. First, recasts constitute a single corrective strategy, whereas the prompts include four different strategies—i.e. clarification requests, repetition of error, elicitation, and metalinguistic clues. It is possible that the greater effect found for prompts is simply because many strategies are more effective than one. Also—whereas recasts are often implicit—prompts include a mixture of implicit and explicit strategies, so it is possible that they are more effective because they are more salient. Third, the effects of the two types of CF are likely to be mediated by a number of factors, such as the instructional tenor of the classroom (i.e. whether it is primarily meaning or form focused); the proficiency level of the learners; and the nature of the target feature. For example, Lyster and Mori (2006) reported that recasts proved more effective than prompts in an instructional context where the learners were more inclined to pay attention to form.

Recasts are clearly effective in promoting acquisition, especially when they are made salient to the learner. Doughty and Varela (1998) investigated the effect of 'corrective recasts' on ESL learners' use of past verb forms. As they defined them, these consist of an initial prompt—in this case, a repetition of the learner's erroneous utterance—followed by a recast if the learner fails to self-correct. See Example (9). Doughty and Varela reported that the recasts resulted in progress through the acquisition sequence for past tense and also in more target-like use in an immediate and delayed oral post-test.

Example (9)
1 L  I think that the worm will go under the soil.
2 T  I *think* that the worm *will* go under the soil?
3 L  (no response)
4 T  I *thought* that the worm *would* go under the soil.
(Doughty and Varela 1998: 124)

The debate about the relative effectiveness of input-providing and output-prompting types of CF is ongoing. See for example, Goo and Mackey (2013) and Lyster and Ranta (2013). Perhaps this debate is somewhat unnecessary. Recasts provide learners with positive evidence and thus make it possible for them to acquire *new* linguistic features. Prompts—on the other hand—can help learners consolidate their knowledge of those features they have prior knowledge of, so both are important. Arguably, learners benefit most when they receive a mixture of these two types of CF.

## Implicit vs explicit corrective strategies

Studies that have investigated the relative effects of implicit and explicit CF have typically compared recasts (an implicit strategy) with one or more types of explicit strategies (for example, metalinguistic comments or explicit correction). It should be noted, however, that recasts (the implicit CF strategy most commonly investigated) differ considerably in how implicit or explicit they are. It is the more explicit types of recasts that have proved more likely to promote learning (Loewen and Philp 2006).

A good example of such a study is Ellis et al. (2006) referred to earlier. The results showed that the group receiving a repetition of an incorrect verb form followed by a metalinguistic comment outperformed both the control group and a group that received recasts. However, the differences only reached statistical significance in the delayed post-tests. Yilmaz (2012) carried out the same comparison in a face-to-face context and a synchronous computer-mediated context and found a clear advantage for explicit correction over recasts in both immediate and delayed tests.

Overall, explicit CF is more effective than implicit CF. However Li (2010), in another meta-analysis, found that overall implicit CF resulted in higher scores in post-tests completed a long time after the instruction. This was because its effect increased over time whereas those of explicit CF did not change. Neither Ellis et al.'s or Yilmaz's study investigated this possibility as their post-tests were administered after only a relatively short interval.

## General comments

A general finding from all the studies I have considered in this section is that corrective feedback is effective irrespective of the type of strategy involved. In this respect, these studies reinforce the conclusion I reached earlier, namely that the negotiation of meaning and of form facilitate acquisition. Li's (2010) meta-analysis of 33 studies involving CF reached exactly this conclusion. However, Li also found that the strength of the effect was influenced by a number of factors. For example, it was much stronger in studies carried out in a laboratory or foreign-language setting than in a classroom or second-language setting perhaps—as I have already suggested—because learners pay greater attention to the feedback they receive in the former settings. Another possibility—which I consider in the next section—is that individual difference factors influence the extent to which learners benefit from CF and also which type of CF is more effective.

## Interaction, working memory, and acquisition

Learner difference factors such as language aptitude, working memory, motivation, and language anxiety can be expected to influence how learners process input and output and thus the extent to which they are able to benefit from interaction. We saw evidence of this in Chapter 3. In this section, I will focus on the individual difference factor that has attracted the greatest attention in interaction research—working memory. Readers might like to refresh their memory of the construct by reading page 45 in Chapter 3.

Working memory is hypothesized to mediate learners' ability to attend to and learn from negotiation. That is, learners with higher working memory may be better able to notice the forms that have been corrected in the feedback, respond to the feedback by modifying their output, and relate information in working-term memory to that held in long-term memory.

Studies (for example, Mackey, Philp, Egi, Fujii, and Tatsumi 2002; Trofimovich, Ammar, and Gatbonton 2007) that have investigated these possibilities have produced mixed results, reflecting perhaps methodological differences in their design. The researchers used different ways of measuring working memory and the interactional treatments they provided differed in how salient recasts were made to learners. Later studies, however, have provided clearer evidence that working memory is indeed a factor influencing how recasts are processed. I will consider one of these here.

Révész (2012) obtained measures of both **phonological short-term memory**—i.e. the capacity to hold aural information in memory—and complex working memory—i.e. the capacity to process information held in short-term memory—and correlated these with test gain scores for two groups of learners. Both groups performed communicative tasks, but only one group received recasts. Révész found that for those learners who did not receive recasts, differences in working memory were not related to gains in the target structure. However, in the group that received recasts, there was a relationship. Phonological working memory was related to accuracy gains in an oral description task, while measures of complex working memory were related to gains in written tests. These results might seem puzzling, but they can be explained in terms of the distinction between **procedural knowledge** and **declarative knowledge**. Those learners with high phonological short-term memory may have benefited from the recasts because they were able to maintain the information in short-term memory longer, which contributed to the development of the procedural knowledge needed for oral production. Those learners with stronger complex working memory may have been able to consciously attend to the information provided by the recasts, which led to the declarative knowledge helpful for written production.

Work investigating the mediating role of working memory is still in its infancy. Révész's results are especially interesting as they suggest that different components of working memory may be important for the development of different kinds of linguistic knowledge—i.e. procedural vs. declarative—resulting from feedback. This suggests that research investigating the effects of interaction on learning needs to pay close attention to how learning is measured. I comment on this in the next section.

## Measuring the effects of input and interaction on acquisition

In Chapter 1, I pointed out that 'acquisition' can be considered in terms of whether learners can comprehend the meaning of a particular feature or in terms of their ability to produce it. I also noted that it is necessary to distinguish different types of knowledge: implicit/procedural and explicit/declarative. Acquisition can also be viewed as progression through developmental sequences.

By and large, the studies we have examined in this chapter have measured acquisition in terms of production rather than comprehension. In most cases, these studies have not attempted to establish whether the acquisition that results from input and interaction is of the implicit or explicit kind. It is, however, clearly important to do so.

How, then, can we tell whether input and interaction lead to 'development' or 'storage'? One way is by administering tests designed to provide separate measures of explicit and implicit knowledge. Here I, will point to two studies that have attempted it. Ellis et al. (2006), in the study discussed above, measured the effects of the two types of corrective feedback by means of an elicited oral imitation test—intended to measure implicit knowledge—and an untimed grammaticality judgement test—designed to measure explicit knowledge. Overall, they found that the explicit correction proved to be a more effective corrective treatment than the implicit in both tests. One interpretation of their study, therefore, is that explicit correction assisted the development of both types of knowledge. Interestingly, however, while there was no evidence that the recasts contributed to explicit knowledge, there was some evidence that they led to gains in implicit knowledge. While no firm conclusions can be drawn from this study, it does suggest that different types of corrective feedback may affect learning in different ways.

Révész (2012), in the study referred to above, also used different tests, designed to tap different types of knowledge. She included an untimed grammaticality judgment test, a written picture description test, and an oral description task. She suggested that the grammaticality judgment test tapped the learners' declarative knowledge; the oral test tapped their procedural knowledge; and the written test potentially both types of knowledge. The results of her study showed that the effectiveness of the feedback strategy she investigated (recasts) varied according to how acquisition was measured. The recasts were found to have the greatest effect on scores in the oral production test; less effect on the written production test scores; and the least effect on the grammaticality judgment test scores. As in Ellis et al (2006), then, the recasts appear to have impacted on learners' implicit knowledge but not on their explicit knowledge.

Some studies have measured acquisition in terms of learners' progress along developmental sequences. Mackey (1999) showed that negotiation enabled learners to advance along the stages for the acquisition for questions. Doughty and Varela (1998) showed that corrective recasts helped learners progress from one interlanguage stage to the next for past tense. Progress through a sequence of acquisition can be seen as indicative of the development of learners' implicit knowledge systems (see Chapter 4). Thus, arguably, this constitutes a better measure of the effect of interaction than tests that simply measure accurate use of specific features.

The assumption of the theories we have examined in this chapter—the Interaction Hypothesis, the Noticing Hypothesis, and the Output Hypothesis—is that input and interaction involve incidental acquisition, which is manifest in gradual changes in learners' implicit knowledge. To demonstrate this convincingly, however, it is necessary to employ methods of assessment capable of providing valid measures of this type of knowledge.

## Conclusion

Input and interaction have been major focuses of research in SLA. Why is this? I think there are several reasons. First, the most obvious case of successful language acquisition—acquisition of our first language—is interaction-driven. Children learn their first language through exposure to input and by interacting with their caretakers. Thus, it is likely that a second language—to some extent at least—is learned in the same way. Second, developments in language teaching have led to greater emphasis being placed on communication and this has served as an incentive for investigating how learners learn from communicating. Third, technological developments have made it easier to collect and transcribe samples of interactions involving learners. Finally, developments in discourse analysis have provided the descriptive tools needed to analyse these samples. There is every sign that input and interaction will continue to figure as a major line of research in SLA.

Below is a summary of the main findings that have emerged from the **interaction approach**:

1 The interaction approach assumes that input and interaction provide learners with L2 data that are processed internally as **intake** in working memory and then potentially incorporated into their developing interlanguages. However, not all intake enters the learner's L2 system.

| Theory | Description |
|--------|-------------|
| Input Hypothesis (Krashen 1985) | The **Input Hypothesis** claims that acquisition takes place automatically and without consciousness when learners are exposed to input made comprehensible through context and simplification. It draws on research into simplified registers (i.e. foreigner talk and teacher talk). |
| Interaction Hypothesis (Long 1983b, 1996) | The **Interaction Hypothesis** proposes that input and output modified through negotiation provide the best data for acquisition. Long (1996) argued that it was the **negotiation of meaning** that is important. However, other researchers (e.g. Lyster and Ranta 1997) have argued that **negotiation of form** (i.e. negotiation triggered by a purely linguistic problem) also assists acquisition. Both the negotiation of meaning and form involve the same set of negotiation strategies which differ in terms of whether they are (1) input-providing or output-prompting and (2) implicit or explicit. |
| Output Hypothesis (Swain 1985, 1995) | The **Output Hypothesis** claims that acquisition is not just dependent on input but that output—especially **pushed output**—also plays a role. One way in which output can be 'pushed' is when a learner modifies an initially non-target like utterance during negotiation. The later version of the Interaction Hypothesis also allows for this. |
| Noticing Hypothesis (Schmidt 2001) | **The Noticing Hypothesis** claims that input works best for acquisition if learners pay conscious attention to linguistic forms and the meanings they convey and, in particular, if **noticing-the-gap** occurs (i.e. learners compare what they have noticed in the input with their own output). |

*Table 7.2 Summary of key theories in the interaction approach*

2 Researchers in this paradigm have identified a number of key constructs about the nature of input and interaction that are theorized to influence intake and incidental L2 acquisition—**pre-modified input, interactionally modified input,** and **modified output.**

3 A number of different theories have informed the interaction approach. These are summarized in Table 7.2.

4 Whereas the Input Hypothesis assumes that acquisition is a subconscious process, both the Interaction Hypothesis and the Output Hypothesis claim that **noticing** facilitates acquisition—i.e. learners benefit from consciously focusing on form while they are communicating. Current accounts of the role of input and interaction accept that noticing is important for acquisition to take place.

5 Researchers have investigated whether **enhanced input** results in noticing. In general, the results have been somewhat disappointing. Enhanced input does induce noticing, but only to a limited extent. Ultimately, it is what a learner chooses to selectively attend to in the input that matters.

6 Researchers have also investigated whether **interactionally-modified input** leads to noticing. Negotiation of meaning and form has been shown to induce noticing of phonological, lexical, semantic, and some grammatical elements (for example, question forms). However, it is much less effective in helping learners to notice morphological features, such as verb tense inflections.

7 Other research has focused on the relationship between **pre-modified input** and acquisition. When learners are exposed to massive amounts of simplified input that they can comprehend, acquisition has been shown to take place incidentally. Input-enhancement, however, has been found to have only a small effect on acquisition.

8 When input is modified interactionally through negotiation, both comprehension and acquisition benefit. However—where acquisition is concerned—the effect appears to be much larger for vocabulary than for grammar, reflecting once again the role of noticing as learners are more likely to pay attention to lexical than to grammatical problems. Another reason why interaction has less effect on grammar is that structures are acquired gradually in stages. Interaction may help learners to advance through a sequence of acquisition without enabling them to achieve target-like accuracy. How learners orientate to interaction—for example, whether they focus exclusively on meaning or whether they also take opportunities to focus on form—influences its effect on acquisition.

9 Modifying output through negotiation provides opportunities for learning as it can 'push' learners to express themselves more clearly and more accurately. Modified output is more likely to occur when learners interact with competent L2 speakers than with other learners. The relative contribution of interactionally modified input and output to acquisition remains a controversial issue.

10 Recent research has focused on the effect of different types of corrective feedback—in particular, input-providing strategies, such as recasts, and output-prompting strategies, such as elicitation or metalinguistic comments. Both types have been found to lead to gains in grammatical accuracy. However, what may be crucial is the extent to which the feedback is salient to learners. Reflecting this, explicit types of feedback have been found to be more facilitative than implicit types.

11 Working memory is believed to play a crucial role in **intake**. Recent research (for example, Révész 2012) indicates that different components of working memory—i.e. phonological short-term memory and the central executive—may be involved in the processing needed to develop different kinds of knowledge—i.e. procedural and declarative.

12 Researchers have begun to pay careful attention to how acquisition is measured. There is increasing recognition that input and interaction can contribute to the development of both procedural/implicit and declarative/explicit knowledge and that it is important to ascertain precisely what their contributions are by designing suitable tests.

As this chapter has shown, interaction researchers have drawn on cognitive theories of L2 acquisition. They see input and interaction as influencing the selective attention that learners pay to linguistic features. They also see cognitive systems as influencing how input is processed. In the next chapter we take a close look at cognitive theories in SLA.

## Notes

1 Swain's hypothesis is also sometimes referred to as the Comprehensible Output Hypothesis.
2 Pushed output can be other-initiated, through interaction, or self-initiated when learners monitor their own output and self-correct.
3 I am grateful to Scott Aubrey for allowing me to use his data.
4 Corrective feedback can occur in both meaning-centred communication when learners perform tasks and in form-centred language exercises. I am only concerned with the former in this chapter.

# 8

# Cognitive aspects of second language acquisition

## Introduction

Cognitive SLA draws extensively on cognitive psychology to investigate the internal mechanisms and processes involved in the representation of L2 knowledge and the way in which the knowledge develops over time—i.e. acquisition. Eysenck (2001) described the subject matter of cognitive psychology in this way:

> ...the subject matter of cognitive psychology consists of the main internal psychological processes that are involved in making sense of the environment and deciding what action might be appropriate. These processes include attention, perception, learning, memory, language, problem solving, reasoning, and thinking. (p. 1).

Cognitive SLA is of course concerned primarily with two of the processes Eysenck mentions—learning and language—but, as we will see, these processes also involve other internal psychological processes. Cognitive SLA, then, is that branch of SLA that examines the mental processes involved in the acquisition of a second language.

## Paradigms in cognitive SLA

A paradigm is the set of practices that define a particular approach to investigating a given phenomenon (Kuhn 1962). These practices concern the kinds of questions that are asked, what kind of data needs to be collected to answer them, and how these data will be interpreted. Within cognitive SLA it is possible to distinguish two distinct paradigms: symbolism and **connectionism** (see Hulstijn 2002).

## Symbolism

Symbolist accounts seek to explain acquisition in terms of a set of abstract constructs—i.e. symbols—and the relationships between these constructs.

They draw on a range of constructs, different psycholinguistic and linguistic theories.

Examples of psycholinguistic constructs that figure in symbolist models are those introduced in the preceding chapter—input, comprehension, noticing, working memory, intake, acquisition, and output. Symbolist models are based on an **information-processing model** of language learning: we perceive features in our environment; we process them in our working memory and sometimes store them in long-term memory; and then use them in output. Information-processing models underscore the research on input and interaction, whilst linguistic constructs—which are derived from linguistic theory—are used to label the architecture of language. In the case of **Universal Grammar** (UG) they take the form of a set of highly abstract principles which constitute 'the mechanisms made available by the brain for building mental grammars for specific languages' (Hawkins 2001: 2). How language is represented in Universal Grammar is considered below.

## Connectionism

Connectionist accounts of language and L2 acquisition differ from both information-processing theories and UG. They have come to the fore in SLA in recent years, driven in particular by the work of N. Ellis. For connectionists such as Ellis there are no rules, only strengths of associations which merely give the impression of rules underlying behaviour. In connectionist accounts, language is represented not in terms of symbols and rules, but as associations of varying strengths, derived from elements encountered in the input. Knowledge of an L2 consists of the stored memories of previously experienced elements. Grammar emerges gradually out of the labyrinth of these stored associations when certain connections become well-established, leading to rule-like linguistic behaviour.

Information-processing theories, Universal Grammar, and connectionist theories all address how knowledge of a second language is represented in the human mind. I will begin, therefore, by examining how these cognitive theories account for L2 representation, including the crucial issue of how the mind stores two languages. I will then move on to consider the role of attention before turning to examine—more broadly—general cognitive theories of L2 acquisition. I will conclude the chapter with a brief look at the research methods that have been used to investigate cognitive aspects of L2 acquisition.

## The representation of L2 knowledge

It is generally accepted that there are two types of linguistic knowledge—implicit and explicit. Both symbolist and connectionist accounts view **implicit knowledge** as primary as it is the type of knowledge that is acquired naturally during L1 acquisition and is needed for fluent, easy communication. However, no cognitive account of L2 knowledge can be complete without also considering the learners' **explicit knowledge**.

## Implicit and explicit knowledge

The fundamental difference between implicit and explicit knowledge lies in whether learners are aware of what they know: in the case of explicit knowledge, learners have this awareness, but in the case of their implicit knowledge, they do not, even though their language behaviour may demonstrate that they have knowledge. Table 8.1 below provides a more detailed specification of the two types of knowledge.

Our knowledge of how to ride a bicycle or tie a shoe lace is implicit. We know how to do these, but would struggle to explain how. In contrast, our knowledge of history dates or of mathematical formulae is explicit: we can tell what we know. Likewise, in the case of language, we may be able to automatically add an -s to third person verbs in the present simple tense without any awareness that we are doing so, or we may consciously draw on a rule to remind ourselves that an -s is needed.

Our actual use of language—whether we are native speakers or L2 learners—can draw on both types of knowledge, but variably so, depending on the type of language use we are engaged in. In everyday conversation, we rely more or less exclusively on our implicit knowledge, but in academic

| Characteristics | Implicit knowledge | Explicit knowledge |
| --- | --- | --- |
| Consciousness | We are not conscious of what we know implicitly; implicit knowledge is only evident in communicative language use. | We have conscious knowledge about the 'facts' of language (e.g. the meanings of words and grammatical rules). |
| Accessibility | Implicit knowledge can be accessed effortlessly and rapidly; it is available for automatic processing. | Explicit knowledge requires controlled processing and thus can typically only be accessed slowly and applied with difficulty. However, with practice, access can be automatized. |
| Verbalization | Implicit knowledge cannot be verbalized unless it is made explicit; learners cannot tell what they know implicitly. | Explicit knowledge is often verbalizable; learners can report what they know. This calls for knowledge of the metalanguage needed to talk about language. |
| Orientation | Implicit knowledge is called upon when learners are oriented towards encoding or decoding the meaning of messages in communication. | Explicit knowledge is called upon when learners are formulating and monitoring sentences to ensure they conform to target language norms or because they lack implicit knowledge. |

*Table 8.1 Distinguishing implicit and explicit knowledge*

writing, we will probably also need to access our explicit knowledge. The kind of knowledge we utilize depends also on the extent of our implicit and explicit knowledge. L2 learners who have only experienced traditional form-focused instruction may have to rely on their explicit knowledge. In contrast, L2 learners who have picked up a language naturalistically may have very limited explicit knowledge and draw primarily on their implicit knowledge.

## Representation in information-processing models

The information-processing model that has proved most influential in SLA is Anderson's **Adaptive Control of Thought (ACT)** (Anderson 1980; 2005). At the level of representation, this model distinguishes 'declarative' and 'procedural' knowledge, which closely resemble the implicit/explicit distinction[1]. Anderson saw the differences between L1 and foreign language speakers in terms of the type of knowledge typically developed. He described foreign language learning in this way:

> We speak the learned language (i.e. the second language) by using general rule-following procedures applied to the rules we have learned, rather than speaking directly, as we do in our native language. Not surprisingly, applying this knowledge is a much slower and more painful process than applying the procedurally encoded knowledge of our own language.
> (1980: 224)

In other words, native speakers develop full **procedural knowledge**, whereas L2 learners rely more on **declarative knowledge** and may not attain the same level of procedural ability as native speakers. However, Anderson acknowledged that foreign language learners are able to use L2 rules without awareness.

Information-processing models draw on the idea of a limited 'processing capacity'. McLaughlin's Information-Processing Model of L2 acquisition (McLaughlin and Heredia 1996) proposes that learners are limited in how much information they are able to process at any one time. Like Anderson, he views language learning as skill-learning. Initially, a skill may be available only through controlled processing, which is demanding on the learner's processing capacity. Practice results in qualitative changes by enabling learners to assemble discrete elements into chunks, thereby facilitating automatic processing. In so doing, it reduces the burden on the learners' information-processing capacity.

These models are symbolic in that they conceive of language representation primarily in terms of rules that differ depending on whether they are subject to controlled or automatic processing. Skehan (1998), however, drew on the idea of limited processing capacity in a somewhat different way. He proposed that L2 learners possess two separate systems that coexist—a **rule-based system** and an **exemplar-based system** consisting of ready-made chunks. The rule-based system consists of powerful 'generative' rules and is utilized to compute complex and well-formed sentences. The exemplar-based system is required for fast, fluent, language use. Skehan argued that 'language users can move between these systems, and do so quite naturally' (p. 54) depending on the demands placed on their information-processing capacity.

These information-processing models differ in one key respect. Both Anderson and McLaughlin view the two types of knowledge as connected; that is, declarative knowledge requiring controlled processing transforms through practice into procedural knowledge, which is available for automatic processing. Skehan, however, views the two systems as distinct and disconnected[2]. These alternative positions regarding representation have implications for how learning takes place. Is procedural knowledge the same as implicit knowledge or is qualitatively different but functionally equivalent as suggested by Husltijn (2002)? Is explicit knowledge the starting point for acquiring implicit knowledge or do the two types of knowledge involve fundamentally different learning processes? We will revisit these questions later in the chapter.

## Representation in Universal Grammar

**Universal Grammar** was a term coined by Chomsky (1981) to refer to the abstract knowledge of language which children are claimed to bring to the task of learning their native language and which constrains the shape of the particular grammar they are trying to learn[3].

The theoretical case for Universal Grammar is based on a number of assumptions. First, it is argued that the grammar of a language is so complex that it is impossible for anyone to learn it simply through exposure to input and, thus, it is necessary to posit an innate capacity for learning language. The claim is that input alone cannot explain how children acquire their mother tongue and therefore the child must be equipped with knowledge that enables the deficiencies of the input to be overcome. Second, this capacity is highly specific in nature. That is, although it is clearly cognitive, it is a specialized cognitive resource, separate from the general cognitive apparatus involved in other types of learning. Third, Universal Grammar is biologically determined—i.e. it is only found in humans.

It should be clear that these assumptions are in direct opposition to those of information-processing models, which assume that input and practice suffice for learning a language; that the cognitive mechanisms involved are the same as those involved in any other kind of learning; and—that to some extent at least—these mechanisms can be found in other species—for example, chimpanzees.

What then is the nature of the abstract knowledge that comprises UG? The specification of this knowledge has changed as linguistic theory has developed over the years. According to one specification, UG consists of linguistic principles and parameters. Principles are the highly abstract properties that underlie the grammatical rules of all languages. Parameters define the restricted ways in which different languages vary. For example, all languages manifest the grammatical category of 'subject'. However, the 'null subject parameter' allows two settings—a plus and a minus setting—for this principle. In some languages, such as Spanish, the subject can be supressed—for example, 'Es el Presidente de los Estados Unidos'—whereas in other languages, such as English, it is required—'He is the President of the United States'.

According to UG, then, such principles and parameters are part of our innate knowledge about the forms that a specific grammar can take. In L1 acquisition, the task facing children is simply to discover which parameter settings apply in the language they are learning. The child 'knows' what the possible settings are. In SLA, one of the key questions is whether L2 learners have continued access to Universal Grammar. A number of different views have been advanced; L2 learners have (1) complete access; (2) no access; (3) partial access; and (4) dual access—i.e. adult learners have continued access to UG, but also make use of a general problem-solving module. More recently, however, SLA researchers have moved away from asking whether L2 learners have 'access' to UG and focused instead on 'the nature of the representations that L2 learners achieve' (White 2003: 27).

UG is a symbolist theory of implicit knowledge. It has nothing to say about explicit, metalinguistic knowledge. For this reason alone, it can provide only a very limited account of how knowledge is represented in the mind of the L2 learner. It is also limited in another way: it is a property theory and aims to provide an explanation of the ideal speaker's linguistic **competence**; it says nothing about how this competence is used in **performance** or how it differs in individuals. By distinguishing competence from performance in this way—and dismissing performance as of little or no relevance—it limits the role that experience of the L2 plays in the representation of L2 knowledge.

## Representation in connectionism

Like information-processing models, connectionist accounts of L2 representation make a clear distinction between implicit and explicit knowledge. They assume that 'humans have separate implicit and explicit memory systems, that there are different types of knowledge of and about language, that these are stored in different areas of the brain, and that different educational experiences generate different types of knowledge' (N. Ellis 2007: 18).

Connectionist accounts of language representation treat implicit and explicit knowledge as disassociated. Evidence for this comes from studies of aphasia and amnesia (Paradis 2004). In some cases, people lose access to their explicit memories, in others their implicit memories. An implication of this dissociation for SLA is that L2 learners will differ in the type of knowledge they acquire depending on their learning experiences. Learners with ample exposure to L2 input will be able to develop implicit knowledge. Those whose experiences consist primarily of explicit language instruction in a classroom context will develop explicit knowledge although—as Hulstijn (2002) pointed out—the learning processes responsible for implicit knowledge are unstoppable and so, even in a traditional classroom, some implicit knowledge is acquired. Some learners, of course, develop rich repositories of both types of knowledge.

Evidence concerning how different learning conditions—for example, education and access to English in the broader community—shape the type of knowledge L2 learners develop comes from a study of different groups of L2 learners by Philp (2009). Using a battery of tests designed to provide relatively separate measures of the two types of knowledge, Philp showed that a group of Malaysian students had developed high levels of both implicit and explicit knowledge, whereas many of the Chinese and Korean learners in her study demonstrated little implicit knowledge, but had high scores on the tests of explicit knowledge.

In connectionist accounts, implicit knowledge is conceptualized as a **complex adaptive system** that is in continual flux. It takes the form of an elaborate neural network comprised of connections between elements that do not correspond to any of the symbols or rules that figure in linguistic descriptions of language. To picture this, imagine a series of dots scattered over a page and a computer equipped with software for drawing lines between these dots. Over time, the software programme generates a maze of lines: some of them are faint—suggesting a low weight of connection—others are heavier—suggesting more firmly established connections. Some dots will be connected to only a few other dots, whilst others will be connected to a large number of other dots—some with faint lines, others with stronger lines. As the software continues to run, so the network of dots grows, gradually becoming more complex; new connections emerge, but also some old ones fade and eventually disappear. Of course, the software will need some input that will determine what lines to draw, where to draw them, how faint or heavy they should be, and when some of them should be eliminated. In the case of language, the input consists of the language learner's encounters with a particular language. The software corresponds to the human capacity to constantly and unconsciously register what has been selectively attended to in the input as the network develops.

It is common to talk of this kind of network as a 'system'. However, implicit knowledge can only be thought of as a 'system' in the sense that the patterns of connections that emerge become so well-established that they reflect (rather than represent) the categories and rules found in linguistic descriptions. What people learn and store in their implicit memories are 'memorized sequences' (N. Ellis 1996)—for example, the **formulaic sequences** which we noted are so characteristic of learner language in Chapter 4. Memorized sequences exist at every level: at the level of word (as a sequence of sounds); at the level of discourse (as sequences of ready-made lexical phrases); and at the level of grammar (as pre-set sequences of words). However, connectionist theories of language also allow for the emergence of abstract schema that are not exactly 'rules', but are 'rule-like'. The human capacity for language includes the ability to extract abstract categories from memorized sequences. These arise through the unconscious 'positional analysis of word order' (N. Ellis 1996: 100). That is, the emerging network recognizes that a certain type of element occurs in a specific slot in a set of formulaic sequences. This element then takes on an abstract value. So something resembling what we refer to as a 'verb' emerges when the network recognizes that words such as 'know', 'understand', 'want' are of the same type because they can all fill the empty slot in the sequence beginning 'I don't ...'. Similarly, something resembling a 'noun' emerges from the recognition that 'pencil', 'book', 'crayon', etc. can all complete the sequence 'Can I have a ...?'. As N. Ellis (1996) put it: 'the abstraction of these regularities is the acquisition of grammar' and formulas are 'the concrete seeds of abstract trees' (p. 111).

The process of abstraction is primarily unconscious. Learners, however, may choose to dwell on its products and formulate explicit rules to account for them. Thus, implicit knowledge—or rather the language usage that results from it—can serve as a basis for developing explicit representations. In this way, explicit knowledge of a language can arise inductively through the analysis of output derived from implicit knowledge. It can also be taught deductively—as is the case in much traditional language teaching. Explicit knowledge—whether arrived at inductively or deductively—is dependent on a different set of cognitive processes from those involved in implicit knowledge. It arises through the conscious identification of patterns which are stored as declarative representations.

## Summing up

In both symbolist and connectionist theories of language, the distinction between implicit and explicit knowledge is central. Furthermore, both paradigms view implicit knowledge as primary; it underlies our ability to use language effectively for communication. However, symbolist and connectionist theories afford different answers to a number of key questions.

1  Are the two types of knowledge distinct or closely related?
   In **Anderson's Adaptive Control of Thought Model**, declarative knowledge provides the basis for the development of procedural knowledge. Thus, the relationship between the two types of knowledge is continuous: there is no modularity. However—in both Skehan's Cognitive Theory and connectionist accounts—the two types of knowledge are seen as disassociated. In these theories, representation involves a dual system.
2  Are language systems symbolic or associative in nature?
   Both information-processing theories and UG view language as symbolic in nature. The categories and rules of linguists have some kind of psychological reality. **Information-processing models** also acknowledge an important role for exemplar-based representation and chunking, but view

these as distinct from the **rule-based system**. In **connectionism**, language systems are seen as a conspiracy of associations. Rule-like behaviour becomes evident only when more abstract linguistic schemata emerge out of well-established associations.

3  Are the cognitive mechanisms that underlie language specialized or general? **Universal Grammar** assumes that language involves a cognitive mechanism distinct from that involved in other types of learning. Principles and parameters are innately available to children. However, older L2 learners may have to rely on strategies of general learning. In contrast, in information-processing theories and connectionist theories, there is no distinct language 'module' in the brain. Knowledge is widely distributed in the same memory systems that store other forms of knowledge.

4  Is language an individual or a collective phenomenon? UG is focused on the **competence** of the ideal native speaker and thus takes no account of individual variability, which it views as a feature of **performance**. In connectionist theories, the linguistic systems that individuals build will differ in accordance with their varied experiences of the language they are exposed to. There is no such thing as an 'ideal native speaker'. However—given that individuals have similar experiences and a need for social identification—they will converge towards the representation of a communal language.

5  What is the relationship between 'learning' and 'representation'? UG is a property theory: it aims to specify the innate knowledge that learners must possess for learning a language, given the inadequacies of the input they are exposed to. In information-processing models, learning takes place when declarative knowledge transforms into procedural; the system changes as learning takes place. In connectionist accounts, there is no clear distinction between learning and representation. The network that houses implicit knowledge is constantly and dynamically evolving.

The differences between symbolic and connectionist models of representation make it unlikely that any integrated theory of L2 representation will arise in the near future. Both approaches continue to figure in SLA, but—as time passes—connectionist accounts are clearly assuming greater importance.

## Representation of two languages

L2 learners come to the task of learning an L2 with their L1 already firmly established in their minds. As we saw in Chapter 6, the effects of the L1 are substantial and ubiquitous. Here I will consider how two languages are represented in the mind and why it is so difficult for learners to establish the representation of a new language.

The first issue is whether the two languages are stored separately or together. Traditionally, two types of bilingualism have been distinguished. In co-ordinate bilingualism, the two languages are kept separate. The forms and meanings of words in the two languages are stored and accessed separately. In compound bilingualism, the two languages are fused in the brain; there is a single store of word meanings linked to separate word forms. It was claimed that co-ordinate bilingualism results when the two languages are learned separately and compound bilingualism when they are learned together.

Current research on bilingual representation indicates that the learner's L1 and L2 are not necessarily housed in separate stores. Paradis (2004) noted that both language systems are located in the same gross anatomical areas of the brain, but in distinct microanatomical subsystems within these areas. Dehaene (1999)—after reviewing the results of neurolinguistic studies of brain activation patterns—suggested that the extent to which the L1 and L2 systems are linked depends on the L2 learners' level of fluency. Highly fluent L2 users make use of the same micro-circuitry as native speakers, but less fluent L2 users rely on different neurological circuits. The degree of linkage, therefore, may depend on the learner's L2 proficiency.

The second and more crucial issue concerns the effect of the L1 on the development of L2 representations. N. Ellis (2006) draws on connectionist models of representation to explain why L2 systems are rarely (and, in the opinion of some, never—see discussion of the **Critical Period Hypothesis** in Chapter 2)—as fully developed as the L1 system. He draws on the key concept of 'learned selective attention' to explain how the L1 impedes the development of the learner's implicit system. Two general processes interfere with our ability to attend to new information. **Overshadowing** occurs when two cues are associated with an outcome and the more subjectively salient of the two cues overshadows the weaker. Overshadowing leads to **blocking** where the learner attends selectively to only the more salient of the two cues. Ellis' point is that L1 cues overshadow L2 cues and block attention. This explains why restructuring of existing categories is especially difficult.

A good example of blocking can be found in Jiang's (2000) account of L2 lexical representation. Jiang points out that semantic, syntactical, morphological, and phonological/orthographic information are all integrated in an L1 lexical entry and that—as a result—the activation of one aspect of an entry simultaneously activates the other aspects—for example, visual recognition of a word automatically activates its phonological representation. In contrast, an L2 lexical entry is tied to the semantic information of the equivalent L1 entry. Jiang argues that it is very unlikely that a new concept or new semantic information is created. The established L1 semantic system blocks the development of a separate L2 semantic system. He concludes that an L2 lexical entry initially contains only formal specifications—i.e. there is no semantic or syntactic information. The repeated association of the formal L2 lexical entry with the L1 lexical entry's meaning strengthens this link to a point where the semantic and syntactic information in this entry is copied into the L2 lexical entry. However, Jiang argues that it is rare that a point is reached where a fully integrated L2 lexical entry is achieved.

Blocking prevents learners from attending to cues in the input and results in L2 representations that are firmly tied to L1 representations. However, when no blocking occurs—for example, when the input provides evidence of a word's meaning for which there is no equivalent L1 representation—new wiring can ensue, and a separate L2 representation can develop. Evidence for this comes from the fact that phonemes that are dissimilar from L1 phonemes are easier to acquire than those that are similar (see Chapter 6). Explicit L2 knowledge can also help to overcome the blocking effect of the L1.

## Attention

Any discussion of the role played by **attention** in L2 acquisition must necessarily draw on a model of **working memory**. As previously explained (see Chapter 3), working memory is the limited capacity part of the human memory system that serves two different functions: it stores information temporarily in **phonological short-term memory**—or, in the case of orthographic information, in the visuo-spatial sketch pad—and it also binds this information with information from long-term memory in the central executive component of working memory. I will draw on this model to account for—and also try to reconcile—some of the conflicting views about attention in SLA.

I will refer extensively to the work of Schmidt on attention as this has proved seminal in SLA. Schmidt (2001) claimed that 'the orthodox position in psychology is that there is little if any learning without attention' (p. 16). He argued that an understanding of attention is necessary to understand just about every aspect of L2 acquisition, including interlanguage development; variability in learner language; L1 transfer; the role of individual differences; and how interaction facilitates acquisition—in other words, all the topics we have considered in previous chapters. However, not all SLA researchers are in complete agreement with Schmidt's views about the nature and role of attention.

### Key characteristics of attention

Schmidt (2001) identified six key characteristics of attention. These are summarized in Table 8.2. The broad picture is as follows. Attention takes place in working memory—wherein the learner selects which information to rehearse and supresses other information. Attention is required to process stimuli obtained from the input together with information accessed from long-term memory, and—since this process of reconciling the old with the new is the very stuff of learning—attention is a necessary condition of learning. Attention, then, involves much more than perception—i.e. the cognitive registration of a stimulus—it also involves establishing links with previously stored information.

| Characteristic | Description |
| --- | --- |
| Attention is limited | Attention takes place in working memory which is limited in capacity. That is, only limited amounts of information can be processed at one time. |
| Attention is selective | This is the corollary of the first characteristic. Because capacity is limited, it is necessary to allocate attention strategically. For example, if the learners' attention is focused on meaning, it may be difficult for them to simultaneously focus on form. (VanPatten 1990). |
| Attention is subject to voluntary control | Learners can decide what to focus their attention on. Voluntary attention is top-down and directed at outside events. However, there is also involuntary attention which is experience driven; learners can attend to elements of the output without having any intention to do so. |
| Attention controls access to consciousness | The role of attention is to bring stimuli or thoughts into awareness. The process of focusing attention on specific stimuli or thoughts gives rise to the subjective feeling of awareness (i.e. consciousness). |
| Attention is essential for the control of action | Novice behaviour requires controlled processing; expert behaviour can make use of automatic processing. Less attention is required for automatic than for controlled processing. |
| Attention is essential for learning | Attention is the mechanism that makes input available for further processing. However, not everything attended to enters long-term memory. Thus attention is essential for learning but does not guarantee it. |

*Table 8.2  Six key characteristics of attention (based on Schmidt 2001)*

## Two SLA theories of attention

There are a number of psychological theories that account for the role of attention in L2 acquisition. Two of these theories have been especially influential.

### Schmidt's Noticing Hypothesis

This was briefly introduced in Chapter 7 as it has informed research on the role of input and interaction. Schmidt's ideas about the importance of 'noticing' originated in his experiences of learning L2 Portuguese in Brazil (Schmidt and Frota 1986). Schmidt kept a diary to establish which features in the input he consciously attended to. His output was then examined to see to what extent the noticed forms turned up in his communicative speech. In nearly every case, the forms that Schmidt produced were those that he had previously noticed in the input. Schmidt also reported that he noticed the differences between his own attempt to produce Portuguese and the native-speaker input he was exposed to—a process he called **noticing-the-gap**.

The fullest account of the Noticing Hypothesis can be found in Schmidt (2001). He distinguished 'perception' and 'noticing'. He acknowledged that while perception need not involve consciousness, noticing is necessarily conscious. That is, while learners may be able to perceive elements in the input without conscious attention, they will not be able to process this information for storage in long-term memory unless they consciously attend to it. However, attention need not be intentional—i.e. learners may not deliberately set out to attend to some specific stimuli—it can also take place incidentally: for example, when linguistic forms have been noticed while learners are primarily focused on meaning. In either case, however, attention involves consciousness.

In his earlier publications, Schmidt promoted the strong version of the Noticing Hypothesis—learners can *only* learn what they have consciously attended. However, in his 2001 publication, he advanced a weaker version of the hypothesis: 'people learn about the things they attend to and do not learn *much* about the things they do not attend to' (p. 30; italics added).

## Tomlin and Villa's Theory of Attention

Tomlin and Villa (1994) distinguished three distinct attentional processes: (1) alertness, which involves a general readiness to deal with incoming stimuli and is closely related to the learner's affective/motivational state; (2) orientation, which entails the aligning of attention on some specific type or class of sensory information at the expense of others—for example, on form as opposed to meaning—and (3) **detection**, when the cognitive registration of a sensory stimulus takes place. It is during the last of these processes that specific stimuli are processed in working memory.

Tomlin and Villa went on to make two claims. The first is that detection can take place without alertness and orientation. In other words, learners can register an input feature even when they are not in an ideal state to attend and their attention is not focused on the feature in question. The second claim is that all three attentional processes can occur without awareness. Tomlin and Villa commented 'awareness requires attention, but attention does not require awareness' (p. 193).

These two theories are often presented as oppositional: Tomlin and Villa consider attention need not involve consciousness, while Schmidt argues that consciousness is a necessary condition of attention. However, a close inspection of these theories suggests that the differences are a matter of emphasis rather than absolute. 'Alertness' and 'orientation' seem to be closely related to the distinction that Schmidt makes between **incidental** and **intentional** learning. Learners may be alerted to attend to form and so will consciously orientate to specific aspects of the L2; this involves intentional learning. However, even if they are not alerted to attend to form and not oriented towards any specific aspect of the L2, incidental attention to form can occur. Finally, if 'detection' is equated with 'perception', then, the two theories agree that it can occur unconsciously, although Schmidt argues that acquisition generally requires conscious attention.

The main difference between the two theories lies in what happens when detection has taken place. Tomlin and Villa point out that detected information allows for further processing. However, they have very little to say about what learners do with the information they have detected, except to note that when particular exemplars are registered in memory, they can be 'made accessible to whatever the key processes are for learning, such as hypothesis formation and testing' (p. 193). Schmidt's notions of 'noticing' and 'noticing-the-gap', however, address not just 'detection' but also—crucially—what learners do with what they have detected. In this respect, the Noticing Hypothesis can be considered a fuller account of the role of attention in L2 learning.

## Detection

The key construct in both theories is **detection**. Detection is the cognitive registration of information in short-term memory. It can be seen as the first stage in a theory of attention. What is not detected cannot be subjected to further processing.

What do learners pay attention to when they detect elements in the input? Do they just detect linguistic exemplars, or do they also identify the symbolic category that an exemplar represents? For example—when exposed to the sentence 'I attended a wedding ceremony'—do learners simply take note of the *-ed* ending on the verb, or do they also recognize that *-ed* denotes the past tense for referring to a past action? There are, in fact, three possibilities: (1) learners only detect a form—for example, *-ed*—(2) they detect a form and map it onto the meaning that it conveys—for example, *-ed* denotes past time reference—and (3) they detect a form and also its metalinguistic category—for example, *-ed* constitutes a linguistic marker of the past tense.

Schmidt suggests that what learners detect is not the raw data or input, but is still concrete—they detect words and parts of words that serve as examples of categories such as noun, adverb, past tense, etc., but the exemplars they detect do not come with such labels. In other words, detection is local and non-metalinguistic. Learners register that the word 'gestern' in the German sentence 'Gestern regnete es' (literally, 'yesterday rained it') can appear at the beginning of this sentence, but may not register that 'gestern' is an adverb or that adverbs can appear as the initial word in a sentence in German. What learners detect in the input is individual tokens and their association with other tokens.

Less clear, however, is whether detection also involves **form-function mapping**. On this point, Schmidt appears to have changed his position. Schmidt (1994) argued that noticing refers 'only to the registration of the occurrence of a stimulus ... not the detection of form meaning relationships' (p. 179). However, Schmidt (2001) clearly sees noticing as involving form-meaning mapping. He comments: 'to acquire morphology ... one must attend to both the forms of the morphemes and their meanings and in order to acquire syntax one must attend to the order of words and the meanings they are associated with' (p. 31).

The Noticing Hypothesis is not without its critics. Truscott and Sharwood Smith (2011) pointed out the contradiction between Schmidt's early and later view about whether noticing entails form-meaning mapping. They also disputed his claim that detection—the registration of some feature of a stimulus—does not involve any abstract understanding of the feature. They commented that 'a pure case of noticing or apperception, with no understanding, is difficult to imagine' (p. 503).

## Executive control

To a large extent, the problems that Truscott and Sharwood-Smith identify with Schmidt's account of noticing can be resolved by distinguishing between 'detection'—the registration of some part of a stimulus—and 'cognitive manipulation'. Detection may indeed be a matter of just perceiving tokens in the input. If detection is a transitory phenomenon—dependent on phonological-short term memory—it is difficult to see how it can also entail symbol-recognition, which requires greater depth of processing. However—as Schmidt makes clear—noticing also entails executive control processes which, it can be argued, make possible form-meaning mapping, symbolic formation, and 'understanding'. Detection may occur consciously or unconsciously—as proposed by Tomlin and Villa—but it involves only shallow processing. In contrast, the complex processing involving the central executive will more clearly involve consciousness.

Information that enters short-term memory—i.e. is detected—may connect directly with long-term memory. However—as Robinson (2003) pointed out—this involves unaware recognition as it entails only matching what has been attended to with pre-existing knowledge. Thus, its function is to strengthen existing categories, but it is unlikely to lead to modification of these categories. However, when detected information is subjected to further processing in working memory, changes in long-term memory can occur. Robinson suggests that this involves **rehearsal** processes. He distinguishes two kinds: maintenance rehearsal and elaborative rehearsal.

Maintenance rehearsal involves data-driven, instance-based processing. Robinson does not explicitly say so, but potentially this allows for noticing-the-gap. By maintaining a chunk—for example, 'made me go'—in working memory and comparing it to a pre-existing chunk—'made me to go'—in long-term memory, the learner has the opportunity to notice the difference in the two chunks. This can lead to a weakening of the association between 'made me' and 'to go' in long-term memory and the formation of new connection between 'made me' and 'go'. In this way, learning takes place. Maintenance rehearsal, therefore, provides an opportunity for the **cognitive comparison**, which—as I have argued—allows for new learning to occur (R. Ellis 1994). Clearly, too, if the two chunks are juxtaposed in interaction—for example, when the learner's erroneous utterance is recast—maintenance rehearsal is made easier and cognitive comparison is more likely to occur.

Elaborative rehearsal involves conceptually-driven, schema-based processing. This is what leads to 'understanding' and explicit learning. The learner does more than simply attend to the difference between 'made me go' and the pre-existing construction 'made me to go'. Symbolic knowledge comes into play leading the learner to understand that the verb 'make' takes a bare infinitive not a *to* infinitive. Schmidt (1994) was hesitant to claim that noticing leads to awareness at the level of understanding in this way, but he did not rule it out.

## Factors affecting attention

Why do learners sometimes fail to attend to things in the input and their own output? Why do they attend to some elements in the input/ output and ignore others? What factors are likely to cause learners to pay attention?

In part, the answer to the first question lies in Tomlin and Villas' theory of attention. Attention is unlikely if learners are not alerted to attend. In other words, if—like Schmidt's Wes (see Chapter 4)—learners are not interested in becoming more grammatically correct and are adept at using existing linguistic resources to meet communicative needs, they will not be alerted to grammatical tokens in the input and—even if they do attend to them—will not engage in the rehearsal needed for learning. Orientation is also needed. Learners—like Wes—who are focused more or less exclusively on meaning, may extend their vocabulary, but are unlikely to pay attention to grammatical features. Working memory is limited in capacity and—as VanPatten (1990) showed—if learners attend to one aspect of language (for example, vocabulary) it is likely to be at the expense of some other aspect (for example, grammar).

Furthermore—as the above discussion of detection and executive control processes makes clear—what learners register and what they process in their working memory is influenced by their existing linguistic schemata. We have seen that L1 schemata block attention to L2 forms preventing detection and processing from taking place. L2 sounds—for example—are filtered through the L1 phonological system. Existing L2 schemata can also block attention to form–meaning mapping. In accordance with the One-to-One principle, (Andersen 1984) learners typically map a particular meaning onto a single invariant linguistic form (for example, they select a single pronoun form to express possession, irrespective of gender or number). This can block attention to variation in possessive pronoun forms in the input.

Some linguistic forms, however, are inherently less 'noticeable' than others. Redundant forms such as third-person -*s* in English are not detected in the input because they play no role in understanding the grammatical meaning of a sentence. Loewen, Erlam, and Ellis (2009) investigated whether learners who were exposed incidentally to an input flood of sentences containing third-person-*s* demonstrated any acquisition of this feature and found that they did not. Even features such as verb + -*ed* may remain unattended to if pastness is encoded by a more salient item (for example, an adverbial such as 'yesterday').

To explain why learners are predisposed to attend to some linguistic features rather than others VanPatten (1996) proposed a number of **input-processing principles,** which he claimed constitute natural processing tendencies that determine how learners allocate attention during online processing. Table 8.3 gives two of these principles. VanPatten has continued to work on these principles over time, modifying them slightly and adding to them. See for example VanPatten (2004b).

| Principle | Description |
| --- | --- |
| P1 | Learners process input for meaning before they process it for form. |
| P1 (a) | Learners process content words in the input before anything else. |
| P1 (b) | Learners prefer processing lexical items to grammatical items (for example, morphological markings) for semantic information. |
| P1 (c) | Learners prefer processing 'more meaningful' morphology before 'less or non-meaningful morphology'. |
| P2 | For learners to process form that is not meaningful, they must be able to process informational or communicative content at no (or little) cost to attention. |

*Table 8.3 Examples of input processing principles (Van Patten 1996: pp. 14–5)*

One factor that can induce noticing is the frequency with which linguistic forms appear in the input. N. Ellis (2002) argued that learners have a built-in capacity to 'count'—i.e. to register the frequency with which tokens and types occur in the input—and that every time a form is registered, some change in the learner's connectionist network takes place. However, frequency—i.e. **positive evidence**—does not guarantee noticing. As Ellis pointed out, the learner's L1 prevents learners from registering incidences of a token. The most frequent form in the input to English learners is the article 'the', but this form is late acquired and—in the case of many learners whose L1 lacks articles—may never be acquired. For some features, then, **negative evidence** may be needed. Negotiation involving **corrective feedback** that provides learners with negative evidence (see Chapter 7) may be crucial for ensuring that adult L2 learners pay attention to forms that would otherwise not be salient to them.

There are other ways of making features salient in the input and thus of increasing the chances they will be attended to. In Chapters 10 and 11, we will examine the roles played by **explicit** and **implicit instruction** in enabling learners to focus their attention on specific linguistic features in both the input and their own output.

## Summing up

What can reasonably be concluded about the nature of attention and its role in L2 acquisition?

1. **Attention** is a complex construct. It involves both **detection**—i.e. the registration of attributes of a stimulus—and what Robinson (2003) calls **rehearsal**. Detection involves short-term memory and may not lead to rehearsal. Rehearsal allows for connections to be made between what has been registered and existing L2 knowledge, as in **noticing-the-gap**.
   For some—for example, Schmidt—attention is necessarily a conscious process: it involves **noticing**. For others—for example, Tomlin and Villa—however, it can take place without consciousness. I have tried to reconcile these different positions by suggesting that whether attention is conscious or not depends on whether it entails only detection or also complex processing.
2. Learners detect exemplars of symbolic categories, not the categories themselves. However, category formation can arise in working memory as a result of rehearsal.
3. Attention can lead to changes in both **implicit** and **explicit knowledge** systems. Elaborative rehearsal is needed for the development of explicit representations.
4. Attention is involuntary—i.e. it happens without any intention on the part of the learner—but can also be voluntary—i.e. learners can consciously elect to attend.
5. In the case of involuntary attention, input frequency—i.e. positive evidence—drives attention but learners' natural processing tendencies (for example, VanPatten's **Input Processing Principles**) and the **blocking** effect of the L1 can prevent detection occurring.
6. Interaction that involves negotiation—especially **corrective feedback**—provides learners with **negative evidence** that may be necessary for some linguistic forms—i.e. those that are redundant or non-salient—to be noticed.
7. Instruction that directs learners' conscious attention to linguistic forms can also help to overcome the limitations in detection.

I have two further points to make—one generally recognized, the other more speculative. First, not everything that is processed in short-term or complex working memory results in observable changes in interlanguage. Second—more speculatively—the different processes involved in detection and rehearsal may account for differences in how children and adults process input. Children detect but are less likely to rehearse. Adults with their more developed working memory are more likely to rehearse what they detect. Perhaps it is children's rich capacity for detection that enables them to develop native-like competence in an L2. In contrast, the adult's complex processing of input leads to a faster rate of learning initially, but also interferes with the **implicit learning** required for achieving full competence.

## Cognitive theories of L2 acquisition

Cognitive theories of L2 learning address how attention leads to change in L2 representations and therefore draw heavily on the constructs and research I have considered in the previous sections of this chapter. I begin by considering how implicit and explicit learning differ and then move on to skill-learning theory and Processability Theory. I will conclude by examining Complex Adaptive System Theory.

## Implicit and explicit L2 learning

There are two different traditions in cognitive SLA research. One has investigated the difference between **incidental** and **intentional learning** and the other between **implicit** and **explicit learning**. Incidental acquisition occurs when learners 'pick up' linguistic features from input. Much of the research we considered in Chapter 7 examined incidental acquisition. Intentional learning occurs through the learners' deliberate efforts to learn a specific feature. Implicit learning is generally defined as learning that occurs without intention and without awareness although—as we have already seen—there are differing views about whether any learning without some level of awareness is possible. Explicit learning involves reflection about language that leads to 'understanding'. Here I will focus on research that has addressed implicit/ explicit learning.

Research on implicit/explicit learning began with a series of studies by Reber (for example, Reber 1976; Reber, Walkenfeld, and Hernstadt 1991). In these studies, the implicit learning condition involved asking people to memorize a set of letter strings generated by an artificial language. In the explicit condition, they were asked to figure out the underlying rules of the same letter strings. Both groups then completed a judgement test where they had to decide if the strings of letters followed the same rules as the strings in the learning conditions. The main findings of these studies were: (1) there was clear evidence of implicit learning—i.e. learning without awareness; (2) there was no difference between the test scores of the implicit and explicit learning groups in the case of simple rules, but implicit learning proved more efficient for complex rules; and (3) the test scores of the explicit group demonstrated much greater individual variation than those of the implicit group—reflecting the mediating role of the learner's analytical skills. It should be noted, however, that—because the artificial grammars that Reber used in his studies were purely formal in nature—his research only addressed whether people can learn linguistic form implicitly, not whether they can learn how form maps onto meaning.

Other cognitive psychologists have also disputed Reber's claim that learning can occur without awareness. The main problem in resolving this issue lies in the way in which learning is measured. Learning without awareness is generally considered to be evident if learners demonstrate learning in a judgement test following training but are unable to report on what they have learned. Shanks (2003), however, argued that a better measure of awareness is reaction time at the point of learning—i.e. during training. He concluded that when this measure is used, there is no clear evidence of null-awareness. Current work in cognitive psychology—for example, Rebuschat 2013—is directed at identifying valid ways of determining whether learning involves awareness. Similar work is taking place in SLA—for example, Leow and Hama 2013. I address methodological issues involved in investigating implicit learning in a later section in this chapter.

A number of SLA studies claim to provide evidence of learning without awareness. Foremost among these are studies conducted by John Williams and his co-researchers—for example, Williams 2005; Leung and Williams 2011. However, such studies continue to be criticized on the grounds that they do not clearly distinguish between learning as a process and learning as a product and that to convincingly show learning without awareness it is necessary to examine the cognitive processes involved at the point of learning. DeKeyser (2003) reviewed a number of L2 studies of implicit learning and concluded 'there is very little hard evidence of learning without awareness' (p. 317). As we have seen, Schmidt (2001) reached a similar conclusion.

However, if implicit knowledge is seen as consisting of a complex of weighted connections between neurons that do not encode symbolic categories—as in connectionist models of representation—it is difficult to see how else knowledge can develop other than through implicit (unaware) learning. Similarly, if learners consciously set about trying to learn a grammatical rule, explicit learning is clearly involved. In other words, distinguishing implicit and explicit learning at the theoretical level seems unproblematic. The problem arises because implicit and explicit processes are intertwined in any use of language, with some types of use—for example, carefully editing a piece of writing—drawing heavily on explicit processes and other types—for example, free conversation—drawing on implicit processes. As learning takes place through language use, implicit and explicit processes are potentially always involved.

This is the position that N. Ellis (2005) evinces when he talks about the 'collaborative mind'. He accepts the disassociation of the implicit and explicit processing systems, but also recognizes that they are 'dynamically involved together in every cognitive task and in every learning episode' (p. 340). According to N. Ellis, learning commences with the explicit representation of a formula—a holistic form that encodes a particular semantic or pragmatic meaning. At this point, learning is a conscious process. However, once a form–meaning conjunction has been established, noticing is no longer necessary and the pattern-recognition mechanisms of connectionist memory involved in implicit learning automatically take over. Gradually more abstract schema evolve as chunks are subconsciously analysed.

In Chapter 1, we examined a number of **interface positions**. The **non-interface position** (Krashen 1981) claims that 'acquisition'—i.e. implicit learning—and 'learning'—i.e. explicit learning—are distinct processes. This is compatible with the N. Ellis' claim—as he acknowledges. However, the other claim of the **non-interface** position, namely that 'acquisition' and 'learning' are unrelated and that the products of 'learning' play no role in 'acquisition' are clearly incompatible with Ellis' position, which is more supportive of a **weak-interface position**. I too have argued for this, claiming that the interface arises when learners bring their explicit knowledge to bear on processing input and monitoring their own output (R. Ellis 1993)[4]. If we accept that the mind is 'collaborative' in the way N. Ellis proposes, then a non-interface is not defensible. However, acknowledging a role for explicit processes does not necessitate abandoning the distinction between implicit and explicit learning and implicit and explicit knowledge.

There is, however, another interface position—the **strong interface position** – that draws on a symbolist rather than connectionist model of language representation and perceives of language learning as a type of skill learning.

## Skill-learning theory

**Skill-learning theory** draws on the distinction between declarative and procedural knowledge and between controlled and automatic processes discussed earlier in this chapter. It is a symbolist theory. It has provided a justification for the **presentation-practice-production** (PPP) so popular in language teaching (see Chapter 10).

The theory claims that language learning is like any other form of learning. It involves a progression from an initial **declarative knowledge** stage involving controlled processing, to a final stage where knowledge is automatic. L2 learners proceduralize their declarative knowledge through extensive practice. DeKeyser (2007) defined practice as 'specific activities in the second language, engaged in systematically, deliberately, with the goals of developing knowledge of and skills in the second language' (p.1). However, DeKeyser (1998) argued that the transformation of declarative knowledge into **procedural knowledge** is only likely to occur when the cognitive operations involved in the practice activity match those in natural communication. That is, it requires practice activities that involve 'real operating conditions' and not just decontextualized mechanical practice.

Skill-learning theory, as explained by DeKeyser, is in part compatible with the idea of **Transfer Appropriate Processing** (TAP)—the fundamental tenet of which is 'that we can use what we have learned if the cognitive processes that are active during learning are similar to those that are active during retrieval' (Lightbown 2008: 27). Lightbown suggests that this can explain why linguistic forms learned in isolation are not available for use in communicative interaction.

When learners experience having to use linguistic forms in communication, deeper processing occurs than when attention is purely on surface form. TAP serves as a rationale for communicative and task-based language teaching. However, it does not constitute a clear justification for PPP, as it makes no claims about a direct link between declarative and procedural knowledge and, in this respect, differs from skill-learning theory.

In another respect, however, skill-learning theory and TAP are more clearly in line. According to skill-learning theory, the knowledge that characterizes the later stages of development—i.e. the procedural stage—is highly specific and so does not transfer to tasks that are dissimilar from those used to develop the knowledge. In other words, the effects of practice are skill specific: practice in listening improves listening, but does not assist speaking and vice versa. This claim directly contradicts VanPatten's (1996) views about input-processing, according to which practice in comprehending the meaning of specific grammatical structures leads to restructuring of the interlanguage system which can then be drawn on for both reception and production. Skill-learning theory predicts that there is no single knowledge store, but rather different knowledge stores that support receptive and productive language skills. VanPatten's theory—and, one might add, connectionist accounts of L2 representation—suggest a single store, drawn on irrespective of the language skill involved.

Skill-learning theory is perhaps best seen as explaining how declarative knowledge becomes automatized rather than how explicit knowledge transforms into implicit. It is difficult to see how skill learning can account for the sequences of acquisition we discussed in Chapter 4 if the starting point is symbolic knowledge of linguistic rules, and if there is no allowance for the automatic tallying of information in implicit learning[5]. DeKeyser (2009) appears to acknowledge this when he comments that it may be the case that 'highly automatized knowledge is still not necessarily qualitatively the same as implicit knowledge' (p. 127). He does suggest, however, that such knowledge is functionally equivalent to implicit knowledge—i.e. it enables learners to perform in a near-native way.

## Processability Theory

A brief account of **Processability Theory** was provided in Chapter 4. Central to the theory is the claim that the processing strategies are hierarchical in nature and mastered one at a time. As Pienemann (2005: 13) put it 'it is hypothesized that processing devices will be acquired in their sequence of activation in the production process'. Thus, the failure to master a low-level procedure blocks access to higher-level procedures and makes it impossible for the learner to acquire those grammatical features that depend on them. The theory, then, focuses on production, but has nothing to say about how L2 forms enter the interlanguage system. It was designed to explain the sequence of acquisition of grammatical structures in learner language (see Table 4.5 in

Chapter 4). Pienemann (2005) claimed 'once we can spell out the sequence in which language processing routines develop we can delineate those grammars that are processable at different points of development' (p. 2).

Following extensive research into the developmental sequences of different languages, Pienemann (2005) proposed the hierarchical processing routines shown in Table 8.4. The strength of Processability Theory is that it provides not only an explanation for attested sequences of acquisition, but also has predictive power. The cognitive dimension afforded by the identification of underlying processing strategies and operations allows researchers to form hypotheses regarding which grammatical structures will be acquired at different stages of development.

The theory claims that the processing operations are specific to language—rather than of a general cognitive nature—and in this respect, differs from connectionist theories. Pienemann (2011) argued that grammatical processing takes place in a 'grammatical memory store'. He also proposed that the grammatical memory store was part of procedural—rather than declarative—memory. In other words, Processability Theory is a theory of implicit rather than explicit learning.

| Level | Routine | Structures |
|-------|---------|-----------|
| 1 | word/lemma | Production based entirely on words/ formulaic chunks which are invariant in form. |
| 2 | category procedure (lexical category) | Production based on lexical entries that are now annotated with a number of diacritic features (e.g. 'possessive' and 'number'). |
| 3 | phrasal procedures (head) | Production of grammatical phrases that involve matching one element with another now occurs. At this level, learners can handle such structures as articles, plural agreement, and 'do' fronting (e.g. 'Do he like it?'). |
| 4 | s-procedure and word order rule | Production involving the exchange of information *between* structural phrases is now possible. The learner can exchange information between a noun phrase and a verb phrase as required for subject-verb agreement (e.g. 'Mary lives in London'). |
| 5 | matrix/subordinate clause | The final procedure to be acquired enables learners to process the word order of subordinate structures such as that found in embedded questions in English (e.g. 'He asked where I lived'). |

*Table 8.4 Processing routines involved in the production of different grammatical features*

Processability Theory is limited in a number of ways. It relies on emergence as the criterion of acquisition—i.e. a feature is considered acquired when it first appears in learner production—and thus does not account for how learners achieve gradual control over a grammatical structure. Also, it does not account for how learners develop receptive knowledge of grammatical structures. The major limitation, however, is that it tells us nothing about how learners obtain **intake** from input, and how this is then used to construct and restructure internal grammars. However, the theory is useful in that it complements other theories—such as Van Patten's Input Processing Principles—that focus exclusively on input-driven learning.

## Complex adaptive systems and L2 acquisition

Finally we turn to a group of theories: the **Competition Model, Complexity Theory, usage-based theories, Dynamic Systems Theory**. As these have in common the idea that language is a **complex adaptive system** I will not consider each of these theories separately but instead consider the general principles that underlie all of them. The theories all draw heavily on connectionist and emergentist models. That is, they reject the idea of a **language acquisition device** and top-down, rule-symbolic processing and instead assert that linguistic systems emerge gradually, driven by the exemplars people are exposed to in social interaction, which are processed by domain-general cognitive mechanisms such as those that regulate attention. I will consider what is meant by 'complex' and 'adaptive' and in what sense a 'system' arises.

### L2 systems are complex

Like any complex adaptive system, everything in an L2 system is interconnected:

> Complexity theory aims to account for how the interacting parts of a complex system give rise to the system's collective behaviour and how such a system simultaneously interacts with its environment.
> (Larsen-Freeman and Cameron 2008: 1).

Larsen-Freeman and Cameron noted that the term 'complex' does not just mean 'complicated', but also refers to the idea that 'its behaviour emerges from the interactions of its components' (p. 2). A complex adaptive system is complex in the sense that it includes social, psychological, and linguistic components all interacting with each other. An implication for the study of L2 acquisition is that one component of the complex system (say grammar) cannot be understood in isolation from other aspects.

The components of a complex system are in competition with each other. Beckner et al. (2009) suggest that there is 'a tug-of-war of conflicting interests between speakers and listeners' (p. 18). Speakers prize production economy whereas listeners want clarity and explicitness. Beginner L2 speakers necessarily simplify (see Chapter 4), but are under pressure to make the meanings of their messages more explicit to meet the needs of their listeners. Thus there is competition between the need to simplify and the need to elaborate the L2 system.

There is also competition within the L2 system. The **Competition Model** (MacWhinney 2001) takes its name from the 'competition' that arises from the different devices or cues that signal a particular language function. For example, in a sentence like 'Mary bit the dog', there is competition between 'Mary' and 'dog' for the role of agent. Semantic expectancy would suggest that 'dog' is the agent but word order indicates that 'Mary' is the agent. The crucial clue in English is word order, which overrides semantic expectancy, but in other languages—for example, Japanese—semantic expectancy or morphological features constitute the stronger cue. L2 learners are influenced by their L1 processing strategies. For Japanese learners to overcome their natural tendency to assign agency on the basis of semantic expectancy, they need to attend to the word order cue to identify 'Mary' as the agent of the sentence. Research has shown that the processing strategies utilized by L2 learners are located somewhere on a continuum between the strategies required to process the input and the strategies of the L1 (Harrington 1987).

A final note: the complexity of a system makes prediction difficult, if not impossible. Just as it is impossible to make reliable predictions about what the weather will be like at any one moment in a particular location, so it is impossible to predict how the interlanguage of an individual learner will develop over time. As Larsen-Freeman (1997) put it 'the best we can do is to explain the occurrence of change *a posteriori*, not actually look at the language and make exact predictions of what change will transpire next' (p. 148).

## Systems are adaptable

Any linguistic system is open rather than closed. It is constantly changing as a result of the interactions among the components. This is what makes precise predictions difficult as it is not possible to foretell with accuracy how the individual L2 learner will respond to the configuration of elements in the system. A good example of a system's adaptability is Dörnyei and Ottos' (1998) process model of motivation (see Chapter 3). L2 learners' motivation undergoes constant change in response to a variety of influences—for example, their subjective values and norms; their learning experiences; and their perceptions of their progress.

The adaptability of a system is never-ending. Beckner et al. (2009) noted that 'even adult grammars are not fixed and static but have the potential to change with experience' (p. 7). L2 grammars are inherently unstable. Thus, from the perspective of a complex adaptive system, **fossilization** is not possible, although periods of **stabilization** can arise. The human brain never ceases responding to the linguistic environment and some change—however small—in the language network will occur.

Evidence for the adaptability of systems comes from **usage-based theories** of grammar. These propose that the organization of a grammar is based directly on the learner's experience with the language. From this perspective, grammar is a process rather than a product. At any one moment in its evolution, it contains memories of how words co-occurred in the interactions the learner participated in and, also, of the probabilities of their occurrence and co-occurrence. Subsequent usage brings about change in these memories.

A central claim of complex adaptive systems theory is that higher-level properties arise from the interaction of lower-level properties and these higher-level properties are gradable rather than categorical. Consider, for example, how learners learn to attach an -*s* to the third person singular of present tense verbs in English. Initially, they develop memories of combinations of third-person pronouns and verb + -*s* (for example, 'he comes', 'she works'). However, at this point the learner may still fail to produce third-person -*s* verbs following noun subjects (for example, * 'John come', * 'Mary work'). Pronouns belong to a closed class, whereas nouns are members of an open class. As a result of differences in input frequency and contingency, the learner more readily establishes an association of pronoun + verb + -*s* than one between noun + verb + -*s*. A higher order category emerges out of the memories of pronoun and specific verb combinations—i.e. 'he/she' + verb + -*s*—leading to regular use of -*s* following a pronoun. However, this falls short of a still higher-order category that can account for all cases—i.e. subject + verb + -*s*—which in some L2 learners never emerges[6].

## Unstable systems

In what sense, then, can a complex adaptable system claim to be a 'system'? The essence of a system is that its parts are constituted in such a way that the behaviour that results from the system is systematic. However, as complex adaptable system theories make clear, much of the behaviour that results from the system is non-systematic and chaotic. In Chapter 5—where I introduced **Dynamic Systems Theory**—we saw that chaotic variation—what I called 'free-variation—is endemic. But if variation is entirely chaotic, there would be no basis for claiming that there is a 'system'. The solution to this problem is to propose that—although systems are in flux resulting in unpredictable behaviour—from time to time, they settle into **attractor states**. De Bot and Larsen-Freeman (2011) defined an attractor state as 'the state the system prefers to be in over other states at a particular point in time' (p. 14). Thus, when a complex system evolves into an attractor state, systematic behaviour—probabilistic rather than categorical—will arise until further experience leads to further change. The **Basic Variety**—i.e. the highly simplified system that beginner learners construct—can be seen as an attractor state. For some learners, it constitutes a stable state, but they can escape from it if the learning conditions change and promote greater attention to formal accuracy. No state is fixed.

An implication of complex adaptive systems theory is that the systems that individual learners build are different. Learners develop idiolects that reflect their own specific language learning experiences. This raises two key issues. First, if learners' systems are all different, how does a communal language— i.e. a shared linguistic code—develop? Second, if learners' systems are idiolects, to what extent is it possible to claim that interlanguages manifest universal properties?

Beckner et al. (2009) provide an answer to the first question. They argue that while there will be linguistic differences in the connectionist networks of individual learners, reflecting the particular interactions they have participated in, commonalities will develop because to a considerable extent their experiences will be similar—for example, in terms of the frequency with which specific linguistic forms appear in the input—and also because of the inbuilt human tendency to converge towards, rather than diverge from, the usage of our interlocutors (Giles 1971). In other words, we need to talk about both 'interlanguages'—the systems of individual learners—and 'interlanguage'—the general properties of the systems of all learners.

Of course, it is only possible to talk about 'interlanguage' as opposed to 'interlanguages' if there are some properties that are universal. In Chapter 4, we provided evidence that there are indeed universal properties: for example, in the progression from the Pre-Basic to a Post-Basic variety and in the stages of acquisition that learners pass through in acquiring L2 negation. Complex adaptive systems theory acknowledges these universal properties. They can be explained in terms of the attractor states that arise in the course of acquisition. However, stages of development are not neat, encapsulated affairs. Learners do not progress abruptly by abandoning an earlier stage in favour of a later one. Development is gradual and dynamic, characterized at each stage by variability, some of it chaotic. Also, care needs to be taken not to overstate the universality of developmental patterns. As de Bot, Lowie, and Verspoor (2007) noted 'it is very well possible that if we look close enough, the general developmental stages individuals go through are much less similar than we have assumed so far' (p. 19).

Complex Adaptive Systems Theory has implications for how L2 acquisition needs to be investigated. The focus needs to be on individual learners rather than groups. Learners need to be studied longitudinally so that the path of development can be carefully plotted. Attention needs to be given to the fine details—i.e. variation, including chaotic variation, cannot be ignored as messy 'noise'. Also—ideally—the L2 learner needs to be investigated holistically to capture the nature of the interactions between the components of the system. A simplistic linear relationship between a cause and an effect is not possible.

To some extent, the research to date adheres to these research ideals. However, researchers have not yet found a way of investigating the totality of a system by taking into account the social, psychological, and all the linguistic components of the system. Rather, they have focused quite narrowly on specific linguistic properties of systems in much the same way as researchers with different theoretical leanings have done. Larsen-Freeman (2006) readily admitted that 'the issue of finding a suitable methodology with which to capture the "fuzziness"... and dynamism of language development is a challenging one' (p. 594). It would seem, then, that researchers are stuck with looking at relatively discrete parts of an L2 complex adaptive system.

## Researching cognitive processes in SLA

Finally, I turn to briefly consider some of the ways in which SLA researchers have investigated cognitive processes—which are of course not available to direct observation. We cannot see in the minds of the L2 learners, but only observe their behaviours and infer the processes involved. In Chapter 7, we considered the methods used by researchers to investigate what learners take from the interactions they participate in—**stimulated recall,** for example. Here I will focus on three other ways of investigating cognitive processes.

## Modelling L2 acquisition

Modelling is a tool that has figured strongly in cognitive SLA. In some studies, computer models have been built to simulate what occurs during actual learning tasks and to examine whether the learning outputs of these models accord with those reported in descriptive L2 studies. A good example of this approach can be found in Nelson (2013). He devised a computer simulation of lexical learning to test the theoretical claim that there is a clear distinction between the storage of the phonological/orthographic form of a word and its meaning—as proposed in Jiang's (2000) model, which we considered earlier in the chapter. The simulation involved feeding in translation pairs (English–Spanish)—along with 48 other words that were related either formally or semantically—in 'training runs'. The results of the simulation gave support to the separation of form and meaning representations. Nelson argued that computer-simulations of this kind can be used to test the claims of symbolic models of L2 representation.

## Neuropsychological research

**Neuropsychological SLA** aims to identify the neurological mechanisms and circuits in the brain that are responsible for regularly occurring linguistic behaviour. It raises the possibility of matching cognitive constructs and neurological activity. Two different approaches can be distinguished: neurolinguistic studies examine how damage to different parts of the human brain affects a person's ability to use an L2, whilst neurobiological studies use techniques for measuring brain imaging or electrical activity in the brain to establish which parts of the brain are activated when L2 learners undertake different tasks.

Neurolinguistic studies have shown that implicit and explicit memory function separately—as claimed in cognitive SLA. Ullman (2001) reported that neurological impairment to different parts of the brain results in differential loss of these two memory systems. For example, the implicit/procedural memory system is damaged in the case of Parkinson Disease, while the explicit/declarative memory system is impaired in Alzheimer's Disease. Damage to one system does not lead to a loss of functions associated with the other system. Paradis (2004) reviewed studies of bilingual aphasic patients and concluded that loss of implicit memory did not prevent access to explicit knowledge. Interestingly, such people generally struggled to communicate in their L1—which he suggested was because they had minimal explicit knowledge of their L1. In contrast, they were better able to use their L2 because of their more developed explicit knowledge in this language.

Neurobiological studies also support a two-system account of language functioning. Ullman (2001) provided evidence to show that the brain consists of two largely separate systems—the lexicon and the grammar, each with distinct neural bases. He illustrated this model with reference to the processing of English regular and irregular past tense verbs forms. He proposed that procedural memory is needed for the computation of regular morphological features—for example, 'mov*ed*'—while declarative memory handles irregular forms—for example, 'ate'.

Neurobiological studies have also investigated the mechanisms involved in attention. In this case, however, it has proved difficult to establish the specific mechanisms involved. Suchert (2004), for example, concluded that the psychological distinctions between attention, perception, cognition, and action have no biological correlates and that attention is 'an ongoing, interactive process that defies singular definition' (p. 173). The distributed nature of attention allows for an interface between explicit/declarative and implicit/procedural memory. Recently activated neurons in explicit memory may remain primed and become active again when exposed to subsequent stimuli that are the same or related. In this way, the learning of a grammatical rule that is held in explicit/declarative memory can exert an influence over the processing of L2 input and output.

Neuropsychological SLA research is still in its infancy and in many cases the evidence it has provided is mixed—making it difficult to reach clear conclusions. However, the research does demonstrate quite clearly that there is no biological correlate of **Universal Grammar**. Language functions are highly distributed in the brain. It also lends clear support to the neurological separation of explicit/declarative memory and implicit/procedural memory. As Schumann (2004b) pointed out, the value of the neuroscientific approach to SLA lies in the constraints it imposes on the metaphors used to explain L2 acquisition.

## Eye-tracking

One of the most recent methods employed to investigate cognitive processing is **eye-tracking** (see Winke, Godfried, and Gass 2013). Eye-tracking machines have been used to investigate the cognitive processes involved in attending to visual information—for example, when reading texts in the L2. This involves examining the fixations—i.e. the words a learner fixes attention on—and saccades—i.e. the movement of the eyes from one location to another. Movement is typically in a forwards direction but sometimes regressions—i.e. backward movements—occur. The length of time that learners spend on a particular word or phrase and the number of regressions to that word indicates the extent of the learners' attention to it.

Winke (2013) used eye-tracking to investigate what effect **input enhancement** has on learners' attention to English passive constructions in a text. Her results showed that the enhanced forms were attended to more than unenhanced forms—i.e. the learners spent more time fixating on them and rereading them—but that this was not found to promote learning. One interpretation of this study is that—although detection of the highlighted forms took place in short-term memory—little complex processing in working memory took place.

## Conclusion

In this chapter, I have tried to survey the rich body of theory and research on cognitive aspects of L2 acquisition. It is not easy to reach clear conclusions given the multitude of perspectives evident in SLA and their obvious differences: cognitive SLA is replete with conflicts. Nevertheless, there does appear to be a growing consensus about a number of issues. I will conclude this chapter by summarizing where there is consensus and pointing out where theoretical differences continue to exist.

1   There is general agreement—and clear evidence—to support the existence of two separate linguistic systems, variably referred to as explicit/declarative and implicit/procedural. There is also general agreement that it is the implicit/procedural system that is primary and that the main goal of SLA is to elucidate how this system works and how it is acquired.

2   There are—however—different views concerning the nature of the implicit/procedural system. According to Universal Grammar (a symbolist theory), implicit knowledge of grammar takes the form of highly abstract properties that are innate and domain-specific and that make possible the acquisition of the grammar of specific languages. According to connectionist theories, implicit/procedural knowledge takes the form of an elaborate and highly-interconnected network, the nodes of which do not correspond to any linguistic categories. Connectionist theories claim that language learning draws on the same cognitive apparatus as any other kind of

learning. In this chapter, I have emphasized the connectionist perspective as this is clearly gaining ground in SLA. However, the debate about whether language learning involves domain-specific or domain-general mechanisms continues. Processability Theory, for example, assumes a domain-specific set of processing procedures to account for the acquisition of L2 grammar.

3 Information-processing and connectionist theories recognize the importance of both explicit/declarative systems and implicit/procedural systems. Both acknowledge that receptive and productive language use draw on these systems; both recognize that L2 acquisition involves both systems; and both see the implicit/procedural system as primary.

4 However, information-processing and connectionist models differ in two key respects. First, Skill-learning Theory and Processability Theory—both information-processing theories—assume skill specificity: that is, they maintain that different systems underlie receptive and productive language use and learning. Connectionist theories, however, assume that learners draw on a single network. Whilst Skill-learning Theory proposes a direct interface between declarative and procedural knowledge, in connectionist models, the interface is only indirect—i.e. explicit knowledge fine-tunes the processes involved in the development of implicit knowledge. If proceduralized explicit knowledge is indeed functionally equivalent to implicit knowledge—as DeKeyser (2003) claims—it is difficult to see how the various positions can be tested empirically.

5 All cognitive theories—with the exception of Processability Theory—emphasize the importance of attention for language learning. They draw on a model of working memory to explain the role that attention plays. Because working memory capacity is limited, L2 learners (especially those of low L2 proficiency) experience difficulty in attending simultaneously to both form and meaning and are likely to prioritize one over the other. They employ top-down processes when processing for meaning, but need bottom-up processing to process and acquire linguistic forms.

6 Theories differ in terms of whether they see attention as a conscious process—what Schmidt called 'noticing'—or as unconscious—as in subliminal learning. In this chapter, I have suggested that both are possible. Detection of exemplars—but not of symbolic categories—takes place in phonological short-term memory. This can occur unconsciously: what is detected can feed directly into the implicit system. However, when complex processing takes place in working memory—when detected information is rehearsed and compared with information in long-term memory—consciousness is involved. Complex processing contributes to both explicit and implicit systems.

7 Various factors influence whether and what learners attend to in the input: the learner's alertness and orientation; the learner's working memory capacity; the intrinsic properties of specific linguistic features—for example, their salience and frequency in input—the learner's natural default processing strategies; and the correspondence between L2 and L1 forms.

8  Two types of learning can be distinguished—implicit and explicit. Implicit learning can occur without awareness. Explicit learning always involves awareness. The main area of controversy concerns whether learning without any awareness is possible. This reflects the disagreement about the nature of attention and its role in learning—see point 6. To resolve this controversy, some researchers have argued that it is necessary to demonstrate whether awareness is demonstrated at the point of learning—i.e. during training—and not just in a post-test that measures whether any learning occurred.

9  Ideally, a complete cognitive theory of L2 acquisition needs to account for both how input is processed and how output is produced. Both play a role in L2 development. Currently, however, different theories deal with these two key aspects of L2 acquisition separately. The most complete theory to date is one that views the L2 system as a dynamic adaptive system. Theories that draw on this concept emphasize the interconnectedness of the components that comprise the system and its emergent nature. Usage-based accounts of L2 acquisition acknowledge the importance of accounting for both how input is processed and output is produced.

10  All cognitive theories acknowledge the important role played by language transfer. There is general recognition that the L1 can inhibit the development of the L2 system by blocking detection and influencing executive processing.

Understanding L2 acquisition necessarily involves the study of the cognitive processes involved. No theory of L2 acquisition is complete without an explanation of how the L2 is represented in the mind of the learner, the role played by attention in reception and production, and the processes that can account for interlanguage change. Equally, however, no theory can ignore the importance of the social context of learning. In their exposition of complex systems, Larsen-Freeman and Cameron (2008) emphasized that 'the social dimension of language is indispensable' (p. 126). However—by and large—the theories I have addressed in this chapter focused on the cognitive aspects of L2 acquisition rather than the social. In the next chapter, I will examine the body of research that has given precedence to the social dimension of L2 learning.

# Notes

1  Eysenck (2001) noted that 'it remains the case that declarative memory resembles explicit memory, in that it involves the **integration** or linkage of information' while 'procedural memory still resembles implicit memory'. (p. 213).

2  Pinker (1999) also argues for a dual-mode system. He claimed that regular morphological features such as past tense -*ed* in English involve rule-based or symbolic processing, whereas features that are not constrained by readily identifiable rules—such as irregular past tense forms like 'swam'—are stored as items.

3 In an earlier version of UG, Chomsky referred to the 'language acquisition device', which he claimed was necessary to explain children's ability to acquire the grammar of their mother tongue.

4 The **interface hypothesis** continues to be debated. Paradis (2009), for example, critiques N. Ellis's **weak-interface position** on the grounds that the acquisition of implicit knowledge involves entirely unconscious processes and therefore excludes conscious 'noticing'.

5 DeKeyser (2007) only makes a limited claim for Skill-Learning Theory, namely that it best accounts for the early stages of acquisition, adult learners with above-average aptitude, and instructed learners.

6 See Chapter 5 for R. Ellis's (1988) account of learners' following pronouns and nouns.

# 9

# Social aspects of second language acquisition

## Introduction

In Chapter 5, we saw that it was necessary to consider social factors to account for variability in learner language and in Chapter 7, we saw that social interaction plays an important role in acquisition. In general, though, the perspective so far has been a cognitive one. Social factors were only invoked to account for how learners obtained input and to explain the characteristics of their output. No consideration was given to the possibility that language learning itself is essentially a social rather than a cognitive enterprise.

The turn of the last century saw a strongly argued critique of cognitive SLA emerge. Firth and Wagner (1997) criticized the predominant cognitive model on the grounds that it was 'individualistic and mechanistic' and 'failed to account for the interactional and sociolinguistic dimensions of language' (p. 285). They considered such an approach 'flawed' and sought to reconceptualize SLA in terms of an integrated account of the social and cognitive dimensions of L2 use and acquisition. Atkinson (2002) pointed out that 'just as surely as language is social, so is its acquisition' (p. 527). Block (2003) noted that mainstream studies of L2 acquisition typically failed to provide rich descriptions of the learners under study and there was a 'certain monolinguistic bias' (p. 33) in the assumption that the learners have a single L1 which remains intact despite contact with the L2. In short, what Block called 'the social turn' had very clearly arrived in SLA.

## Two senses of 'social context'

But what exactly does it mean to talk about the 'social turn' in SLA? In what sense is L2 acquisition a social rather than a cognitive phenomenon? To answer this question, it is helpful to distinguish two different senses in which acquisition can be viewed as social. Central to both is the notion of **social context**. Siegel (2003) distinguished a structural view of social context where social factors such as power and prestige are seen as *determining* the context in which learners learn and an interactional view where social context is seen as *constructed* dynamically in each situation. Applied to SLA, this suggests two ways of investigating the 'social turn':

1 By examining how social factors impact on the individual learner's acquisition of an L2. In such a view, social factors are seen as just affecting the learner's access to input (see Chapter 7) and the learner's motivation to learn (see Chapter 3). In this view, social factors do not alter the cognitive/psychological processes responsible for acquisition but merely influence the data made available to the learner and the learner's propensity to make use of the data.

2 By viewing learning itself as primarily a social activity—albeit one that involves cognitive processes. This view sees learning as embedded in the processes by which social contexts are constructed through interaction. In other words, learning is no longer seen as essentially an individual, cognitive affair but as a participatory and social affair.

It is this latter sense of the 'social turn' that critics of cognitive SLA have promoted and which is the focus of this chapter. However, my starting point will be SLA research based on a structural view of social context and its role in L2 acquisition. This research predated the later research and thus—from a historical perspective—is an appropriate starting point. I will then move on to examine in some detail the objections to 'cognitive SLA' and consider the alternative social (and social-cognitive) theories that this critique gave rise to.

## Social factors and L2 achievement

The social context in which learners live and work has an effect on how successful they are in learning an L2. This is especially true of learners in a second language context—i.e. a context where the majority or official language is the target language as in the case of L2 learners of English who are living in the United States or United Kingdom. However, it is also true of learners in a foreign language context (i.e. a context where the target language is not the official or majority language as, for example, with Chinese learners of English in China). In both cases, social factors determine the opportunities that learners have to engage with the L2 and their motivation to do so.

The two theories I will now consider focus respectively on the role of social factors in second language settings and foreign language classrooms.

## Schumann's Acculturation Model

Schumann's **Acculturation Model** aimed to account for the variable success of immigrants in second language settings. The key concept was 'acculturation'. As Schumann (1978a) put it:

| Learner's background | Alberto was a 33-year-old lower middle class Costa Rican working in a factory in the USA with other non-native speakers of English. He lived within a small Spanish-speaking minority in a Portuguese area. |
| --- | --- |
| Data collection | Three types of audio recorded data were collected:<br>1 spontaneous speech recordings of conversations with the researcher<br>2 experimental elicitations (e.g. transforming a positive into a negative utterance)<br>3 pre-planned sociolinguistic interactions involving taking Alberto to parties, restaurants, and sports events in order to collect speech in varied natural situations. |
| Analysis | The analysis focused on specific grammatical structures (e.g. negatives, interrogatives, and auxiliary verbs). It involved **frequency analysis** (see Chapter 4). |
| Main findings | Alberto showed very little linguistic development during the period of study—for example, his negatives were predominantly of the 'no' + verb type ('I no use television'), a large proportion of his interrogatives were not inverted ('Where you get that?'), and only one auxiliary (copula *is*) was mastered. In short, Alberto's English was 'pidginized' (i.e. manifested the same features as pidgin languages). |
| Discussion | Schumann considered a number of factors that could explain Alberto's lack of development. He dismissed ability and age as factors and instead examined the factors that could result in **pidginization**. Schumann also suggested that Alberto experienced substantial psychological distance (for example, displayed negative attitudes and little motivation to learn English). |

*Table 9.1 Schumann's (1978b) study of Alberto*

…second language acquisition is just one aspect of acculturation and the degree to which a learner acculturates to the target-language group will control the degree to which he acquires the second language (1978a: 34).

Schumann focused on one of the six learners (Alberto) studied by Cancino, Rosansky, and Schumann (1978). Whereas the other five manifested considerable development over the ten-month period of the study, Alberto did not advance in most of the structural areas Schumann investigated. Table 9.1 provides a summary of Schumann's ten-month study of Alberto.

The extent to which learners acculturate determines the level of their **social distance** from the target language community. Schumann identified a number of social factors that influence the degree of social distance:

1 Social dominance—i.e. whether the L2 group is politically, culturally, technically, or economically superior (dominant), inferior (subordinate), or equal to the target language group.

2 Integration pattern—i.e. whether the L2 group assimilates (gives up its own lifestyle and values in favour of those of TL group), seeks to preserve its lifestyle and values, or acculturates (adopts lifestyle and values of TL group while maintaining its own for intra-group use).

3 Enclosure—i.e. the extent to which the L2 group shares the same social facilities (low enclosure) or has different social facilities (high enclosure).

4 Cohesiveness—i.e. the extent to which L2 group is characterized by intra-group contacts (cohesive) or inter-group contacts (non-cohesive).

5 Size—i.e. whether the L2 group constitutes a numerically large or small group.

6 Cultural congruence—i.e. whether the culture of the L2 group is similar or different from that of the TL group.

7 Attitude—i.e. whether the L2 group and TL group may hold positive or negative attitudes towards each other.

8 Intended length of residence—i.e. whether the L2 group intends to stay for a long time or a short time.

A learning situation can be 'bad' or 'good' (Schumann 1978a) depending on social distance. Overall, Alberto's situation was a bad one: he belonged to an L2 group that was socially inferior to the TL group; neither his group nor the target language group sought assimilation; his L2 group was characterized by high enclosure; the L2 group was relatively cohesive and large; the level of cultural congruence was not high; negative attitudes predominated in both groups. As a result, Alberto did not acculturate and had very little need to communicate with members of the TL community.

While the Acculturation Model affords a convincing explanation of Alberto's lack of progress in learning English, a true test of the theory would require proof that learners who vary in the extent of their social distance also vary in the extent to which they acquire the L2. A number of studies (see Schumann 1986b) attempted to show this, but with mixed results. One reason for this lies in the difficulty of measuring the social variables that are claimed to influence acculturation. Apart from the problem of obtaining reliable measures of each social factor, there is no principled way of weighting the different variables. Another problem with the theory is that it has nothing to say about how social factors influence the *quality* of contact that learners experience. The model is premised on the assumption that social distance determines the *quantity* of contact. Finally, the theory is clearly deterministic; that is, social factors determine the extent to which learners participate (or do not participate). It takes no account of learner agency—i.e. the ability of learners to confront and overcome potentially negative social conditions through their own actions.

## The Socio-educational Model

**The Socio-educational Model** was introduced briefly in Chapter 3. In contrast to the Acculturation Model, it was developed to explain L2 learning in classroom settings, in particular the foreign language classroom. The model is socio-psychological in nature—it sought to relate social and psychological factors to explain differences in L2 achievement—and was based on the importance that Gardner (1985) attached to 'integrativeness' (i.e. the individual's willingness to identify with members of the target language group). The model plots the connections between four aspects of L2 learning: (1) the social and cultural milieu; (2) **individual learner differences**; (3) the setting, and (4) learning outcomes. It proposes that L2 learning—even in a classroom setting—is not just a matter of learning new information but of 'acquiring symbolic elements of a different ethnolinguistic community' (Gardner 1979: 193).

Our primary interest here lies in the role the model attributes to the social/cultural milieu. It predicts that the relationship between the social/cultural milieu and L2 achievement is an indirect one. Factors in the social and cultural milieu are seen as causally related to 'integrativeness', which—in turn—is causally related to motivation and—via this—to achievement. Gardner's research (for example, Gardner 1985) lends support to the basic claim of the model, namely that there are identifiable causal paths between the different components of the model. Social factors impact on the nature and level of the individual learner's motivation, which in turn affects achievement.

Missing from the model, however, is any account of how particular social factors operative in a social/cultural milieu influence attitudes. In this respect, the socio-educational model is much more limited than the Acculturation Model. Like the Acculturation Model, however, the Socio-educational Model is deterministic. There is no allowance for the possibility that learners can themselves influence their social/cultural milieu.

## SLA—a cognitive or a social enterprise?

Both the Acculturation Model and the Socio-educational Model are *de facto* input-output models. That is they assume that L2 learning is a mental phenomenon involving individual learners. Learning is conceptualized in terms of 'success' and 'achievement' with social factors having an indirect effect through learners' access to input and their motivation to make use of it for learning. This is a position that has been challenged by post-modernist accounts of L2 acquisition which dispute the existence of a simple linear relationship between social context and learning.

### Critiques of cognitive SLA

One of the first critiques of cognitivist SLA was Firth and Wagner (1997). They claimed that there was an imbalance in SLA research in favour of cognitive-oriented theories and methodologies and argued that there was a need to reconceptualize SLA as a more balanced enterprise by acknowledging the social dimension of L2 acquisition. They suggested that this required three major changes:

> (a) a significantly enhanced awareness of the contextual and interactional dimensions of language use, (b) an increased emic (i.e. participant-relevant) sensitivity towards fundamental concepts, and (c) the broadening of the traditional SLA data base.
> (Firth and Wagner 1997: 286)

In relation to (a), they emphasized the importance of recognizing that meaning 'is not an individual phenomenon consisting of private thoughts executed and transferred from brain to brain, but a social and negotiable product of interaction, transcending individual intentions and behaviours' (p. 290). They objected, for example, to the input modification studies we considered in Chapter 7 on the grounds that there is no such thing as a base-line way of talking and interacting. They also challenged the assumption that talk involving L2 learners is inherently problematic, arguing that what cognitivist researchers view as deviant and problematic forms may simply reflect learners' resourceful and strategic use of their available linguistic resources. They emphasized the need to consider the 'local agenda' that figures in specific interactions rather than applying a pre-determined universal model for the **negotiation of meaning**.

In relation to (b), they challenged the status of some fundamental SLA concepts—in particular those of 'native speaker' and 'non-native-speaker'. They argued that these terms ignore the participants' own sense of social reality. When learners speak, they do not do so as 'non-native speakers' but as a friend, a guest, an expert or a novice, a stranger, etc. Similarly, when so-called native speakers talk to learners they do not do so as native speakers, but from whatever social identity is relevant to the social context.

'An approach that takes the participants' own perspective into account—i.e. an emic approach—requires acknowledging that they have particular social identities which shape how specific encounters unfold. They also rejected the view of the learner as a 'defective communicator' that is implicit in cognitive-interactionist SLA.

For Firth and Wagner (1997), the traditional SLA data base is overly narrow as it consisted mainly of interactions from a laboratory or classroom setting. They argued that the L2 is a means of participating in a whole range of different social contexts, with typical encounters involving multilingual participants communicating with each other for social purposes. Thus, it is necessary to investigate how learners communicate in real-world situations. This criticism of cognitivist SLA, however, is perhaps less valid for—as we have seen—there has been plenty of research that has drawn on a rich, 'naturalistic' data base, including Schumann's study of Alberto; the European Science Foundation work on the basic variety (see Chapter 4); and—from a structural perspective—the work on variability in learner language (see Chapter 5).

Like Firth and Wagner, Block (2003) sought to broaden the scope of SLA by adopting a more interdisciplinary and socially-informed approach. He critiqued the way that the terms 'second', 'language', and 'acquisition' are conceptualized in the input-output model of L2 acquisition. He argued that the term 'second' fails to capture the experiences of multilingual speakers and proposed that a better term would be 'other' or 'additional'[1]. Block pointed out that in mainstream SLA 'language' has been interpreted as referring to **linguistic competence** and that it has failed to examine **communicative competence**. He noted that 'acquisition' has been understood in terms of **information-processing models** (as we saw in Chapter 7) and that such models typically fail to recognize that the processes involved are social and external as much as they are mental and internal. Above all, Block argued for rich, contextualized descriptions of learners and the interactions they participate in.

It is important to note, however, that both Firth and Wagner and Block did not reject the importance of cognitive aspects of L2 acquisition. Firth and Wagner concluded their article by emphasizing that language is both a social and a cognitive phenomenon and that what was needed was to investigate 'how language is used *as it is being acquired* through interaction' (p. 296, italics in original). Block considered it possible to integrate information processing and sociocultural approaches in a single theory. However, by and large the 'social turn' has prioritized the social over the cognitive.

## Responses to the critique

Firth and Wagner's (1997) article led to a number of responses published one year later in *The Modern Language Journal*. Some of these responses (for example, Rampton 1998) were clearly sympathetic to Firth and Wagner's position whilst others were dismissive. The central point of contention was the site of acquisition. Is acquisition a matter of taking in and thereby possessing knowledge of the L2? The term 'acquisition' implies this—i.e. that we can 'acquire' a language in the same way we acquire a house or car. Alternatively, is acquisition best conceived of as 'participation'—the taking part in social activity, which becomes the site of learning? It was this latter view of acquisition-as-participation that was the focus of the objections. Long (1998), for example, argued that changes in the social setting have not been shown to have any effect on the way in which learners acquire an L2 (for example, no differences in error types or developmental sequences are evident). In a similar fashion, Gass (1998) argued the approach that Firth and Wagner advocated 'is not actually part of SLA, but part of the broader field of L2 studies' (p. 84). She emphasized the need to distinguish 'participation' and 'acquisition'. In effect, Long and Gass simply reasserted the legitimacy of the input-output model and SLA as a branch of cognitive science.

## Summarizing the differences between cognitive and social SLA

This debate is on-going. Table 9.2 provides a summary of the principal differences between cognitive and social SLA. As Larsen-Freeman (2007) noted these paradigms are both internally consistent and 'exist in parallel worlds' (p. 781).

| Dimensions | Cognitive SLA | Social SLA |
|---|---|---|
| Scope | Focus on the universal aspects of L2 acquisition. Priority is given to linguistic competence. | Focus on the discursive characteristics of interactions involving L2 learners and how learning of both the micro and macro aspects of language is embedded in these interactions. |
| Social context | The structural view is dominant—the social context determines the L2 data made available to the learner and the learner's attitudes to learning. | The interactional view is dominant—the social context is seen as jointly constructed by the participants through interaction. |
| Learner identity | The learner is viewed as a 'non-native speaker'. Learner identity is static. | The learner is viewed as having multiple identities that afford different opportunities for language learning. Learner identity is dynamic. |
| Learner's linguistic background | The learner has full linguistic competence in his/her L1. | Learners may be multilingual and may display varying degrees of proficiency in their various languages. |
| Input | Input is viewed as linguistic 'data' that triggers acquisition. | Input is viewed as contextually constructed; it is both linguistic and non-linguistic. |
| Interaction | Interaction is viewed as a source of input and an opportunity for output. | Interaction is viewed as a socially negotiated event and a means by which learners are socialized into the L2 culture. |
| Research methodology | Methodology is quantitative and confirmatory—inquiry is seen as 'scientific' and value-free, aimed at testing specific hypotheses with a view to making generalizations. | Methodology is qualitative and interpretative—emphasis is placed on uncovering the 'local agenda' through detailed analysis of naturally-occurring interactions. Learning is demonstrated by tracking specific learning objects over time to demonstrate that change has occurred. |

*Table 9.2  Cognitive and social SLA compared*

So far, we have painted a picture of social SLA as a uniform approach, but in fact there are a number of different theories that lay claim to being 'social'. To some extent, these theories do share a common epistemology, as portrayed in Table 9.2: in particular, they all provide socially-oriented explanations of language learning; they all aim to provide local, situated accounts of learning; and they all reject the cognitivist view that 'use' and 'acquisition' are distinct. However, as Atkinson (2011b) pointed out, these theories have been developed in isolation from each other, drawing on very different epistemological bases. One clear difference lies in how the theories conceptualize 'language'. In some of the theories, the focus is on how learners use and acquire specific linguistic features and—in this respect—they accord with cognitive approaches. In other theories, however, the emphasis is more on the learner's social world—how relations of power affect opportunities for language learning or on how social forms of knowledge needed to become a member of a language community are developed. I will begin by examining theories that are clearly socio-cognitive in nature and conclude with theories that are more purely social.

# Sociocultural SLA

Sociocultural accounts of L2 acquisition pre-dated the advent of the 'social turn' in SLA: the first (Frawley and Lantolf) appearing in 1985. Lantolf—the person most closely associated with sociocultural SLA—was also one of the first to critique the competence-performance dichotomy that lies at the heart of cognitive SLA. In Lantolf (1996), for example, he disputed the idea of the human mind as 'containing' the knowledge that results from processing linguistic input and argued for broadening the scope of SLA by 'letting all the flowers grow'. Subsequently, however, Lantolf has single-mindedly promoted sociocultural SLA and challenged many of the precepts on which cognitive SLA is based, including what he called the **Universal Acquisition Hypothesis** (Lantolf 2011), namely the claim that the acquisition of L2 grammar follows a natural and universal route (see Chapter 4).

## Vygotsky

**Sociocultural SLA** draws extensively on the work of the Russian psychologist Vygotsky (1978). Whereas Piaget saw cognitive development as involving progression through a set of universal and biologically determined stages—analogous, in some ways, to the order and sequence of development in L2 acquisition we examined in Chapter 4—Vygotsky viewed development as arising out of the interaction between biologically endowed abilities and culturally organized artefacts. Our biological inheritance equips us with lower mental functions of the same kind as are found in some primates; our higher mental functioning, however—for example, memory, attention, rational thinking—develops through the 'interweaving of our cultural and biological inheritances' (Lantolf and Thorne 2006: 59). Sociocultural theory aims to explicate the nature of this 'interweaving'

For Vygotsky, then, the pattern of cognitive development is not predetermined as the potential always exists to bring about cognitive change through external means. In his own research with children, Vygotsky emphasized the importance of examining what children do when they are given a task that is beyond their current level of development along with some form of external assistance to help them solve it. His interest lay in studying how children make use of this assistance and how over time they internalize the assistance to the point where they no longer need it.

Drawing on these ideas, sociocultural SLA has focused on learning-as-a-process rather than leaning-as-a-product by investigating the use that learners make of the assistance available to them. Learning is both a social and cognitive process in sociocultural theory because new concepts (including new linguistic forms) originate in social interaction and are only subsequently internalized as mental schemata.

## Mediation

Lantolf and Thorne (2006) define **mediation** as 'the process through which humans deploy culturally constructed artefacts, concepts, and activities to regulate—i.e. gain voluntary control over and transform—the material world or their own and each other's social and mental activity' (p. 79). Mediation involves the use of 'tools' that help learners to perform a task which they cannot perform successfully with their existing linguistic resources.

Let me give an example. A beginner-level learner was shown a card depicting a man holding an umbrella with rain falling onto the man inside the umbrella and asked to say what is wrong with the picture. The learner lacked the vocabulary to accomplish this task. The learner might have made use of a 'culturally constructed artefact'—a bilingual dictionary—to access the necessary L2 vocabulary to mediate her performance of the task. However, this was not available. Instead, she performed the task with the help of her teacher. In other words, the mediation took the form of social activity. Extract 1 below shows what transpired. The learner demonstrated independent control only over one of the words she needed to perform the task ('man') but the teacher helped her to produce two other key words—'raining', which she repeated after the teacher, and 'umbrella' which she was able to say with the help of a prompt from the teacher. In socio-cultural terms, we can see learning-as-a process taking place. Interestingly, when this learner performed the same task two weeks later, she was able to produce both 'raining' and 'umbrella' without assistance from the teacher. In other words, she had now gained 'voluntary control' over the use of these words. We see here how the **other-regulation** evident in Extract 1 transformed into **self-regulation** at a later time. Clearly, though, further mediation was needed to enable this learner to perform the whole task successfully.

**Extract (1)**

1 T   Look at this one.
2 L   Man and a...
3 T   What's it doing?
4      It's...
5      It's raining.
6 T   Huh?
7 L   Raining.
8 T   Raining.
9 T   What's the man holding in his hand?
10 T   D'you know what this is called?
11      Begins with 'u' – 'um...'
12 L   *(sounds of trying to remember)* Umbrella.
13 T   Umbrella, yes.
14 T   And where's the rain coming from?
15 L   Water.
16 T   Water yes. Where from?
17 T   Is it inside or outside the umbrella?
18 L   No.
19 T   Yeah, should be outside, yes?

Social interaction serves as the primary means for mediating learning. In the case of the example above, the mediation was provided by an expert (i.e. a teacher), but learners can also mediate each other's learning. Ohta (2001) identified four major mediating devices that learners use: waiting; prompting; co-construction; and explanation. In a study of peer interaction in a Japanese as a foreign language classroom in the United States, Ohta found that 'peer interlocutors tend to provide their partners with ample wait time' (p. 89). Prompting was a more explicit technique involving repeating a word or syllable just uttered, thereby helping the interlocutor to continue. Co-construction consisted of one learner contributing some linguistic material (a word, phrase or grammatical particle) to complete another learner's previous utterance. Explanations, often provided in the L1, were used to address errors the partner had made.

Individual learners can also mediate their own L2 use and learning through **private speech**. Ohta (2001) defined private speech as 'audible speech not adapted to an addressee' (p. 16). She suggested that it can take a number of forms including imitation, vicarious response as when a classroom learner produces a response to a question the teacher has addressed to another learner, and mental rehearsal. The defining characteristic of private speech is not whether it is silent but whether it is self-directed. Children frequently resort to talking to themselves, even when they are in the company of others (Saville-Troike 1988). Adults do this too, but, in many cases, their private speech is silent. L2 learners may resort to the use of their L1 in self-directed speech[2].

There is a close relationship between social and private speech. Lantolf (2011) explained the relationship in this way:

> In its communicative function, language entails interaction between 'I' and 'You'. Eventually, however, a new function emerges, in which conversation becomes intrapsychological, i.e. between 'I' and 'Me', where 'I' formulates plans and makes decisions and 'Me' (the counterpart of 'You' in social interaction) evaluates, critiques, and revises these as necessary (pp. 25–6).

This quotation reveals two important points. Firstly, both social and private speech are forms of interaction. However, there are differences: private speech is not constrained by the same norms that affect social speech; even if learners can use the correct target language forms in social speech, they may not do so in self-directed speech. Thus what may appear to be 'errors' may simply be the private forms that learners use in their struggle to maintain control over a task (Frawley and Lantolf 1985). The second point is that interpersonal mediation through social talk serves to establish intrapersonal mediation through private speech (i.e. what requires social mediation at one time can be handled by means of private speech at a later time). Perhaps, though, the reverse is also possible. Learners may rehearse privately before attempting social speech. In a study of Japanese children in an American kindergarten, Saville-Troike (1988) found that only those children who engaged actively in self-directed talk for a period went on later to participate in social talk.

There is also another type of mediation—concept mediation. Lantolf (2011) defined concepts as 'the meanings that cultures construct to make sense of the world' (p. 32). He distinguished two types of concepts: every-day/spontaneous concepts and scientific concepts. The former are learned by observing entities and events as these appear to our senses in the social world. They involve only superficial learning as the concepts so attained operate below the level of full consciousness: the vocabulary learning that took place in Extract 1 above might be considered an example of this. In contrast, scientific concepts are highly explicit and available for conscious manipulation and analysis. Their power lies in their generative capacity i.e. they are generalizable across diverse situations. Unlike everyday/spontaneous concepts, scientific concepts require some kind of educational intervention such as **concept-based instruction** where learners are given very precise 'scientific' descriptions of grammatical rules to mediate their learning (see Chapter 10).

To sum up, all learning is mediated. That is, learning is initially an external phenomenon that is other-regulated and only later becomes internalized when self-regulation takes place. Thus, the primary focus in research in sociocultural SLA is on the process by which concepts are mediated. Different types of mediators have been identified: cultural artefacts (such as dictionaries); social interaction; private speech (itself an internalized form of social interaction); and scientific concepts made available through education. Primary among these is social interaction. As Lantolf (2011) put it, 'mediation is realized through social, largely communicative interaction' (p. 37).

## Zone of Proximal Development

There are two levels of development: 'the actual developmental level, that is the level of development of the child's mental functions that has been established as a result of certain already completed developmental cycles' (Vygotsky 1978: 85) and the level of potential development as demonstrated in problem solving undertaken with the assistance of an adult (an expert) or through collaboration with peers (novices). There is also a third level where a particular mental function lies beyond the learner, even if mediation is available. The Zone of Proximal Development (ZPD) is the second of these levels; the level of potential development. To use Vygotsky's own metaphor, it is the 'bud' rather than the 'fruit' of development.

The ZPD is a key construct in sociocultural theory. It works 'by achieving through collaborative mediation what is unachievable alone' (Lantolf 2011: 29). In other words, the ZPD is not so much a cognitive level present in the mind of the learner, but a socially constructed activity. As Newman and Holzman (1997) put it 'the ZPD is not a place at all; it is an activity....' (p. 289). Thus, it is not equivalent to the built-in syllabus that the learner is pre-ordained to follow, as claimed by some cognitively-oriented researchers (for example, Corder 1967; Krashen 1981). There are of course developmental limitations on the possibility of constructing a ZPD with a learner, but these are not universal; they vary from one learner to another. Success in constructing a ZPD depends very much on the quality of the mediation provided. The ZPD, then, far from supporting the **Universal Acquisition Hypothesis**, actually challenges it.

Aljaafreh and Lantolf's (1994) study of **corrective feedback** illustrates the application of the ZPD in SLA (see Table 9.3). Lantolf (2011) listed the important findings of this study: (1) It showed that different learners benefit from qualitatively different types of mediation (i.e. more implicit or explicit corrective feedback) for the same grammatical structure; (2) individual learners may require different types of mediation for different grammatical features depending on their developmental level; (3) mediation needs to be withheld sometimes to establish whether learners have achieved independent control over a feature; and (4) evidence that learning has occurred consists of showing that a lower level of mediation (in this case, more implicit corrective feedback) can achieve **other-regulation** than at an earlier time (when more explicit feedback was needed). This last point is of special importance as it offers a radically different view of what learning involves to the standard cognitive view which emphasizes the importance of demonstrating (often through tests) that a learner has achieved full independent control over a linguistic feature.

| Purpose | To investigate how the negotiation of corrective feedback in the ZPD promotes learning |
|---|---|
| Participants | Three students with different levels of L2 proficiency enrolled in an eight-week ESL writing-and-reading course; a researcher who was not an instructor. |
| Procedures | The students wrote an initial essay which was used to identify grammatical structures that were problem areas. Students then wrote a number of essays and participated in one-on-one tutorials with the researcher. Before the tutorials began, the students were asked to underline any errors and correct them if they could. The tutorials consisted of the researcher working collaboratively with the students to help them correct the errors. |
| Corrective feedback | The nature of the corrective feedback the researcher provided was not pre-determined. Rather the researcher worked collaboratively with individual students to help them self-correct their errors. This typically involved beginning by directing the learner's attention to a sentence containing an error and asking a general question (e.g. 'Do you notice any problem here?') If this failed to elicit a self-correction, the researcher used increasingly more explicit strategies (e.g. 'pay attention to the tense of the verb'). Only if necessary did the researcher correct the error himself. |
| Analysis | To measure development over time in the learners, four levels were distinguished. (1) The learner failed to even notice an error. (2) The learner noticed an error but failed to correct it even with assistance. (3) The learner noticed and corrected an error but only after other-regulation. (4) The learner noticed and corrected the error with minimal intervention from the researcher but still repeated the same error later. (5) The learner was able to use the target structure correctly in all contexts. |
| Results | The results were presented in terms of detailed analyses of the interactions that took place between the individual learners and the researcher at different times. Although not pre-planned, the feedback provided by the researcher reflected a regulatory scale ranging from very implicit to very explicit use of corrective strategies. The learning evident in the students was clearly a collaborative and dynamic endeavour. Development was reflected in progression from one level to another and reflected changes in the extent of the other-regulation required. |

*Table 9.3   Summary of Aljaafreh and Lantolf's (1994) study of second language learning in the Zone of Proximal Development*

Subsequent work on learning in the ZPD has involved **dynamic assessment**. In Poehner and Lantolf (2005), learners constructed a past tense oral narrative in French after watching a short video clip. They were given no feedback or mediation in this first task. Then they repeated the task after watching a second clip. This time 'they interacted with a mediator who offered suggestions, posed questions, made corrections, and helped them think through decisions concerning selection of lexical items, verb tense, and other language difficulties' (p. 246). This interactive assistance, which was provided in the learner's L1, was 'highly flexible, emerging from the interaction between the student and the mediator' (p. 14). Poehner and Lantolf showed how the native-speaker interlocutor varied the specific mediating strategies he used at different times with the same learner and also with different learners. For example, in the case of one learner, he initially used quite direct clues (for example, 'in the past') and subsequently, when addressing the same linguistic problem, more indirect means (for example, 'there's something there with the verb'). Poehner (2008) reported a four-month study of dynamic assessment. This included an examination of what Poehner called 'transcendence'—i.e. the ability of the learner to appropriate the mediation provided in the performance of one task to the performance of a new and more complex task. This study provided evidence of the development of full self-regulation where learners were able to generalize what they had learned to challenging new contexts.

## Collaborative dialogue and 'languaging'

Up to this point, I have drawn largely on the work of Lantolf, but I will now turn to look at the contribution made by Swain and her co-researchers. In Chapter 7, we considered Swain's **Output Hypothesis**. This was framed within the cognitive paradigm. That is, output constituted data that fed into the mental mechanisms held responsible for learning. Swain (2000), however, subsequently reframed her understanding of the role of output in sociocultural terms. She now viewed it as a socially constructed cognitive tool for mediating learning and, accordingly, focused on examining the role of 'dialogue' and, in particular, 'collaborative dialogue', which she defined as 'dialogue in which speakers are engaged in problem solving and knowledge building' (p. 102).

Swain and her co-researchers conducted a whole series of studies designed to examine the contribution of collaborative dialoguing to language learning. These studies typically involved asking learners to complete a challenging task in pairs, recording the conversations they took part in as they did so, and then investigating the **language-related episodes** (LREs) that occurred when they ran into problems. See Example eight in Chapter 7 for an example of a LRE. Swain was interested in two main questions: Were learners successful in jointly solving linguistic problems? Were these learners subsequently able to use the linguistic forms that figured in their solutions independently? In other words, Swain looked for evidence to show that collaborative dialogue in problem-solving was knowledge-building. The methodology she employed was to carry out detailed analyses of the LREs that occurred in collaborative dialogue and then investigate—sometimes by means of post-tests—whether these had contributed to the learners' self-regulated use of the linguistic forms.

A good example of the kind of study Swain conducted is Swain and Lapkin (2002). In this study, two Grade seven immersion learners first viewed a videotape of a mini-lesson on French reflexive verbs and watched two learners modelling writing a story. They then wrote a story collaboratively based on a picture jigsaw task. Their text was then reformulated by a native speaker after which the learners worked together to notice the differences between their text and the native speaker's. There was also a stimulated recall interview where they were asked to comment on the features they had noticed. Finally, they were given a copy of their original story and asked to rewrite it. Swain and Lapkin examined the LREs that arose when the learners were writing the initial story and during the noticing activity. They then compared the learners' initial and final texts, treating them as a pre-test and a post-test. 80 per cent of the changes that the learners made were correct. Some of the correct changes corresponded to the changes in the reformulated text but other changes were directly traceable to the LREs.

In a later study, with a very similar design, Swain and Lapkin (2007) investigated the role played by 'interaction with the self' (p. 82) (i.e. private speech). The key difference between this and the earlier study was that a single learner performed the writing tasks independently. The focus was on the differences that this learner reported noticing between his original text and the reformulated text and how these related to the changes he made to his original text. Swain and Lapkin reported similar results to the earlier study. By interacting with himself, this learner was able to focus his attention on problematic linguistic forms, construct new understandings, and consolidate existing knowledge[3].

The attention to linguistic form that occurs in talk—whether social or private—when a problem arises constitutes **languaging** (Swain 2006). Languaging can occur when any kind of problem arises but the particular type that Swain was interested in was 'languaging about language'. She argued that it constitutes one of the principal ways in which advanced levels of language learning can be achieved as it involves learners (1) articulating and transforming their thinking into 'an artefactual form' and, thereby, (2) providing a means for further reflection on this form. Languaging, then, is not just a facilitator of learning; it is where learning takes place.

## Final comments

Sociocultural SLA has attracted increasing interest among both researchers and language educators. It is the most established of the 'social' theories I will consider in this chapter. It differs from the input-output model informing the research we considered in Chapter 7 by its insistence that the 'social' and the 'cognitive' are dialectally connected. It disputes the dualism inherent in cognitive SLA by claiming that social and cognitive processes are not distinct and separate, but two sides of the same coin. It also provides a basis for what Lantolf (2011) called 'educational praxis', a process whereby theory and the practice of teaching are mutually informing. The importance sociocultural SLA attaches to learning as a mediated external, not just a mental internal phenomenon, is of obvious relevance to language pedagogy. In fact, many of the studies by Lantolf and Swain involved instructed L2 learners. We might ask, however, to what extent sociocultural SLA truly belongs to the 'social turn', which—as I have already noted—it pre-dates. In some respects it clearly does. It rejects the idea of a universal order and sequence in L2 acquisition—since learning in the ZPD varies from one individual to another—and it adopts a constructivist stance to the role played by interaction in learning whereby the social context is the actual site of learning. Moreover, its methodology emphasizes the importance of detailed analyses of interactions involving learners as, for example, in Swain's investigation of language related episodes.

But in other respects, sociocultural SLA does not conform to the key features of the 'social turn' (see Table 9.1). Much of the research has focused quite narrowly on adult foreign or second learners in 'social' contexts, largely restricted to those created by some kind of instructional activity. There is, of course, no reason why sociocultural theory cannot be studied in the naturalistic contexts found in the real world but—by and large—this has not happened. As a result, there has been no exploration of the myriad social identities that L2 learners can and do draw on in their social encounters in the real world. The L2 learner is positioned as a 'novice' and the teacher/ native speaker is an 'expert'. In its methodology, too, it is not adverse to using tests as a complement to detailed analyses to establish whether self-regulation has taken place. However, I do not intend to suggest these aspects of sociocultural theory constitute a limitation. In fact, they can be construed as signs of its main strength, namely that it is clearly both a social and a cognitive theory and therefore manifests epistemological and methodological aspects of both paradigms.

# The sociocognitive approach

Like sociocultural SLA, the **sociocognitive approach** acknowledges that there is both a social and a cognitive dimension to all forms of language use and thus it follows that to understand language acquisition it is necessary to understand how these two dimensions interrelate (Batstone 2010). Thus, like sociocultural theory, the sociocognitive approach emphasizes learning-as-participation when mind and body come together in and through the interactions that occur in specific situational contexts.

The question, of course, is exactly how the social and the cognitive dimensions interrelate. For Batstone, there are distinct cognitive and social dimensions that come together when we engage in social interaction. He acknowledges that we have prior conceptions—i.e. schematic knowledge, scripts derived from previous interactions and personal identities—which we draw on while simultaneously attending to the linguistic signs that signal how speakers are orienting to the discourse in a particular context. In this way, speakers achieve a convergence of their internal and external worlds. Learning takes place when the exigencies of a particular interaction challenge pre-existing schematic knowledge, causing modification to take place.

Atkinson (2011c) takes a different view of the interrelationship of the social and the cognitive. He sees language as simultaneously in the world and in the learner's head and, thus, it is neither 'social' nor 'cognitive', but both together. Thus there is no hard division between 'inner' and 'outer' processes. For Atkinson, language co-exists in cognitive and social space. For example, the simple activity of exchanging greetings involves 'facial expression, physical orientations, affective stance, a conventionalized social scene in a social setting with a social purpose performed by social actors and the effective deployment of the social tool of language' (2002: 531–2). Cognition, then, is not something mental but is 'fundamentally continuous with the world' (2011: 149). In Atkinson's sociocognitive approach 'neither language acquisition nor language use – nor even cognized linguistic knowledge – can be properly understood without taking into account their fundamental integration into a socially-mediated world' (2002: 534).

Atkinson argues for the inseparability of the social and the cognitive. A sociocognitive event is 'profoundly integrative'. However, unlike Batstone, and also unlike sociocultural theory, Atkinson rejects a view of learning as something that begins in the social world and then ends up in the learner's head. There is no such thing as 'internalization' in Atkinson's theory. Learning is a purely external phenomenon.

The key construct in Atkinson's theory of L2 learning is 'alignment'. Through interaction learners and their co-participants align adaptively to the 'ever-changing mind-body-world environment' in which they are jointly functioning (Atkinson, Churchill, Nishino, and Okada 2007: 171). To illustrate this, Atkinson et al. describe a series of interactions between a Japanese high school student (Ako) and her aunt as they work collaboratively on an English exercise, practising the 'have you ever' construction in order to demonstrate Ako's 'growing ability to participate meaningfully in conversations using the *Have you (ever)* experience construction' (p. 182). An implication of Atkinson's sociocognitive approach—reflected in the study of Ako—is that knowledge of an L2 is not abstract but a situation-dependent process. Learners participate in 'situated activity systems' that 'support language growth' and what they come to do and know is embedded in these systems. Learners learn by doing, so what they learn is tied to the activity in which they learned it. Interaction is central to this process as it is through interaction that alignment takes place. Alignment is 'the necessary condition' for acquisition to occur.

To date, there is little research to support the claims of a sociocognitive approach. As Atkinson (2011c) admitted, it is 'new and undeveloped'. Ideally, it requires longitudinal studies of L2 learners to show how the world-body-mind interface manifests itself in interaction at different times so that change can be identified. It also requires a methodology for examining the details of the interactions in which learners participate. Atkinson drew on **conversation analysis** to achieve this. This is the next approach we will consider.

## The conversation-analytic approach

Like sociocultural theory, the **conversation-analytic approach** emphasizes the importance of learning as a process—i.e. as something that happens *in* social interaction. It also resembles sociocognitive theory methodologically through its insistence on the detailed analyses of the sequential talk and the non-verbal behaviour that accompanies it in specific interactions involving L2 learners. I will begin with a brief exposition of the conversation-analytic approach and its methodology and then examine how it has been used to investigate L2 learning.

### Theoretical principles

Conversation analysis (CA) grew out of branch of sociology—ethnomethodology—the aim of which is to describe and explain the methods that ordinary people use to participate in everyday events and to make sense of their daily lives. Drawing on many of the theoretical premises of ethnomethodology, it developed a methodology for analysing how conversations are constructed, how participants make sense of what transpires in a conversation and—of special relevance to conversations involving L2 learners—how problems that arise are dealt with.

A key construct in the conversation-analytic approach is **interactional competence**, conceived of not as a cognitive ability, but as how interaction is accomplished in different situations. Interactional competence includes how the participants in an interaction mutually co-ordinate their turns, how roles are established and role-relationships enacted, how linguistic and non-verbal resources are used to produce and interpret turns and actions, and how problems are repaired. Interactional competence is highly situated. That is, it consists of the know-how about how to behave in specific situations—for example, in service encounters; in language proficiency interviews; and in pharmacist-patient consultations. Examples of how **conversational analysis** was used to investigate interactional competence in these situations can be found in Hall, Hellerman, and Pekarek Doehler (2011).

As Kasper and Wagner (2011) noted, 'interactional competence is understood to serve a double duty as both a fundamental condition for and (as an) object of learning' (p. 119). That is, learners need to know how to interact, but through interaction they develop the routines associated with specific interactional events. In developing these routines, L2 learners also expand the linguistic resources needed to participate in them. Thus, the conversation analytic approach is concerned with how learners learn to do talk-in-interaction and how this leads to the acquisition of conversational structures and also how specific linguistic forms—i.e. sounds, words, and grammatical structures—are used and learned. In this respect, it has a broader agenda than cognitive SLA, which by and large has only addressed the acquisition of linguistic forms.

## The methodology of conversation analysis

Conversation analysis seeks to describe 'how participants understand and respond to one another in their turns at talk' (Hutchby and Wooffitt 1998: 14). Analysis is entirely bottom-up and data driven (i.e. there is no reference to *a priori* norms or structures). Conversation analysts make no assumptions about or reference to inner, cognitive states. They base their work on very narrowly transcribed conversations in order to examine them in minute detail. Markee (2005) listed what he considered the minimal requirements for a CA transcript. It needs to show:

> ... how members hesitate, pause, or become silent during talk, how they speed up or slow down their delivery, how they modulate the volume of their speech, how they emphasize certain words or sounds through stress, and how they overlap each other's talk. (p. 358)

He then added that if conversations are video-recorded it will also be possible—and desirable—to include information about gestures, embodied actions, and eye-gaze behaviours.

Two aspects of conversations have received particular attention—**turn-taking** and **repair**. Conversation analysts have identified a number of rules that underlie speaker selection and change: only one speaker speaks at a time; a speaker can select the next speaker by nominating or by performing the first part of an adjacency pair (for example, asking a question that requires an answer); a speaker can alternatively allow the next speaker to self-select; and, in everyday conversations, there is usually competition to take the next turn. However, turn-taking in classrooms—and in other institutional settings—differs in that 'the organization of turn-taking is constrained and related to the institutional goal' (Seedhouse 2004: 168).

Conversational analysts define repair as the treatment of 'trouble'—i.e. anything that the participants consider is impeding communication—and treat it as a joint production. In this respect, then 'repair' includes much more than the **negotiation of meaning** and **corrective feedback**, see Chapter 7 and Chapter 10. Schegloff, Jefferson, and Sacks (1977) distinguished different types of repair work in terms of who initiates the repair (the speaker or the hearer) and who carries it out. The four basic types they found were: (1) self-initiated self-repair; (2) self-initiated other repair; (3) other-initiated self-repair; and (4) other initiated-other repair.

There is now a rich literature on the application of conversation analysis in SLA (CA-SLA for short), although much of this work is purely descriptive. As our interest here is on what CA can show about learning, I will examine research that has explored three themes: 'doing learning'—i.e. how learners and their conversational partners engage in explicit learning events—'short-term development', and 'long-term development' (Markee 2000).

## Doing learning

'Doing learning' involves the 'interactional moments where the participants' focal concern of their interactions is learning' (Kasper and Wagner 2011: 127). In other words, 'learning' becomes the topic of social practice resulting in the participants foregrounding the identity of the learner as 'learner', as opposed to some other identity, such as customer or patient. In such interactions, the learner's interlocutor (another learner or a native speaker) becomes a resource from which the learner can obtain new input. 'Doing learning' is clearly very similar to Swain's **languaging**.

One common way of doing learning is when one of the participants experiences a vocabulary problem and repair work ensues to address the problem. Kasper and Wagner (2011) provide a detailed analysis of part of a business phone call between two sale representatives—one Danish (J) and the other English (T). J begins by suggesting they have lunch when T arrives in the afternoon, but then—believing he has used the wrong word for the meal-time—self-repairs by substituting 'breakfast'. Further repair work follows. As the conversation continues, it becomes clear that J has a very uncertain understanding of the English names for mealtimes. Recognizing this, T now helps out by explicitly telling J the names. In this way 'a repair sequence transforms into a lecturing/instruction sequence' (p. 131).

Doing learning in this way is, of course, not surprising given that—even in naturally occurring interactions such as that between J and T—occasions will arise where it becomes necessary or helpful for the more competent speaker to help out the less competent, not just by engaging in repair work, but by adopting the role of a tutor. In instructional settings, of course, this constitutes an authorized social practice.

If learning is 'participation', then doing learning *is* learning. This is the position taken by sociocultural theorists and also by some conversation analysts. Such a position would be disputed by cognitive theorists who require evidence that 'doing learning' results in some change in the learner's linguistic system. Some conversation analysts also acknowledge that 'learning is understood as changes in doing, rather than as doing in itself' (Sahlström 2011: 45). We do not know for sure that J will remember the names of the English mealtimes following T's input. As Kasper (2006) noted 'CA does not provide a ready-made framework to examine learning, whether language learning or the learning of other things' (p. 91). How then does CA-SLA endeavour to show that learning has taken place?

## Short-term development

Given CA-SLA's commitment to relying exclusively on the evidence provided in the naturally-occurring interactions that learners participate in—i.e. eliciting additional data by means of tasks and tests is not allowed—it is necessary to look for evidence within the same or in successive interactions involving the same learner to demonstrate that change has occurred. 'Short-term development' is demonstrated if change occurs within a single interaction or within subsequent interactions that occur shortly afterwards (for example, within the same lesson).

## Long-term development

To investigate how learning takes place over time, Markee (2008) advocated a 'learning tracking methodology'. This consisted of (1) learning object tracking and (2) learning process tracking. The former involved identifying when a specific learning object (for example, a word or a grammatical structure) occurred in the interactions involving the same learner(s) over a period of time. The latter involved showing 'how and when participants orient to, and potentially incorporate, particular learning objects that occur in different speech events in their interactional repertoires' (p. 409).

An example of this kind of approach can be found in Firth and Wagner (2007). They focused on a lexical item—'blowing'—as this occurred in telephone conversations between a Danish cheese exporter (H) and an Egyptian importer (A). These extracts are reproduced below. On the first occasion, A refers to the problem with the cheese he has received from (A), noting that it is 'blowing' (a non-standard way of referring to the fact that the cheese has started to ferment). A self-initiated/other-repair sequence ensues where H indicates he does not understand 'blowing' and A responds by providing synonyms (i.e. 'bad' and 'fermenting'). Finally—in l.6—H demonstrates he has understood by providing his own synonym ('gone off'). In this extract, however, H only produces 'blowing' when repeating the word following A's turn. In the second extract (Extract 3 below)—which occurred in a telephone conversation between the same two people two weeks later—H is able to produce 'blowing' without any assistance from A. Firth and Wagner argued that this second encounter shows how learning 'is carried over in time and space' (p. 808) and that 'H has now learned this lexical item in a way that extends beyond the concrete local context where he first became acquainted with it' (p. 809).

**Extract (2)**

1 A  We don't want the order after the cheese is uhh blowing.

2 H  See, yes.

3 A  So I don't know what I can we can do uh with the order now. (.)
     What do you think we should do with this is all blowing Mister
     Hansen (0.7)

4 H  I am not uh (0.7) blowing uh what uh, what is this uh too big or
     what?

5 A  No the cheese is bad Mister Hansen (0.4) it is like (.) fermenting in
     the Customs cool rooms.

6 H  Ah it's gone off.

7 A  Yes, it's gone off.

**Extract (3)**

1 A  Yes (.) Mister Hansen.

2 H  Hello Mister Akkad (.) hh we haf some informations for you
     about the cheese (.) with the blowing.

3 A  Yes Mister Hansen

(Firth and Wagner 2007: 808)

Firth and Wagner aim to show how 'learning in action' takes place. In CA-SLA this involves 'being contingently adaptable as the unfolding context requires' (2007: 808). The analyses they provide also illustrate another important claim of the conversation analytical approach, namely that change occurs as learners discover how to become members of a particular **community of practice**—a cheese exporter/importer in the case of Firth and Wagner's study. It is in this sense that language learning is a social practice.

Conversation analysts are also concerned with how learners acquire the discursive practices associated with particular social events. Young and Miller (2004), for example, investigated an adult Vietnamese learner's participation in the revision talk that occurred in weekly writing conferences. They documented how this changed over time from peripheral to fuller participation. They described a participation framework for this particular social event consisting of eight speech acts. Initially, the instructor performed seven of these. Four weeks later, however, the student performed many of the acts himself (for example, he now identified problems, explained the need for revision, and suggested possible ways of carrying out revision) without any direction from the instructor. In other words, the student demonstrated that he had now acquired 'interactional competence in the practice of revision talk' (p. 533).

## Final comments

The conversation-analytic approach views language learning as social activity. Perhaps, more than any of the other social approaches examined in this chapter, it is representative of the 'social turn' in SLA. It avoids consideration of exogeneous factors as explanations of learning[4]. It is broad in scope – it addresses both how linguistic items are acquired and how interactional competence is developed – and it views the former as embedded in the latter. It asks questions such as 'How do learners learn to do disagreement, repair, etc. as members of specific communities?' and 'In so doing how do they acquire L2 linguistic resources in the process?' It views identity as multiple and negotiated rather than fixed and situationally determined. Thus identity is not something that is 'accessed' by learners when they interact but rather is 'interactionally produced, locally occasioned, and relationally constituted' (Kasper and Wagner 2011: 122). At times it is the learner's identity as learner that is made prominent but at other times other social identities emerge.

The greatest challenge facing conversation analytical approaches is being able to provide evidence of long-term learning. Naturally-occurring data do not readily afford instances of reoccurring 'learning objects' and it is difficult to know what constitute comparable interactional events. The rejection of tests to establish long-term learning can perhaps be justified on the grounds that tests do not show what learners can do in naturally occurring interactions but this creates problems[5]. CA-SLA is also limited because it declines to consider how psychological factors (for example, working memory or motivation) affect how specific interactions unfold.

## The social identity approach

Sociocultural theory, sociocognitive theory, and conversation analysis all acknowledge the importance of social identity. I turn now to a theory that foregrounds the role of social identity. The **social identity approach** constitutes an 'unequivocally social approach to SLA' (Norton and McKinney 2011: 87).

## Social identity as a postmodern phenomenon

From a postmodern viewpoint, social identity is understood as a relational rather than an individual phenomenon: our social identities do not constitute fixed traits, but rather exist in a state of flux as they are discursively constructed through participation in interactions with different people in different contexts. Nevertheless, we do tend to think of our own and other people's identities as 'inscriptions'. We view our identities in terms of gender (male or female); race (African or European); marital status (married or single); occupation (university professor or chef), etc. Language learners may similarly see themselves as native or non-native speakers—despite Firth and Wagner's rejection of such inscriptions—although they do not necessarily always act out these identities. These two ways of conceptualizing social identity, however, are not necessarily contradictory. As Miller and Kubota (2013) pointed out our identities are constructed and reconstructed repeatedly so that 'our ongoing social performances become sedimented into recognizable durable identities that persist over time' (p. 233). By and large, however,—as Miller and Kubota acknowledged—SLA research that has investigated the role of social identity has drawn on these sedimented identities.

Postmodern accounts of social identity emphasize the following:

1 Social identity is multiple and non-unitary. The language learner is not just a 'language learner', but can draw on a number of different social identities when interacting in the L2. This is most obviously the case for learners functioning in multilingual naturalistic settings, but is also true for classroom learners.

2 Social identity is complex and inherently subjective. For example, learners' sense of what it means to be 'male' or 'female' intersects with their other identities (race, ethnicity, social class, etc.) and thus varies from one learner to another. Thus, it is not possible to generalize how gender affects learning opportunities across all male or all female learners. McKay and Wong (1996), for example, found little commonality in how four male Chinese students in a Californian secondary school enacted gender in their social contact with other students.

3 Because social identity is multiple, conflicts can arise when the behaviour associated with one identity becomes incompatible with that of another. Skilton-Sylvester (2002) reported that Ming—a Cambodian learner of English—was unable to balance her identity as a student with that as a wife when her husband demanded she discontinue her language classes because he perceived her expanding social networks as a threat to their marriage. She felt obliged to give up her literacy studies.

4 Power relationships are inextricably linked to the social identities that are evoked when learners engage in interactions with other speakers of the language and thus impact on the learning opportunities available to learners. Inequitable power relationships can impede learners' rights to speak and to be heard and thus restrict their access to the L2. Learners, however, have 'agency'. That is, they can resist how they have been positioned by drawing on an identity option that affords them more equal status with their interlocutors and, in this way, they can achieve ways of participating in the kinds of social exchanges that foster opportunities for learning. Social identities, then, are a site of struggle.

5 The social identities of learners need to be understood not just in terms of those identities that they have already constructed but also in terms of imagined communities and identities they envisage for their future lives. Learners conceive of groups of people who are not yet accessible, but who may become so in the future. 'Imagined communities are no less real that the ones in which learners have daily engagement and might have a stronger impact on their identities and investments' (Norton and McKinney 2011: 76).

6 Language learning requires 'investment' on the part of the learner. This notion—first introduced by Norton Peirce (1995)—differs from that of instrumental motivation (see Chapter 3). It acknowledges that when learners speak, they are not just concerned with the material benefits of learning a language, but also with organizing and reorganizing who they are. Learners' decisions whether or not to invest in language learning depends on how they see themselves in relation to their existing or imagined social communities[6].

7 Social identities are dynamic: they evolve over time and new identities are constantly being formed. This is clearly so in the case of the 'language learner'. In the opinion of some researchers this results in a 'third space'— a hybrid identity that evolves when learners come to see themselves as multilingual and transnational individuals, rather than as language learners. Kramsch (2009) proposed that the third space allows learners to take over the language and 'give it meanings other than the native speaker would' (p. 238).

## Norton's theory of social identity in L2 learning

The importance of social identity in L2 learning came to prominence in a series of publications by Norton in the 1990s (for example, Norton Peirce 1995; Norton 1997). Norton sought to 'rethink language acquisition in its social, cultural, and political contexts, taking into account gender, race, and other relations of power as well as the notion of the subject as multiple and formed within different discourses' (Norton Peirce 1995: 20).

Norton (1997) defined **social identity** as 'the relationship between the individual and the larger social world, as mediated through institutions such as families, schools, workplaces, social services, and law courts (p. 420). She argued that it was related to but distinct from both 'cultural identity' ('the relationship between individuals and members of a group who share a common history, a common language, and similar ways of understanding the world') and 'ethnic identity' ('the relationship between the individual and members of the race to which the learner belongs'). Norton elected to investigate social identity because she believed that it best captured the heterogeneous and dynamic nature of identity in the learners she investigated.

Implicit in Norton's view of social identity, L2 use, and L2 learning is the importance of 'ownership' of the language being learned. Norton rejected the view that native speakers own the language and asserted that learners need to see themselves as legitimate speakers of it and challenge being positioned as illegitimate. Thus—like Firth and Wagner—she rejected the traditional notions of 'native speaker' and 'non-native speaker'.

Norton (2000) reported on a number of case studies of adult immigrant women in Canada. She documented how these women often had social identities imposed on them which denied them opportunities to speak and be heard and which they were uncomfortable with. In some cases, this resulted in them withdrawing from contact with native speakers. In other cases, however, they fought to establish a preferred social identity in their interactions with native speakers which afforded more equal discourse rights and—in Norton's view—greater opportunities for learning English. Mai is an example of the first. She became the subject of derision in her workplace because of the preferential treatment she received from the management on account of her single status. As a result, she was not able to establish an identity that created the conditions where she could comfortably interact with other speakers. In contrast, Martina—a Czech woman who came to Canada with her husband and children at the age of 37—was able to make use of her identity as the primary caregiver in her family to engage in 'counter-discourses'. She refused to be silenced despite experiencing frequent feelings of shame. Instead, she challenged the 'rules' governing interactions between immigrants and Anglophones—for example, by entering into an argument with her landlord about the terms of her lease. However, Norton provided no evidence that the learning opportunities afforded to Martina led to learning.

## Transnational identity

Where Norton was concerned with under-privileged immigrant learners, other researchers studied L2 learners who were not so socially disadvantaged. Block (2006), for example, investigated the multilingual identities of five Japanese female graduate students in London. These learners were all middle-class, highly educated, and economically secure and thus possessed 'the requisite social and cultural capital to make the move from Japan to London' (p. 104). While there were some marked differences in these learners' identities, they were 'internationalist women'—that is, women who had elected to live their lives, to some degree at least, outside the confines of traditional Japanese society. They viewed English as 'a language of liberation in which they can develop new femininities' (p. 97).

An increasing number of studies have focused on the **transnational identity** of multilingual learners. Rampton (1995)—for example—documented the insider identities that arise in the multiracial communities found in urban settings. He described the 'language crossing' (i.e. 'the use of speech varieties which are not normally thought to belong to the speaker') that occurred in White and Asian adolescents' use of West Indian Creole. Rampton suggested that these speakers' access to minority languages enabled them to play with different identities when interacting with members of their peer group. Li and Hua (2013) investigated the 'translanguaging' of a group of Chinese university students in London. Originating from different countries and social backgrounds, they developed a transnational and multilingual network amongst themselves. Li and Hua illustrated how these students developed fluid identities—not as Chinese from specific countries, nor as Chinese in Britain—but as Chinese students at universities in London.

## Final comments

A limitation of these—and other—studies is that, although they address how 'learning opportunities' are created through the social identities learners assume, they do not demonstrate to what extent these opportunities actually result in learning. There is a tendency to uncritically equate 'learning opportunities' with 'learning'. In part, this limitation is a result of the methodology researchers have adopted. By and large, the research has consisted of short-term case studies. In such studies it is not possible to document how social identity and learning interrelate over time. Also, as Miller and Kubota (2013) pointed out, there has been a reliance on learner narratives collected through interviews. Researchers have tended to take what learners say about their learning experiences at face value without questioning the veracity of self-report data.

Miller and Kubota also pointed out the lack of clarity in the terms commonly used to discuss the role of social identity in L2 learning. They noted that despite the insistence on poststructuralist accounts of identity, there is still a tendency to view identity in terms of inscriptions such as 'female' or 'Japanese'. Constructs such as 'agency' and 'subjectivity'—central to theories of social identity—need to be elucidated more fully and grounded more closely in data drawn from the social interactions in which learners participate.

## Language socialization and L2 learning

**Language socialization** is the practice by which novices in a community are socialized both into the forms of a language and—through language—into the values, behaviours, and practices of the community in which they live. It entails 'socialization through the use of language and socialization to use language' (Schieffelin and Ochs 1986: 163). Thus, in the process of learning to become a member of a community, learners learn the L2, and, conversely—through learning an L2—they become a member of the community that speaks it.

Central to language socialization accounts of L2 learning is Lave and Wenger's (1991) notion of a **community of practice**. This refers to specific social groups—for example, classroom L2 learners or insurance claim processors—that share a common set of practices related to a particular social domain—for example, a workplace or a classroom. Wenger (1998) proposed that a community of practice is characterized by (1) mutual engagement—i.e. through participation in a community, members establish norms and build collaborative relationships); (2) joint enterprise—i.e. members develop a shared understanding of what unites them); and (3) shared repertoire—i.e. members establish a common set of communal resources including ways of speaking). From this perspective, learning an L2 entails becoming a member of a community of practice. L2 learners entering such a community may at first be able to participate only in peripheral ways but, over time, they may become increasingly involved as they establish a shared repertoire of resources—including linguistic resources—and, a result an insider identity may evolve. From this perspective, social practice and learning—including language learning—are inseparable.

Language socialization theory acknowledges that 'practices come with ideologies' (Zuengler and Cole 2005: 313). This is especially the case with immigrant or refugee populations where power and ideology play a major part in the discourses experienced by such learners. Language socialization, then, is not necessarily a smooth and seamless process as learners may demonstrate agency and contest being positioned as novices. In some communities of practice, what constitutes expertise is disputed and so-called experts are themselves socialized into accepting new norms. Thus, communities of practice should not be seen as fixed and stable, but as evolving dynamically as new members enter.

Nevertheless, socialization research has primarily focused on how more capable members of a community assist those who are linguistically, communicatively, and culturally less capable to become legitimate members of the community. This assistance takes place through interaction and can be both explicit and implicit. Explicit socialization consists of prompts, directives, and corrections while implicit socialization takes place experientially when learners engage with more competent members as they perform the tasks that characterize the life of the community.

Research on language socialization has blossomed in recent years—one of the clearest indications of the 'social turn' that has taken place in SLA. Much of this research has focused on macro aspects of language: for example, how learners are socialized into the practices of academic oral and written discourse communities (Duff 2010). Duff and Talmy (2011) acknowledged that in general research based on language socialization 'pays more attention to the interactional and linguistic *processes* of socialization in real interactional time than to the systematic study of *outcomes*' (p. 100, italics in original). In other words, researchers do not typically document how socialization into a community of practice results in the acquisition of specific linguistic forms. As Ortega (2009) pointed language socialization research focuses on 'access' and 'participation' rather than acquisition of the L2 code.

However, some studies have paid attention to the L2 code. Duff and Kobayashi (2010) examined how Japanese international students in Canada, who were enrolled in a content-based course, learned to participate in a specific cultural practice—a group oral presentation in English about their experiences as volunteers with local organizations and with their classes on campus. The rich data collected for this study consisted of recordings of the interactions that took place and the participants' self-reports and relevant documents (for example, class handouts). Duff and Kobayashi described the iterative, longitudinal nature of the socialization processes as these students were explicitly and implicitly inducted into the discursive practices leading up to the group presentation. Explicit socialization consisted of modelling by the teacher and by the students themselves. Implicit socialization was evident in the teachers' and students **scaffolding** that supported the development of effective argument and also the choice of linguistic forms. As the students engaged with the project, they also internalized the institution's ideology of collaborative learning. Duff and Kobayashi argued that the socialization process was both social and cognitive in nature: it involved both the development of social understandings and the negotiation of linguistic forms in what Swain called language-related episodes. However, unlike many of Swain's studies (see the earlier section on Sociocultural SLA), this study provided no evidence of longer-term learning.

Another study that sought to marry a broad scope account of socialization with a narrow, linguistic focus is Bongartz and Schneider's (2003) study of two English-speaking brothers learning German in Germany. This study investigated two aspects of these boys' socialization through the interactions they took part in with their German-speaking playmates: language play—for example, sound play, narratives, insults and 'tough' talk—and negotiation—for example, about what, when, and how to play. They examined the boys' linguistic inventories by analysing their syntactic development—for example, sentence types and negation—and phrasal structure—for example, prepositions and determiners. They found that there were marked differences in the frequencies of the different tokens used by the two boys. For example, whereas the older brother used dependent clauses more frequently, the younger boy used imperative verbs more often. Bongartz and Schneider suggested that these differences were linked to the different patterns of socialization experienced by the two boys. Whereas the older boy interacted with his playmates through narratives, the younger boy interacted by attempting to initiate and control interactions. Bongartz and Schneider concluded that the 'lexical and syntactic choices for both boys are directly related to their interactional practices' (p. 32).

A number of other socialization studies have focused on pragmatic aspects of the L2. Matsumura (2003), for example, compared a group of Japanese learners of English in Canada with a group in Japan in terms of their perceptions of status and their ability to give advice appropriately. Whereas the group in Japan only made modifications in how they gave advice for higher-status addressees, the group in Canada showed a finer-grained awareness of status and were able to give advice accordingly. This study suggests that these learners' perception of status and advice-giving went hand in hand and that the opportunity to interact with and become socialized into a target-language community led to their L2 use becoming more pragmatically target-like.

## Final comments

Duff and Talmy (2011) concluded their review of the L2 socialization approach by claiming that it 'holds tremendous promise' for elucidating 'the complex phenomenon that is typically referred to as L2 learning' (p. 111). This claim is to some extent justified. A major strength of many of the studies is the richness of the data collected. Duff and Kobayashi's (2010) study, for example, combined self-report and observation which allowed both an emic account of social events and the detailed analysis of actual interactions involving the learners. L2 socialization research acknowledges that L2 learning is both social/cultural and cognitive in nature and, thus, can justifiably be considered sociocognitive in orientation. However, the cognitive aspect of learning remains under-theorized as a result of the focus on participation and access. In this respect, it has much in common with a number of other approaches in the 'social turn' in SLA.

## Conclusion

The importance of social factors in SLA has been recognized from early days. Both Schumann's **Acculturation Model** and Gardner's **Socio-educational Model** acknowledged that that the social context influences how successful learners are in acquiring an L2. However, these theories are structuralist in orientation: they view social factors as determining the conditions of learning and the effort that individual learners make to learn. They were investigated using a quantitative methodology that involved correlating measures of various social factors with measures of learning outcomes. These theories are entirely compatible with the interactionist-cognitive theories we considered in Chapter 7. They simply articulate how social factors affect learners' access to input and their motivation to attend to it. Implicitly, then, these theories acknowledge that acquisition is a mental phenomenon—something that takes place inside the minds of learners.

It was this basic assumption that was challenged in the 'social turn' and the 'alternative' theories that belong to it. While there are notable differences in these theories, they all adopt an interactionist view of the social context. That is, while acknowledging that external factors do indeed determine the social context to some extent, they emphasize that contexts are always constructed by those who take part in them and that learners are able to influence how they are constructed. In so doing, they challenge one of the mainstays of cognitive theories, namely that there are relatively fixed, universal trajectories of learning (see Chapter 4). They rejected the prevailing view of the 'language learner' as an abstract input-processing machine and insisted on treating learners as individuals who act on the world in different ways and who consequently manifest different learning trajectories.

There is considerable diversity in the research that has followed the 'social turn' but it is possible to identify a number of underlying premises:

1 Above all, the social turn emphasizes the importance of investigating learners within their **social context**. It distinguishes different levels of context—the wider social context in which the learner lives, the context created as

the interaction unfolds, and the remembered contexts of previous interactions. All the social turn theories emphasize the importance of providing detailed, process descriptions of the social context of learning.

2  Social interaction is the site in which learning takes place. In **sociocultural SLA**, interaction is the primary means of mediating higher forms of learning. In **sociocognitive theory**, learning takes place when interaction achieves an alignment of the mind-body-world. In the **conversation-analysis** approach, conversation is where learning starts and where it is consolidated. In the **social identity approach**, interaction is a site of struggle as learners jockey for the right to be heard and to speak. In **language socialization** theory, learners are socialized into a community of practice through interaction and, in the process, learn language. Interaction, then, is not just a source of input but it is where learning takes place.

3  Learners have agency and can dispute how they are positioned in an interaction. In many situations, learners will find themselves in an inequitable power relationship with their interlocutors as when, for example, they are positioned as a 'language learner' or an 'immigrant' and their other social identities ignored. However, they can challenge this by insisting on a social identity that redresses the power imbalance. Social identity theory claims that in so doing they create 'learning opportunities'.

4  All L2 learning is 'situated' and local. Learners learn discursive practices and the linguistic forms linked to them in the particular situation in which they experienced them. Language is tied to context and can only be modified or extended through experiencing the use of routines and linguistic forms in the same or new contexts. Above all, learning is seen as an ongoing process, not a product[7].

5  Learners sometimes have 'learning conversations': they make language the topic of talk, often when they experience a problem in expressing themselves clearly. Swain's term **languaging** best captures this important aspect of learning-through-interaction but we can find the same idea rooted in other social turn theories (for example, the conversation analytic approach and language socialization theory).

6  Learning an L2 is not just a question of learning linguistic forms but of developing **interactional competence**. The development of interactional competence and the acquisition of linguistic forms are intertwined. An implication of this is that SLA researchers need to investigate the macro aspects of a language—for example, how to repair problems that arise in a conversation—as well as the micro aspects—i.e. how to express past time in the L2. This aspect of the 'social turn' is most clearly evident in the conversation-analytic approach and in language socialization theory but is, arguably, implicit in the other theories as well.

7  L2 acquisition is not a process of adding a new language or a new identity. It involves the development of a hybrid language system and identity sometimes referred to as 'third space' where learners find themselves mediating between their languages and cultures in their interactions with different

speakers. From this perspective, learners can no longer be seen as directed at acquiring the 'target language'. Rather they develop a **transnational identity** and a 'translingual competence'. This involves the ability to deploy linguistic forms drawn from more than one language in accordance with context in communication that, as likely as not, is with other learners rather than native speakers.

8 Research in the 'social turn' calls for an emic approach that investigates how individual learners behave in specific social contexts and how they think about themselves in these contexts. It seeks an insider perspective through interviews and through the detailed analysis of the interactions that learners participate in. It contrasts with the etic approach characteristic of much of the research in the cognitive SLA paradigm, which utilizes objective measures of specific variables—both social and cognitive—with the aim of identifying cause-effect relationships.

The social-turn has undoubtedly enriched our understanding of L2 acquisition by insisting on the need to consider the social and personal factors involved. As Block (2007) put it, the social turn has provided us with 'a bigger toolkit' (p. 90) for looking at both the micro/local level of how interactions take place and the exogenous factors (for example, individual learners' biographies and their membership in different communities of practice) that both impact on the interactions learners participate in and are shaped by them.

The weakness of much of the research in the social turn is its emphasis on learning-as-participation and its neglect of learning-as-change. It was this that led Long (1998) to assert that changes in the social setting have not been shown to have any effect on error types or developmental sequences. All too often, social-turn researchers have been content to show how the social context affords 'learning opportunities' or how so-claimed 'new' linguistic forms are brought into play through interaction. They have provided only limited evidence to show that these 'learning opportunities' actually result in the learning of language that is then available for subsequent use in the same and, more importantly, in different contexts.

Central to any theory of L2 acquisition is the notion of 'change'—in particular linguistic change. As Larsen-Freeman (2007) noted 'any definition of learning must involve the transcendence of a particular time and space' (p. 783). What is missing from much of the social turn research is any attempt to demonstrate that linguistic change has occurred, or even to conceptualize what this constitutes in L2 learning. In Ellis (2010) I argued that to demonstrate change it is necessary to show that:

1 The learner could not perform $x$ at time $a$—i.e. there is a 'gap' in the learner's linguistic knowledge.
2 The learner co-adapted $x$ at time $b$—i.e. through participating in social interaction the learner is able to deploy $x$.
3 The learner initiated $x$ at time $c$ in a similar context as in time $b$—i.e. partial internalization of $x$ has taken place.

4  The learner employed *x* at time *d* in a new context—i.e. full internalization has occurred and allowed for the transfer of learning.

Here 'x 'refers to some micro or macro feature of language—for example, a specific lexical item, structural property, or discursive practice. Viewed in this way, change—and therefore acquisition—can occur at three different levels:

- Level 1 is where change originates in social activity—it is evident in participation.
- Level 2 is where the learner demonstrates the ability to initiate use of the newly learned feature in a similar context to that in which it first appeared.
- Level 3 occurs when the learner can initiate the use of the feature in an entirely different context.

Thus, while these theories do address change in terms of the learners' experiences of learning a language and their social identity, they have—in general—failed to document the incremental and continuous nature of change in the linguistic systems of the L2.

Of the social theories we have considered in this chapter, only sociocultural theory addresses how linguistic change takes place by recognizing that L2 learning is a process involving progress from **other-regulation** to **self-regulation**. Markee's learning tracking methodology also affords a means of showing how learning-as-participation can lead to learning-as-change. By and large, however, researchers drawing on these theoretical frameworks have been content to investigate Level 1 learning (i.e. learning-as-participation). Norton's Social Identity Theory stops short of even that by limiting its application to a consideration of how 'learning opportunities' are created. The problem facing research in the social turn is how to provide evidence of Level 2 and 3 learning, given the insistence on examining only naturally-occurring social interactions and the attendant difficulty of obtaining data relating to the use of the same specific linguistic feature over time. Only sociocultural researchers have been prepared to supplement the qualitative data they obtain from the analysis of social interactions with pre- and post-test data that can more easily reveal learning-as-change. The insistence on a purely emic account of learning in much of the social turn research has definitely contributed much to our understanding of learners and the role of the social context, but it has resulted in research that has shed only limited light on actual learning.

As Sfard (1998) argued, both the 'participation' and 'acquisition' metaphors are needed along with the recognition that it is not possible to make a clear distinction between the two. Cognitive SLA is arguably guilty of under-theorizing the nature and importance of the social context. Some social turn researchers are guilty of failing to theorize what acquisition entails and struggle to handle the cognitive side of L2 learning. As Veronique (2013) argued 'an integrated research perspective is highly desirable' (p. 270)—one that combines social, psychological, and linguistic perspectives and gives weight to all three. At present, though, there is little sign of this happening. As Firth and Wagner (2007) observed when they revisited the arguments in their 1997 paper in support of a social dimension in SLA, the field may not be able to 'withstand the current bifurcations, competing methods, critiques, and internal tensions, and remain generally cohesive' (p. 813).

## Notes

1 Block (2003) is clearly right to point out the problem with the term 'second' as, for many learners 'additional' is clearly a more appropriate term. However, 'second' continues to be the preferred term. For example, the title of Atkinson's (2011a) book, which provides an account of alternative, more socially-oriented approaches, refers to 'second' language acquisition. Once established, labels are not easily replaced.

2 Lantolf (2006) suggested that when even advanced L2 learners are faced with a difficult task, they have difficulty in sustaining use of the L2 and are likely to resort to the use of their L1 in their private speech.

3 Swain's research demonstrates that both collaborative dialogue and self-verbalization can mediate learning. It would be interesting to know if one is more effective than the other. Lantolf (2011), however, noted that this interesting question remains unresearched.

4 However, CA-SLA has recently begun to acknowledge that Discursive Psychology might have a role to play. Discursive Pyschology acknowledges that there are psychological phenomena, but sees these as things that are constructed, attended to, and understood in interaction.

5 Sociocultural researchers have not been so reluctant to avoid testing. Also, see Ellis and Shintani (2013) for a study that combined a conversation analytic approach by tracking learning objects with pre- and post-tests.

6 Norton Peirce (1995) argues that 'investment' is not the same as either 'integrative' or 'instrumental motivation. However, as she describes it has clear connections with Dörnyei's (2005) 'ideal self' in his L2 Motivational Self System (see Chapter 3).

7 In this respect, the theories of the 'social turn' view language in a very similar way to the theories that see language as a **complex adaptive system**, which can also lay claim to being 'social' in their epistemology (see Chapter 8).

# 10

# The role of explicit instruction

## Introduction

All language instruction constitutes a form of intervention in the process of learning a second language (L2). In this respect, instructed language learning differs from the naturalistic language learning that takes place in first language (L1) acquisition and in untutored L2 acquisition. However, it does not follow that contextual differences are necessarily reflected in differences in the cognitive and social processes involved in acquisition. Indeed, what is of interest to SLA researchers is precisely whether instruction does involve different learning processes. Investigating the effects of instruction, therefore, serves as a means of testing different claims about the nature of the processes involved in L2 acquisition. In this and the next chapter, I will examine this research. My main purpose is to use the research to examine some of the competing theories discussed in previous chapters in order to further understanding about the nature of L2 acquisition. In so doing, however, I will also address a question of paramount importance to teachers—namely, how can instruction best foster language learning?

## Types of intervention

Instruction as intervention in the process of language learning is of two basic kinds—direct and indirect. Direct instruction involves providing learners with explicit information about the target of the instruction, often together with opportunities to practise the target. I will henceforth refer to this type of instruction as **explicit instruction**. Explicit instruction invites **intentional learning** on the part of the learner. Indirect instruction involves setting up opportunities for learners to learn without specifying what the target of the instruction is: in other words, there is no provision of explicit information about the target feature, although there are opportunities to engage in the use of it. I will refer to this second type of instruction as **implicit instruction**. It caters to **incidental learning** on the part of the learner, although learners may

| Implicit instruction | Explicit instruction |
|---|---|
| • attracts attention to target form<br>• is delivered spontaneously (e.g. in an otherwise communication-oriented activity)<br>• is unobtrusive (minimal interruption of communication of meaning)<br>• presents target forms in context<br>• makes no use of metalanguage<br>• encourages free use of the target form. | • directs attention to target form<br>• is predetermined and planned (e.g. as the main focus and goal of a teaching activity<br>• is obtrusive (interruption of communicative meaning)<br>• presents target forms in isolation<br>• uses metalinguistic terminology (e.g. rule explanation)<br>• involves controlled practice of the target form. |

*Table 10.1  Implicit and explicit forms of form-focused instruction (based on Housen and Pierrard 2006: 10)*

sometimes choose to focus on specific linguistic forms and try to learn them intentionally. Table 10.1 provides a more detailed specification of these two types of instruction (see also Ellis and Shintani 2013: Chapter 4).

There is also another distinction commonly referred to in the literature. **Focus-on-form** refers to an approach that involves an attempt to draw learners' attention to a linguistic form while they are primarily focused on meaning—i.e. trying to communicate. It contrasts with **focus-on-forms**—seen as the 'traditional approach'—in which the primary goal is to help learners master the structural features listed in the syllabus by making the linguistic target of each lesson quite explicit. Here 'the aim is to *direct* learner attention and to *exploit pedagogical grammar*' (Doughty and Williams 1998: 232). These definitions suggest that focus-on form involves implicit instruction and focus-on-forms explicit instruction. This is broadly the case. However, these distinctions are not the same. Implicit instruction does not necessarily involve a primary focus on meaning. Some researchers have investigated implicit instruction by simply telling students to read and memorize a set of discrete sentences—an activity that, arguably, does not require a primary focus on meaning. Also, explicit instruction can include practice activities that require learners to focus on meaning. The terms 'focus-on-form' and 'focus-on-forms' are perhaps best used to distinguish specific kinds of instructional activities that may figure in both implicit and explicit instruction.

The focus of this chapter is on explicit instruction and the following chapter examines research that has investigated implicit instruction. Where appropriate, I will use the terms 'focus-on-forms' and 'focus-on-form' to refer to specific activities that figure in studies that have investigated these two types of instruction.

# Types of explicit instruction

Explicit instruction is not a uniform approach. It can be provided in a number of different ways, involving different theoretical assumptions concerning the role of explicit information and different kinds of practice activities. Table 10.2 outlines the different approaches along with the theoretical positions that support them.

A general distinction can be made between **deductive** and **inductive instruction**. In deductive instruction, learners are provided with metalinguistic information about the target of the instruction. This can occur in the presentation stage of the lesson or while learners are engaging in practice activities. Deductive instruction also differs in terms of the nature of the explicit information provided. Generally, the explicit information is typically drawn from a pedagogic grammar—i.e. it is simplified—but, in some types of explicit instruction, it consists of 'scientific concepts'—i.e. very detailed linguistic descriptions of grammatical features. In inductive explicit instruction, no metalinguistic information is provided. In the Audiolingual Method, for example, controlled production practice is employed to develop correct 'habits', whilst in Consciousness-Raising Instruction, learners complete a series of tasks that guide them to an understanding of the target feature, but without being asked to practise it. Both deductive and inductive instruction also vary in terms of whether the practice activities involve production or comprehension of the target feature. Later, we will consider different types of explicit instruction that incorporate these various options.

In Chapter 1, I outlined three different positions relating to the relationship between explicit and implicit knowledge (see also Chapter 8). The different instructional approaches listed in Table 10.2 reflect two of these positions: the **strong interface position,** which views explicit knowledge as transformable into implicit knowledge (or its equivalent), and the **weak interface position,** which views explicit knowledge as a facilitator of implicit knowledge but not directly transformable into it[1]. Investigating these instructional approaches, then, can help to shed light on the legitimacy of these two positions. Each of the instructional approaches draws on a different theoretical base: for example, whereas **presentation-practice-production** (PPP) draws on **skill-learning theory** and emphasizes the importance of production practice, **Processing Instruction** draws on VanPatten's **Input Processing Principles** and emphasizes the need for comprehension-based practice. Thus, investigating studies that have compared these two instructional approaches enables the claims of the theories that support them to be evaluated. In the sections that follow, I will review some of the key studies that have investigated these instructional approaches and their theoretical underpinnings.

| General types of explicit instruction | Instructional approaches | Interface position | Theoretical basis |
|---|---|---|---|
| Deductive | pedagogic grammar and production practice (as in presentation-practice-production, i.e. PPP) | strong | Skill-learning theory (DeKeyser 1998) |
| Deductive | integrated instruction (i.e. explicit explanation provided during communicative practice) | strong | Transfer Appropriate Processing (Lightbown 2008) |
| Deductive | concept-based instruction (involving presentation of 'scientific concepts' and production practice | strong | Sociocultural theory (Lantolf and Thorne 2006) |
| Deductive | comprehension-based instruction (as in Processing Instruction) | strong | Input Processing Theory (VanPatten 1996) |
| Inductive | pattern practice (as in the Audiolingual Method) | strong | Behaviourism (habit formation) |
| Inductive | consciousness-raising instruction (involving consciousness-raising tasks) | weak | Theory of Instructed Language Learning (R. Ellis 1994) |

*Table 10.2  Different kinds of explicit instruction*

## Presentation-Practice-Production instruction

Presentation-practice-production (PPP) constitutes the dominant approach promoted in teacher guides (e.g. Scrivener 2005; Ur 1996). As noted in Chapter 9, it is supported by Skill-Learning Theory, which claims that language learning is like any other kind of learning. The starting point is **declarative knowledge** (i.e. explicit knowledge of specific linguistic forms), which is then proceduralized through practice until eventually it becomes automatic. Acquisition of linguistic forms, therefore, is conceptualized as involving a shift from controlled to automatic processing. The role of instruction is to facilitate this process by first providing learners with explicit knowledge of a target feature and then, through practice, facilitating the cognitive changes needed for automatic processing. In effect, then, PPP assumes a strong interface between explicit and implicit knowledge although, as DeKeyser (2003) pointed out, the end result may not be 'true' implicit knowledge but rather speeded-up declarative knowledge, which he argued was functionally equivalent. The extent to which even this takes place, however, is disputed with some researchers (e.g. Hulstijn 2002; Paradis 2009) claiming that there are limits to how automatized explicit knowledge can become and that it is not equivalent to implicit knowledge.

The test of skill-learning theory is whether PPP results in the learners' ability to communicate freely using the language feature targeted by the instruction. To investigate this, I have chosen a number of carefully designed studies whose instructional components reflect the principles of PPP. That is, the explicit component should provide a clear explanation of the target feature and the practice component should include a variety of activities including communicative tasks. The inclusion of communicative tasks is seen as of special importance because—as DeKeyser (1998) emphasized—for automatization to happen, learners need to practise the target feature under 'real operating conditions'. Three further criteria for the selection of the studies were: (1) they included a control group that did not receive the instruction; (2) the testing regime included a measurement of learning based on free production (i.e. not just discrete point tests); and (3) there was a delayed test to provide some evidence of long-term learning. I have also selected studies that investigated a variety of linguistic features—grammatical, lexical, socio-pragmatic, and phonological. Table 10.3 summarizes six studies that meet these specifications.

These studies all involved the explicit presentation of the target feature(s). All of them—with the possible exception of Housen et al. (2005)—involved practice activities that included communicative tasks. However, they varied in a number of ways, in particular regarding the length of the instruction provided. The overall results are clear: explicit instruction, together with practice, led to gains over time and to statistically significant differences when the experimental groups were compared to control groups. These gains were evident when the target features involved grammar (Harley 1989; Housen et al. 2005; Akakura 2012), vocabulary (Shintani 2011), a pragmalinguistic feature (Lyster 2004), and pronunciation (Saito and Lyster 2012). In the case of the studies that investigated grammatical features, the gains were evident both in simple features—for example, French negation—and also in more complex features known to cause problems to L2 learners—for example, the contrast between French passé composé and imparfait for French learners of L2 English; English articles for Asian learners; and French passive constructions. Only Akakura failed to find any effect of instruction on one of the features she investigated—generic uses of English articles—but the learners in her study rarely made any attempt to use this feature. One might conclude, therefore, that the type of instruction in these studies—explicit presentation combined with practice that included focus-on-form activities—can result in the development of implicit knowledge or, at least, automatized declarative knowledge.

Those studies in Table 10.3 that were directed at grammar learning reflect the general finding of Norris and Ortega's (2000) **meta-analysis** of different types of form-focused instruction, namely that explicit instruction involving Focus-on-Form activities has a large effect on grammar learning.

| Study | Target feature | Participants | Instruction | Tests | Results |
|---|---|---|---|---|---|
| Harley (1989) | two French verb tenses—*passé composé* and *imparfait* | 319 grade-six students in a French immersion programme in Canada | explicit description of the target structures followed by eight weeks of practice activities including communicative tasks | ratings based on written compositions; cloze test scores; errors scores based on an oral interview. | The instructed learners outperformed the control group on all measures derived from both the immediate and delayed post-tests—including those based on the oral interview. |
| Lyster (1994) | French address forms *tu* and *vous* | 106 grade-eight students in a French immersion programme in Canada | explicit techniques (e.g. comparing use of *tu* and *vous*); structured exercises; intensive reading activities, free writing, role plays. | an oral production test, a written production test, and a multiple-choice test. | Immediate and delayed tests showed clear gains in both oral and written production and also awareness of socio-stylistic differences. |
| Housen, Pierrard, and van Daele (2006) | 69 14–15-year-old Dutch speaking learners of L2 French in Belgium | French sentence negation (a 'simple structure'); French passive constructions (a 'complex structure') | four weeks of instruction consisting of: (1) pedagogical rule; (2) reading text; (3) identification of exemplars in the text; (4) description of these examples; (5) sentence-transformation and answering semi-open questions. | an unplanned production task consisting of oral questions about pictures and objects, which the learners had to answer instantly. | No difference between experimental and control groups on absolute number of tokens of target structure produced on the immediate post-test, but experimental group significantly outperformed the control group in accuracy of production. Same pattern for delayed post-test. The complexity of the target structure did not affect the results. |

| Study | Target feature | Instruction | Tests | Results |
|---|---|---|---|---|
| Akakura (2012) | Non-generic and generic uses of English articles (*a* and *the*) | computer-based; explicit explanation of functions performed by articles; controlled and free production activities. | an elicited imitation task and an oral production task to measure implicit knowledge; a grammaticality judgement task and a metalinguistic knowledge test to measure explicit knowledge (see R. Ellis 2005c) | The instructed learners outperformed the control group in the immediate and delayed metalinguistic knowledge test and elicited imitation task. However, no effect was evident for the generic use of articles in the oral production task. Effects of instruction stronger in delayed tests. |
| Shintani (2011) | 24 nouns and 12 adjectives | explicit presentation of the target words followed by controlled and free practice activities. | discrete word production test; same or different task | The PPP group outperformed the control group. Significant gains for both nouns and adjectives evident in both tests. The gains were maintained in the delayed post-test. |
| Saito and Lyster (2012) | English /r/ as in 'red' | Four hours of form-focused instruction integrated into argumentative skills lessons containing 38 minimally paired words. Instruction carried out with and without corrective feedback to two experimental groups. Control group received no instruction and no corrective feedback. | ratings and acoustic analyses conducted on /r/ tokens of familiar and unfamiliar items elicited via a word reading test, a sentence reading test and a timed picture description task. | The group that received corrective feedback demonstrated improvement in pronunciation of /r/ in both controlled and free production both immediately after instruction and later. In contrast, the group that received instruction without corrective feedback did not improve. |

*Table 10.3 Selection of studies investigating effects of explicit instruction*

However, the situation is different for pronunciation. Saito's (2012) meta-analysis of pronunciation studies reported that while six studies that involved focus-on-form activities reported improvement at a controlled level, only two of them did so at the spontaneous level. All eight studies that involved only focus-on-forms failed to demonstrate any improvement in spontaneous language use.[2]

A number of caveats are also in order. All the studies—with the exception of Shintani's—investigated learners whose knowledge of the target features was already established. In other words, the studies demonstrate that explicit instruction helps learners achieve greater accuracy in the use of linguistic forms than they have already partially acquired. One might ask whether such instruction is also effective in helping learners acquire completely new linguistic features. Shintani's study demonstrated that it is effective for teaching new words, which involves **item-learning**. It does not follow, however, that it is also effective for teaching new grammatical items, which involves **system-learning**. One interpretation of Akakura's study is that instruction had no effect on implicit knowledge of a structure—generic articles—which constituted a relatively 'new' structure for most of her learners. There is an obvious need to test skill-learning theory in studies that investigate the system-learning of new grammatical structures as DeKeyser (2007) argued that the theory is most clearly applicable to the fairly early stages of learning.

A second caveat concerns *how* the instruction facilitated learning. In general, the studies were product based—i.e they examined the effects of the instruction in terms of performance on post-tests of various kinds. They did not provide much information about what actually occurred in the 'black box' of the classroom—for example, whether and in what ways the learners received **corrective feedback**. In Chapter 7, we saw that corrective feedback during interaction has been shown to have a positive effect on learning. Saito and Lyster's (2012) study also showed that the corrective feedback received by one of their experimental groups was crucially important, as only this group showed improvement. Corrective feedback was almost certainly provided in all the studies and this may have been a factor in the effectiveness of the instruction. Later in this chapter, I will return to an examination of the role of corrective feedback.

All the studies provided learners with input including the target feature, often in ways designed to draw attention to the target feature. In other words, these studies examined the joint effect of both input and production practice. This raises another question. Is production-practice needed or does input-based practice by itself suffice? This question is of obvious theoretical importance to SLA, as theories differ in whether they see learning as input- or output-driven or both. I will also examine this issue in a later section of the chapter.

A final issue concerns the nature of the metalinguistic information learners are given in explicit instruction. Norris and Ortega pointed out the lack of consistency across studies in the way in which this is handled. In general, the rules presented to learners are based on pedagogical grammar—i.e. they emphasize 'clarity' and 'simplicity' over 'truth'. See Swan (1994) for a list of criteria that pedagogical rules need to satisfy. However, there is considerable variability. Later, I examine a type of explicit instruction that emphasizes the importance of presenting learners with 'scientific concepts' about grammar in a way designed to ensure they are internalized. Studies also differ in terms of when the explicit rules were provided—either prior to the instruction or during it. In the next section, I consider instruction where explicit explanations of the target structure occurred within the communicative practice.

## Integrated explicit instruction

Whereas PPP takes as its starting point the presentation of explicit information about the target structure, **integrated instruction** embeds explicit explanation into communicative practice activities. Thus, the difference rests in *when* the explicit information is provided. The theoretical basis for integrated explicit instruction lies in the **Transfer Appropriate Processing Hypothesis,** which I introduced in Chapter 8. In accordance with this hypothesis, explicit information will be more effective if it is provided while learners are communicating as they are more likely to remember it and be better able to access it in a subsequent communicative activity.

Spada et al. (2014) reported a study that compared isolated and integrated explicit instruction. Both types of instruction drew on the same topics and themes (e.g. medical practices, famous places) and both involved providing learners with explicit information about the target structure (English passive). In the **isolated instruction,** the target structure was first explained to the learners who then engaged in communicative/content-based activities without any further explicit focus on the passive. In the integrated instruction, a specific theme was first introduced focusing purely on content. Then, the learners performed the communicative activities during which the teacher provided brief interventions by means of quick explanations and corrective feedback. Learning was assessed by means of a written error-correction test and a picture-cued oral production task. Both types of instruction proved effective and there were no significant group differences. However, the group receiving the isolated instruction gained higher scores for passive on the error-correction test while the integrated instruction group did better on the oral production task.

This study provides further evidence that instruction consisting of an initial explanation of the target structure followed by communicative practice—i.e. isolated instruction—is effective. It indicates, however, that integrated instruction is also effective. While no firm conclusions can be drawn from this study, it points to a differential effect of the two types of instruction. Isolated instruction may contribute mainly to explicit knowledge—the kind of knowledge tapped by the error-correction test—while integrated instruction may be more beneficial for the development of implicit knowledge—the kind of knowledge tapped by the oral production task. As such, it lends some support to the Transfer Appropriate Processing Hypothesis.

## Concept-based instruction

As we saw in Chapter 9, sociocultural theory emphasizes the importance of developing 'conceptually organized grammatical knowledge' by means of accounts of grammatical features that explain in detail the link between form and semantic/functional concepts. Such accounts are seen as an important mediational tool. Lantolf (2007) questioned the usefulness of 'rules-of-thumb' drawn from pedagogic grammar. He commented 'rules of thumb are not necessarily wrong, but they generally describe concrete empirical occurrences of the relevant phenomenon in a fairly unsystematic fashion and, as a result, fail to reveal deeper systematic principles' (p. 36). He argued that learners need access to 'scientific concepts', a term taken from Vygotsky (1986). The kind of explicit instruction that Lantolf favours consists of the direct presentation of scientific concepts about grammar followed by activities that provide for spoken and written communicative practice.

Lantolf drew on Gal'perin's (1989) proposal for systemic-functional instruction. This is based on three fundamental principles: (1) the instruction needs to be organized around coherent theoretical units; (2) it needs to provide a material instantiation of the target concepts; and (3) learners need to verbalize the concept-based explanation to foster full understanding and internalization of the concepts. Principle (1) involves the direct presentation of the 'scientific concepts' relevant to the target of the instruction. Principle (2) is achieved by means of charts and diagrams representing the concepts. Principle (3) is seen as crucial—learners need to verbalize the concepts as they perform production activities.

Neguerela and Lantolf (2006) reported a study illustrating this approach. The study investigated 12 students in a typical university Spanish-as-a-foreign-language course. The class met three times a week for 15 weeks. The explicit instruction involved a 'Schema for the Complete Orienting Basis of Action' for presenting grammatical aspect. It consisted of a flow chart that led the learners through a series of questions to help them understand when to use the preterite and imperfect tenses in Spanish. The students were asked to verbalize the schema six times while carrying out a number of oral and written activities based on interactive scenarios in which learners argued for their preferred course of action. They then produced a written version of the scenario. The aim was to assist internalization of the information in the schema so the learners could use it automatically when communicating.

The students' verbal explanations of the grammatical structures were collected at the beginning and end of the course. Initially, these were simplistic and incomplete, reflecting the rules of thumb in in the student textbooks that the students were familiar with. Their explanations at the end of the course—although not always complete—were generally more coherent and accurate, reflecting the complex factors that determine choice of aspectual form in Spanish. Neguerela and Lantolf suggested that this was indicative of internalization of the concept taking place.

The study also provided evidence to show that the learners were able to use the formal features associated with the target concepts more accurately at the end of the course—i.e. their improved conceptual understanding was reflected in improved accuracy in production. However, the effects of the instruction were more clearly evident in students' written work, which allows for **monitoring** using explicit knowledge, than in their oral production, which is more likely to draw on their implicit knowledge. Thus, while the study demonstrates that conceptually-organized instruction may help students develop clearer explicit knowledge, it does not convincingly show that the instruction resulted in implicit knowledge of the target features[3].

Neguerela and Lantolf 's study can be seen as lending support to the central claim of **Sociocultural SLA**—namely that learning is mediated by cultural artefacts—i.e. the scientific descriptions of linguistic phenomena presented directly to learners—and by social interaction in the performance of communicative activities. However, the study was not comparative in design and so does not allow us to conclude that giving learners scientific descriptions makes explicit instruction more effective than giving them simplified pedagogical rules. Also, this study and others like it to date have all involved university-level students of foreign languages and doubts must remain about the suitability of **Concept-based Instruction** for other kinds of learners—for example, young beginner learners or adult learners with low language analytical ability—and in other settings—for example, in second language contexts.

## Comprehension-based instruction

So far, I have focused on research that investigated the effects of explicit explanation in combination with production-based practice activities. This reflects the way in which explicit instruction is generally executed. However, as I noted earlier, some cognitive theories of L2 acquisition emphasize the importance of input in learning. Thus, we can ask whether metalinguistic explanation followed by comprehension-based activities—in which learners are induced to process the meaning of the target features in the input—is sufficient for learning to take place and—in fact—whether it is more effective than production-based instruction.

The case for comprehension-based language teaching was first made in the 1960s. Asher (1977) reported the results of a number of studies investigating the effects of his Total Physical Response Method (TPR), which involved learners listening to and responding to commands without any production practice. Overall, TPR proved superior to traditional production-based instruction, although the studies suffered from a number of design problems. In 1981

Winitiz published an edited collection of papers on **comprehension-based instruction**. In the same decade, Krashen and Terrell (1983) proposed their **Natural Approach**, which was premised on the assumption that ability to produce in an L2 emerges only after learners have acquired some language through comprehending input. Later, VanPatten (1996) also argued that the acquisition of grammatical features originates in input. However—unlike Winitz and Krashen—he rejected the view that learning will always occur 'naturally' and automatically if learners are exposed to comprehensible input and argued that it was necessary to focus learners' attention on specific grammatical forms and their meanings. The approach he developed—called **Processing Instruction**—is considered below.

## Theoretical positions

Comparative studies of comprehension- and **production-based instruction** are of theoretical importance in SLA as they provide a means of testing a number of different theoretical positions:

1 Comprehension-based instruction benefits receptive, but not productive L2 knowledge, whereas production-based instruction benefits productive knowledge, but not receptive knowledge. This position is supported by **Skill-Learning Theory** which views the effects of instruction as skill-specific (DeKeyser 2007).

2 Production-based instruction will prove superior to comprehension-based instruction in developing both types of knowledge. This position receives support from theories that emphasize the importance of production in L2 acquisition. The **Output Hypothesis** (Swain 1985; 1995), for example, proposes that advanced acquisition requires opportunities for **pushed output** (See Chapter 7).

3 Comprehension-based instruction will prove superior to production-based instruction in developing both types of knowledge. This is supported by models of L2 acquisition that propose a single knowledge store that is drawn on for both comprehension and production and that develops as a result of processing input. VanPatten (2007) argued that input processing (defined as the process by which a form-meaning connection is established) leads to changes in the learner's internal grammar, which will be manifest in both reception and production (see Chapter 8).

4 Production-based instruction will only benefit acquisition if it takes account of the learners' level of L2 development, but no such constraint exists in the case of comprehension-based instruction. This position is evident in Pienemann's (1985) claim regarding the learnability and teachability of grammatical structures. Pienemann proposed that the ability to produce a specific grammatical structure depends on whether the learner has mastered the specific processing operation that it requires (see Chapter 4). The **Teachability Hypothesis** predicts that:

'instruction can only promote language acquisition if the interlanguage is close to the point when the structure to be taught is acquired in the natural setting so that sufficient processing prerequisites are developed'. (Pienemann 1985: 37).

However, this only applies to the acquisition of productive ability. I will examine these different theoretical positions, first by examining studies that compared comprehension-based and production-based instruction and, second by examining studies that investigated a particular type of comprehension-based instruction: Processing Instruction.

## Comprehension-based vs production-based studies

Shintani, Li, and Ellis (2013) reported a **meta-analysis** of studies that have compared the effects of comprehension-based and production-based instruction on L2 learning. Of the 35 studies included in the analysis, 29 involved explicit instruction—i.e. they included an explicit presentation of the target structure catering to intentional language learning. All of these studies measured the effects of instruction using both tests of receptive and productive knowledge. The results for these 29 studies showed that both types of instruction benefitted both receptive and productive knowledge of the target features. Comprehension-based instruction was more effective than production-based instruction for the acquisition of receptive knowledge but only in the immediate tests—i.e. the advantage was not sustained over time. The opposite was the case for production-based instruction: it was more effective than comprehension-based instruction for productive knowledge in the delayed tests, but there was no difference in the immediate tests. The meta-analysis also investigated the relative effects of the two types of instruction depending on the nature of the production-based instruction—i.e. whether it involved focus-on-forms activities or also included focus-on-meaning activities. The comprehension-based instruction was more effective that the production-based instruction for developing receptive knowledge when the latter only consisted of focus-on-forms activities.

The results of this meta-analysis provide some support for Skill-Learning Theory. Both types of instruction were beneficial for both receptive and productive knowledge but, overall, comprehension-based instruction was more effective for developing receptive knowledge in the short term, and production-based instruction more effective for productive knowledge in the long term.

All in all, however, there was no clear evidence to support the superiority of either type of instruction. The meta-analysis did not enable Pienemann's Teachability Hypothesis to be tested. This hypothesis applies only to acquisition of productive knowledge of 'new' grammatical features and it was not possible to establish whether the target structures investigated in the studies were 'new' or already 'partially acquired'.

## Processing Instruction

I now turn to look in more detail at a sub-set of the input-based studies based on VanPatten's (1996) **Input Processing Principles**, which were introduced in Chapter 8. VanPatten argued that it is difficult for learners to attend concurrently to different stimuli in the input and so they need to decide how to prioritize their attentional resources during online processing. Due to limited working memory capacity, they typically resort to a number of default processing strategies captured in Input Processing Principles such 'Learners prefer processing lexical items to grammatical items—for example, 'morphological markings' (p. 14) for semantic information' and the First Noun principle, i.e. 'Learners tend to process the first noun or pronoun they encounter in a sentence as the subject/agent' (p. 33). For VanPatten, two points followed. First, the purpose of instruction should be to help learners overcome these default processing strategies. Second, only grammatical features that are governed by these principles are deemed suitable targets for investigating the effects of Processing Instruction on acquisition. For example, English past tense is a good candidate for instruction because learners are likely to fail to notice the inflection on the verb if the sentence also contains an adverbial marker of past time, as in 'Yesterday I visited an old friend in London'.

Because the problem learners face in acquiring certain grammatical features relates to perception—i.e. attending to them in input—it follows that what is needed is 'a type of grammar instruction whose purpose is to affect the ways in which learners attend to input data' (VanPatten 1996: 2). VanPatten argued that such instruction will prove more effective than traditional production practice—i.e. practice involving text-manipulation activities. While not dismissing production practice, VanPatten (2004a) claimed that it only assists skill development—i.e. it increases control over the use of a grammatical feature in production—and that input alone is sufficient for acquisition.

Processing Instruction, then, aims to help learners overcome their default processing strategies. It consists of three components:

1 explicit explanation of the target structure
2 explicit strategy training to enable learners to overcome the default processing strategy
3 structured input activities.

The most important component is **structured input**. Lee and VanPatten (2003) proposed the following guidelines for the development of structured input activities:

- Present one thing at a time.
- Keep meaning in focus.
- Move from sentences to connected discourse.
- Use both oral and written input.
- Keep the learner's processing strategies in mind.

Structured input consists of both referential and affective activities. The former require the learner to choose between two interpretations of a sentence—for example whether it refers to the 'present' or 'past'—when responding to sentences like 'Maria visited her sister during the holidays'. The latter require learners to indicate an opinion or belief and so allow for more than one correct answer. Thus referential activities force attention onto the target form, whereas affective activities simply provide learners with input containing the form[4].

The studies we will now consider examined position (3) above—namely, the claim that Processing Instruction is more effective than production-based instruction in helping learners acquire L2 grammar. In an early study, VanPatten and Cadierno (1993) compared the effects of two instructional treatments, one directed at manipulating learners' output through production practice, and the other aimed at changing the way the learners perceived and processed input. Learners of Spanish in a university level course, who received input-processing practice relating to Spanish word order rules and the use of clitic pronouns (as in the sentence 'La sigue el señor'—'Her follows the man') performed better in comprehension tests than a group of similar learners who received production practice involving both purely form-focused and more meaning-centred activities. This input-processing group also performed at the same level as the production practice group in a production task. This study, then, suggested that Processing Instruction was superior to traditional production practice.

The instruction provided to both groups in this study also contained explicit explanation about the target. A later study (VanPatten and Oikennon 1996) investigated whether the provision of explicit explanation had contributed to the effect of the processing instruction. In this study, there were three groups: (1) received explicit information about the target structure followed by structured input activities; (2) received only explicit information; and (3) just completed the structured input activities. Acquisition was measured by means of both comprehension and production tests. In the comprehension test, significant gains were evident in groups (1) and (3), but not in (2). In the production test, group (1) did better than group (2). VanPatten and Oikennon interpreted these results as showing that it was the structured input, rather than the explicit information, that was important for acquisition. Other studies—for example, Sanz and Morgan-Short (2004) and Benati (2004)—have since replicated these results. However, more recent studies—for example, Fernández (2008); Henry, Culman, and VanPatten (2009)—have shown that explicit information plays an important role at least for some grammatical structures, such as those that are redundant and therefore less noticeable in the input.

There have now been a large number of studies that have investigated Processing Instruction—with and without explicit explanation. Shintani (2015) conducted a meta-analysis of 42 comparative research experiments. The main finding was that Processing Instruction had a greater effect in the receptive tests than in the productive tests, while the opposite was the case for production-based instruction.

Shintani noted that the learners who received production-based instruction fared relatively poorly in the receptive tests. To investigate why this might be the case, she considered the role played by explicit strategy training. She showed that the effectiveness of the Processing Instruction was not influenced by the presence or absence of explicit explanation plus strategy training: structured input by itself proved sufficient, as in VanPatten and Oikennon's study. However, the presence of explicit strategy training did have an effect in the case of production-based instruction. When Shintani compared those production-based groups who had received strategy training with those that had not, she found that the former scored notably higher in the receptive tests. In other words—while strategy training played a non-significant role in the Processing Instruction—it contributed significantly to the effect that production-based instruction had on receptive knowledge. She concluded that production-based instruction could be as effective as Processing Instruction for receptive knowledge, but only if it included explicit strategy training.

Another issue concerns the durability of the effects of the two types of instruction, as seen in the results for the immediate and delayed tests. Shintani found that the effects of the Processing Instruction in both the receptive and productive tests atrophied over time, suggesting that its impact on acquisition is not long-lasting. She interpreted this result as showing that the knowledge resulting from the Processing Instruction was of the explicit rather than implicit kind, as **explicit knowledge** is more likely to atrophy. The effects of the production-based instruction also reduced over time, but only in the production tests. The receptive test scores did not decline. Shintani speculated that—because the production-based instruction did not typically involve explicit strategy training—the learners did not develop explicit knowledge and so relied on their more resilient **implicit knowledge.**

There is, in fact, little evidence that Processing Instruction results in the implicit knowledge (or proceduralized explicit knowledge) needed for fluent communication. Very few of the studies included measures of learning based on free oral production. Clearly, there is a need for further research to ascertain whether Processing Instruction has any effect on accuracy in free oral production.

The following are the main conclusions regarding the effectiveness of Processing Instruction:

1 Processing Instruction is effective. It results in development of both receptive and productive knowledge.
2 However, its positive effect is more evident in tests of receptive knowledge than productive knowledge.
3 Also, there is no clear evidence that it leads to the kind of implicit knowledge needed for communicative language use.

4 In the case of more complex grammatical structures, explicit explanation together with explicit strategy training may be needed, while for simpler grammatical structures, structured input by itself may suffice.

## Final comments

This review of the research that has investigated the comparative effects of comprehension-based and production-based instruction lends general support to skill-learning theory—i.e. position (1) above. By and large, comprehension-based instruction facilitates the development of the knowledge needed for comprehending grammatical structures and production-based instruction the knowledge required for producing them. However, the studies also demonstrate that both types of instruction can have an effect on both comprehension and production. This is not surprising, as the two types of instruction may not be as distinct as assumed. It is quite possible that learners receiving comprehension-based instruction engage in silent production practice—i.e. what is termed **private speech** in sociocultural theory—while the learners receiving production-based practice will also be exposed to input when they listen to other students' attempts to produce the target structure and to the teacher's **corrective feedback**.

DeKeyser and Prieto Botana (2015) noted that the research investigating Processing Instruction is quite limited as relatively few grammatical structures have been examined. From a pedagogic perspective, however, there is sufficient evidence to suggest that structured-input activities are a useful addition to the battery of instructional devices for teaching grammar. As I pointed out in Ellis (2002a), many published grammar teaching materials make little use of such activities.

## Pattern practice

Up to now, I have focused on explicit instruction of the deductive kind. Some of the Input Processing studies I considered, however, involved inductive instruction—i.e. there was no explicit explanation of the target structures. These studies indicated that instruction consisting of structured input alone was effective for some structures. I turn now to examine studies that involved inductive production-based instruction of the pattern practice kind.

Pattern practice is closely associated with the **Audiolingual Method**. This was based on **behaviourist learning theories**, which view L2 learning as the development of habits, that become ingrained so that learners can automatically use the L2 correctly. Habits are developed by systematically engaging learners in drills of various kinds—for example, repetition, substitution, and transformation—which present learners with stimuli and carefully control their responses to ensure they do not make errors. Mimicry and memorization of these stimuli play a major role.

The effectiveness of the Audiolingual Method was investigated in a number of large-scale studies that compared it with deductive methods involving explicit presentation. The best of these studies was the Gothenberg Project (Levin 1972). In this project, different groups of learners engaged in pattern practice either with or without grammatical explanations. No significant differences between the inductive and deductive groups of school learners were found. In fact, very little learning occurred in either. In the case of an older group of high school students, however, a clearer advantage was found for the deductive instruction. Also, older learners benefitted most from the deductive method. This project, like the other global method comparisons, failed to show that one method was superior to another in terms of overall language proficiency. Short-term differences were sometimes evident, but these disappeared over the long term. A general conclusion is that pattern practice—even when accompanied by explicit explanation—contributes little to L2 learning.

Other studies have investigated whether there is any relationship between the amount of practice that individual learners engage in and L2 learning—i.e. whether learners who engage in more practice learn more. The results are very mixed. In some studies, learners who practised more learnt more. In others, the opposite proved to be the case. In still others, there was no significant relationship. Again, then, there is no clear evidence to suggest that pattern practice is effective. A reasonable conclusion is that practice of the more controlled kind does not make perfect. In fact, sometimes it can even have a deleterious effect on learning by interfering with natural acquisition processes and causing learners to overuse the structure they have practised intensively (Lightbown 1983).

There is a strong theoretical reason for doubting the effectiveness of pattern practice. The Transfer Appropriate Processing Hypothesis predicts that there is a direct relationship between the type of practice and the kind of learning that takes place. Pattern practice of the audiolingual kind positions learners as responders to stimuli and thus is unlikely to prepare them to participate in spontaneous face-to-face communication where they will need to play an initiating as well as a responding role.

## Consciousness-raising Instruction

All the types of explicit instruction we have examined so far involve consciousness-raising in the sense that they aim—deductively or inductively—to make learners aware of the properties of the feature that is the target of the instruction. However, in a series of publications (e.g. Ellis 1991; 1993; 2012) I have used the term **Consciousness-raising Instruction** to refer to instruction based on tasks designed to help learners to construct their own explicit rules about structural features. This type of explicit instruction differs from other types in that it does not include any comprehension or production-practice activities.

The theoretical justification for Consciousness-raising Instruction rests on the claim that explicit instruction of any kind is unlikely to affect implicit knowledge because of developmental constraints (see Chapter 4), but that it can contribute to explicit knowledge, which is not subject to such constraints. The **weak-interface position** makes two claims: (1) implicit and explicit knowledge are neurolinguistically distinct (Paradis 2009) making the transformation of explicit into implicit knowledge impossible; and (2) explicit knowledge of linguistic features can facilitate the processes involved in the development of implicit knowledge (e.g. **noticing** and **noticing-the gap**—see Chapter 8). It follows, then, that instruction should focus on the development of explicit rather than implicit knowledge and that this is justified by the role that explicit knowledge plays in the subsequent, natural development of implicit knowledge. Consciousness-raising Instruction requires learners to engage in **languaging** (see Chapter 9).

Consciousness-raising Instruction makes use of consciousness-raising tasks—i.e. activities for helping learners construct an explicit representation of a target feature. They consist of data illustrating the use of the target feature and require one or more operations—for example, identification of the feature and rule-formation—that guide learners in analysing the data in order to enable them to arrive at the explicit representation. They do not require production of the feature and—unlike structured-input activities—they do not provide practice in input processing. The focus is entirely on representation.

A number of studies have investigated consciousness-raising tasks. A good example is Eckerth (2008). This study investigated university-level learners of German who completed two tasks—a text-reconstruction task and a text-repair task—where the learners worked in pairs to agree on a correct version of a text given to them. Although not framed by sociocultural theory, this study demonstrated the importance of the 'learner-learner **scaffolding**' (p. 102) that occurred while learners performed the tasks as they attended to the ways in which form, meaning, function, and context interrelated. Eckerth also investigated the effects of the tasks in tests designed to provide measures of explicit knowledge of the target features. He reported significant gains between both the pre-test and the immediate post-test, and also between the immediate and delayed post-tests. In other words the learners showed incremental gains across the period of the study.

Consciousness-raising Instruction has been shown to be effective in helping learners develop explicit knowledge[5]. But does this knowledge facilitate the processes involved in subsequent development of implicit knowledge? In fact, this has been little studied. Fotos (1993) showed that the explicit knowledge that learners gained from performing consciousness-raising tasks helped subsequent noticing of the targeted features. Several weeks after the completion of the tasks, the learners in her study completed a number of dictations that included exemplars of the target structures. They were then asked to underline any particular bit of language they had paid special attention to as they did the dictations. Fotos reported that they frequently underlined the structures that had been targeted in the consciousness-raising tasks.

# Feedback

Providing learners with feedback is an important element of all the forms of explicit instruction we have examined. Feedback can be positive—i.e. it shows learners their response is correct—or negative—i.e. it shows them their response is incorrect. The nature of the feedback differs in comprehension-based and production-based instruction. In the former, it simply indicates whether learners have succeeded in processing the target feature correctly in the input. In the latter, it enables them to see if they produced the target structure correctly and sometimes provides the correct form.

Somewhat surprisingly, there is little mention of feedback in many of the studies that have investigated comprehension-based instruction. Potentially, the timing of the feedback is significant. It can be provided *within* a structured input activity—i.e. immediately after learners have responded to an input stimulus—or *at the end* of the activity—i.e. by the teacher informing the learners of the correct answers for all the stimuli. The former is perhaps more likely to assist input-processing as learners can use the feedback they receive on one item to adjust their response to the following item. In one study that did report feedback procedures (Marsden 2006), feedback was only provided at the end of an activity. In another study (Toth 2006), feedback was provided—sometimes by the teacher and sometimes by learners—on learners' responses to individual stimuli. No study has investigated the comparative effects of providing feedback in these different ways.

All the different types of **corrective feedback** I considered in Chapter 7—i.e. input-providing vs output-prompting; implicit vs explicit—can occur in explicit instruction involving production activities. The conclusion I reached in that chapter was that all the types assist learning but that—on balance—the explicit types are more effective than the implicit types. The importance of corrective feedback in explicit instruction is demonstrated in Tomasello and Herron's (1988) 'down the garden path' approach. This involved deliberately eliciting errors in learners' production and then correcting them explicitly. They found this type of production practice more effective than simply providing learners with explanations of the target structures. The corrective feedback enabled the learners to carry out a **cognitive comparison** between their own deviant utterances and the correct target-language provided by the teacher.

Saito and Lyster (2012; see Table 10.3) compared the effects of production-based explicit instruction with and without corrective feedback and found that only those learners who received the feedback improved. This suggests that corrective feedback is an essential element in explicit instruction where pronunciation is concerned. Is it possible, then, that corrective feedback by itself suffices for learning to take place—i.e. there is no need for explicit grammar lessons? Spada and Lightbown's (1993) study suggests this might be the case. In this study, an experimental group received explicit instruction consisting of explicit explanation, focus-on-forms and focus-on-form activities, and corrective feedback. A comparison group did not receive the explicit instruction but the teacher regularly corrected their errors. The experimental group improved accuracy in the use of the target structures. But so too did the control group. This study suggests that as long as learners receive feedback, there may be no need for explicit grammar lessons.

Feedback is viewed as important for acquisition in all theories of L2 acquisition—cognitive and social. It is tempting to conclude that it is the single most important factor in explicit instruction, especially if the feedback is sustained over time. In terms of cognitive theories, it promotes attention to form, it helps learners to carry out a cognitive comparison, and it pushes them to produce the correct form. In terms of social theories, new linguistic forms can emerge in the repair work that occurs in form and accuracy contexts.

## The interface positions revisited

The perspective I have adopted in this chapter is to consider research that has investigated explicit instruction in relation to different theories of L2 acquisition. As shown in Table 10.2, these theories (and the types of explicit instruction they lend support to) differ in terms of the interface position they adopt—i.e. a strong or a weak position. I will now reconsider the research in relation to these positions.

The ultimate purpose of all types of explicit instruction is to help learners use the linguistic features targeted by the instruction in unplanned language use without the need for conscious monitoring. Instruction can achieve this directly by facilitating an interface between explicit and implicit knowledge—the **strong-interface position**—or indirectly by developing explicit knowledge which subsequently, and over time, can promote the usage-based processes involved in the development of implicit knowledge—the **weak interface position**. Inherent in both positions is the claim that explicit instruction can lead to implicit knowledge and in this respect they differ from the **non-interface position**. The strong and weak interface positions differ primarily in how and when this is achieved.

In order to investigate these different positions, it is necessary to examine how the learning that results from instruction is measured. That is, separate measures of explicit and implicit knowledge are required. Obtaining such measures is no easy task as language users are likely to draw on whatever knowledge resources they have. However, in R. Ellis (2005c) I proposed a number of criteria for designing tasks that would bias learners to the use of either explicit or implicit knowledge and went on to report a study that investigated the validity of measures of the two types of knowledge based on these criteria. Tasks likely to elicit explicit knowledge are those that focus learners on linguistic correctness and allow them plenty of time to respond—for example, untimed fill-in-the-blank exercises or grammaticality judgements. Tasks more likely to elicit implicit knowledge are those that focus learners' attention on meaning and are time-pressured—for example, elicited oral imitation tests and oral production tasks. However, if implicit and proceduralized explicit knowledge are functionally equivalent—as suggested by DeKeyser (2003)—the measures I have proposed for implicit knowledge cannot be used to investigate the strong-interface position as currently formulated. Perhaps, though, this does not matter as we can still ask whether explicit instruction results in the type of knowledge (implicit or proceduralized explicit knowledge) needed in spontaneous communication.

## The strong-interface position

The studies we have examined in previous sections of this chapter afford mixed evidence. There is little evidence to show that the Processing Instruction studies or the Concept-based Instruction studies resulted in improved accuracy in free oral production tasks—for the simple reason that very few of these studies included such tasks. There is, however, evidence to show that explicit instruction involving focus-on-form activities and corrective feedback does have a positive effect on free oral production. All the studies in Table 10.3 included an oral production task and gains in accuracy were seen in grammatical, lexical, and phonological features. However, there are other studies that have not reported gains. We saw in Saito's (2012) meta-analysis of pronunciation studies that only two out of six reported positive results. In Ellis (2002b) I reviewed 11 grammar studies that included a measure of free oral or written production. Of these, seven reported improved accuracy as a result of the instruction, but four did not.

Is it possible, then, that there a strong-interface for some structures, but not for others? One possibility is that instruction will work if it focuses on a target feature that learners are developmentally ready to acquire. Pienemann (1984) reported a study that indicated this was the case, which led him to formulate his **Teachability Hypothesis**. However, there is very limited support for this hypothesis. Spada and Lightbown (1999) conducted a study to explicitly test its claims by investigating whether the stage of development that learners had reached in the acquisition of English question forms constrained the effect of the instruction. They reported that the learners followed the sequence of development predicted by Pienemann's Processability Theory, but that the beneficial effect of the instruction did not depend on the specific developmental stage individual learners had reached. This study, then, did not provide convincing support for the Teachability Hypothesis.

Another possibility is that a strong interface will be found for easy-to-acquire structures. In Ellis (2002b), I suggested that instruction was more likely to result in implicit knowledge of simple morphological features than of complex syntactic features. However, Spada and Tomita (2010) reached the opposite conclusion. They found that explicit instruction directed at those grammatical forms they considered complex—for example, relative clauses—had a larger effect on accuracy in free communication than instruction directed at simple forms—for example, plurals. The problem here is that there are no agreed criteria for determining what constitutes a complex or simple grammatical form. The only conclusion possible at the moment is that explicit instruction can sometimes lead to improved accuracy in oral production for both simple and complex structures.

One other type of evidence can be used to test the strong-interface position and might also help to decide whether explicit instruction results in implicit knowledge or proceduralized explicit knowledge. As we saw in Chapter 8, implicit knowledge resides in the connectionist networks of implicit memory, which—once established—are tenacious and enduring. Explicit knowledge consists of declarative facts in explicit memory and more readily atrophies. We can ask, then, whether explicit instruction results in knowledge that is durable. The results of Norris and Ortega's (2000) meta-analysis indicated that there was some loss of learning between immediate and delayed post-tests, but that this was relatively small. Some studies (e.g. White 1991), however, have reported substantial loss over time. Whether the effects of instruction are durable may depend on whether learners are subsequently exposed to input containing the target structure and whether they have a communicative need to use it in their own output. One interpretation, then, is that explicit instruction does result in proceduralized explicit knowledge—rather than implicit knowledge—but that implicit knowledge may subsequently develop if the environmental conditions are right. Such an interpretation is more compatible with the weak-interface position.

One important caveat is in order. Just about all the studies examined in this chapter investigated the effects of explicit instruction on features that were already partially acquired. That is, it demonstrated that instruction can lead to greater control—improved accuracy. Arguably, a clearer test of the strong-interface position requires examining whether instruction has any effect on the acquisition of features that learners have no prior knowledge of.

## The weak-interface position

It is important to recognize that the weak-interface position does not reject a role for explicit instruction, but rather re-evaluates it. That is, it supports explicit instruction as a means for developing explicit knowledge, which can subsequently be used to facilitate the development of implicit knowledge by tuning attention to form in communicative input and output. Thus—arguably—the weak-interface position supports a lesser but more manageable role for explicit instruction as there is no expectancy that the instruction will lead to immediate implicit or proceduralized explicit knowledge. The weak-interface position assumes that implicit knowledge can only develop naturally through communicative experiences, but that teaching explicit knowledge will help to speed up this process.

What evidence can we cite in support of this claim? Fotos (1993) study showed that teaching explicit knowledge does tune attention to form in subsequent input. We know, too, that learners rely on explicit knowledge to monitor their communicative output, which can then function as auto-input to implicit learning processes (Schmidt and Frota 1986). There are also studies (for example, Spada 1986) that show that learners who have access both to formal instruction and to exposure to English outside the classroom make the greatest gains in proficiency. Spada commented, 'attention to both form and meaning works best' (p. 133). An implication of her study is that form-focused instruction functions in conjunction with later communicative experiences. However, all this evidence is indirect. As things currently stand, the case for the weak-interface hypothesis rests more on theoretical arguments than on empirical evidence.

## Conclusion

Irrespective of whether the research supports a strong or weak interface position, it is clear that explicit instruction 'works' and has durable effects for at least some linguistic features. Its effects are evident in all levels of language—phonological, lexical, grammatical, and pragmatic. Thus Long's (1983a) early conclusion that 'there is considerable evidence to indicate that second language instruction does make a difference' (p. 374) has been borne out by subsequent research.

The focus of this chapter has been on investigating the effects of different kinds of explicit instruction. The following are the tentative conclusions I have reached:

1 Presentation-practice-production (PPP) instruction results in improved accuracy that is manifest not just in controlled language use but also in free production. Crucial to the effect of this kind of instruction is the presence of activities that cater for the use of the target features under real operating conditions—i.e. communicative language use. Instruction consisting only of pattern practice is unlikely to lead to improved accuracy in free communication.

2 Instruction that includes an explicit explanation of the target feature is, on the whole, more likely to be effective than instruction that does not—i.e. consists only of practice activities.

3 Explicit explanation can be provided prior to practice activities as in isolated instruction or during communicative activities as in integrated instruction. The timing of the explicit information may affect the type of knowledge—explicit or implicit—that results, but this awaits fuller investigation.

4 Further research is needed to investigate the relative effects of presenting learners with simplified explicit explanations of grammatical features or 'scientific concepts'. The former is typical of the PPP studies; the latter figures in Concept-based Instruction. PPP draws on skill-learning theory and Concept-based Instruction on sociocultural theory. The relative effects of these two types of explicit instruction remain unclear.

5 Consciousness-raising tasks provide a means of allowing learners to induce explicit knowledge of a grammatical feature, and have been found to be as effective in this respect as giving learners explicit information.

6 Both comprehension-based and production-based practice activities have been found to be effective. The former contribute mainly to receptive knowledge of the target features and the latter to productive knowledge as predicted by skill-learning theory. However, both types of practice activities contribute to both types of knowledge.

7 Feedback—especially corrective feedback—plays an important and possibly essential role in the effect that explicit instruction has on learning. Practice activities that do not include feedback—in particular explicit corrective feedback—are less effective than those that do.

The studies investigated in this chapter have been premised on the assumption that explicit instruction works in the same way for all learners. However, this is not always the case. Individual difference factors such as the learners' age, language aptitude, and working memory are likely to mediate the effects of instruction. DeKeyser (2007), for example, claimed that high-aptitude learners are more likely to benefit from explicit instruction. Studies that have investigated the mediating role of individual learner factors were considered in Chapter 3.

## Notes

1 The non-interface position does not lend support to any form of explicit instruction and so is not considered in this chapter. It is relevant to the following chapter when implicit instruction is considered.

2 Jeon and Kaya (2006) reported a meta-analysis of studies investigating the effects of L2 instruction on pragmatic development. However, the small number of studies precluded any firm conclusion about the effects of explicit instruction when development was measured using natural language data.

3 Lantolf and Thorne (2006: Chapter 11) summarize a number of other studies that have investigated concept-based instruction. None of them, however, showed that the instruction resulted in improvement in free, spontaneous language use.

4 Henshaw (2012) compared groups that received only referential activities, only affective activities, and a mixture of both. All the groups improved on the receptive post-tests. The two groups that completed affective activities were better able to maintain their learning in the delayed tests.

5 However, not all studies have found consciousness-raising instruction effective (see Ellis 2012). While some studies have reported substantial gains in explicit knowledge, others report little. This may reflect the learning difficulty of the target structure. The studies also report considerable individual variation in learners' ability to benefit from performing CR tasks, suggesting a role for individual difference factors such as **language aptitude**.

# The role of implicit instruction

## Introduction

In the last chapter, we examined the research that has investigated the role of explicit instruction, defined as instruction that invites **intentional learning** of specific features of the second language (L2) and typically includes explicit information about the target feature. In this chapter, we will consider research that has investigated the role of **implicit instruction**, which I have defined as instruction that caters to **incidental acquisition** and aims to attract rather than direct attention to form. See Table 10.1 for a more detailed specification of the differences between these two types of instruction.

Implicit instruction needs to be distinguished from **implicit learning**. In Chapter 8, I defined implicit learning as learning that takes place without any awareness. I also noted that there is disagreement as to whether in fact any learning can occur without some level of awareness—for example, awareness at the level of 'noticing'. Implicit instruction does not assume that the learning that results is necessarily of the implicit kind. Indeed, a major feature of most types of implicit instruction is that learners attend, albeit unobtrusively, to linguistic form and that this is necessary for acquisition to occur. It is for this reason that I have defined implicit instruction as instruction aimed at facilitating incidental acquisition—i.e. the picking-up of linguistic features when learners are not making deliberate efforts to learn them. However, when learners learn incidentally, they may well pay conscious attention to specific target features and this **noticing** may be needed for learning to take place. Implicit instruction, however, does not aim at inducing metalinguistic understanding of target features and it is in this respect that it differs most clearly from explicit instruction.

## Theoretical issues in implicit instruction

The rationale for implicit instruction draws on a number of theoretical constructs that we have considered in previous chapters. First, it assumes that incidental acquisition is possible—even by adults: learners do not have to be told what it is they are supposed to learn. Indeed, in implicit instruction, learners are not told what the target of the instruction is. Rather—as Housen and Pierrard (2006) put it—the instruction is designed so as to 'attract attention to the target form'. Second, it can be argued that incidental acquisition is the main way in which learners develop high levels of proficiency in an L2. Krashen (1982) pointed out that there are limits to how much learners can deliberatively 'learn'—i.e. as explicit knowledge—and that they need opportunities to 'acquire' implicit knowledge. It is difficult to see how the kind of elaborate connectionist network that comprises implicit knowledge—see Chapter 8—can be constructed other than through incidental acquisition. In other words, implicit instruction can help learners to acquire the kind of capacity needed to engage in communication. Of course, this is not to deny a role for explicit instruction, but rather to point out that it is not sufficient.

## Focus-on-form

Arguably, the key theoretical construct that informs implicit instruction is **focus-on-form** (Long 1991). In Chapter 7, I introduced this construct to explain how input and interaction provide opportunities for learners to attend to linguistic form while they are primarily focused on meaning. Implicit instruction aims not just to expose learners to the target language, but to do so in ways that will induce incidental attention to linguistic forms. In Chapter 7, I examined various ways in which this can take place, for example by pre-modifying the input that learners are required to comprehend and through the **interactionally modified input, corrective feedback,** and **pushed output,** which can arise when negotiating a communication or linguistic problem. Activities that give rise to focus-on-form, then, have a central role in implicit instruction. They provide the means for ensuring that **noticing** and **pushed output** take place. In Chapter 10, we noted that focus-on-form activities also play a part in explicit instruction; in particular in the free production stage of a lesson. In implicit instruction, however, such activities comprise the totality of the instruction; that is, there is no explicit presentation of the instructional targets. Attention to form only occurs *while* learners are experiencing use of the L2.

## Limited resources model

However, not all implicit instruction has been based on focus-on-form – or, at least, not as defined by Long. Skehan (1998) draws on his **Dual-Mode Model** (see Chapter 8) as a basis for his own proposals for implicit instruction. This model is premised on the assumption that learners have limited processing capacity and thus will experience difficulty in focusing on form and meaning at the same time and, thus, will need to prioritize one or the other at different times by accessing either their **rule-based system** (when concerned primarily

| Aspects of language production | Description |
|---|---|
| Complexity | The extent to which the learner produces more complex constructions using the rule-based system. It is distinguished from 'accuracy' in that it demonstrates that the learner is taking the risks that will lead to 'restructuring' of the L2 system. |
| Accuracy | The extent to which the learner conforms to target language norms. Accuracy is achieved by the learner drawing on the rule-based system and engaging in syntactic processing in order to avoid making errors. |
| Fluency | The extent to which the learner can speak rapidly without undue pausing, repetition, or reformulation. Fluency is achieved by drawing on ready-made chunks of language and by using communication strategies to address any problems that arise. |

*Table 11.1  Three aspects of language production as described by Skehan (1998)*

with form) or their **exemplar-based system** (when concerned primarily with meaning). Skehan distinguishes three aspects language production: **complexity, accuracy,** and **fluency** (CAF) (see Table 11.1)[1].

Skehan's principal argument is that instruction needs to create the cognitive conditions that will cause learners to prioritize one aspect of production over another. His **Trade-off Hypothesis** proposes that learners will prioritize one aspect of production over the others. Implicit instruction for Skehan, then, is not a means for attracting learner's attention to specific linguistic forms (as in focus-on-form) but rather as a means for orienting learners generally to either meaning or form and—in the case of the latter—to either accuracy or complexity.

To explain how this takes place Skehan (2009) drew on **Levelt's** (1989) **Model of Speech Production.** This distinguishes three basic processes: 'conceptualization', 'formulation', and 'articulation'. Conceptualization concerns the propositional content of the message that a speaker wishes to convey and its communicative intent. Formulation involves developing a linguistic plan for encoding the propositional content by accessing lexis and grammar from long-term memory. Articulation occurs when the plan is performed. In native speakers, these phases occur in parallel. However, L2 learners, especially those with limited proficiency, have difficulty in executing the three phases simultaneously, and thus engage in more linear processing. Thus, if they first conceptualize what they want to say before having to speak, they will then be able to allocate greater attention to formulation and articulation.

This—Skehan suggested—results in language that is both more fluent and more complex, but not necessarily more accurate. If they are pressured to conceptualize, formulate, and perform messages in parallel, L2 learners' speech becomes less fluent and less complex. When they talk about a very familiar topic there is less need to conceptualize, allowing more time for formulation. In this case—because the message-content is ready-made and they do not need to express complex ideas—they can concentrate on accuracy. Skehan also pointed out that when learners have difficulty in formulating a message—in particular because of limitations in their mental lexicon—they are likely to resort to **communication strategies**, such as avoidance, circumlocution, and paraphrase: for example, if they do not know or cannot access the lexical item 'gallery' they might paraphrase its meaning by saying 'place with pictures on the walls'.

In effect, Skehan envisages a tension between performance and acquisition. In performance, learners need to prioritize meaning when they are communicating; however, acquisition requires that they also attend to form so that new linguistic material can be transferred from **working memory** to long-term memory. Thus, the role of implicit instruction is to balance the demands of performance with the requirements of acquisition. Skehan argued that asking learners to perform communicative tasks that pose varying processing demands on them can guide learners to focus their attention on specific aspects of language and thus help to ensure balanced language development.

## The Cognition Hypothesis

As we will see later, Skehan's research has focused on identifying the design features of tasks and the different ways of implementing them that predispose learners to attend to a specific aspect of production. Robinson's (2007) **Cognition Hypothesis** has a similar goal. It constitutes a framework for classifying the relevant design and implementation variables that influence complexity, accuracy, and fluency. Robinson (2001) distinguished 'resource-directing' variables and 'resourced-dispersing' variables of a task. The former affect the demands the task can make on the learner's attention and—in so doing—cause the learner to focus on specific linguistic forms (i.e. accuracy and complexity) and thus potentially promote interlanguage development. Task variables that are resource-directing include whether the task requires: (1) reference to events happening in the 'here-and-now' or to events that took place in the past elsewhere (in the 'there-and-then); and (2) transmission of simple information or provision of reasons for intentions, beliefs, or relations. Resource-dispersing variables affect the procedural demands on the learners' attentional and memory resources, but do not affect the extent to which they draw attention to specific linguistic forms. They do not promote the acquisition of new L2 forms, but do enhance automaticity (i.e. fluency). Examples are (1) providing **pre-task planning** time, and (2) whether or not a task has a clear structure.

There is also a third set of variables in Robinson's model which influence how learners respond to implicit instruction: 'task difficulty'. These involve factors relating to the learner rather than the complexity of the task itself. Robinson identifies two sets of learner factors that influence how learners respond to an activity: cognitive factors—i.e. **working memory** and reasoning skills—and affective factors—**motivation** and **language anxiety**.

Based on the Cognition Hypothesis, Robinson makes somewhat different predictions from those of Skehan. Skehan argues that the nature of the task will not just predispose learners to attend to fluency or form, but that it will also lead them to focus on a specific aspect of form—i.e. either accuracy or complexity. Robinson, however, sees the essential trade-off as being between fluency and form: a task which is complex in terms of resource-directing variables will cause learners to make greater effort to control and monitor their production, thus affecting *both* accuracy and complexity. He argued that 'pedagogic tasks should be sequenced solely on the basis of increases in their cognitive complexity' (Robinson 2011: 14).

Robinson (2007) further developed his model into what he called 'The Triadic Framework for Task Classification'. The three parts of the model are: (1) 'task complexity'—which included the resource-directing and resource-dispersing variables; (2) 'task condition'—which covered participation and participant variables (for example, whether the task required one-way or two-way interaction and whether the task participants were familiar with each other); and (3) 'task difficulty'. The main addition in this later framework, then, was a list of variables relating to 'task condition'. These were hypothesized to affect the quantity and quality of the interactions that occur when a task is performed—for example, **negotiation of meaning**. These variables, however, are only relevant to tasks that require learners to interact (i.e. dialogic tasks).

## Types of implicit instruction

The various types of implicit instruction are shown schematically in Figure 11.1 and described below. In Chapter 8, I considered how implicit learning is investigated in cognitive psychology. Typically, this involves asking participants to memorize a set of sentences which provide exemplars of particular syntactic structures and then assessing whether the participants can distinguish whether new sentences containing the same structures are grammatical or ungrammatical. Implicit learning is said to have taken place if the participants are able to judge the grammaticality of the new sentences correctly, but are unable to report how they made their judgements. This approach has also been used in some SLA studies—for example N. Ellis (1993) and Robinson (1996). Asking learners to memorize sentences can be considered a type of implicit instruction. However, it is not a type that figures in language pedagogy.

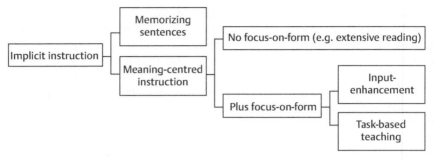

*Figure 11.1  Types of implicit instruction*

Implicit instruction in language pedagogy is meaning centred: it involves engaging learners in the comprehension and production of the L2 for a communicative purpose. Two broad types of such instruction can be distinguished, the first of which is entirely meaning focused; that is to say, there is no attempt to attract the learners' attention to form. Examples of this type are extensive reading and Krashen and Terrell's (1983) Natural Approach. In both 'acquisition' (as defined by Krashen 1981) is claimed to occur automatically, as in L1 acquisition when learners comprehend input[2].

The second type is also meaning focused, but employs various instructional strategies to induce learners to attend to form: although the instructional activities require primary attention to be paid to meaning, they also invite peripheral or periodic attention to linguistic form. One way in which this can occur is through **enhanced input**—specific linguistic forms (words or grammatical structures) are made prominent in input that learners are asked to comprehend. Prominence can be achieved by highlighting the specific features, using intonation in the case of oral input, or typographically in the case of written input. Another way is simply to ensure that the specific features occur with high frequency in the input. The aim in both cases is to increase the saliency of the features so that they will be noticed by the learners while they are trying to comprehend.

The second way of inducing attention to form while learners are primarily engaged in communicating is through **task-based language teaching** (TBLT). In TBLT, learners are asked to perform various types of tasks which create contexts for the interactionally authentic use of language. A **task** is an instructional activity that satisfies four criteria (R. Ellis 2003): (1) it requires a primary focus on meaning; (2) there is some kind of gap—for example, an information gap that motivates the learners to communicate; (3) learners use their own linguistic resources—i.e. they are not provided with the language needed to perform the task; and (4) there is a communicative outcome—i.e. not just the display of correct language. Learners' attention to form can be motivated either by the way the task is designed—for example, a task that involves reporting an accident will provide a natural context for the use of the past tense—or by the way the task is implemented—for example, by allowing learners opportunity to plan before they perform the task. As we will see, TBLT has drawn extensively on SLA research and, indeed, has served as one of the main ways of investigating hypotheses in SLA.

I considered research that investigated memorizing sentences, extensive reading, and text enhancement in Chapter 6 and so will not consider these further here. Instead the main focus of this chapter will be the theory and research that underpins TBLT. The following sections address how tasks have been investigated in SLA and the extent to which TBLT constitutes an effective form of instruction. In the final section of this chapter I consider the relative effectiveness of explicit and implicit instruction.

## Investigating task-based teaching

The investigation of task-based instruction in SLA has addressed two basic questions:

1 What effect do task design and implementation variables have on the way a task is performed?
2 What effect does the way in which a task is performed have on L2 acquisition?

The first question concerns the relationship between (A) and (B) in Figure 11.2. The second question addresses the relationship between (B) and (C). The bulk of the research to date has been directed at the first question. It has examined how task design and implementation variables affect learners' comprehension of input, the nature of their language production—in terms of CAF—and the nature of the interactions the task gives rise to—in particular, whether any focus-on-form occurs. This research has been cross-sectional: it involves recording learners' performance of a task and analysing the language use that occurred. Subsequently, on the basis of theory, implications are drawn regarding the effect the performance of the task might have on L2 acquisition. Far fewer studies have investigated the second question, in part because it is difficult to demonstrate that the performance of a single task (or even of several tasks) results in measurable changes in learners' interlanguage.

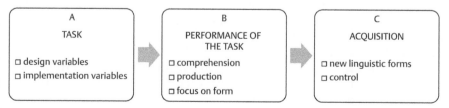

*Figure 11.2 Tasks, task performance, and acquisition*

Tasks can be input based or output based. In an input-based task the learner is positioned as a receiver of information and production is not required although it is not prohibited (i.e. learners can elect to speak if they wish to); output-based tasks require production by the learners. Tasks can also be either focused or unfocused. A focused task is designed in such a way as to create a context for the use of some specific linguistic feature—for example, a set of vocabulary items or a particular grammatical structure. An unfocused task has no pre-determined linguistic target and—thus—is designed to elicit general samples of language use. Both focused and unfocused tasks must satisfy the criteria for a task listed earlier. Researchers have investigated all these different types of tasks. Focused tasks—especially of the input-based type—make it much easier to investigate the effects of the instruction on acquisition, as it is possible to design experimental studies that measure whether performing the task resulted in new linguistic knowledge or increased control over partially acquired linguistic forms.

The approach I will adopt in reviewing the research that has investigated tasks is to select representative studies rather than attempt a comprehensive review of the research. Such reviews can be found in R. Ellis (2003), Samuda and Bygate (2008), Skehan (2011), and Robinson (2011). In the sections that follow, I will first examine studies based on input-based tasks and then those that have investigated output-based tasks. My main purpose is to consider each study in relation to the theoretical constructs that informed it and the extent to which the results of the study lend support to these constructs. It should be noted, however, that there is also a rich pedagogic literature on tasks (e.g. Prabhu 1987; Willis and Willis 2007). Indeed, interest in tasks as a vehicle for learning a language originated in proposals for language pedagogy (Candlin 1987).

# Input-based tasks

In an input-based task, learners are presented with L2 input (oral or written), which they need to comprehend in order to achieve the outcome of the task. Thus, an input-based task does not require production on the part of the learner. However, learners are not prevented from speaking and, in fact often do when they fail to comprehend. Input-based tasks are based on the assumption that learners will pick up new linguistic forms through exposure to the input providing that (1) they are able to comprehend the input and (2) notice the new forms. Thus, they draw on those SLA theories that emphasize the importance of **comprehensible input** (Krashen 1985) and **positive evidence**. Input-based tasks can also help to develop comprehension skills in learners.

Many of the input-based studies involved 'listen and do' tasks. Ellis, Tanaka, and Yamazaki (1994), for example, used a kitchen task, which required learners to listen to directions about where to place various objects in a matrix picture of a kitchen. The objects were depicted in small numbered pictures. The outcome of the task was the matrix picture of the kitchen with the numbers of the small pictures marked in different locations. In this experimental study, different groups of high school Japanese learners of English listened to the directions in baseline form—i.e. the input was unmodified—in premodified form—i.e. the input was simplified to aid comprehension—and in interactionally-modified form—i.e. the students were allowed to request clarification when they did not understand a direction. In this way, it was possible to investigate the effects of exposing learners to different kinds of input on their comprehension of the directions. The results were clear. Every direction was comprehended better by the interactionally modified group than by the baseline or premodified group, lending support to the **Interaction Hypothesis**. However, a likely explanation for this is that the learners had more time to process the input in the interactionally modified condition. Ellis and He (1999) carried out a similar study, but this time took care to ensure that the amount of time allocated to the **premodified input** and **interactionally modified input** conditions was the same. In this case, there was no statistically significant difference in the comprehension scores of the two groups.

Ellis, Tanaka, and Yamazaki did not just investigate the effects of the different kinds of input on comprehension, they also embedded a number of words—i.e. the names of different kitchen objects—that were new to the learners. This allowed them to examine whether or not the different input conditions had any effect on vocabulary acquisition. Overall, none of the groups learned many of the new words, as demonstrated in tests administered after the task was completed. However, significantly more words were acquired by the learners who received interactionally-modified input. Again, this may reflect the additional time afforded learners and the fact that they were exposed to the new words more frequently in this condition. In Ellis and He's study—where time for each condition was controlled—there was no difference in the vocabulary scores of the premodified and interactionally modified groups.

Ultimately, then, what emerges as important for both comprehension and vocabulary acquisition in these studies, is the fact that learners need both time to process the input and multiple exposures to the target words. Interactionally modified input can guarantee both time and multiple exposures. Premodified input can do likewise, but only providing that care is taken to build sufficient repetition into the linguistic material.

These studies investigated vocabulary acquisition. The question arises as to whether input-based tasks also cater to the incidental acquisition of grammatical features. Shintani and Ellis (2010) and Shintani (2015) investigated this. The learners in these studies were young Japanese children with no prior knowledge of English—i.e. they were complete beginners. The input-based tasks consisted of teacher commands that required the learners to identify objects—represented by picture cards displayed in front of them—and to take them to either a supermarket or a zoo, represented by friezes pinned to the walls of the classroom. Thus the learners displayed their understanding of the commands by selecting the correct card and taking it to the correct location.

The same tasks were repeated nine times over a five week period. The commands were designed to expose the learners to two grammatical structures—plural -s (a grammatical feature not present in Japanese and therefore difficult to acquire) and copula *be*. Some of the commands required the students to identify a singular object—for example, 'Please take the crocodile to the zoo; while others referred to a plural object—for example, 'Please take the crocodiles to the zoo'. Although the tasks were input based, they inevitably led to interaction as the learners struggled to understand the teacher's commands. Acquisition was investigated by means of tests that measured learners' receptive and productive knowledge of plural -s and productive knowledge of copula-*be*[3].

The results of these studies are interesting. The learners were successful in acquiring receptive knowledge of plural -s, but only a few of the them developed productive knowledge of this structure and none of the learners acquired productive knowledge of copula-*be*. The learners' successful acquisition of receptive knowledge of plural -s can be explained by the fact that the tasks created a functional need to process this feature: they could only achieve a successful outcome if they were able to distinguish singular and plural nouns in the input. In the interaction that resulted from the tasks, the learners sometimes checked whether the noun was plural or singular—for example by asking 'one? two?'—and they also received feedback on whether they had selected the right card(s). However, only a few of the learners ever produced the plural form of a noun during the tasks. This might be due to the fact that because they did not have to produce plural nouns the learners did not develop productive knowledge of them. In the case of copula *be*, ample exposure in the input did not lead to the ability to produce this structure, probably because this feature is redundant and non-salient in the input or—again—because the learners did not produce it.

Input-based tasks are well suited to low-proficiency learners of the kind that figured in these studies because they can be designed to expose learners to the kinds of input that research has shown can assist comprehension. They can also incorporate specific target features—both lexical and grammatical—making it possible to investigate if acquisition takes place. When implemented in the classroom, learners can be given—or just take—opportunities to request clarification, leading to the negotiation of meaning and form that has been shown to facilitate both comprehension and acquisition (see Chapter 7). Input-based tasks can facilitate incidental acquisition of vocabulary and of grammatical items that are functionally important for performing the task.

However, the studies I have considered in this section suggest that input-based tasks have their limitations. They showed that the learners developed receptive knowledge of the target features, but not productive knowledge. To acquire productive knowledge, learners may need opportunities to produce the target features. Also, the studies make it clear that sheer exposure to target features may not be enough. Acquisition becomes evident only when tasks create a functional need for the learners to attend to form. For this reason, redundant and non-salient features may not be attended to and not acquired.

## Output-based tasks

Output-tasks require learners to speak or write. However, by and large, the research that has investigated output-based tasks has focused on oral production. Output-based tasks can be monologic or dialogic. An example of a monologic task is when learners are asked to produce (or reproduce) a narrative, as in Skehan and Foster (1999) or Yuan and Ellis (2003). Dialogic tasks that require learners to interact require information-exchange and are typically of the information-gap or opinion-gap kind. For example, Foster and Skehan (1996) included a decision-making task where the learners had to work in pairs to reach agreement about suitable prison sentences for a number of offenders.

Monologic and dialogic tasks differ in some fundamental ways. In the former, learners have to rely entirely on their own resources, while in the latter, they work collaboratively and can scaffold each other's production. Dialogic tasks also allow for online corrective feedback as in Lyster's studies (for example, Lyster 2004), which we considered in Chapter 7. For some researchers, tasks are necessarily dialogic. McDonough and Mackey (2000), for example, claimed that the aim of a task is to 'provide learners with opportunities to engage in meaningful interaction and to direct their attention to form' (p. 83). This, however, is an over-narrow view of a task.

Central to all the research involving output-based tasks is the identification of the design and implementation variables that influence how learners perform a task. Design variables refer to features of the task-as-workplan— i.e. the task materials. Implementation variables refer to ways in which the task is carried out and thus relate to the methodology of task-based teaching. A large number of variables have been identified and investigated. Table 11.2 lists some of the major ones.

The extent to which it is possible to influence the way in which learners perform a task by manipulating design and implementation variables is a matter of some controversy. Sociocultural theorists have argued that it is not possible to predict the 'activity'—i.e. the process—that results from a 'task' as learners are likely to interpret the task-as-workplan differently in accordance with their own goals and motives. Coughlan and Duff (1994) reported a study that showed that the 'activity' that took place when the same task was performed by different learners varied considerably. This study also showed that the 'activity' varied when the same learner performed the task on different occasions. Seedhouse (2005) argued that the discrepancy between the predicted and actual language use resulting from a task was so great that a task should only be defined with reference to the language processes that arose in its performance. However, as we will see, there is plenty of evidence

| Design variables: task workplan | Implementation variables: task performance |
|---|---|
| 1  Contextual support | 1  Learners' role (i.e. listener vs interactive participant) |
| 2  Number of elements to be manipulated | 2  Pre-task planning |
| 3  Topic familiarity | 3  Time pressure |
| 4  Shared vs split information | 4  Rehearsal (task-repetition) |
| 5  Dual vs single task | 5  Post-task requirement |
| 6  Closed vs open outcome | |
| 7  Inherent structure of the outcome | |
| 8  Discourse mode (e.g. description vs narrative) | |
| 9  Here-and-now vs there-and-then | |

*Table 11.2  Selected task design and implementation variables*

to show that specific design and implementation variables are predictive of the language use that results from performing a task[4].

I will begin by considering design features of tasks: first in monologic tasks and then in dialogic tasks. I will then turn my attention to an examination of a number of implementation variables that have attracted the attention of researchers, such as **pre-task planning**. In the process, I will examine the competing claims of Skehan's **Trade-off Hypothesis** and Robinson's **Cognition Hypothesis**.

## Effect of task design features on L2 production

### Monologic tasks

The research that has investigated monologic tasks has examined how the complexity of a task affects CAF in learners' production. As you may recall, there are different theoretical positions concerning this. Skehan (2009) argued that because learners' processing capacity is limited, they will prioritize one aspect of production over others—for example, either accuracy or complexity, but not both—depending on the difficulty of the task. Robinson (2007) proposes that a complex task will have an effect on both accuracy and complexity.

Tavakoli and Foster (2011) investigated a narrative task performed by two separate groups of learners—a group of 60 EFL learners in Tehran and a group of 40 ESL learners in London. The study involved four tasks that differed in terms of whether the storyline had a tight or loose structure, and whether the story did or did not include background events. They hypothesized that (1) the narrative with tight structure would lead to learners prioritizing accuracy; and (2) the more complex narrative that involved encoding background events as well as foreground events would result in learners prioritizing complexity—both lexical and grammatical—but not accuracy.

The results showed that the design of the tasks did indeed affect the production of both groups with the tight narrative structure promoting accuracy and the two story lines greater syntactic complexity. Tavakoli and Foster then went on to note:

> As a result, a narrative with loose structure and only foreground events elicits a performance of relatively low accuracy and low syntactic complexity, whereas performance in a narrative of tight structure and both foreground and background events elicits relatively higher accuracy and complexity.
> (Tavakoli and Foster 2011: 57)

As Tavakoli and Foster then pointed out, parts of these results fit both Skehan's Trade-off Hypothesis and Robinson's Cognition Hypothesis. Both tasks with a clear ordering of narrative elements were performed more accurately than the tasks with a loose structure, thus supporting Skehan's model and replicating the results of previous studies—for example, Foster and Skehan 1999. In terms of Levelt's speaking model, when learners have to spend less effort on conceptualization, they are free to focus more on formulation and—hence—accuracy increases. However, there was also some support for the Cognition Hypothesis as the task which had a tight structure and two story lines and which therefore incorporated both a source-dispersing and a resource-directing variable resulted in both greater accuracy and complexity, as predicted by the hypothesis[5].

This study also reported on the effect of the learning context (i.e. Tehran or London). It had no effect on accuracy or fluency, but it did affect lexical complexity although not grammatical complexity. They suggested that London learners' opportunity to use the target language in everyday tasks outside the classroom primarily benefits lexical development.

There have been a number of studies that have investigated the claims of the Cognition Hypothesis. Jackson and Suethanpronkul (2013) reported a **meta-analysis** of nine studies that investigated simple and more complex narrative tasks. Overall, the results of the analysis did not support Robinson's hypothesis. The more complex tasks resulted in measurable greater accuracy. However, they were not found to have a significant effect on complexity whether of the grammatical or lexical kind. In other words, task complexity was not shown to have a joint effect on both accuracy and complexity. Jackson and Suethanpronkul concluded that resource-directing variables, presumed to enhance task complexity, appear to only affect accuracy.

It is difficult to come to any firm conclusions about the effects of task-design variables on different aspects of learner production in monologic tasks. Overall, increasing task complexity does appear to result in greater accuracy and also has a negative effect on fluency, which in part supports the Cognition Hypothesis. But there is limited evidence to show that it also has an effect on complexity. Rather—as claimed by the Trade-off Hypothesis—simpler tasks have been shown to support production complexity. However, the studies that have investigated these theoretical positions have operationalized task complexity in very different ways and also have employed different measures of CAF. This makes any attempt at synthesizing the results of the studies problematic.

## Dialogic tasks

Researchers have investigated the effects of design features of dialogic tasks by examining how they influence (1) the quantity and quality of the interactions that arise when the tasks are performed, and (2) CAF.

In Chapter 7, I examined features of the interaction—for example, the **negotiation of meaning, the negotiation of form**, and **modified output**—that arise when learners perform dialogic tasks that have been hypothesized (and have indeed been shown) to assist acquisition. In this chapter, I will focus on a number of design features of tasks that have been found to affect the incidence of these interactional features.

In Ellis (2003), I summarized the findings of some of the early work on tasks by identifying a number of design variables that had been shown to influence interaction and that constituted 'psycholinguistically motivated dimensions' of tasks (Long and Crookes 1987). Two key variables were (1) whether the information to be exchanged was required or optional, and (2) whether the outcome of the task was closed—i.e. there was only one possible outcome—or open—i.e. there were many possible outcomes. The results of the studies that investigated these tasks are quite mixed, but overall required information-exchange as in information-gap tasks was found to be more likely to promote the negotiation of meaning than optional information-exchange, as in opinion-gap tasks (Pica, Kanagy, and Falodun 1993). Closed tasks were also found to be more likely to result in negotiation of meaning than open tasks. Thus—from the perspective of the Interaction Hypothesis—tasks that require information exchange and have closed outcomes are more likely to promote acquisition. However, my review of this early research also showed that different task variables impacted differently on different aspects of interaction. For example, some studies showed that optional information-exchange tasks with an open outcome could lead to greater complexity in learner output. I concluded that the research was only suggestive of what design features promoted the kinds of interactions hypothesized to be important for acquisition.

Research on how task design variables affect interaction has continued apace since my 2003 review. There is further support for the importance of required information exchange and closed outcomes as a means of promoting the negotiation of meaning. Pica (2002) pointed out the limitations of the open-ended discussions she observed taking place in content-based classrooms with high-intermediate level learners:

> The discussions were interesting and meaningful with respect to subject-matter content. However, as open-ended communication activities, they drew attention away from students' need for input and feedback containing negative evidence on crucial form-meaning relationships in their L2 development
> (Pica 2002: 16).

We might ask what evidence is there that tasks that trigger attention to form through the negotiation of meaning actually result in acquisition? In other words, do task design features influence learning via the types of inter-action they give rise to? In terms of Figure 11.1 this means examining the relationship between (1) task design and (3) acquisition.

A number of studies that have attempted this were meta-analysed by Keck et al. (2006). Overall, this meta-analysis showed that tasks that give rise to interaction do result in acquisition gains for both lexis and grammar and also that these gains are maintained over time. This constitutes clear support for task-based learning. But did different types of tasks have different learn-ing effects? Keck et al. compared the effect of two types of task—jigsaw (which involves optional information exchange) and information-gap (which involves required-information exchange). Both proved effective but—as predicted by the Interaction Hypothesis—information-gap tasks that trigger greater negotiation of meaning were more effective than jigsaw tasks. Keck et al. also compared the effects of two types of focused tasks. Drawing on Loschky and Bley-Vroman (1993), they distinguished tasks that made the use of the target feature(s) essential and tasks where the use of the target feature(s) was just useful. They reported little difference in the immediate effect of these two types of task, but a clear advantage for task essentialness when learning was measured in delayed tests. This meta-analysis, then, indicates that task design does effect acquisition and in ways that can be predicted on the basis of the theories that inform the design of tasks.

## Effects of task implementation variables on L2 production

A task-based lesson can consist of a pre-task phase, the main task phase when learners perform the task, and a post-task phase. See Table 11.2 for a list of implementation variables that can be linked to the first two of these phases. For example, pre-task planning and task rehearsal involve the pre-task phase. Time pressure, focus-on-form strategies, and setting a post-task requirement are relevant to the main-task phase. The post-task phase can involve a variety of activities including explicit language instruction (see R. Ellis 2003). My concern here is only with those implementation variables that impact on how the task is performed—that is, those associated with the pre-task and main task phases.

### Pre-task implementation variables

The variable that has attracted the greatest attention is pre-task planning. See, for example, chapters in Ellis (2005a) and Skehan (2014a). At stake here is whether giving learners an opportunity to plan before they perform the task affects the complexity, accuracy, and fluency of their production when they perform the task. The theoretical models we considered earlier make different predictions. According to Skehan's **Limited Resources Model**, planning facili-tates deeper conceptualization and thus—when learners perform the task—they are able to devote more attention to formulation with corresponding effects on complexity. In contrast, pre-task planning constitutes a resource-dispersing variable in Robinson's Cognition Hypothesis and so is not predicted to result in joint increases in accuracy and complexity.

In Ellis (2009) I reviewed 19 studies (mainly monologic tasks) that have investigated **pre-task planning**. I concluded that it has a clear effect on the way a task is performed. The main finding was that planning aids fluency irrespective of whether the task was performed in a laboratory or classroom setting but that it had no effect on fluency in a testing context. Thirteen of the studies reported that pre-task planning also has an effect on complexity (i.e. it resulted in more complex language especially grammatical). Planning also resulted in more accurate language in 13 of the studies. Interestingly, if the planning affected complexity it did not affect accuracy and vice versa. In other words, planning led to greater fluency and *either* greater complexity or accuracy.

Pre-task planning is, of course, not a homogeneous activity. It can vary in a number of ways: for example, the amount of time allocated to it and whether it is unguided—learners are left to their own devices about what and how to plan—or guided—learners' attention is directed to meaning, form, or to both. Individual learner factors are also likely to play a role. However, I was unable to come to any clear conclusions about how these various factors impacted on the effect of planning, as they have not been systematically investigated. I also noted that the studies were all cross-sectional and only investigated the effects of planning on performance, not acquisition. There is a clear need for longitudinal studies that can address what effect planning a task performance has on acquisition. There is also a need for studies that examine what learners actually do when they plan and whether this affects task performance[6]. Finally, as we will shortly see, pre-task planning interacts with online planning conditions.

Another pre-task variable that has received attention is task-rehearsal. This involves asking learners to repeat a task one or more times. In this way, the performance of a task at one time prepares learners for a subsequent performance. In Ellis (2009) I reviewed three studies that have investigated rehearsal. I concluded that there was clear evidence that rehearsal has beneficial effects on the performance of the same task, especially for fluency and complexity, and sometimes also for accuracy. However, there was no transference of these effects to a new task even when the new task was of the same type as the original task. This suggests that repeating a task may not contribute to acquisition. However, as Bygate (2001) pointed out 'massed' repetition practice may be needed to bring about transfer of training. Shintani's (2012) study lends support to this claim. It found that asking young beginner learners to repeat a task nine times did have a measurable effect on their acquisition of new words and one grammatical structure (plural -*s*).

To sum up, the results of the planning and rehearsal studies give support to both Skehan's and Robinson's models. Pre-task planning and rehearsal do result in greater fluency and complexity, as Skehan predicts, but in some studies they also lead to greater accuracy, which his model does not predict. In the majority of the studies, pre-task planning affects either complexity or accuracy but not both. There is scant evidence of either pre-task planning or rehearsal facilitating acquisition through the performance of a task.

## Main task implementation variables

If what learners do before they perform a task is important, the conditions under which they actually perform it are likely to be even more important. We can distinguish two kinds of main task implementation variables—those that impose external constraints on how the task is to be performed, and those that involve online intervention during the performance of the task.

One kind of external constraint is time pressure. That is, learners can be asked to perform the task in their own time or they can be pressured to complete it within a fixed amount of time. I have suggested that this affects the nature of the online-planning that learners engage in (Ellis 2005b). When learners can engage in unpressured **online-planning** they have time to access their linguistic resources during formulation and also to monitor their utterance plans both prior to and after articulating them. I predicted that in this condition linguistic accuracy would benefit. In contrast, when learners are pressured to speak rapidly, accuracy would suffer. This prediction was supported by Yuan and Ellis (2003), who reported greater accuracy in the unpressured performance of a monologic narrative task by Chinese university students than in their pressured performance. Complexity also benefited to a lesser extent but, interestingly, there was no difference in fluency. Yuan and Ellis also investigated pre-task planning, reporting that it had an effect on complexity but not accuracy. One possible explanation for this is that the two types of planning have differential effects, with pre-task-planning primarily assisting fluency and complexity and online planning primarily accuracy[7].

Another way of imposing an external constraint on the performance of a task is by setting some post-task requirement that learners know about before they start to perform the task. An example of a post-task requirement is informing learners that when they finish the task they will have to transcribe it. Foster and Skehan (2013) hypothesized that knowing this would induce learners to avoid error and thus enhance accuracy when they performed the task. In fact, the results of their study showed that this requirement had a general effect on form—i.e. on both complexity and accuracy.

There is a rich literature dealing with how various kinds of online interventions affect both learners' production and acquisition. These studies have drawn on cognitive-interactionist theories of L2 acquisition and concern in particular how techniques for focusing learners' attention on form during meaning-focused interaction can assist acquisition. A number of the studies I considered in Chapter 7, in particular those investigating corrective feedback and modified output, indicate that focus-on-form during the performance of a task has clear effects on acquisition when this is measured in terms of increased accuracy in post-tests or in progression along an acquisition sequence.

I will consider one further study (Samuda 2001) that investigated within-task intervention in some detail. Samuda was concerned with the role played by the teacher in a task-based lesson, noting that this must involve 'ways of working with tasks to guide learners towards the types of language process-ing believed to support L2 development' (p. 120). The lesson was based on a focused task designed to provide learners with communicative opportunities for using and learning epistemic modals (e.g. *might* and *must*). It began with an activity where learners were told the contents of a mystery person's pocket and were asked to work together in groups, speculating about the person's possible identity. However, the students failed to use the target modal forms in this stage of the lesson. In the following class discussion the teacher attempted to shift the students' focus from meaning to form by interweaving the target forms into the interaction mainly by means of **recasts**. However, the students still failed to use the target structures. The teacher then resorted to direct explanation of the target feature. At this point, the students started to try to use the target forms and the teacher corrected them when they failed to use them or used them erroneously. This was not an experimental study but Samuda did provide some evidence to suggest that the task resulted in acquisi-tion of the target feature. In this lesson, the teacher used a skilful amalgam of implicit and explicit focus-on-form techniques to draw attention to the target structure. Throughout, however, there was a primary focus on meaning[8].

## Some general comments on research involving tasks

There is now a very rich research literature on task-based learning and I have only scratched the surface. Researchers have adopted two different approaches. In one approach, they have investigated how task design features and implementation conditions affect the way tasks are *performed* and then proposed how this will affect acquisition, but without demonstrating that it does. Theoretically-based taxonomies of design and implementation variables have been developed as a basis for making predictions about how specific variables—such as task complexity—affect CAF. There is now ample evidence to show that these variables do have differential effects on these different aspects of production contrary to the claims of sociocultural theorists who consider the activity that results from a task is unpredictable. However, this approach is not without its problems. As Skehan (2014b) pointed out 'any task is likely to subsume a bundle of features' (p. 6). Is it possible then to isolate the effect of specific variables as much of the research has attempted to do? The justification for attempting this is it allows for the testing and devel-opment of theories of task-based learning and also that it can contribute to empirically-grounded teaching. By and large, however, the research to date has not produced results that enable us to choose between competing theories (e.g. Skehan's Trade-off Hypothesis and Robinson's Cognition Hypothesis) and, given the fundamental nature of tasks as bundles of features, it is doubtful whether the research ever will.

There is a further problem with the first approach. As Révész (2014) pointed out, researchers have generally failed to provide independent evidence of the key independent variable—task complexity. She commented that it was important to(1) not just assume that a complex task is more cognitively demanding, but to demonstrate that it is and (2) provide independent evidence of the the causal processes claimed to enhance learning when the task is performed, rather than just relying on the performance itself. For example, learners' subjective rating scales could be used to measure learners' perceptions of task complexity after they had performed a task. Cognitive effort can be measured by using dual tasks and measuring reaction time on the secondary task to provide an indication of the cognitive load imposed by the primary task.

The second approach has involved investigating how tasks can promote acquisition. It entails examining how learners' attention can be attracted to form in the interactions that tasks give rise to. Its theoretical premise is that for acquisition to take place, focus on form—viewed as both an instructional strategy and as a mental process—is needed for acquisition to take place. This approach typically involves designing focused tasks so that the effects of performing the task on acquisition can be investigated experimentally by means of pre-test and post-tests. The studies investigating input-based tasks I considered earlier are good examples of this approach. It is, however, more problematic to design focused, output-based tasks as learners are adept at avoiding the use of linguistic features they find difficult, although there are some successful examples of these (e.g. Samuda's study and the studies considered in Chapter 7). This approach to investigating tasks has provided convincing evidence that incidental acquisition does take place when learners are primarily focused on meaning and when there is focus on form.

## Explicit vs. implicit instruction

Task-based instruction has been subjected to a number of critiques, in particular from teacher educators who espouse the need for explicit instruction. Swan (2005), for example, accuses advocates of task-based teaching, such as Skehan, Robinson, and R. Ellis of 'legislating by hypothesis'. He claimed there is no evidence that task-based instruction is more effective than explicit instruction (PPP) and that researchers were extrapolating unconvincingly from theory. We have seen, however, that there is in fact substantial evidence that task-based instruction does promote the kinds of performance likely to facilitate acquisition and also a growing body of evidence to show that it can result in acquisition. However, the question remains as to the relative effectiveness of explicit and implicit instruction. Is Swan right in claiming that, in an instructed context, explicit instruction and the intentional learning it fosters is more effective?

One way to address this question is by a meta-analytic comparison of the two broad types of instruction. Norris and Ortega (2000) reported a clear advantage for explicit instruction in their meta-analysis of 29 studies involving implicit treatments and 69 involving explicit treatments. In fact, they considered this the single trustworthy finding regarding the effect of form-focused instruction. Spada and Tomita's (2010) meta-analysis also compared the effectiveness of the two types of instruction. They reported that both types were effective for both simple and complex grammatical features, and that this was evident irrespective of whether learning was measured in controlled or free language production. As in Norris and Ortega, explicit instruction was found to be more effective than implicit instruction. In a narrative review of instructed second language vocabulary learning, Schmitt (2008) concluded:

> Although research has demonstrated that valuable learning can accrue from incidental exposure, intentional vocabulary learning—i.e. when the specific goal is to learn vocabulary, usually with an explicit focus— almost always leads to greater and faster gains, with a better chance of retention and of reaching productive levels of mastery.
> (Schmitt 2008: 341)

Thus, it would seem that for both grammar and vocabulary explicit instruction is superior.

However, it is not quite as simple as that. For a start, both explicit and implicit instruction can take many different forms. As we saw in Chapter 10, not all forms of explicit instruction are successful, especially when learning is measured in free production. Also—as we have seen in this chapter—task-based instruction (as the principal type of implicit instruction) also differs in many ways. In addition, little is currently known about the role that individual difference factors such as **language aptitude** and age play in the efficacy of the two types of instruction. It would seem very likely that learners vary in their ability to benefit from implicit and explicit instruction. Analytically-minded learners may do better with explicit instruction, but functionally-minded learners may gain more from implicit instruction. Thus blanket comparisons of explicit and implicit instruction are of doubtful validity.

There is also a bigger issue. The general advantage for explicit instruction is evident in studies where the instruction is directed at learning specific linguistic features—i.e. a particular grammatical structure or a set of vocabulary items. But, as we saw in Chapter 9, there is more to learning a language than acquiring new linguistic features and items. Learners need to also develop **interactional competence** (i.e. the ability to utilize their linguistic resources in communicative routines in relevant communities of practice). Thus, to establish the relative contributions of explicit and implicit instruction, it is necessary to investigate not just which type of instruction is superior in helping learners acquire isolated linguistic elements but also the relative effects of the two types of instruction on L2 development more generally and, in particular, on learners' ability to engage confidently and easily in the use of the L2. Arguably, implicit instruction, which adopts a more holistic view of L2 proficiency and seeks to develop not just linguistic but also interactional competence, is better equipped to foster L2 development overall.

Few studies have taken this broader approach to comparing explicit and implicit instruction. One that has done so is Shintani's study of young beginner learners of English (Shintani and Ellis, 2010; Shintani 2012; Shintani 2015), which was referred to earlier in this chapter and also in Chapter 10. Here is a summary:

1  This study compared the relative effects of implicit instruction consisting of input-based tasks and explicit instruction consisting of **presentation-practice-production (PPP)** on the acquisition of a set of new words. The results indicated that both types of instruction were effective, but that overall the implicit instruction was superior.
2  The study also reported that the implicit instruction resulted in superior incidental acquisition of a grammatical feature (plural *-s*). This feature was not explicitly taught in either the task-based instruction or in the PPP.
3  The study also undertook a micro-genetic analysis of the interactions that occurred in the two types of instruction to examine how affordances for the use of the target items (both lexical and grammatical) arose. It showed how opportunities for learners to initiate discourse and to negotiate for both meaning and form were common in the input-based lessons and how—in contrast—the explicit instruction largely constrained learners' contributions to responding in **initiate-respond-follow up (IRF) exchanges**.

If we want to have a clearer idea of the relative effects of implicit and explicit instruction we need more studies like Shintani's including those involving adult learners who are, perhaps, better equipped to take advantage of explicit instruction. We need studies that measure the effects of implicit and explicit instruction on both planned and unplanned linguistic features and that also document the kinds of interactions that occur and how these, to a greater or lesser extent, foster interactional competence.

# Conclusion

The goal of implicit instruction is the same as that of explicit instruction, namely the development of the kind of knowledge needed to engage effectively in communication (especially oral communication). However, it differs from explicit instruction in that it does not assume that explicit knowledge is the starting point. Instead it assumes that classroom learners, irrespective of their age, are able to acquire implicit knowledge by participating in activities that foster its incidental acquisition.

Such a position is clearly in opposition to the **strong-interface position**, but can be seen as compatible with the **non-interface position**—i.e. explicit knowledge and implicit knowledge are cognitively differentiated and involve different learning processes. Implicit instruction assumes that learners will acquire the L2 naturally and easily through participating in instructional activities that provide them with **comprehensible input**, opportunities for **pushed output**, and also attract attention to form. Thus—like explicit instruction—it emphasizes the importance of conscious attention to form. The difference is that implicit instruction draws on theories that claim that attention to form needs to be achieved while learners are trying to communicate. In this way, as the weak-interface position proposes, explicit knowledge can help to activate the processes involved in acquiring implicit knowledge.

There can be no doubt that much of language learning occurs incidentally. As Schmitt (2008) commented, there are limits to how often a teacher can ensure explicit exposure to new words and thus 'many of the meetings that learners need to consolidate and enhance their knowledge of lexical items must come from the extensive exposure generated by the meaning-focused strand, from which incidental learning can occur'. (p. 246).

The same is true for grammatical items and, perhaps, for phonological features too. It is, however, not just a question of 'extensive exposure'. As this chapter has attempted to show, it is how opportunities for incidental acquisition can be engineered by the kinds of tasks used and how they are implemented. The theories I have examined may not provide conclusive evidence about how this is best achieved, but they illuminate the factors that are involved and provide a basis for research-informed implicit language pedagogy.

Finally, there is no need for teachers to make a choice between explicit and implicit forms of instruction. Chapter 10 provided clear evidence that explicit instruction is effective. This chapter has shown that implicit instruction is also effective. A language curriculum that includes both explicit and implicit instructional components is perhaps most likely to ensure that language pedagogy is efficient and effective for ensuring balanced L2 development.

# Notes

1  A wide range of specific measures have been used to investigate complexity, accuracy, and fluency. See Ellis and Barkhuizen (2005) and Housen, Kuiken, and Vedder 2012) for details of the measures that have been used.

2  Of course, even in implicit instruction that is entirely meaning centred, individual learners may elect to attend to engage in intentional language learning. However, meaning-centred instruction is not designed to encourage this.

3  It was not possible to measure receptive knowledge of copula *be* as this grammatical structure conveys no meaning—i.e. it is redundant—and thus does not have to be processed for comprehension to take place.

4  Both Coughlin and Duff's and Seedhouse's point about the lack of correspondence between the task-as-workplan and the activity that arises when it is performed was made with reference to output-based tasks. Arguably, the same point is relevant to input-based tasks. Shintani (2012), for example, documents in detail how the performance of the input-based

tasks in her study varied considerably when they were repeated nine times.

5 However, Tavakoli and Foster (2011) suggested that the increase in complexity may have simply reflected the learners' use of co-ordinators such as 'while' and 'during', rather than the complexity involving greater subordination.

6 A number of studies have examined what learners do when they engage in pre-task planning. See for example Pang and Skehan (2014).

7 Wang (2014) investigated two pressured online-planning conditions. In one, they watched a video whilst speaking, while in the other, they watched the video first and then spoke. The effects for online planning were only evident in the first of these conditions. In fact, this condition corresponded closely to the condition in Yuan and Ellis (2003) as the learners in this study were allowed to look at the picture story for a short time before they spoke and also while speaking. This suggests that the online planning condition works in conjunction with another variable—i.e. here-and-now vs there-and-then. In other words, unpressured online planning benefits accuracy when there is also visual support.

8 Samuda's (2001) study can be seen as an example of Integrated Instruction, which I discussed in Chapter 10. However, Samuda intervened only once and only briefly to explain the use of the modal verbs in a manner I consider more compatible with task-based teaching.

# Understanding and applying second language acquisition

## Introduction

SLA is still quite young as a field of study—much younger than well-established disciplines such as psychology or sociology. While there has always been an interest how people acquire second languages, the systematic study of L2 acquisition did not start until the 1960s when Chomsky's (1959) critique of Skinner's *Verbal Behavior* liberated researchers from what Larsen-Freeman (2007) termed the 'bondage of behaviorism', making it possible to investigate language learning as a cognitive enterprise. Since then, SLA has developed exponentially and, arguably now manifests all the characteristics of an academic discipline (see Table 12.1).

However, while a case can be made for viewing SLA as a discipline, it is in many respects interdisciplinary in nature: that is, it draws on the knowledge and methodologies of a range of other disciplines. Like other interdisciplinary academic areas, it is subject to continuous change; it is fragmented and heterogeneous; and it interacts with other disciplines in complex ways. For some SLA researchers, this is problematic as it raises questions regarding the boundaries of the discipline, what constitute appropriate methodologies for investigating L2 acquisition, and what the ultimate goal of SLA should be. Klein (1998) considered SLA among 'the bottom dwellers in the language science' (p. 53). This is perhaps overly harsh but it is clear that SLA is far from coalescing to provide a uniform account of how an L2 is acquired.

## The boundaries of SLA

What constitute the boundaries of SLA is perhaps the area of greatest contention. As we have seen, SLA was originally positioned as a cognitive enterprise (i.e. language is viewed as a mental construct and acquisition as taking place inside the mind of the learner) and the task facing the researcher as that of identifying the mental processes—such as **noticing**—that account

| Characteristics of a discipline | SLA |
| --- | --- |
| 1  A discipline has a particular object of research. | SLA investigates the acquisition of a language acquired after the learner's mother tongue. |
| 2  A discipline has a body of accumulated specialist knowledge referring to a specific object of enquiry, which is not generally shared with another discipline. | SLA has drawn on a range of other disciplinary areas but has now developed specialist knowledge related to such issues as individual differences in learning outcomes, the trajectory of development in an L2, variability in L2 systems, L1 transfer, the role of input and interaction, and the cognitive and social processes involved in L2 learning. |
| 3  A discipline has theories and concepts that can organize the accumulated specialist knowledge effectively. | SLA has spawned a plethora of theories to explain L2 acquisition although, to date, no widely-accepted general theory has emerged. |
| 4  A discipline uses specific terminologies or a specific technical language adjusted to the research object. | SLA borrows technical terms from its source disciplines but also increasingly coins its own special terminology—as can be seen by a brief inspection of the Glossary in this book. |
| 5  A discipline has developed specific research methods according to its specific research requirements. | SLA has borrowed research methods from other disciplines but has adapted these to its own needs and developed new methods. |
| 6  A discipline must have some institutional manifestation in the form of subjects taught at universities or colleges, respective academic departments, and professional associations connected to it. | There are now departments of SLA in universities while courses in SLA figure regularly in postgraduate programmes. SLA has its own conferences. |

*Table 12.1  SLA as a discipline (based on Krishnan's 2009 criteria for a discipline)*

for how learners extract information from the input and how **interlanguage** systems develop over time. This perspective emphasizes the universal aspects of L2 acquisition as manifested, for example, in the orders and sequences of acquisition of an L2 grammar we considered in Chapter 4. For some researchers, SLA is necessarily a 'branch of cognitive science' (Long and Doughty 2003: 4). For other researchers, however, L2 acquisition is primarily a social phenomenon. In Chapter 9, I examined a number of theories belonging to the 'social turn' in SLA. These emphasize the local and situated nature of L2 acquisition and point to its heterogeneity and the inevitability of individual differences in the trajectories it follows. As Larsen-Freeman (2007) pointed out, researchers in these two branches of SLA do not ask the same questions and they draw on different kinds of data. The bifurcation that arose in SLA as a result of these competing accounts of L2 acquisition remains unresolved, although in recent years there have been attempts to find a larger lens that incorporates both perspectives in work on **complex adaptive systems** and—in particular—in **Dynamic Systems Theory** (see Chapter 8). Nevertheless, arguments over the boundaries of SLA are far from over and SLA continues to reflect parallel epistemologies. For many SLA researchers (myself included), however, this is no bad thing as, arguably, multiple metaphors—'acquisition' and 'participation (Sfard 1998), for example—are needed to account for the full complexity of L2 acquisition.

## Research methodology in SLA

As the boundaries of SLA have expanded, so too have the research methodologies employed to investigate L2 acquisition. The methods that researchers have employed vary according to how 'acquisition' is conceptualized. In Ellis (2006), I distinguished three different ways of defining 'acquisition' and discussed the different ways of measuring acquisition associated with each:

### Acquisition as emergence

When acquisition is conceptualized in this way, it is necessary to show that learners can demonstrate they use a particular L2 feature that they could not use previously. The primary way of demonstrating this is to take 'emergence' as the measure of acquisition. This has been defined as the use of the feature in at least three different contexts in the learner's spontaneous production. This approach to investigating acquisition has been employed in research based on Pienemann's (1998) **Processability Theory** (see Chapters 4 and 8) and it is also the principal way of investigating acquisition in the social turn (see Chapter 9).

### Acquisition as increased control

When acquisition is conceptualized as increased control, the metric applied is target language accuracy—i.e. the extent to which the learner demonstrates a gain in the ability to use a specific linguistic feature in accordance with target language norms. In experimental studies, this is generally achieved by means of tests. Increasingly, however, researchers have used tasks to elicit more spontaneous language use and then examined the accuracy of specific linguistic forms by examining suppliance in **obligatory contexts** (see Chapter 4).

### Acquisition as progress along an acquisitional sequence

All SLA theories acknowledge that there are developmental trajectories as learners' interlanguages advance. To investigate these, longitudinal studies involving a series of data collection points are required. The research then plots the use of specific linguistic features over time, identifying when and how change takes place. It is the required method for investigating L2 acquisition as a **complex adaptive system**.

In order to avoid the **comparative fallacy**, many researchers reject target-like accuracy as an adequate measure of acquisition, although this continues to be the preferred approach for investigating the effects of explicit instruction (see Chapter 10). The **usage-based approaches** for investigating acquisition which have become so influential in SLA view acquisition as emergence and then plot the development of specific linguistic features over time. An example of this approach is Eskildsen's (2012) study discussed in Chapter 4.

A major development in SLA has been the use of **meta-analysis** to provide summative accounts of the results of experimental studies that have investigated various aspects of SLA. Meta-analysis is a statistical technique used to examine the results obtained from a large number of studies that have investigated the same phenomenon in order to arrive at a generalized statement about the effect of a particular treatment—for example, **form-focused instruction** or **input enhancement**—on acquisition. Norris and Ortega (2006) published a collection of meta-analyses and several more have since appeared in the journal *Language Learning*. Previous chapters in this book have drawn on the results of a number of these meta-analyses.

Increasingly, SLA researchers have sought out methods for investigating the cognitive processes involved in acquisition. For example, in Chapter 7 we saw that researchers interested in the role of interaction have used **stimulated recall** to investigate what learners attend to in the interactions they participated in. Computer simulations of learning, techniques for measuring brain activity, and **eye-tracking** have also been used to investigate how input is processed (see Chapter 8). The methods employed by cognitive SLA researchers have become increasingly more sophisticated over time as have the statistical tools used to analyse quantitative data.

Social SLA has employed a different set of methods to investigate acquisition in flight. In particular, they have drawn on **conversation analysis** to investigate in detail how learners participate in conversations and how such participation assists the development of both **linguistic competence** and **interactional competence** (see Chapters 1 and 9). Social SLA has also drawn on the methods employed in ethnography—for example, the use of diaries, interviews, and learner autobiographies—to explore the social worlds that learners inhabit.

Looking back over some 50 years of SLA research, it is clear that there have been huge advances in the methods researchers have employed, reflecting the general tendency to look beyond SLA itself and borrow from other fields, in particular from cognitive psychology and branches of sociology.

## The goal of SLA

Given the disputes over the boundaries of the discipline, it is not surprising that there is also no clear agreement over the goal of SLA. For much of the history of the discipline, the goal has been the description and explanation of how people acquire a *second* language, viewed as separate and distinct from the first language. This is how I defined it in Chapter 1—L2 acquisition is the 'learning of *any* language after the first'. I also noted, however, that there are moves to reframe it as the study of bi/multilingualism. Ortega (2012) argued that L2 acquisition should not just be contrasted with L1 monolingual acquisition from birth, but also with bilingual acquisition from birth. She made the case for what she called the 'bi/multilingual turn for SLA'—that is, making the goal of SLA not just the study of a *second* language, but of how later-learned languages figure in making a person bi- or multilingual. In a similar vein, Cook (1991) has argued for investigating **multicompetence** on the grounds that the L1 and the L2 should not be treated as separate linguistic systems but as intertwined, each affecting the other. In general, however, SLA has continued to focus on how learners acquire a second language.

For some SLA researchers, SLA is seen as 'central to the wider goal of understanding the ontogeny of the human language capacity' (Ortega 2012: 8). In other words, SLA is seen as contributing alongside other language sciences to an explanation of the special human capacity for language—what this consists of; how it has evolved; and how people draw on it when acquiring a specific language. This has not been a major goal of this book, but there are several areas of research I have covered that are relevant to it. In Chapter 2, we examined the **critical period hypothesis**, which addresses the key issue of whether the human language faculty is still available for late-starting L2 learners. Chapter 4 reported research that had investigated **learner varieties,** which—according to Klein (1998)—are a reflection of our innate, genetically endowed capacity for learning a language. Other branches of SLA have also proposed that language learning is only possible because of a highly specialized capacity for language—see, for example, the account of **Universal Grammar** in Chapter 9. In contrast, the connectionist view of language outlined in Chapter 1 proposes that there is no special language faculty and that language learning depends on the same cognitive abilities as those involved in all learning and that language learning is primarily driven by learners' experiences of language. By and large, then, just as there is no consensus about the boundaries of SLA, so there is no agreement about what the human language capacity consists of. The contribution that SLA has made to our understanding of this issue, however, is not negligible as it has served as a useful testing ground for the competing nativist and environmentalist theories of language.

There is another goal that has figured strongly in SLA: to provide guidance about how second languages can be most effectively taught. This was the goal that motivated much of the early research in SLA. It is premised on the reasonable assumption that for language instruction to be effective, it must take account of how learners acquire a language. As Long (2006) noted:

> Many SLA researchers have witnessed firsthand the relatively few successes and the widespread failures of even the best-intentioned classroom instruction, and many were first motivated to undergo training as SLA researchers with a view to improving that state of affairs.
> (Long 2006: 156)

The hope was that SLA would help to identify ways of teaching that were compatible with how learners learn. In Chapters 10 and 11, we examined a number of proposals for language instruction that have emanated from SLA and have been empirically investigated by SLA researchers. In this respect, SLA constitutes an applied rather than a pure discipline. It aims to utilize theoretical understanding of L2 acquisition and the results of empirical research to propose instructional approaches that will foster learning. However, exactly how SLA can best inform language pedagogy remains uncertain, and is the subject of the final section in this chapter. First, though, I will attempt a summary of what SLA—as a discipline—has told us about the nature of L2 acquisition.

## What do we know about L2 acquisition?

The conclusion chapter to the previous edition of this book provided a summary of the main theories of L2 acquisition. However, such an approach no longer seems appropriate as I have already examined the key theories in earlier chapters. Ideally, I would like to conclude this book with a general theory of L2 acquisition but—as will have become clear—this is not possible given the diversity of the theoretical positions on offer and their fundamental epistemological differences as, for example, in how 'acquisition' is conceived in the cognitive and social theories discussed in Chapters 8 and 9. Instead, therefore, and at the risk of over-simplification, I will attempt to formulate a set of general statements that encompass what SLA has shown us about the nature of L2 acquisition.

## L2 acquisition is complex

All theories acknowledge the complexity of L2 acquisition. It is complex because a multitude of factors influence how an L2 develops: individual difference factors, such as **language aptitude** and **motivation**; the learner's L1; the nature of the input that learners are exposed to; the kinds of interactions they participate in; the **social context** in which learning takes place; and whether or not **form-focused instruction** is available. These factors interact in different ways with different learners, influencing the rate at which learning takes place, the ultimate level of achievement, and also the process of acquisition itself. The sheer complexity of the factors involved and of the interactions among them is the main reason why no general theory of L2 acquisition has been forthcoming. Instead—as we have seen—theories have been developed to account for the influence of specific factors.

Language itself is a **complex adaptive system** (Larsen-Freeman and Cameron 2008). It incorporates phonological, lexical, and grammatical subsystems which are interlocked in complex ways. These linguistic systems are connected to meaning systems that enable us to behave in pragmatically appropriate ways. The process of acquiring this complex adaptive system is a slow and gradual one. The initial L2 system is a simple one—it consists of **formulaic sequences** and vocabulary, which learners use as best they can to serve their communicative needs. Gradually, as the system becomes more complex, grammar emerges. This process is not a linear one. Learners do not accumulate discrete grammatical elements in a neat and ordered way. As new linguistic forms are internalized, earlier acquired forms are re-organized and the developing system is restructured. Development is dynamic, uneven, and at times chaotic. Unsurprisingly, acquiring an L2 involves hard work and persistence on the part of the learner—as Hatch (1978) pointed out many years ago.

## There are universal patterns of L2 acquisition

In Chapter 4, I reviewed research that testifies to a relative fixed **order of acquisition** of grammatical morphemes, such as verb + -*ing* and third-person -s, and to **sequences of acquisition** involving identifiable stages in the development of grammatical structures, such as negation. Klein and Perdue (1997) documented remarkable consistency in the **language varieties** that learners construct as they progress from the pre-basic variety to the **basic variety** and finally to the post-basic variety. Pienemann, Johnston, and Brindley (1988) drew on earlier research to show that there was an invariant order in the acquisition of different English grammatical structures. This and other research points to universal patterns in the acquisition of a second language. Long (1990) considered this one of the 'well-established findings' that a theory of L2 acquisition needs to explain:

> ... learners of different ages, with and without instruction, in foreign
> and second language settings, follow similar developmental sequences
> for such items as English negation.
> (Long 1990: 659)

However, not all SLA researchers are in agreement with what Lantolf called the **Universal Acquisition Hypothesis.** It is clearly incompatible with **sociocultural theory** which emphasizes the importance of mediation in enabling learners to overcome the limitations of their own cognitive resources. For example, the theory claims that mediation in the form of language instruction can help learners 'beat' the natural route of development[1]. The hypothesis is also disputed by **Dynamic Systems Theory,** which views learning as unpredictable with individual learners following distinctively different trajectories (see Chapter 5). **Usage-based approaches** to investigating L2 acquisition—for example, Eskildsen (2012)—also question the existence of universal sequences for specific grammatical structures. However, they do recognize that there is a general pattern of development common to all learners involving a 'developmental sequence from formula, through low-scope pattern, to construction' (N. Ellis 2002: 170).

These differences can be reconciled if we accept that the Universal Acquisition Hypothesis constitutes an idealization and serves as a useful simplification of the complexity evident in the real system that is empirically adequate within accepted limits (Ellis 2014). There are clearly regularities in how all learners acquire the linguistic systems of an L2. In general, learners do follow a similar developmental pattern and it is important to acknowledge this.

## L2 systems are variable

At any stage of development, learners deploy a variety of forms for realizing a particular grammatical structure. For instance, a learner may have begun to produce negative utterances containing an auxiliary—for example, 'Maria is not coming today'—but at the same time continues to use the earlier acquired 'no' + verb construction as in, 'Maria no coming today'. Much of the variability in learner language is systematic: that is, it is possible to identify the factors that predict which forms a learner will deploy in accordance with the situational or linguistic context. More advanced constructions are likely to occur in the learner's **careful style** when attention is paid to form; earlier acquired forms occur more frequently in the **vernacular style** where the focus is on spontaneous communication. Some linguistic contexts elicit the use of the more advanced form, others the use of the more primitive form. Learners also make systematic use of their variable linguistic resources to realize different functions. Schachter (1986), for example, observed that one learner systematically used the 'no' + verb form to express denial and 'I don't know' for the 'no information' function. Learners deploy their resources communicatively, mapping whatever forms are available to them onto the functions they need to perform. Over time the configuration of these **form-function mappings** changes.

Not all L2 variability is systematic, however. When new forms first enter the L2 system they are likely to be used as alternatives to existing forms. The result is **free variation**. Researchers working within the framework of Dynamic Systems Theory have documented the chaotic nature of learner language. They emphasize that those points at which variation appears most chaotic are precisely the times when development is likely to occur. Learners look to maximize the efficiency of their linguistic resources by rapidly organizing and then re-organizing them into functional systems that serve their communicative purposes.

To claim that L2 systems are variable is, at first sight, to deny of the existence of a natural route of L2 development. However, the fact that L2 systems are variable does not necessarily contradict the claim that there are orders and sequences of acquisition. Some grammatical forms do typically emerge before others. All learners, for example, start on the path to acquiring English negation with the 'no' + verb construction. Over time, early forms are supplanted by later forms, but this is a gradual process with the result that the variable use of the different forms is evident at any particular stage of development.

**Processability Theory** (see Chapter 8) seeks to account for both developmental regularities and variability. It proposes that some features are developmental in nature and are acquired in sequence as learners master a set of hierarchically ordered processing procedures. As each procedure is mastered, a range of grammatical structures governed by that procedure become available. But individual learners may not demonstrate immediate acquisition of *all* the structures associated with a procedure. There is individual variation in the structures activated by the procedure. The theory also proposes that some grammatical features—for example copula *be*—are not subject to processing constraints and thus will be acquired by learners at different times. This theory, then, affords an account of both the universal and variable aspects of acquisition.

## The effects of the L1 are pervasive

The learner's L1 influences all aspects of L2 acquisition—phonology, lexis, grammar, and pragmatics. It is also evident in all stages of L2 development. Transfer—both **negative** and **positive transfer**—is linguistic, semantic, and conceptual in nature. Linguistic transfer takes place when learners incorporate an L1 structure into their L2 system as, for example, when Spanish learners of English persist in using the 'no' + verb negation structure over time because it is the same as the L1 structure. **Semantic transfer** involves the mapping of a concept shared by two languages onto a translation equivalent. as when Finnish learners of English use 'tongue' in place of 'language'. **Conceptual transfer** occurs when the concept itself differs in the two languages as for example when an English learner of Russian refers to a paper cup as 'chaska' (= cup) rather than 'stakanchik' (= little glass) as a result of differences in how the two languages conceptualize 'cup' and 'little glass'. Transfer is also evident in the gestures that learners employ when speaking.

Much of the research on L1 transfer has focused on the issue that Kellerman (1983) identified many years ago—'now you see it, now you don't'. Various factors have been shown to influence when transfer occurs: the relative **markedness** of the equivalent L1 and L2 forms; the distance between the two languages; the learners' intuitions about the transferability of specific linguistic forms; the context in which learning takes place (for example, the formal language classroom may inhibit transfer); the learner's age (for example, older learners tend to transfer more than younger ones); and psychological factors (for example, learners with larger working memories are better able to overcome negative transfer).

The pervasiveness of transfer effects raises once again the legitimacy of claiming universal patterns in L2 acquisition. At the most general level, however, L1 transfer affirms universality: all learners do it. The strength of L1 representations blocks attention to L2 forms in the input. More interestingly, however, research has shown that transfer effects are themselves developmental. They interact with the universal processes responsible for the relatively fixed orders and sequences of grammatical features in L2 development. Transfer tends to occur when learners have reached a stage of 'natural' development that allows them to access an L1 form that is similar or equivalent to an L2 stage. Thus—in recognizing the prevalence of transfer—it is not necessary to abandon the idealization that L2 acquisition is subject to universal constraints.

## The learner's starting age plays an important role

The differential achievement of learners who commence learning at different ages—i.e. as young children or as adolescents/adults has been an abiding topic of interest in SLA (see Chapter 2). Granena and Long (2013) reported that there have been over 100 empirical studies published during the last 50 years that have investigated this issue. This reflects its importance for both understanding the nature of the human capacity for language and for educational decision making.

The research demonstrates conclusively that starting earlier results in higher levels of L2 proficiency. The crucial issue, however, is whether learning needs to start before a certain age for learners to achieve native-like ability. According to the **Critical Period Hypothesis** native levels of ability are only possible if learning commences within a critical period. However, the existence of a 'critical' period is disputed on the grounds that there is no clear discontinuity between learning during the period and after it ends, but rather a gradual falling-off in ability[2]. For this reason, many researchers prefer to talk about a 'sensitive' period. That is, they claim that children are more likely to achieve native-like ability but acknowledge that learners who start as adults may also sometimes succeed in doing so. Long (2013) defined the sensitive period as consisting of a 'peak'—i.e. a period of intense sensitivity to language that starts at age zero—followed by an 'offset' (a period of gradual but not sharp decline) and thereafter a sharper 'discontinuity' in language learning ability. Thus, for example, learners who start learning before the age of six are likely to achieve a native-like pronunciation and can still do so if they start between the ages of six and 12, but are very unlikely to do so after that.

Why are children generally more successful in learning an L2 than adults? There is no consensus on the answer to this question. The explanation may be social—children are more likely to seek membership of a native-speaking peer group. It is tempting, however, to look for a cognitive explanation. Children are more likely—and perhaps better equipped—to engage in **implicit learning** while adults are more likely to learn explicitly. Even if adult learners still possess the capacity for implicit learning—and there are reasons for believing that this is the case—this ability may decline with age. Also, their greater analytical skills can interfere with 'natural' learning.

The fact that the age of onset influences ultimate achievement in an L2 has been used to justify introducing foreign languages in the elementary school rather than waiting—as is traditional—until the secondary school. There is, however, no clear justification for such an educational decision. The advantage of starting early only applies if learners have intense exposure to the L2. This cannot be achieved by a few hours of classroom instruction each week. Also, the research has shown that adolescent learners initially learn more rapidly than child learners. Thus—in a context where learners are reliant on the classroom—starting later may still be preferable. Studies that have investigated the relative benefits of starting at the elementary level have failed to show it results in higher levels of proficiency than starting later.

## Psychological factors influence all aspects of L2 acquisition

In Chapter 3, I examined a number of psychological factors that contribute to individual differences in L2 learning. I elected to focus on two of these factors—**language aptitude** and **motivation**—as these have been shown to be especially influential and have attracted the most attention in SLA. As with age, there is a long history of research investigating both factors.

Both language aptitude and motivation are complex constructs, reflecting again the complex nature of L2 acquisition. Language aptitude is composed of different cognitive abilities—phonemic coding ability, language analytical ability, and rote-learning ability. More recently **working memory**—i.e. the memory system that stores and processes information making links with long-term memory—has also been incorporated into models of language aptitude. Motivation is comprised of the learner's motivational orientation—i.e. the reasons a learner has for needing or wanting to learn an L2—behavioural motivation—i.e. the effort a learner makes to learn the L2, persistence with the learning task, and the impact the immediate context has on these—and attributional motivation—i.e. the effect that the learner's evaluation of his/her progress has on subsequent learning behaviour. Whereas language aptitude is generally seen as a relatively stable factor, not unduly influenced by learning experiences, motivation is increasingly viewed as dynamic, changing not just from day to day, but also moment by moment.

Initially, research that investigated these two factors was correlational in nature. That is, measures of language aptitude and motivation were obtained by means of tests—for example, the **Modern Language Aptitude Test**—and questionnaires—for example, the Attitude Motivation Test Battery—and their relationship to measures of L2 achievement, or proficiency, investigated. Both factors were found to account for up to 35% of the variance in achievement/proficiency scores. In other words, learners with a strong aptitude and motivation were more likely to learn quickly and achieve higher levels of L2 proficiency.

More recent research on language aptitude has attempted to show how it influences the process of L2 acquisition. In so doing, researchers have sought to bring research on language aptitude into line with mainstream SLA. Skehan (2002), for example, proposed a model of language aptitude that links the different components to different stages in the process of language acquisition. The model proposes that phonemic coding ability and working memory are important for **noticing**, while language analytical ability contributes to the **restructuring** that occurs during L2 development. Researchers have also addressed the role that language aptitude plays in implicit and explicit learning, although no firm conclusions have yet been reached. It seems likely that different components of aptitude are involved in these two types of learning—**phonological short-term memory** in implicit learning, and **language analytical ability** in explicit learning.

A major shift has also occurred in how motivation is conceptualized. Initially it was seen as a state, measurable by means of a questionnaire. Currently it is seen as a process as in Dörnyei and Otto's (1998) **Process Model of Motivation**. In line with social accounts of L2 learning, researchers have re-conceptualized motivation as a highly situated phenomenon, influenced by the specific settings that learners find themselves in. This has led to an emphasis on qualitative case studies of individual learners in place of the earlier quantitative, survey-based studies. Many years ago, McNamara (1973) argued that 'the really important part of motivation lies in the act of communication' itself. This observation has now been taken up in current research, linking the study of motivation to another major stream in SLA—the **interaction approach**.

## Social interaction plays a crucial role in L2 acquisition

No matter whether acquisition takes place inside or outside the classroom, social interaction plays a central role. Allwright (1984) argued that interaction is 'the fundamental fact of classroom pedagogy' because 'everything that happens in the classroom happens through a process of live person-to-person interaction' (p. 156). Similarly, in naturalistic settings, the major source of data for learning is that obtained through interaction with other speakers of the languages. Early on, Hatch (1978) observed 'one learns how to do conversations, one learns how to interact verbally, and out of this interaction syntactic structures are developed' (p. 252).

The importance attached to interaction in SLA is reflected in what Gass and Mackey (2007) called the **interaction approach** (see Chapter 7). This approach grew out of Krashen's (1985) **Input Hypothesis** and Long's (1983b) **Interaction Hypothesis**. Krashen argued that acquisition takes place naturally as long as learners have access to **comprehensible input**. Long took up this idea and developed it further by proposing that one of the main ways in which input is made comprehensible is through the **negotiation of meaning** when learners experience a communication problem. Swain (1985) hypothesized that **comprehensible output** also plays a role as it forces learners to engage in syntactic processing in order to make their meaning clear. Pica (1992) developed a framework that incorporated these various hypotheses by proposing that interaction provides learners with comprehensible input; helps them segment the input into its component parts; provides them with feedback on their use of the L2; and pushes them to modify their output by making it more target-like.

These theoretical perspectives have informed a wealth of research investigating both the nature of the interactions involving learners and the specific ways in which these interactions facilitate acquisition. They have shown that **interactionally-modified input, corrective feedback,** and **interactionally-modified output** all contribute to L2 development. Influenced in particular by Schmidt's (2001) **Noticing Hypothesis**—which claims that 'people learn about the things they attend to and do not learn much from the things they do not attend to' (p. 30)—researchers demonstrated that interaction works for acquisition because it induces noticing of linguistic forms in the input and output that interaction affords. In other words, learners learn from interaction because it activates cognitive processes, such as **noticing** and **noticing-the-gap**—i.e. the difference between an erroneous and a target linguistic form—required for acquisition to take place. These theoretical constructs have led to pedagogic proposals, in particular **task-based language teaching** and **focus-on-form**, where the emphasis is placed on providing opportunities for classroom learners to engage in meaning-focused activities while their attention is drawn to features in the input and output that arise in the interactions the activities generate.

The importance of work on interaction for language pedagogy is perhaps most clearly seen in the research that has investigated **corrective feedback**. This is a topic that has always been of interest to SLA researchers and has a long history. Much of the recent research is experimental in nature, investigating the effects of different types of feedback—for example input-providing strategies, such as recasts, and output-prompting strategies, such as elicitation or metalinguistic comments. The research has shown that the corrective feedback that occurs in meaning-focused interaction helps acquisition—especially when the correction is made salient to learners. For older learners, corrective feedback may be essential to help them overcome entrenched interlanguage forms.

While emphasizing the importance of interaction, we need to also recognize that not all learning is dependent on the opportunity to interact in the L2. Learning can also occur through exposure to non-interactive input—for example, through extensive reading. There is plenty of evidence to show that such input—especially if pre-modified to make it comprehensible to the learner or if specific linguistic features are made salient through **input enhancement**—can lead to acquisition.

## L2 acquisition is a cognitive phenomenon

The interaction approach is founded on a cognitivist view of L2 acquisition. It is premised on what Block (2003) called the input-output model: that is, the input made available through interaction and the output that it triggers activate the internal cognitive processes involved in acquisition. Acquisition, then, is conceived as essentially a mental phenomenon. SLA has drawn increasingly on theories and research in cognitive psychology (see Chapter 9). Two theories in particular have been influential in SLA—Reber's theory of implicit and explicit learning and Anderson's Adaptive Control of Thought (ACT) Model.

Drawing on Reber's research, N. Ellis (1994) proposed that **implicit learning** and **explicit learning** are fundamentally different. Implicit learning is learning that takes place without intention and without awareness—i.e. learners cannot report what their language behaviour shows they must have learned. This is because the implicit L2 system is connectionist in nature: it does not consist of 'rules', but of an elaborate network of associations of linguistic elements of different sizes. It is emergent—its development is driven by the learners' ongoing experiences of language in use and their unconscious tallying and analysis of the linguistic forms they are exposed to. Rule-like behaviour emerges gradually as learners unpack formulaic sequences and discover how to use and combine the linguistic elements that comprise them. **Implicit knowledge**, then, is largely exemplar-based, and this allows for rapid and easy communication. In contrast, explicit learning is intentional and thus takes place with awareness—i.e. learners can report what they have learned. The **explicit knowledge** that results is metalinguistic in nature. In the case of grammar, it consists of 'rules' that learners can draw one when formulating utterances and when monitoring their output. However, whereas implicit knowledge can be processed automatically, explicit knowledge requires controlled processing and is not readily available in spontaneous face-to-face communication. Thus, if learners wish to develop effective communicative skills in an L2 they need **implicit L2 knowledge**.

Anderson's model is based on a distinction between **declarative** and **procedural knowledge**, which—broadly speaking—matches the explicit/implicit distinction. However, whereas N. Ellis views the two types of knowledge as distinct, Anderson sees them as connected. Learning commences with forming declarative representations—i.e. 'rules' in the case of language learning—which are gradually restructured into procedural representations that allow for automatic language use. Anderson's theory underlies **skill-learning theory** (DeKeyser 1998). This claims that L2 learning begins with declarative rules which learners use as crutches during practice—especially communicative practice—until the rules are subsequently proceduralized.

Cognitive theories of SLA draw on two other important constructs imported from cognitive psychology—**attention** and **working memory**. The importance of attention in L2 acquisition owes much to the work of Schmidt.

He saw what he called **noticing** as a conscious process of attending to exemplars of linguistic features in the input. Noticing, however, does not guarantee learning—as learners may fail to store what they have attended to in long-term learning—but it makes learning possible. Attention takes place in the learner's working memory, which is seen as limited in capacity. This explains why learners often fail to attend to L2 features in the input or fail to access knowledge stored in long-term memory in their output. Attention is selective. It is influenced by the learner's L1 and it is governed by **input-processing principles** (VanPatten 1996) that account for why some grammatical features (e.g. verb + -*ed*; passive voice) go unnoticed and so are typically learned late. It follows, therefore, that one way of enhancing learning is by helping learners to attend consciously to such features. This can occur incidentally—for example, through communicative interaction that induces a focus-on-form—or intentionally, through **structured input** activities that force attention onto problematic forms.

Cognitive SLA has been characterized as 'mainstream'. That is, cognitive accounts of L2 learning have tended to dominate in SLA. However, there has always been interest in social aspects of L2 acquisition and from the 1990s these have attracted increasing interest from researchers.

## L2 acquisition is also a social phenomenon

Concern for the social factors that influence L2 development—especially the rate of learning and ultimate achievement—was evident from an early period in SLA as, for example, in Schumann's (1978a) claims about the influence of the social distance between the learner and the target language community. Firth and Wagner's (1997) critique of cognitive SLA, however, set out the case for viewing L2 learning as pre-eminently social in nature. This led to what has been called 'a social turn' in SLA (Block 2003).

The fundamental claim of the social turn is that L2 acquisition is embedded in the social world that learners inhabit and that they themselves help to construct. Whereas Schumann saw factors such as social dominance and the cohesiveness and size of the L2 group as determining learners' access to the L2 and their motivation to learn and thereby influencing learning, social-turn researchers saw learning itself as a social activity that learners actively shape through their own agency. They saw learning as local and highly situated and emphasized the importance of investigating learners within specific social contexts. Researchers focused on investigating learning-as-participation rather than on learning-as-acquisition. That is, L2 learning was conceptualized as happening *within* social interaction rather than *through* it. It was seen as an external rather than an internal phenomenon. Learners learn to become members of a **community-of-practice** through speaking the language. Socialization and language learning go hand in hand.

In Chapter 9, I reviewed a number of social turn theories—presented as alternatives to cognitive theories of L2 acquisition. Of these theories, by far the most influential is **sociocultural SLA**, which also has the longest history in SLA. Like other social theories, it emphasizes learning-as-process rather than learning-as-product. Drawing on Vygotsky's work, it treats development as potentially always open to external influence rather than cognitively pre-determined. Thus, the key concept is **mediation**—the process by which culturally-determined artefacts are deployed to regulate activity. The primary artefact is social interaction. Interaction with both 'experts'—for example, teachers or native speakers of a language—and 'novices'—for example, other learners—enables learners to understand and produce linguistic forms that they have not yet internalized. Through the **other-regulation** afforded by interaction, **self-regulation** develops: that is, the linguistic forms are internalized and made available for independent use. It should be clear that sociocultural theory is, in fact, not just a social theory, but a cognitive one as well. It accounts for how external language—the starting point—becomes internal. In this respect, sociocultural theory affords a much more complete account of L2 acquisition that most of the other social turn theories which address only learning-as-participation.

The social turn has had a major impact on SLA. It has led to research that focuses on individual learners in their own social contexts, rather than on groups of learners in laboratory contexts. By its concern for how **interactional competence** develops, it has shifted the focus of SLA away from **linguistic competence**. It has also introduced a methodology—**conversation analysis**—that provides a powerful resource for investigating learning-as-participation and has expanded our understanding of how learning takes place in social interaction. The social turn rightly emphasizes that learners have agency; they are not just subject to input, but can insist on the right to speak and so actively shape their learning experiences. It has shown us the importance of **social identity** in L2 learning and that the learners' social identities are actively constructed through the process of learning. No account of L2 acquisition is complete without a social perspective.

## Instruction helps acquisition

In Chapters 10 and 11, I examined research that has investigated the effects of instruction on acquisition. For many learners, the classroom provides the only opportunity for learning an L2. Thus, it is important to understand whether instruction benefits L2 learning and what kind of instruction benefits it the most.

I distinguished two broad types of instruction: **explicit instruction** directs attention to target language forms and caters to **intentional learning** and provides learners with explicit information about target language features; **implicit instruction** attracts attention to linguistic forms while learners are engaged in performing communicative activities and caters to **incidental learning**. Both types aim to develop the **procedural knowledge** that enables learners to communicate effectively in the L2.

Different types of explicit instruction draw on different theories of L2 learning, but, in the main, they are based on a **strong-interface position**: that is, they assume that **declarative knowledge** can be transformed into procedural knowledge by providing explicit information about a target feature, together with opportunities for practice. They differ in terms of how the explicit information is provided (i.e. by means of simplified descriptions based on a pedagogical grammar or by detailed descriptions including 'scientific concepts'); when the explicit information is to be provided (i.e. before or during the practice activities); and also the nature of the practice activities (i.e. whether these are input-based or output-based and—in the case of the latter—whether they involve controlled or free-production). There is plenty of evidence to show that explicit instruction 'works', in the sense that it leads to improved accuracy in the use of target features—especially when learners can access their declarative knowledge through controlled processing. There is, however, less clarity about the relative effectiveness of different types of explicit instruction, especially if the criterion of effectiveness is the learners' ability to use the target feature accurately in free production.

Given that the acquisition of implicit knowledge of a grammatical feature is a slow and dynamic process, it is difficult to see how short-term, explicit interventions can have anything but a superficial effect on the acquisition of entirely new features. It was this that led Krashen (1982) to support the non-interface position and propose the virtual abandonment of explicit instruction. However, research has shown that explicit instruction is effective in helping learners gain more control over grammatical features that they have already partially acquired. Also, explicit instruction may have a long-term indirect effect. According to the **weak-interface position**, instruction facilitates rather than causes acquisition. That is, the explicit knowledge that results from explicit instruction can assist the gradual development of implicit knowledge by facilitating **noticing** and **noticing-the-gap** when the learner subsequently experiences input. In other words—even if explicit instruction does not have an immediate effect on the acquisition of implicit knowledge—it can have an indirect, facilitative effect.

Implicit instruction makes use of 'tasks' to provide opportunities for meaning-centred interaction in the classroom. Through careful task-design and choice of implementation options, research has shown that it is possible to vary the extent to which learners attend to **complexity, accuracy,** or **fluency** when they perform different tasks. Task-based teaching also affords opportunities for a **focus-on-form:** that is learners are encouraged to pay attention to specific linguistic forms while they are communicating. This can be achieved in a variety of ways but in particular through **corrective feedback**. As noted earlier, corrective feedback in the context of meaning-focused communication can assist acquisition. It has also been shown to help learners progress along developmental sequences.

The relative merits of explicit and implicit instruction continue to be debated—not least because they entail different theoretical positions about L2 acquisition. The non-interface position has few supporters these days: the debate centres on the strong and weak-interface positions. Can explicit instruction lead directly to the knowledge needed for accurate use of the target feature in spontaneous language use? There is evidence that it can, but this might be because it results in automatized explicit knowledge rather than true implicit knowledge. However, if there is no functional difference between these two types of knowledge—as DeKeyser (2003) argues—then, it does not matter as explicit instruction clearly 'works'. Implicit instruction is also effective. One advantage of implicit instruction is that it not only assists the development of **linguistic competence**—i.e. implicit knowledge—but also fosters **interactional competence**—for example, how to initiate and manage conversations in the L2.

The research investigating explicit and implicit instruction also offers teachers some useful tools for teaching grammar. **Concept-based Language Instruction, Processing Instruction, Consciousness-raising Instruction** and **Task-based Language Teaching** are all fully-theorized approaches that also offer the practical means for implementing them. The study of explicit and implicit instruction has not only increased our understanding of L2 acquisition, but has also enriched language pedagogy.

# Applying SLA

I have argued that SLA constitutes an academic discipline in its own right (see Table 12.1). That said, the origins of SLA lay in a wish to improve language pedagogy—just about all the early figures in SLA were at one time teachers or language teacher educators. Research in SLA has continued to be driven by these same motivations, leading to discussion about how SLA can best serve the needs of language pedagogy. This is not an easy issue to address, for—as Bardovi-Harlig (1995) noted—the 'relationship of pedagogy to second language acquisition is a complex one that is not clearly agreed on by applied linguists' (p. 151). I will consider a number of different ways of making use of SLA for language pedagogy.

## Basing pedagogical proposals on the findings of SLA

For some researchers, SLA provides 'hard evidence' which should be used to advise teachers about what approaches and techniques work best (Long 1990). In general, however, SLA researchers have been wary of prescribing or proscribing how to teach, preferring instead to exercise caution about applying SLA findings.

One way in which researchers have tried to make the results of their research of practical value to teachers is by an 'implications' section tacked on to the end of a research report. There is, however, an obvious danger in such an approach. It does not follow that the implications drawn from a single study are of relevance to all teachers in all instructional contexts. It is also doubtful whether teachers or, indeed, many teacher educators read research articles. so their 'implications' are likely to have little impact on language pedagogy.

A more promising approach, perhaps, is to base advice on a theory of L2 acquisition that has been tried and tested through research. This is the approach that Krashen adopted. His theory—the **Input Hypothesis**—has had a considerable influence on language pedagogy. It is frequently referred to in popular guides for language teachers (e.g. Ur 1996; Hedge 2000) and many teachers have heard of him. However, Krashen's theory is no longer accepted in its entirety and no other single theory has replaced it as a guide for pedagogy. We are currently in a situation where there is a plethora of SLA theories offering different—and often conflicting—accounts of L2 acquisition. Thus, while there might be merit in exploring the applications of individual theories to language pedagogy, it would be asking a lot of teachers and language educators to find their way through the varying applications of the different theories, especially as much of the SLA literature is highly technical and so not readily accessible to lay readers.

A much better way is that adopted by Lightbown (2000). She proposed a set of generalizations which were 'consistent with the research to date' and which could serve as a 'source of information which could help teachers set appropriate expectations for themselves and their students' (2000: 431). Examples of her generalizations are:

> There are predictable sequences in L2 acquisition such that certain structures have to be acquired before others can be integrated.
>
> Knowing a language rule does not mean one will be able to use it in communicative interaction.
>
> For most adult learners, acquisition stops...before the learner has achieved native-like mastery of the target language.

These generalizations were formulated with teachers in mind. Wisely, Lightbown did not propose specific pedagogical practices based on them. She saw SLA research as a body of knowledge that can help to shape teachers' 'expectations' rather than as a source of specific recommendations. She called for researchers to 'enter into a dialogue with classroom teachers', listening to what they are saying as well as informing them about SLA. However, there is a problem with such generalizations. They are challengeable, especially as new research becomes available. We have seen—for example—that not all SLA researchers currently accept the idea of 'predictable sequences' or the idea that 'acquisition stops' for learners.

## Practitioner research and SLA

A second way of making use of the findings of SLA is to encourage teachers themselves to participate in investigating L2 learning in their own classrooms.

There are two ways of going about this. One is to carry out small-scale action research projects to investigate specific problems that teachers have identified in their own teaching (see Burns 2010). For example, teachers may be uncertain about how to go about correcting their students' errors in speaking activities, so they could consult the SLA literature on corrective feedback and then design a study to examine whether a particular type of corrective feedback—for example, elicitation—works for them.

The second way is to encourage teachers to replicate an existing SLA study. Vasquez and Harvey (2010) demonstrated the value of this. They asked a group of MA and doctoral students taking a course in SLA to replicate Lyster and Ranta's (1997) study of corrective feedback. To help them, they broke down the research process into a number of steps. First, they asked them to video record their own classes, then to prepare transcripts of the lessons, and then—after extensive discussion of Lyster and Ranta's categories—to code the data. Vasquez and Harvey reported that the teachers were surprised to find how prevalent **recasts** were in their own teaching and became more inclined to acknowledge the cognitive rather than the affective dimension of corrective feedback as a result of their research. Replicating SLA studies in this way can help teachers to examine their own beliefs about teaching and their actual practices.

Practitioner research provides an excellent way of making the link between SLA and teaching. However, it is time-consuming and probably not something that most teachers are likely to undertake regularly. One way that might appeal to teachers is small-scale investigations of particular instructional activities. For example, they could carry out an evaluation of an information-gap task to see whether it provokes **negotiation of meaning** and **modified output** when performed by their own students.

## Exploring language pedagogy through SLA

A third way of making use of SLA for language pedagogy is to take pedagogic issues as the starting point and then scrutinize them from the perspective of SLA. Ellis and Shintani (2013) adopted this approach. They examined a number of popular teacher guides—ones that figure frequently in teacher education programmes of various kinds—and extracted from them a number of key pedagogic topics, such as how to teach grammar and vocabulary; the importance of 'authenticity' in teaching materials; error correction; and the use of the students' L1 in the classroom. Such topics constitute 'persistent concerns in the professional practice of teachers' (Hedge 2000: 1). Ellis and Shintani first reviewed the pedagogic proposals about these issues in the guides before turning to the findings of SLA relevant to each issue. In other words, they did not so much 'apply' SLA as explore the validity of the proposals that figured in the guides.

One example of how this approach can help to illuminate language pedagogy will have to suffice. The guides typically advise teachers not to engage in corrective feedback while students are engaged in performing communicative tasks on the grounds that this will detract from the main purpose of the tasks, namely to promote 'fluency'. The corrective feedback research in SLA, however, indicates a clear advantage in correcting errors while learners are primarily focused on meaning (see Chapters 6 and 11). The research also shows that corrective feedback need not interfere unduly with fluency, especially if it takes the form of **recasts** or elicitation. It would seem, then, that—in this case—there is a mismatch between what is promoted as 'good practice' in the teacher guides and what SLA has demonstrated.

Many teacher education programmes include a course on SLA. Perhaps the time has come to rethink how SLA is incorporated into such programmes. Relevance and transfer of knowledge may be better achieved by identifying interface issues—i.e. issues like corrective feedback that are relevance to both pedagogy and SLA—and then examining the extent to which current pedagogic views are supported or challenged by SLA research. SLA is—of course—not the only source of knowledge of relevance to language pedagogy, but it is surely an important one if language pedagogy is to ensure teaching-for-learning.

## Conclusion

I concluded the first edition of *Understanding Second Language Acquisition* with the comment 'there is no consensus about the overall direction that SLA research should follow' (p. 290). This is perhaps even more clearly the case today. If anything, the epistemological differences that divide cognitive and social SLA—both with regard to theoretical positioning and to research methodology—are greater than ever. Ortega (2011) commented that there is 'unheeded and unprecedented theoretical diversity in SLA' (p. 176). For some SLA researchers, this is a problem. To my mind, however—given the complexity of L2 acquisition—it is both inevitable and desirable. Debate is healthy, and I do not know of any discipline in the social and psychological sciences where similar debate is not to be found.

## Notes

1 Zhang and Lantolf (2014) report a study that shows that instruction can override the natural tendency of learners to acquire grammatical structures in a fixed sequence. To some extent at least, the route that learners follow is teachable.

2 Birdsong's (2006) review of the research concluded that there was no sharp discontinuity, but rather a gradual decline in ability, starting from an early age.

# Glossary

**Acculturation Model** This theory treats L2 acquisition as one aspect of acculturation (the process by which the learner becomes adapted to a new culture). Various factors influence the social and psychological 'distance' of the learner from the target-language culture and thereby the rate and ultimate success of L2 acquisition. See also *social distance* and *psychological distance*.

**accuracy** Accuracy 'concerns the extent to which the language produced conforms to target language norms' (Skehan 1996: 22). A typical measure of accuracy is percentage of error-free clauses.

**accuracy order** This refers to the order in which different grammatical features of an L2 reach native-like accuracy. See also *morpheme studies*.

**Adaptive Control of Thought (ACT) Model** This is Anderson's model of skill-learning. The model accounts for how learners' ability to perform a skill develops from a declarative stage, where information is stored as facts, to an automatic stage, where information is stored as easily accessed procedures.

**Aspect Hypothesis** The Aspect Hypothesis claims that acquisition of verbal morphology is determined by the lexical aspectual class of the verb, i.e. whether the verb refers to a state—for example, 'seem' and 'know'—an achievement —for example, 'arrive' and 'fall asleep'—, an activity—for example, 'sleep' and 'study'— or an accomplishment—for example, 'build a house' or 'paint a picture'.

**attention** In SLA, attention is the cognitive process by which learners perceive and rehearse L2 features in working memory. The extent to which attention is an entirely conscious process or is subconscious remains a matter of some controversy. See also *Noticing Hypothesis*.

**attractor state** This is a term used in *Dynamic Systems Theory*. De Bot and Larsen-Freeman (2011) defined it as 'the state the system prefers to be in over other states at a particular point in time' (p. 14). Such states are not permanent but depending on the strength of the attraction may resist change for a period of time.

**Attribution Theory** The term 'attributions' refers to the subjective reasons by which we explain our past successes and failures. These can have a positive or negative effect on our motivational disposition.

**Audiolingual Method** A method developed in the United States based on *behaviourist learning theory*. It emphasizes the importance of pattern practice through mimicry and repetition in order to develop correct 'habits'.

**avoidance** Avoidance is said to take place when specific target-language features are under-represented in the learner's production in comparison to native-speaker production. Learners are likely to avoid structures they find difficult as a result of differences between their native language and the target language.

**basic variety** This constitutes an early stage of L2 acquisition identified by researchers in the *European Science Foundation Project*. It is characterized by the absence of grammatical functors. Learners rely instead on pragmatic means to convey semantic concepts such as pastness. Verbs are non-finite. The 'basic variety' is preceded by the 'pre-basic variety'—characterized by nominal organization—and is followed by the 'post-basic variety'—where finite verb forms appear.

**behaviourist learning theory** Behaviourist learning theory is a general theory of learning—i.e. it applies to all kinds of learning. It views learning as the formation of habits when the learner is confronted with specific stimuli which lead to responses, which are, in turn, reinforced by rewards, or are corrected. Behaviourist learning theory emphasizes environmental factors as opposed to internal, mental factors.

**blocking** See *overshadowing*.

**careful style** This is a term used by Labov (1970) to refer to the language forms evident in speech that has been consciously attended to and monitored. A careful style is used in formal language tasks such as reading pairs of words or doing a grammar test. See also *vernacular style* and *stylistic continuum*.

**Cognition Hypothesis** This constitutes a framework developed by Robinson (2001) for classifying the design and implementation variables that influence the complexity, accuracy, and fluency of L2 production.

**cognitive comparison** This is a term used to refer to the mental process involved when learners compare their own output with the input made available to them and identify the differences. See also *noticing-the-gap*.

**communication strategy** A communication strategy is employed when learners are faced with the task of communicating a meaning for which they lack the requisite linguistic knowledge—for example, when they have to refer to some object without knowing the L2 word.

**communicative competence** Communicative competence consists of the knowledge required to understand and produce messages in a language. Various models of communicative competence have been proposed, but most of them recognize that it entails both linguistic competence—for example, knowledge of grammatical rules—and pragmatic competence—for example, knowledge of what constitutes appropriate linguistic behaviour in a particular situation.

**community of practice** This refers to specific social groups—for example, classroom L2 learners or insurance-claim processors— that share a common set of social and linguistic practices related to a particular social domain—for example, a workplace or a classroom.

**comparative fallacy** Bley-Vroman (1983) referred to methods that seek to account for

learner language solely in terms of target-language norms as inadequate because they fail to acknowledge that learners develop their own unique systems. He called this the comparative fallacy.

**competence** This term refers to a language user's underlying knowledge of language, which is drawn on in actual *performance*. Theories of language vary in how they define competence.

**Competition Model** This is a functional model of language use and language acquisition (Bates and MacWhinney 1982). It views the task of language learning as that of discovering the particular form-function mappings that characterize the target language. These mappings are viewed as having varying 'strengths' in different languages. For example, in English, case is a relatively weak signal of agency, whereas in Russian, it is a strong signal. See also *emergentism*.

**complex adaptive system** Interlanguage is a complex adaptive system. In the sense that it emerges gradually, driven by the exemplars learners are exposed to in social interaction, which are processed by general cognitive mechanisms. A complex adaptive system is comprised of a number of interconnected systems which develop unevenly at different points in time during L2 development.

**complexity** Language is complex when there is of a range of vocabulary and grammatical structures used. A common measure of the grammatical complexity of language is the amount of subordination used.

**Complexity Theory** Complexity Theory views all systems as complex and constantly adaptive involving interactions among the many components that comprise the system. Complexity Theory has been applied to L2 acquisition by Larsen-Freeman.

**comprehensible input** Input that can be understood by a learner has been referred to as 'comprehensible input' (Krashen 1985). Input can be made comprehensible in various ways: through simplification, with the help of context, or by negotiating non-understanding and misunderstanding. Krashen considers comprehensible input a necessary condition for L2 acquisition.

**Comprehensible Output Hypothesis** 'Output' is language produced by the learner. It can be comprehensible or incomprehensible to an interlocutor. Swain (1985) has proposed that when learners make efforts to ensure that their output is comprehensible—i.e. produce *pushed output*—acquisition may be fostered.

**comprehension-based instruction** This is an approach to teaching a language through input rather than through production. It consists of listening and reading activities that expose learners to input and facilitate acquisition of the L2. See *input processing instruction*.

**concept-based instruction** This is a type of explicit instruction that emphasizes the importance of providing detailed descriptions of grammatical features through charts and diagrams and asking learners to verbalize the metalinguistic information as they perform oral and written practice activities.

**conceptual transfer** This addresses how an L1-specific world view affects the acquisition of another language. That is, transfer effects are seen as not just linguistic but as reflecting the underlying ways in which learners perceive and conceptualize the world.

**connectionist theories** Connectionist accounts of L2 learning view language as an elaborative neural network rather than as a set of rules. The network changes over time as a response to input frequencies and productive use of l2 features. The underlying assumption is that L2 learning is a complex phenomenon but can be accounted for by a relatively simple mental mechanism that is not specific to language learning.

**Consciousness-raising Instruction** This is a type of explicit instruction designed to help learners understand a grammatical structure and learn it as explicit knowledge. That is, in this kind of instruction there are no practice activities.

**constructions** Constructions are 'recurrent patterns of linguistic elements that serve some well-defined linguistic function' (N. Ellis 2003: 66). They can be at sentence level or below. Emergentist accounts of L2 acquisition view acquisition as a process of internalizing and subsequently analysing constructions. See also *formulaic sequences*.

**Contrastive Analysis Hypothesis** According to the Contrastive Analysis Hypothesis, L2 errors are the result of differences between the L1 and the L2. The strong form of the hypothesis claims that these differences can be used to predict all errors that will occur. The weak form of the hypothesis claims that these differences can be used only to identify some out of all the errors that actually occur.

**conversational analysis (CA)** CA is a method for analysing social interactions in order to uncover their orderliness, structure, and sequential patterns. CA is used to investigate both institutional interactions (i.e. in the school, doctor's surgery, or law court) and casual conversation. Key aspects of interaction studied in CA are turn-taking and repair.

**corrective feedback** In language acquisition, the term 'feedback' refers to information given to learners which they can use to revise their interlanguage. A distinction is often made between 'positive' and 'negative' feedback—sometimes referred to as *negative evidence*. Corrective feedback can be implicit or explicit and also input-providing or output-prompting.

**Critical Period Hypothesis** This states that there is a period—i.e. up to a certain age—during which learners can acquire an L2 easily and achieve native-speaker competence, but that after this period L2 acquisition becomes more difficult and is rarely—if ever—entirely successful. Researchers differ over the span of this critical period.

**declarative knowledge** Declarative knowledge is characterized by Anderson (1983) as 'knowledge that'. In the case of L2 acquisition it consists of explicit knowledge of L2 grammatical rules.

**deductive instruction** Deductive instruction involves providing learners with an explicit rule which they then practise in one way or another. It contrasts with *inductive instruction*.

**detection** Detection is the cognitive registration of information in short-term memory. It can be seen as the first stage in a theory of attention.

**discourse competence** This refers to the ability to participate in coherent and cohesive conversations.

**Discourse Hypothesis** The discourse hypothesis states that speakers will systematically distinguish between foregrounded and backgrounded information when performing a narrative.

**Dual-Mode Model/System** Skehan (1998) proposed that a person's knowledge of language (first and second) is comprised of two distinct systems—a rule-based system and a memory-based system where 'exemplars' are stored. These systems are drawn on differentially depending on whether the speaker prioritizes *complexity, accuracy,* or *fluency.*

**dynamic assessment** This term refers to a mode of assessment that has 'the expressed goal of modifying learner performance during the assessment itself' (Poehner and Lantolf 2005: 235) as opposed to obtaining a static measure of a learner's proficiency without feedback or intervention of any kind.

**Dynamic Paradigm** The Dynamic Paradigm figures in sociolinguistic studies of L2 variability. It seeks to account for variation in terms of the evolving form-function systems that characterize interlanguage development.

**Dynamic Systems Theory** This theory views interlanguage as a *complex adaptive system* involving complete interconnectedness; that is 'all variables are interrelated and therefore changes in one variable will have an impact on all other variables that are part of the system' (de Bot, Lowie, and Verspoor 2007: 8). The theory claims that much of the variation evident in learner language is chaotic and acquisition is non-linear.

**emergentism** In the context of SLA, emergentism refers to theories that assume that language use and acquisition are usage-based—driven, in particular by the frequency of linguistic forms in the input. An example of an emergentist theory is the *Competition Model.*

**enhanced input** Input can be enhanced in several ways—by including frequent use of the target feature in the input or by highlighting it through intonation in the case of oral input, or making it bold or italicizing the feature in the case of written input. Enhanced input is intended to facilitate noticing of the target feature and thus increase the chance of learning.

**exemplar-based system** This is an L2 system comprised of ready-made chunks—i.e. sequences of sounds, words, and grammatical inflections—as opposed to generative rules. See *formulaic sequences.*

**explicit correction** This is a type of feedback that provides the learner with the correct form while at the same time indicating that an error was committed.

**explicit instruction** Explicit instruction involves 'some sort of rule being thought about during the learning process' (DeKeyser 1995). That is, learners are encouraged to develop metalinguistic awareness of the rule. This can be achieved by means of *deductive instruction* or *inductive instruction.* Explicit L2 knowledge is declarative knowledge—i.e. knowledge of rules—which learners are able to report. Explicit L2 knowledge is closely linked to metalinguistic knowledge. It contrasts with *implicit knowledge.*

**explicit learning** Explicit learning is a conscious process that is also likely to be intentional. It can be investigated by giving learners an explicit rule and asking them to apply it to data or by inviting them to try to discover an explicit rule from data provided.

**eye-tracking** In eye-tracking research, an eye-tracking machine is used to plot the movement of the eyes across a written text, documenting the fixations and regressions that occur. It has been used to investigate the cognitive processes involved when reading a text.

**fluency** Various definitions exist. Skehan (1996: 22) defines it as concerning 'the learner's capacity to produce language in real time without undue pausing or hesitation'. A common measure of fluency is the number of syllables per minute.

**focus-on-form** Focus-on-form 'overtly draws students' attention to linguistic elements as they arise incidentally in lessons whose overriding focus is on meaning or communication (Long 1991: pp. 456).

**focus-on-forms** Focus-on-forms is a traditional approach to grammar teaching based on a structural syllabus. The underlying assumption is that language learning is a process of accumulating distinct entities one at a time. It involves *explicit instruction.*

**foreign language acquisition** A number of researchers distinguish 'foreign language acquisition'—for example, the learning of French in schools in the United States—and 'second language acquisition'—for example, the learning of English by speakers of other languages in the United States.

**foreigner talk** When native speakers address learners, they adjust their normal speech in order to facilitate understanding. These adjustments, which involve both language form and function, constitute 'foreigner talk'. Foreigner talk has been hypothesized to aid L2 acquisition in a number of ways—for example, by making certain features more salient to the learner.

**form-function mapping** When learners acquire an L2 they need to identify which functions (grammatical, semantic, or pragmatic) map onto which linguistic forms—a process called form-function mapping. It is investigated by identifying all instances of a specific linguistic form in the data and the different meanings realized by this form and how the form-function mappings change over time.

**form-focused instruction** Form-focused instruction involves some attempt to focus learners' attention on specific properties of the L2 so that they will learn them. Different types of form-focused instruction can be distinguished, including *explicit instruction* and *implicit instruction*.

**formulaic sequences** Wray (2000: 465) gives the following definition:

A sequence, continuous or discontinuous, of words or other meaning elements, which is, or appears to be, prefabricated; that is stored and retrieved whole from memory at the time of use, rather than being subject to generation or analysis by the language grammar.

**fossilization** Selinker (1972) noted that most L2 learners fail to reach target-language competence. That is, they stop learning while their internalized rule systems differ from that those of the target system—i.e. they fossilize. Fossilization can also be viewed as a cognitive process whereby new learning is blocked by existing learning. It remains a controversial construct with some researchers arguing that there is never a complete cessation of learning.

**free variation** When a speaker uses two or more variants of a variable structure randomly—for example, selects variants without reference to the linguistic or situational context—free variation occurs. Free variation can arise when learners acquire a new form and use it side by side with a previously acquired form to realize the same meaning.

**frequency analysis** This is the method of analysing learner language that involves identifying the *variants* of a given structure and examining the frequency of occurrence of each variant. For example, a learner may make negative utterances using (1) 'no' + verb, (2) 'don't' + verb and (3) auxiliary + verb. A frequency analysis of the negative utterances produced by this learner would involve counting each occurrence of the three variants at a particular point in L2 development.

**good language learner** Researchers have investigated the individual learner factors that contribute to L2 learning by investigating what expert, successful L2 learners do in order to learn an L2. These studies are known as the 'good language learner studies'.

**Gradual Diffusion Model** Gatbonton's (1978) Gradual Diffusion Model identifies two broad phases in L2 acquisition: an 'acquisition phase', characterized by free variation, and a 'development phase' where free variation gives way to systematic variation and categorical language use.

**grammaticality judgement test** One way of obtaining data on what learners know about specific grammatical structures is by asking them to judge whether sentences containing grammatical and ungrammatical versions of these structures are correct or incorrect.

**horizontal variability** This refers to the variation evident in learner language at a particular moment or stage in a learner's development. It contrasts with *vertical variability*. See also *frequency analysis*.

**immersion programme** In immersion education programmes the L2 is taught by using it as the medium of instruction for teaching the content of other school subjects. Immersion education has been widely used in Canada and has now spread to other countries.

**implicit instruction** Implicit instruction is directed at enabling learners to learn an L2 incidentally by attracting their attention to linguistic forms while they are primarily focused on meaning. There is no direct explanation of the target feature and in this respect it contrasts with *explicit instruction*.

**implicit L2 knowledge** Implicit knowledge of a language is knowledge that is intuitive and tacit. It cannot be directly reported. The knowledge that most speakers have of their L1 is implicit. The study of linguistic competence is the study of a speaker-hearer's implicit knowledge of a language. See also *explicit L2 knowledge*.

**implicit L2 learning** Implicit learning is typically defined as learning that takes place without either intentionality or awareness. It can be investigated by exposing learners to input data, which they are asked to process for meaning. Evidence of implicit learning is obtained if it can be shown that they have acquired some linguistic property even when they cannot report they have learned it.

**incidental L2 learning** This refers to learning of some specific feature that takes place without any deliberate intention to learn it. It can, however, involve consciousness—for example when learners notice a specific feature in the input. It is investigated by giving learners a task that focuses their attention on one aspect of the L2 and, without pre-warning, testing on some other feature.

**individual learner differences (IDs)** The term 'individual learner differences' refers to the differences in how learners learn an L2, in how fast they learn, and in how successful they are. These differences include both psychological factors such as language learning aptitude and motivation, and specific learning strategies.

**inductive instruction** Inductive instruction is a form of explicit instruction that involves asking learners to induce rules from examples given to them or simply by practising the use of the rules. It contrasts with *deductive instruction*.

**information-processing model** An information processing model views the individual as processing information from input, storing it in memory and then drawing on the stored information in output. Individuals are seen as functioning in much the same way as a computer.

**initiate-respond-follow up (IRF) exchange** The IRF exchange is a familiar pattern in classroom talk. It typically consists of the teacher initiating the exchange, the student responding, and the teacher following up on the student's response.

**Input Hypothesis** The Input Hypothesis was advanced by Krashen (1985) to explain how 'acquisition' takes place. It states that 'we acquire...only when we understand language that contains a structure that is "a little beyond" where we are now' (1982: 21). Krashen has referred to the idea of input that is 'a little bit beyond' as 'i + 1'.

**Input Processing Principles** VanPatten (1996) proposed that because learners have a limited working memory capacity they process input in accordance with a set of principles that allocate attention selectively to input. An example of such a principle is 'Learners process input for meaning before they process it for form'. These principles account for why learners make specific errors and why they have difficulty in learning some grammatical structures.

**instrumental motivation** See *motivation*.

**instrumental orientation** Learners have an instrumental orientation when they wish to learn an L2 for functional purposes—for example, to pass an examination or obtain a job—or to please other people—for example, parents.

**intake** Intake is that portion of the input that learners notice and therefore process in their working memory. Intake may subsequently be accommodated in the learner's interlanguage system—i.e. become part of long-term memory.

**integrated instruction** This is a type of *explicit instruction* where the explicit explanation of the target feature is embedded into the practice activities rather than provided prior to the practice. See also *isolated instruction*.

**integration** Integration is a general term that refers to the cognitive processes involved in storing items that have been noticed and processed into long-term memory. These processes involve modification of learners' interlanguage systems. See also *restructuring*.

**integrative orientation** A learner has an integrative orientation when the reason for learning is a genuine interest in coming closer psychologically with individuals who speak the language. See also *motivation*.

**intelligence** Intelligence is the general set of cognitive abilities involved in a wide range of tasks. It constitutes 'a general sort of aptitude that is not limited to a specific performance area but is transferable to many sorts of performance' (Dörnyei 2005: 32).

**intentional learning** Intentional acquisition/ learning takes place when learners make a conscious and deliberate attempt to learn a new L2 item or feature. *Explicit instruction* caters to intentional learning.

**interactional competence** Interactional competence consists of the knowledge of how to interact in specific situations – for example, in service encounters, in language proficiency interviews, and in pharmacist-patient consultations. It includes knowing how to produce and interpret turns and actions and how to repair any 'trouble' that arises.

**interaction approach** In the interaction approach researchers investigate L2 acquisition by examining what happens 'when learners encounter input, are involved in interaction, receive feedback and produce output' (Gass and Mackey 2007: 176).

**Interaction Hypothesis** The Interaction Hypothesis claims that 'negotiation for meaning, and especially negotiation work that triggers interactional adjustments by the NS or more competent interlocutor, facilitates acquisition because it connects input, internal learner capacities, particularly selective attention, and output in productive ways' (Long 1996: 451–2).

**international posture** This is defined as 'a general attitude towards the international community that influences English learning and communication' (Yashima 2002).

**interactionally modified input** This is input that is modified by the learner as a result of the *negotiation of meaning or negotiation of form*. It contrasts with *premodified input*.

**interface position/hypothesis** Theories of L2 acquisition that emphasize the distinctiveness of implicit and explicit knowledge can either maintain that these are completely separate, or that each knowledge type 'leaks', so that explicit knowledge can become implicit and vice-versa. This latter position is known as the 'strong interface position'. See also *non-interface position* and *skill-building hypothesis*.

**interference** According to *behaviourist learning theory*, old habits get in the way of learning new habits. Thus, in L2 learning the L1 interferes with the learning the L2—i.e. results in negative transfer. See also *language transfer*.

**interlanguage** Selinker (1972) coined the term 'interlanguage' to refer to the systematic knowledge of an L2 which is independent of both these learner's L1 and the target language. The term has come to be used with different but related meanings: (1) to refer to the series of interlocking systems which characterize acquisition, (2) to refer to the system that is observed at a single stage of development ('an interlanguage'), and (3) to refer to particular L1/L2 combinations—for example, L1 French/L2 English versus L1 Japanese/L2 English.

**internalization** A term used in sociocultural theory to refer to the process by which a person moves from other-regulation to self-regulation. Ohta (2001) referred to this as 'the movement of language from environment to brain' (p. 11).

**intrinsic motivation** This refers to the motivation that derives from a learner's own curiosity about the target language or the interest generated by participating in a language-learning activity. It is closely linked to the idea of *self-determination* in language learning.

**isolated instruction** This is a type of explicit instruction where the explanation of the target feature is provided prior to the practice activities as in traditional *presentation-practice-production (PPP)* instruction. It contrasts with *integrated instruction*.

**L2 Motivational Self System** This is a comprehensive theory of motivation that distinguishes three primary components:

(1) the ideal-self—i.e. the extent to which learners see themselves as possible successful language learners—(2) the ought-to self—i.e. the extent to which learners consider they ought to learn the L2—and (3) the learners' L2 learning experiences.

**language acquisition device**  Mentalist theories of language acquisition emphasize the importance of the innate capacity of the language learner at the expense of environmental factors. Each learner is credited with a 'language acquisition device' (LAD), which directs the process of acquisition. This device contains information about the possible form that the grammar of any language can take. See *Universal Grammar*.

**language analytical ability**  This is one of the abilities involved in *language aptitude*. It refers to the ability to identify grammatical patterns and the grammatical functions of words in sentences.

**language anxiety**  Different types of anxiety have been identified: (1) trait anxiety—a characteristic of a learner's personality—(2) state anxiety—apprehension that is experienced at a particular moment in response to a definite situation—and (3) situation-specific anxiety—the anxiety aroused by a particular type of situation. Language anxiety is a type of situation-specific anxiety. It can be both facilitating—i.e. it has a positive effect on L2 acquisition—or debilitating—i.e. it has a negative effect.

**language aptitude**  It has been hypothesized that people possess a special ability for learning an L2. Language aptitude is considered to be separate from the general ability to master academic skills, often referred to as *intelligence*. It is one of the factors that characterize individual learner differences. Various tests have been designed to measure language-learning aptitude, for example, the *Modern Language Aptitude Test*.

**language distance**  This refers to fact that differences between the learner's L1 and L2 varies. For example, the distance between Japanese (L2) and Korean (L1) is much less than that between Japanese (L2) and English (L1). This can affect the extent to which L1 transfer occurs.

**language-related episodes**  Swain (1998) defined a language-related episode (LRE) as 'any part of a dialogue in which students talk about the language they are producing, question their language use, or other- or self-correct' (p. 70).

**language socialization**  Schieffelin and Ochs (1986) defined language socialization as the practice by which novices in a community are socialized both to the language forms and, through language, to the values, behaviours, and practices of the community in which they live. Thus, it entails 'socialization through the use of language and socialization to use language' (p. 163).

**language transfer**  Odlin (1989) gives this 'working definition' of 'transfer': Transfer is the influence resulting from similarities and differences between the target language and any other language that has been previously (and perhaps imperfectly) acquired (p. 27). Two types of transfer are commonly identified: negative transfer (resulting in errors) and positive transfer (resulting in correct use of the L2).

**languaging**  This refers to the use of language to mediate cognitively complex acts of thinking. It is 'the process of making meaning and shaping knowledge and experience through language' (Swain 2006). According to sociocultural theory, languaging is indicative of learning in progress.

**learner varieties**  See *basic variety*

**learning strategy**  A learning strategy is a device or procedure used by learners to develop their *interlanguages*. Learning strategies account for how learners acquire and automatize L2 knowledge. They are also used to refer to how they develop specific skills. It is possible, therefore, to talk of both 'language-learning strategies' and 'skill-learning strategies'. Learning strategies can be subdivided into cognitive, metacognitive, and social/affective strategies.

**Levelt's Model of Speaking**  Levelt (1989) proposed that speech production could be accounted for in terms of four overlapping operations: (1) conceptualization; (2) formulation; (3) articulation; and (4) monitoring. His model has been used in studies that have investigated the effects of planning on L2 performance.

**Limited Resources Model** A limited resources model is premised on the assumption that people have limited processing capacity. Skehan (1998) suggested that because of this L2 learners will have difficulty focusing on meaning and form at the same time and also are likely to prioritize either accuracy or complexity but not both. See also *Trade-off Hypothesis*.

**Linguistic Coding Difference Hypothesis** This claims that native language skills play an important role in the success or failure of L2 learning. Learners who have limitations in their native language are predicted to encounter difficulties in learning an L2.

**linguistic competence** Researchers who work within the theoretical framework developed by Chomsky consider it necessary to distinguish *competence* and *performance*. Linguistic competence refers to the knowledge of the rules that comprise the grammar of a language.

**linguistic markedness** See *markedness*.

**markedness** Various definitions of linguistic markedness exist. The term refers to the idea that some linguistic structures are 'special' or 'less natural' or 'less basic' than others. For example, the use of 'break' in 'she broke my heart' can be considered marked in relation to the use of 'break' in 'she broke a cup'. SLA researchers are interested in markedness because it can help to account for *language transfer*.

**Markedness Differential Hypothesis** This is a hypothesis advanced by Eckman (1977). It makes use of 'markedness' to explain why some L1 forms are transferred while others are not. It claims that learners transfer target-language features that are less marked than equivalent features in their L1 but do not transfer those that are more marked.

**mediation** This is a term used in *sociocultural SLA*. Mediation in second language learning includes (1) mediation by others in social interaction, (2) mediation by self through private speech, and (3) mediation by artefacts (for example, tasks and technology).

**meta-analysis** A meta-analysis is a form of research synthesis. It involves investigating a large number of studies that have investigated the same phenomenon—for example, the effect of instruction on learning—and then calculating statistically the overall effect based on the effects reported in the different studies.

**metacognitive strategy** Many L2 learners are able to think consciously about how they learn. Metacognitive strategies involve planning learning, monitoring the process of learning, and evaluating how successful a particular strategy is.

**Modern Language Aptitude Test** This is a test developed by Carroll and Sapon (1959) that measured the different abilities involved in *language-learning aptitude* including phonemic coding ability, language analytical ability, and memory.

**modified output** Modified output occurs when learners modify their own previous utterance. This may occur following feedback or as a result of self-correction. The modification may occur immediately following the original utterance or feedback or some turns later. It may involve repair of an initial error or some other change.

**monitoring** Both native speakers and learners typically try to correct any 'mistakes' they make. This is referred to as 'monitoring'. The learner can monitor vocabulary, grammar, phonology, or discourse. Krashen (1981) uses the term 'Monitoring' (with a capital 'M') to refer to the way learners use explicit knowledge to edit utterances generated by means of implicit knowledge.

**morpheme studies** In the 1970s a number of researchers investigated the acquisition of a group of English morphemes—for example, verb + *-ing*, verb + *ed* and third-person-*s*—with a view to determining their order of acquisition. These studies, which were both cross-sectional and longitudinal, were known as 'morpheme studies'.

**Morphological Congruency Hypothesis** This claims that when a grammatical morpheme with the same function is present in both the native and target languages, language learning will easier than when it is present in the target language but not in the native language.

**motivation** In general terms, motivation refers to the effort that learners put into learning an L2 as a result of their need or desire to learn it. Gardner and Lambert (1972) distinguished *instrumental motivation* and *integrative motivation*. Other types of motivation have also been identified, including (1) *intrinsic motivation* and (2) *attributional motivation*. Dörnyei developed a theory of motivation—the *L2 Motivational Self System*—that incorporates a range of motivational constructs.

**multicompetence** Cook (2002) proposed the idea of 'multicompetence' to refer to knowledge of two or more languages in the same mind. One implication of this is that the linguistic competence of bi- or multi-linguals differs from that of monolinguals.

**Natural Approach** The Natural Approach is based on Krashen's Input Hypothesis. It is an approach to teaching a second/ foreign language that emphasizes comprehensible input rather than production practice in order to foster 'acquisition' as opposed to 'learning'.

**negative evidence** Long (1996: 413) defined negative evidence as input that provides 'direct or indirect evidence of what is ungrammatical'.

**negative transfer** See *interference*.

**negotiation of form** This occurs in interaction when there is no communication difficulty but negotiation still occurs—i.e. when the problem is entirely linguistic. It is uncommon in conversational interaction—although sometimes learners do request it—but has been shown to occur often in some classroom contexts.

**negotiation of meaning** Communication involving L2 learners often leads to problems in understanding and communication breakdown. Frequently, one or more of the participants—the learner or the interlocutor—attempts to remedy this by engaging in interactional work to secure mutual understanding. This work is often called 'negotiation of meaning'. It is characterized by *interactional modifications* such as comprehension checks and requests for clarification.

**neuropsychological SLA** This aims to correlate cognitive operations with neural functioning. Researchers attempt to show the locations and the neural circuits in the brain that are linked to the formation and consolidation of memories for language.

**non-interface position/hypothesis** Theories of L2 acquisition which emphasize the distinctiveness of explicit and implicit knowledge and which claim that one type of knowledge cannot be converted directly into the other type adopt a 'non-interface position'. See also *interface position*.

**noticing** This is a cognitive process whereby linguistic exemplars in the input that learners are exposed to are consciously attended to. It takes place in *working memory*.

**Noticing Hypothesis** The strong version of the hypothesis claims that learners will only learn what they consciously attend to in the input. The weak version allows for the representation and storage of unattended stimuli in memory but claims that 'people learn about the things they attend to and do not learn much about the things they do not attend to' (Schmidt 2001).

**noticing-the-gap** This is a cognitive process whereby learners notice the difference between their own erroneous output and target-like input. It involves making a *cognitive comparison* in working memory.

**obligatory occasion analysis** This involves identifying contexts that require the obligatory use of a specific grammatical feature in samples of learner language and calculating the accuracy with which the feature is supplied in these contexts. See also *target-like use analysis*.

**online planning** Online planning is a term used in task-based research to refer to the planning that learners do while they are performing a task. It contrasts with *pre-task planning*.

**order of acquisition** A number of studies of L2 acquisition—for example, the *morpheme studies*—have produced evidence to suggest that learners achieve mastery of grammatical features in a particular order irrespective of their L1 or their age. For example, verb + *-ing* has been found to be mastered before verb + *-ed*.

**other-regulation** This is a term used in sociocultural theory to refer to the help that learners are given by others—for example, a teacher or another learner—to perform a particular task which they are not yet able to perform by themselves. Other-regulation serves to help learners develop *self-regulation*. See also *zone of proximal development*.

**Output Hypothesis** See *comprehensible output hypothesis*.

**overgeneralization** Language learners in both L1 and L2 acquisition produce errors like 'comed'. These can be explained as extensions of some general rule to items not covered by this rule in the target language.

**overshadowing** Overshadowing in L2 learning occurs when two linguistic cues are associated with a single meaning and the more subjectively salient of the two cues overshadows the weaker. As overshadowing continues over time, *blocking* results—i.e. learners learn to selectively attend to only the more salient of the two cues.

**performance** This term refers to the actual use of language in either comprehension or production. It contrasts with *competence*.

**phonological short-term memory** This refers to a person's ability to retain chunks of speech in their working memory for a short period of time. Common tests for this include the non-word repetition and memory span for words and numerals.

**positive evidence** 'Models of what is grammatical and acceptable' (Long 1996: 413).

**positive transfer** According to *behaviourist accounts* of L2 acquisition, learners will have no difficulty in learning L2 patterns when these are the same as L1 patterns. Support for positive transfer occurs when it can be shown that learners acquire L2 features which are the same as or similar to L1 features with little difficulty.

**pragmalinguistic competence** This is a term used to refer to L2 learners' ability to perform speech acts such as requests and apologies in linguistically appropriate ways according to the situational context.

**pragmatic transfer** Pragmatic transfer occurs when learners attempt to conform to the pragmatic norms of the L1. When these norms are the same as the L2 *positive transfer* occurs; when they differ *negative transfer* is evident.

**pre-modified input** This is input that is modified to make it more comprehensible prior to the learner's exposure to it. It can involve both simplification and elaboration of the input.

**presentation-practice-production (PPP)** This is a type of explicit instruction that involves a fixed sequence of activities, commencing with the presentation of the target feature, followed by controlled practice activities, and finally free-production activities. It constitutes a type of *explicit instruction* of the *isolated instruction* kind.

**pre-task planning** Pre-task planning is a term used in task-based research to refer to the planning that learners do before they start the task. See also *online planning*.

**private speech** This is speech that is addressed to oneself. Some L2 learners who go through a *silent period* engage in private conversations with themselves, thus, perhaps, preparing themselves for social speech later. It constitutes one type of *mediation*.

**procedural knowledge** Two related but different uses of procedural knowledge can be found in SLA research. On the one hand, it is used in contrast to *declarative knowledge* to refer to knowledge that has become proceduralized so that it is available for automatic and unconscious use. On the other hand, it refers to knowledge of the various strategies that learners employ to compensate for lack of L2 knowledge in communication—for example, *communication strategies*.

**Processability Theory** Pienemann's Processability Theory seeks to explain what is known about acquisitional orders/sequences in terms of a set of processing routines. As Pienemann (2005: 2) put it 'once we can spell out the sequence in which language processing routines develop we can delineate those grammars that are processable at different points of development'.

**Processing Instruction** VanPatten (1996) defined Processing Instruction as 'a type of grammar instruction whose purpose is to affect the ways in which learners attend to input data. It is input-based rather than output-based' (p. 2). It is intended to assist learners to construct form-function mappings in line with target language norms.

**Process Model of L2 Motivation** Dornyei and Otto (1998) developed this model of motivation to account for how motivation changes over time. It views motivation as continuously changing both in the short and long term.

**production-based instruction** This is a type of instruction that aims to teach linguistic features by means of activities that involve controlled or free production of the target features.

**prototypicality** This term is used by Kellerman (1977) to refer to perceptions that learners have regarding the structure of their own language.

**psychotypology** Kellerman (1978) has suggested that learners have perceptions regarding the distance between their L1 and the L2 they are trying to learn. These perceptions constitute their psychotypology.

**pushed output** This is a term used by Swain (1985) to refer to learner output that is produced with effort and reflects the outer limits of the learner's linguistic competence. See also *comprehensible output hypothesis* and *modified output*.

**recast** An utterance that 'rephrases the learner's utterance by changing one or more components—subject, verb, object—while still referring to its central meaning' (Long 1996).

**rehearsal** In information processing theories of L2 acquisition, 'rehearsal' refers to the recycling of input that has been attended to—i.e. entered short-term working memory—in complex working memory.

**repair** Repair refers to the conversational work undertaken to deal with 'trouble'—i.e. anything that the interlocutors consider is impeding communication. Repair is viewed as something accomplished jointly by the participants in the conversation. See *conversation analysis*.

**restructuring** This is a term used in information-processing theories of L2 acquisition to refer to the qualitative changes that take place in learners' interlanguage at certain stages of development. For example, learners may begin by representing past tense forms as separate items—for example, 'ate'—and then shift to representing them by means of a general rule for past-tense formation—for example, 'eated'.

**rule-based system** Symbolic theories of L2 acquisition view interlanguage as consisting of abstract rules that are drawn on when processing input and output. Such theories contrast with theories that view interlanguage as consisting of an *exemplar-based system*.

**scaffolding** Scaffolding refers to the process by which one speaker—an expert or a novice—assists another speaker—a novice—to perform a skill that they are unable to perform independently. It is a term used in *sociocultural SLA*. See also *dynamic assessment*.

**Self-determination Theory** This is a theory of motivation and personality that emphasizes the choices people make that are not influenced by external factors—i.e. are self-determined. In terms of motivation in L2 acquisition, it emphasizes the importance of *intrinsic motivation*.

**self-regulation** This is the ability to monitor one's learning and make changes to the strategies that one employs. It involves both the ability to exercise control over one's attitudinal/motivational state and to engage in self-critical reflection of one's actions and underlying belief systems. In *sociocultural SLA*, however, it has a different meaning. It refers to the ability to exercise self-control over a function as a result of the internalization that occurs through *other-regulation*.

**sequence of acquisition** L2 research has shown that learners pass through a series of identifiable stages in acquiring specific grammatical structures such as negatives, interrogatives, and relative clauses. To a large extent, these sequences are viewed as universal—i.e. common to all L2 learners. However, the universality of sequences of acquisition is now challenged. See *Dynamic Systems Theory*.

**semantic transfer** This occurs when the L1 and the L2 share the same concept and the learner attempts to represent this concept by selecting the L1 word or structure. See also *conceptual transfer*.

**Similarity Differential Rate Hypothesis** This hypothesis proposes that L2 sounds that are dissimilar to the L1 may be difficult to acquire initially but over time improvement takes place more rapidly than with similar sounds.

**Skill-learning Theory** Skill-learning Theory is based on the view that language learning, like any other skill, is characterized by a progression from an initial declarative knowledge stage involving controlled processing, to a final procedural stage, involving automatic processing. Skills are developed as a result of 'practice'.

**social context** According to a structural view of social context, social factors such as power and prestige are seen as determining social context. In an interactional view the social context is seen as constructed in each situation through interaction.

**social distance** This is a term used by Schumann (1978a) to account for why some L2 learners learn very slowly or achieve low levels of proficiency. Various factors such as the size of the learner's L2 group and the learner's desire to acculturate influence the 'distance' between the learner and the target-language community.

**social identity** Norton defined 'social identity' as 'the relationship between the individual and the larger social world, as mediated through institutions such as families, schools, workplaces, social services, and law courts' (Norton 1997: 420).

**social identity approach/theory** This approach involves examining the role of social identity in L2 learners' 'right to speak'. Norton (2000) demonstrated through a series of case studies of immigrant women in Canada how the social identity that figured in interactions with native speakers facilitated or impeded their access to opportunities for learning English.

**socialization** See *language socialization*.

**Social-interactionist SLA** In social-interactionist SLA researchers seek to demonstrate how language learning takes place in the social interactions in which learners participate. It contrasts with research based on the Interaction Hypothesis which sees interaction as triggering internal changes in learners' interlanguage.

**sociocognitive approach** The sociocognitive approach emphasizes learning-as-participation when mind, body, and world come together through the interactions that take place in specific situational contexts. L2 acquisition is viewed as involving local, embodied, and situated language use.

**sociocultural SLA** This is a branch of SLA that draws on the work of Vygotsky in viewing learning as the product of mediated activity. Higher order language functions are seen as developing both in and out of social interaction. Learners progress from other-regulation to self-regulation through interacting with others. See also *zone of proximal development* and *scaffolding*.

**Socio-educational Model** This is a model of L2 learning developed by Gardner (1985).

It posits that the social and cultural milieu in which learners grow up determines the attitudes and motivational orientation they hold towards the target language, its speakers, and its culture. These in turn influence learning outcomes.

**sociolinguistic competence** Sociolinguistic competence refers to speakers' knowledge of the social meanings of different linguistic forms and the ability to use these forms in ways that are appropriate in different situations.

**sociopragmatic competence** This is a term used to refer to the L2 learner's ability to perform the right speech act for the situational context. For example, in many English-speaking communities it is considered normal to thank a person after visiting their home for a meal. However, in other cultures—for example, Japanese—it would be more appropriate to apologize for inconveniencing them.

**speech styles** Speech style varies in accordance with the social context or topic. A common distinction is between a *careful style* and a *vernacular style*.

**stabilization** Stabilization refers to a state where L2 development has temporarily ceased. It contrasts with *fossilization*, which refers to the permanent cessation of development.

**stimulated recall** This is a research technique for eliciting a retrospective report. It seeks to explore learners' thought processes at the time they performed an activity by asking them to report their thoughts about it after they have completed the activity. It has been used to investigate *corrective feedback*.

**strategic competence** This concerns the ability to deal with communication breakdown and to cope with gaps in one's linguistic competence. See *communication strategy*.

**strategy instruction** This involves attempts to teach learners how to make use of specific *communication strategies* or *learning strategies*. Strategy instruction studies measure the effect that such instruction has on language learning.

**strong interface position** This claims that explicit knowledge can transform into implicit knowledge and in this respect contrasts with the *non-interface position*. The strong interface position underlies *skill-learning theory*. That is, the transformation can take place through practising the use of a declarative rule.

**structural and semantic simplification** Structural simplification is evident in the omission of grammatical functors—for example, 'I *buy* a car' when referring to a past event. Semantic simplification is evident in the omission of one or more propositional elements—for example, when a learner says 'Hitting sister' instead of 'Kurt is hitting his sister'. Both types of simplification are common in beginner learner language.

**structured input** This is input that has been specially designed to expose learners to exemplars of a specific linguistic feature. It constitutes the essential component of *Processing Instruction*.

**style-shifting** Both native speakers and L2 learners use different *variants* of a linguistic form depending on the degree of attention they pay to their speech (i.e. whether they are accessing their *vernacular* or *careful style*). Labov refers to these changes in speech as 'style shifting'.

**systematic variation** Variation in the use of two or more variants of a feature is systematic if it can be explained (and also predicted) by reference to the situational or linguistic context.

**task** A task is a language-teaching activity where meaning is primary. There is some kind of gap, students are required to use their own linguistic resources, and there is an outcome other than the display of language for its own sake (Ellis 2003).

**task-based language teaching** Task-based language teaching is an approach to the teaching of second/foreign languages based on a syllabus consisting of communicative tasks and utilizing a methodology that makes meaningful communication primary but which also allows for incidental attention to form.

**Teachability Hypothesis** Pienemann's (1985) Teachability Hypothesis 'predicts that instruction can only promote language acquisition if the interlanguage is close to the point when the structure to be taught is acquired in the natural setting (so that sufficient processing prerequisites are developed)' (p. 37).

**teacher talk** Teachers address classroom language learners differently from the way they address other kinds of classroom learners. They make adjustments to both language form and language function in order to facilitate communication. These adjustments are referred to as 'teacher talk'. See also *foreigner talk*.

**token frequency** Token frequency is the frequency with which particular items occur in the input or output. For example 'ate' is a token. Token frequency also affects acquisition; learners are more likely to acquire those tokens that occur with high frequency than those with low frequency. Frequent exposure to 'ate', for example, can lead to it replacing 'eated' which has been overgeneralized from the verb + -*ed* pattern. See *type frequency*.

**Trade-off Hypothesis** This is a hypothesis developed by Skehan (1998) based on his *Limited Processing Model*. It proposes that learners will have difficulty in focusing on all aspects of production (i.e. complexity, accuracy, and fluency) at the same time and this will prioritize one aspect to the detriment of the other aspects.

**Transfer Appropriate Processing** The principle of transfer-appropriate processing states that 'the learning environment that best promotes rapid, accurate retrieval of what has been learned is that in which the psychological demands placed on the learner resemble those that will be encountered later in natural settings' (Lightbown 2006).

**Transfer to Nowhere Principle** In contrast to the *Transfer to Somewhere Principle*, this principle claims that L1 features can be transferred even if they are not licensed by natural acquisition principles.

**Transfer to Somewhere Principle** This claims that L1 transfer is more likely to occur if the L1 feature is compatible with natural acquisition principles. For example, Spanish learners of English are more likely to maintain the 'no' + verb construction as this construction occurs in the natural acquisition of all L2 learners.

**transitional construction** Dulay, Burt, and Krashen (1982) define transitional constructions as 'the interim language forms that learners use while they are still learning the grammar of a language'. For example, before learners master the rule for English negatives, they operate with interim rules (such as 'no' + verb).

**transnational identity**  Migrants have been shown to establish identities related to the social fields in which they operate that cross geographic, cultural, and political borders. Transnational identities arise out of the multiple relations they develop and maintain.

**turn-taking**  Conversation analysts have identified a number of rules or regularities that underlie speaker selection and change in conversations—for example, only one speaker speaks at a time.

**type frequency**  Type frequency refers to the frequency of a pattern in the input or output. For example, verb + -*ed* constitutes a syntactical pattern. It has high type frequency in English because a large number of different lexical verbs can be fitted into this pattern. Learners are more likely to acquire those patterns that have a high type frequency. See also *token frequency*.

**Universal Acquisition Hypothesis**  This is a term used by Lantolf (2011) to refer to the claim that the acquisition of an L2 grammar follows a common route for all learners irrespective of their age or the setting in which learning takes place. See also *order of acquisition* and *sequence of acquisition*.

**Universal Grammar**  This is a term used by Chomsky to refer to the abstract knowledge of language which children bring to the task of learning their native language, and which constrains the shape of the particular grammar they are trying to learn. Universal Grammar consists of various abstract *principles* which govern the form grammatical rules can take. See also *Language Acquisition Device*.

**usage-based theories**  Usage-based theories of L2 acquisition view learning as a process that originates in chunk-learning and progresses gradually towards a more schematic inventory of linguistic resources. In other words, rule-like behaviour is not the starting point but arises out of experience with the use of the L2.

**U-shaped pattern of development**  L2 learners have been observed to manifest a target-language form in their output at an early stage of development, only to manifest an interlanguage form in its place at a later stage. Eventually the correct target-language form reappears—for example, 'came' becomes 'comed' and, later still, 'came' again. This pattern of development is known as 'U-shaped behaviour'.

**variable rule**  A variable rule is used by sociolinguists to describe the uses of a linguistic feature that has two of more variants. For example, there are two variants of the negator 'not' in English – the full form ('not') and the contracted form 'nt' – whose use varies stylistically.

**vernacular style**  This is a term used by Labov (1970) to refer to the language forms evident when speakers are communicating spontaneously and easily with interlocutors familiar to them. It contrasts with *careful style*, and for this reason is also sometimes referred to as 'casual style'. See also *stylistic continuum*.

**vertical variability**  This refers to the differences in learner language evident from one time to another. It reflects the development that is taking place in the learner's interlanguage. It has been proposed that vertical variability mirrors the *horizontal variability* evident at a particular stage of development.

**weak-interface position**  This acknowledges a disassociation between explicit and implicit knowledge but suggests that explicit knowledge plays a role in the processes involved in implicit learning—for example, by priming attention to linguistic exemplars in the input. Thus explicit knowledge contributes indirectly to the development of implicit knowledge.

**working memory**  Working memory is where the key processes of perception, attention, and rehearsal take place. It is believed to play a central role in L2 acquisition and provides a link with long-term memory. There are different models of working memory but the model that figures most strongly in SLA research is the limited capacity model.

**Zone of Proximal Development (ZPD)**  This refers to 'the distance between the actual developmental level as determined by independent problem solving and the level of potential development as determined through adult guidance or in collaboration with more capable peers' (Vygotsky 1978: 86). It is a term used in *sociocultural SLA*. Learning occurs when a zone of proximal development is constructed for the learner through *mediation* of one kind or another.

# Bibliography

**Abdullah, K.** and **H. Jackson.** 1998. 'Idioms and the language learner: contrasting English and Syrian Arabic'. *Languages in Contrast* 1: 83–107.

**Abrahamsson, N.** 2003. 'Development and recoverability of L2 codas: a longitudinal study of Chinese/Swedish interphonology'. *Studies in Second Language Acquisition* 25: 313–49.

**Abrahamsson, N.** and **K. Hyltenstam.** 2009. 'Age of onset and nativelikeness in a second language: listener perception versus linguistic scrutiny'. *Language Learning* 59: 249–306.

**Achiba, M.** 2003. *Learning to Request in a Second Language.* Clevedon: Multilingual Matters.

**Adams, R., A. Nuevo,** and **T. Egi.** 2011. 'Explicit and implicit feedback, modified output, and SLA: does explicit and implicit feedback promote learning and learner-learner interactions?' *Modern Language Journal* 95, Supplementary Issue: 42–63.

**Akakura, M.** 2012. 'Evaluating the effectiveness of explicit instruction on implicit and explicit L2 knowledge'. *Language Teaching Research* 16: 8–37.

**Aljaafreh, A.** and **J. Lantolf.** 1994. 'Negative feedback as regulation and second language learning in the Zone of Proximal Development'. *The Modern Language Journal* 78: 465–83.

**Allwright, R.** 1984. 'The importance of interaction in classroom language learning'. *Applied Linguistics* 5: 156–71.

**Alvarez, E.** 2006. 'Rate and route of acquisition in EFL narrative development at different ages' in Muñoz, C. (ed.): *Age and the Rate of Foreign Language Learning.* Clevedon: Multilingual Matters.

**Andersen, R.** 1983. 'Transfer to somewhere' in Gass, S. and L. Selinker (eds.): *Language Transfer in Language Learning.* Rowley, MA: Newbury House.

**Andersen, R.** 1984. 'The one-to-one principle of interlanguage construction'. *Language Learning* 34: 77–95.

**Andersen, R.** 1991. 'Developmental sequences: the emergence of aspect marking in second language acquisition' in Ferguson, C. and T. Huebner (eds.): *Second Language Acquisition and Linguistic Theories.* Amsterdam: Benjamins.

**Anderson, J.** 1980. *Cognitive Psychology and its Implications.* San Francisco: Freeman.

**Anderson, J.** 1993. *Rules of the Mind.* Hillsdale, NJ: Lawrence Erlbaum.

**Anderson, J.** 2005. *Cognitive Psychology and its Implications.* 6th edn. New York: Worth Publishers.

**Armstrong, N.** 2002. 'Variable deletion of French ne: a cross-stylistic perspective'. *Language Sciences* 24: 153–73.

**Arthur, B., M. Weiner, J. Culver, L. Young,** and **D. Thomas.** 1980. 'The register of impersonal discourse to foreigners: verbal adjustments to foreign accent' in Larsen-Freeman, D. (ed.): *Discourse Analysis in Second Language Research.* Rowley, MA: Newbury House.

**Ashby, W.** 1981. 'The loss of negative particle ne in French: a syntactic change in process'. *Language* 57: 674–87.

**Asher, J.** 1977. *Learning Another Language Through Actions: The Complete Teachers' Guidebook.* Los Gatos, CA: Sky Oaks Publications.

**Aston, G.** 1986. 'Trouble-shooting in interaction with learners: the more the merrier?' *Applied Linguistics* 7: 128–43.

**Atkinson, D.** 2002. 'Toward a sociocognitive approach to second language acquisition'. *The Modern Language Journal* 86: 525–45.

**Atkinson, D.** (ed.). 2011a. *Alternative Approaches to Second Language Acquisition.* London: Routledge.

Atkinson, D. 2011b. 'Introduction: cognitivism and second language acquisition' in Atkinson, D. (ed.).

Atkinson, D. 2011c. 'A sociocognitive approach to second language acquisition: how mind, body and world work together in learning' in Atkinson, D. (ed.).

Atkinson, D., E. Churchill, T. Nishino, and H. Okada. 2007. 'Alignment and interaction in a sociocognitive approach to second language acquisition'. *Modern Language Journal* 91: 169–88.

Baddeley, A. 2003. 'Working memory and language: an overview'. *Journal of Communication Disorders* 36: 189–208.

Bailey, K. 1983. 'Competitiveness and anxiety in adult second language learning: looking at and through the diary studies' in Seliger, H. and M. Long (eds.): *Classroom-oriented Research in Second Language Acquisition*. Rowley, MA: Newbury House.

Bailey, N., C. Madden, and S. Krashen. 1974. 'Is there a "natural sequence" in adult second language learning?' *Language Learning* 21: 235–43.

Bardovi-Harlig, K. 1995. 'The interaction of pedagogy and natural sequences in the acquisition of tense and aspect' in Eckman, F. et al. (eds.): 151–168. *Second language Acquisition Theory and Pedagogy*. Mahwah, NJ: Lawrence Erlbaum.

Bardovi-Harlig, K. 2000. 'Tense and aspect in second language acquisition: form, meaning and use'. *Language Learning Monograph Series*. Malden, MA: Blackwell.

Bardovi-Harlig, K. 2006. 'On the role of formulas in the acquisition of L2 pragmatics' in Bardovi-Harlig, K, C. Félix-Brasdefer, and A. Omar (eds.): *Pragmatics and Language Learning* 11. Honolulu, HI: University of Hawai'i Press.

Bardovi-Harlig, K. and Z. Dörnyei. 1998. 'Do language learners recognize pragmatic violations? Pragmatic vs. grammatical awareness in instructed L2 learning'. *TESOL Quarterly* 32: 233–59.

Batstone, R. 2010. 'Issues and options in sociocognition' in Batstone, R. (ed.): *Sociocognitive Perspectives on Language Use and Language Learning*. Oxford: Oxford University Press.

Bayley, R. 1996. 'Competing constraints on variation in the speech of adult Chinese learners of English' in Bayley, R. and D. Preston (eds.): *Second Language Acquisition and Linguistic Variation*. Amsterdam: John Benjamins.

Bayley, R. 2005. 'Second language acquisition and sociolinguistic variation'. *Intercultural Communication Studies* XIV: 1–14.

Beckner, C., R. Blythe, J. Bybee, M. Chistiansen, W. Croft, N. Ellis, J. Holland, J. Ke, D. Larsen-Freeman, and T. Schoenmann. 2009. 'Language is a complex adaptive system: position paper'. *Language Learning* 59: 1–26.

Beebe, L. 1980. 'Sociolinguistic variation and style-shifting in second language acquisition'. *Language Learning* 30: 433–47.

Bell, H. 2009. 'The messy little details: a longitudinal case study of the emerging lexicon' in Fitzpatrick, T. and A. Barfield (eds.): *Lexical Processing in Second Language Learners*. Bristol: Multilingual Matters.

Benati, A. 2004. 'The effects of structured input activities and explicit information on the acquisition of Italian future tense' in VanPatten, B. (ed.): *Processing Instruction: Theory, Research, and Commentary*. Mahwah, NJ: Lawrence Erlbaum.

Berdan, R. 1996. 'Disentangling language acquisition from language variation' in Bayley, R. and D. Preston (eds.): *Second Language Acquisition and Linguistic Variation*. Amsterdam: John Benjamins.

Bialystok, E. and K. Hakuta. 1999. 'Confounded age: linguistic and cognitive factors in age differences for second language acquisition' in Birdsong, D. (ed.): *Second Language Acquisition and the Critical Period Hypothesis*. Mahwah, NJ: Lawrence Erlbaum.

Bickerton, D. 1975. *Dynamics of a Creole System*. Cambridge: Cambridge University Press.

Bickerton, D. 1981. 'Discussion of "Two perspectives on pidginization as second language acquisition"' in Andersen, R. (ed.): *New Dimensions in Second Language Acquisition Research*. Rowley, MA: Newbury House.

Birdsong, D. 1992. 'Ultimate attainment in second language acquisition'. *Language* 68: 706–55.

Birdsong, D. 2006. 'Age and second language acquisition and processing: a selective overview' in Gullberg, M. and P. Indefrey (eds.): *The Cognitive Neuroscience of Second Language Acquisition*. Malden, MA: Blackwell.

Bley-Vroman, R. 1983. 'The comparative fallacy in interlanguage studies: the case of systematicity'. *Language Learning* 33: 1–17.

Block, D. 2003. *The Social Turn in Second Language Acquisition*. Edinburgh: Edinburgh University Press.

Block, D. 2006. *Multilingual Identities in a Global City*. Basingstoke: Palgrave Macmillan.

Block, D. 2007. '"Socializing" second language acquisition' in Hua, Z., P. Seedhouse, L. Wei, and V. Cook (eds.): *Language Learning and Teaching as Social Interaction*. London: Palgrave.

Bongaerts, T. 1999. 'Ultimate attainment in L2 pronunciation: the case of the very advanced late L2 learners' in Birdsong, D. (ed.): *Second Language Acquisition and the Critical Period Hypothesis*. Mahwah, NJ: Lawrence Erlbaum.

Bongartz, C. and M. Schneider. 2003. 'Linguistic development in social context: a study of two brothers learning German'. *The Modern Language Journal* 87: 13–37.

Brown, R. 1973. *A First Language: the Early Stages*. Cambridge, MA: Harvard University Press.

Burns, A. 2010. *Doing Action Research in English Language Teaching: A Guide for Practitioners*. New York: Routledge.

Burt, M. 1975. 'Error analysis in the adult EFL classroom'. *TESOL Quarterly* 9: 53–63.

Bygate, M. 2001. 'Effects of task repetition on the structure and control of oral language' in Bygate, M., P. Skehan, and M. Swain (eds.): *Researching Pedagogic Tasks, Second Language Learning, Teaching and Testing*. Harlow: Longman.

Bylund, E., N. Abrahamsson, and K. Hystenstam. 2012. 'Does first language maintenance hamper nativelikeness in a second language? A study of ultimate attainment in early bilinguals'. *Studies in Second Language Acquisition* 34: 215–41.

Callies, M. 2013. 'Markedness' in Robinson, P. (ed.): *The Routledge Encyclopedia of Second Language Acquisition* (pp. 406–9). London: Routledge.

Canale, M. 1983. 'From communicative competence to language pedagogy' in Richards, J. and R. Schmidt (eds.): *Language and Communication*. London: Longman.

Cancino, H., E. Rosansky, and J. Schumann. 1978. 'The acquisition of English negatives and interrogatives by native Spanish speakers' in Hatch, E. (ed.): *Second Language Acquisition*. Rowley, MA: Newbury House.

Candlin, C. 1987. 'Towards task-based language learning' in Candlin, C. and D. Murphy (eds.): *Language Learning Tasks*. Englewood Cliffs NJ: Prentice Hall International.

Carroll, J. 1965. 'The prediction of success in foreign language training' in Glaser, R. (ed.): *Training, Research, and Education*. New York: Wiley.

Carroll, J. 1981. 'Twenty-five years in foreign language aptitude' in Diller, K. (ed.): *Individual Differences and Universals in Language Learning Aptitude*. Rowley, MA: Newbury House.

Carroll, J. 1990. 'Cognitive abilities in foreign language aptitude: then and now' in Parry, T. and C. Stansfield (eds.): *Language Aptitude Reconsidered*. Englewood Cliffs, NJ: Prentice Hall.

Carroll, J. and S. Sapon. 1959. *Modern Language Aptitude Test—Form A*. New York: The Psychological Corporation.

Cenoz, J., B. Hufeisen, and U. Jessner. 2001. *Cross-linguistic Influence in Third Language Acquisition*. Clevedon: Multilingual Matters.

Cenoz, J. and U. Jessner. 2000. *The English in Europe: the Acquisition of a Third Language*. Clevedon: Multilingual Matters.

Chaudron, C. 1983. 'Foreigner talk in the classroom—an aid to learning?' in Seliger, H. and M. Long (eds.): *Classroom-Oriented Research in Second Language Acquisition*. Rowley, MA: Newbury House.

Chomsky, N. 1959. 'Review of *Verbal Behavior* by B. F. Skinner'. *Language* 35: 26–58.

Chomsky, N. 1965. *Aspects of the Theory of Syntax*. Cambridge, MA: MIT Press.

Chomsky, N. 1981. 'Principles and parameters in syntactic theory' in Hornstein, N. and D. Lightfoot (eds.): *Explanation in Linguistics: The Logical Problem of Language Acquisition*. London: Longman.

Chomsky, N. 1986. *Barriers*. Cambridge, MA: MIT Press.

Clement, R. 1986. 'Second language proficiency and acculturation: an investigation of the effects of language status and individual characteristics'. *Journal of Language and Social Psychology* 5: 271–90.

Cochrane, R. 1980. 'The acquisition of /r/ and /l/ by Japanese children and adults learning English as a second language'. *Journal of Multilingual and Multicultural Development* 1: 331–60.

Cohen, A. and J. Chi. 2001. 'Language strategy use survey'. Minneapolis, MN: Center for Advanced Research on Language Acquisition, University of Minnesota. http://www.carla.umn.edu/about/profiles/Cohen.

Cook, V. 1991. 'The poverty of stimulus argument and multicompetence'. *Second Language Research* 7: 103–17.

Cook, V. 2000. 'Is transfer the right word?' Paper presented at the 7th International Pragmatics Conference, July 2000. Budapest.

Cook, V. 2003. 'Changing the first language in the L2 user's mind: Introduction to L2 effects on the L1'. http://homepage.ntlworld.com/vivian.c/Writings/Papers/EffectsIntro.htm

Coppetiers, R. 1987. 'Competence differences between native and near-native speakers'. *Language* 63: 544–73.

Corder, S. P. 1967. 'The significance of learners' errors'. *International Review of Applied Linguistics* 5: 161–9.

Corder, S. P. 1983. 'A role for the mother tongue' in Gass, S. and L. Selinker (eds.): *Language Transfer in Language Learning*. Rowley, MA: Newbury House.

Coughlan, P. and P. Duff. 1994. 'Same task, different activities: analysis of a SLA task from an activity theory perspective' in Lantolf, J. and G. Appel (eds.): *Vygotskian Approaches to Second Language Research*. Norwood, NJ: Ablex.

Crookes, G. and R. Schmidt. 1991. 'Language learning motivation: reopening the research agenda'. *Language Learning* 41: 469–512.

Curtiss, S. (ed.). 1977. *Genie: Psycholinguistic Study of a Modern-day 'Wild Child'*. London: Academic Press.

Czinglar, C. 2012. 'The effect of age of acquisition on L1 transfer from Russian to L2 German'. http://www.fcsh.unl.pt/clunl/pl2/wcil2/pdfs/Christine%20Czinglar.pdf

de Bot, K. and D. Larsen-Freeman. 2011. 'Researching second language development from a Dynamic Systems Theory perspective' in Verspoor, M., K. de Bot, and W. Lowie (eds.): *A Dynamic Approach to Second Language Development*. Amsterdam: John Benjamins.

de Bot, K., W. Lowie, and M. Verspoor. 2007. 'A dynamic systems theory approach to second language acquisition'. *Bilingualism: Language and Cognition* 10: 7–21.

de Graaff, R. 1997. *Differential Effects of Explicit Instruction on Second Language Acquisition*. Holland Institute of Generative Linguistics.

de la Fuente, M. 2002. 'Negotiation and oral acquisition of L2 vocabulary: the roles of input and output in the receptive and productive acquisition of words'. *Studies in Second Language Acquisition* 24: 81–112.

de la Fuente, M. 2003. 'Is SLA interactionist theory relevant to CALL? A study on the effects of computer-mediated interaction in L2 vocabulary acquisition'. *Computer Assisted Language Learning* 16: 47–81.

de Swart, H. 2006. 'Negation: an early "window" on language genesis'. igitur-archive.library.uu.nl/ai/2008-0317-200901/preprint055

de Villiers, J. and P. de Villiers. 1973. 'A cross-sectional study of the development of grammatical morphemes in child speech'. *Journal of Psycholinguistic Research* 1: 299–310.

Deci, E. and M. Ryan. (eds.). 1985. *Intrinsic Motivation and Self-Determination in Human Behavior*. New York: Plenum.

Dehaene, S. 1999. 'Fitting two languages into one brain'. *Brain* 122: 2207–08.

DeKeyser, R. 1998. 'Beyond focus on form: cognitive perspectives on learning and practicing second language grammar' in Doughty, C. and J. Williams (eds.): *Focus on Form in Classroom Second Language Acquisition*. Cambridge: Cambridge University Press.

DeKeyser, R. 2000. 'The robustness of critical period effects in second language acquisition'. *Studies in Second Language Acquisition* 22: 499–533.

DeKeyser, R. 2003. 'Implicit and explicit learning' in Doughty, C. and M. Long (eds.): *Handbook of Second Language Acquisition*. Malden, MA: Blackwell.

DeKeyser, R. 2007. 'Introduction: situating the concept of practice' in DeKeyser, R (ed.): *Practice in a Second Language*. Cambridge: Cambridge University Press.

DeKeyser, R. 2009. 'Cognitive-psychological processes in second language learning' in Long, M. and C. Doughty (eds.): *Handbook of Second Language Teaching*. Oxford: Wiley-Blackwell.

DeKeyser, R. and G. Prieto Botana. 2015. 'The effectiveness of processing instruction in L2 grammar acquisition: a narrative review'. *Applied Linguistics* 36(3).

Dewaele, J. 2004. 'Retention or omission of the ne in advanced French interlanguage: the variable effect of extralinguistic factors'. *Journal of Sociolinguistics* 8: 433–50.

Dewaele, J. and V. Regan. 2002. 'Maîtreser la norme sociolinguistique en interlanguage francaise: le cas de l'omission variable de *ne*'. *Journal of French Language Studies* 12: 123–48.

Dickerson, L. 1975. 'The learner's interlanguage as a system of variable rules'. *TESOL Quarterly* 9: 401–7.

Dietrich, R., W. Klein, and C. Noyau (eds.). 1995. *The Acquisition of Temporality in a Second Language*. Amsterdam: John Benjamins.

Dijk, M., M. Verspoor, and W. Lowie. 2011. 'Variability and DST' in Verspoor, M., K. de Bot, and W. Lowie (eds.): *A Dynamic Approach to Second Language Development*. Amsterdam: John Benjamins.

Dimroth, C. 2008. 'Age effects on the process of L2 acquisition? Evidence from the acquisition of negation and finiteness in L2 German'. *Language Learning* 58: 117–150.

Dimroth, C. 2012. 'Learner varieties' in Chapelle, C. (ed.): *The Encyclopedia of Applied Linguistics*. Blackwell.

Dörnyei, Z. 2001. *Motivational Strategies in the Language Classroom*. Cambridge: Cambridge University Press.

Dörnyei, Z. 2002. 'The motivational basis of language learning tasks' in Robinson, P. (ed.): *Individual Differences in L2 Learning*. Amsterdam: John Benjamins.

Dörnyei, Z. 2005. *The Psychology of the Language Learner: Individual Differences in Second Language Acquisition*. Mahwah, NJ: Lawrence Erlbaum.

Dörnyei, Z. 2009. 'The L2 Motivational Self System' in Dörnyei, Z. and E. Ushioda (eds.): *Motivation, Language Identity and the L2 Self*. Bristol: Multilingual Matters.

Dörnyei, Z. 2010. 'The relationship between language aptitude and language learning motivation: individual differences from a dynamic systems perspective' in Macaro, E. (ed.): *Continuum Companion to Second Language Acquisition*. London: Continuum.

Dörnyei, Z. and T. Murphey. 2003. *Group Dynamics in the Language Classroom*. Cambridge: Cambridge University Press.

Dörnyei, Z. and I. Otto. 1998. 'Motivation in action: A process model of L2 motivation'. *Working Papers in Applied Linguistics* 47: 173–210. Thames Valley University.

Dörnyei, Z. and P. Skehan. 2003. 'Individual differences in second language learning' in Doughty, C. and M. Long (eds.): *The Handbook of Second Language Acquisition*. Malden, MA: Blackwell.

Doughty, C. and E. Varela. 1998. 'Communicative focus-on-form' in Doughty, C. and J. Williams (eds.): *Focus-on-Form in Classroom Second Language Acquisition*. Cambridge: Cambridge University Press.

Doughty, C. and J. Williams (eds.). 1998. *Focus-on-form in Classroom Second Language Acquisition*. Cambridge: Cambridge University Press.

Duff, P. 2010. 'Language socialization into academic discourse communities'. *Annual Review of Applied Linguistics* 30: 169–92.

Duff, P. and M. Kobayashi. 2010. 'The intersection of social, cognitive, and cultural processes in language learning: a second language socialization approach' in Batstone, R. (ed.): *Sociocognitive Perspectives on Language Use and Language Learning.* Oxford: Oxford University Press.

Duff, P. and S. Talmy. 2011. 'Language socialization approaches to second language acquisition: social, cultural, and linguistic development in additional languages' in Atkinson, D. (ed.): *Alternative Approaches to SLA.* London: Routledge.

Dulay, H. and M. Burt. 1973. 'Should we teach children syntax?' *Language Learning* 23: 245–58.

Dulay, H. and M. Burt. 1974. 'Errors and strategies in child second language acquisition'. *TESOL Quarterly* 8: 129–36.

Eckerth, J. 2008. 'Task-based learner interaction: investigating learning opportunities, learning processes, and learning outcomes' in Eckerth, J. (ed): *Task-Based Language Learning and Teaching: Theoretical, Methodological, and Pedagogical Perspectives.* Frankfurt am Main: Peter Lang.

Eckman, F. 1977. 'Markedness and the contrastive analysis hypothesis'. *Language Learning* 27: 315–30.

Eckman, F. 1985. 'Some theoretical and pedagogical implications of the markedness differential hypothesis'. *Studies in Second Language Acquisition* 7: 289–307.

Eckman, F. and G. Iverson. 2013. 'The role of the native language phonology in the L2 production of L2 contrasts'. *Studies of Second Language Acquisition* 35: 67–92.

Egi, T. 2007. 'Interpreting recasts as linguistic evidence: the role of linguistic target, length and degree of change'. *Studies in Second Language Acquisition* 29: 511–38.

Ellis, N. 1993. 'Rules and instances in foreign language learning: interactions of explicit and implicit knowledge'. *European Journal of Cognitive Psychology* 5: 289–319.

Ellis, N. 1994. 'Introduction: Implicit and explicit language learning—an overview' in Ellis, N. (ed.). *Implicit and Explicit Learning of Languages.* San Diego: Academic Press.

Ellis, N. 1996. 'Sequencing in SLA: phonological memory, chunking, and points of order'. *Studies in Second Language Acquisition* 18: 91–126.

Ellis, N. 1997. 'Vocabulary acquisition: word structure, collocation, word-class, and meaning' in Schmitt, N. and M. McCarthy (eds.): *Vocabulary: Description, Acquisition and Pedagogy.* Cambridge: Cambridge University Press.

Ellis, N. 1998. 'Emergentism, connectionism, and language learning'. *Language Learning* 48: 631–64.

Ellis, N. 2002. 'Frequency effects in language processing: a review with implications for theories of implicit and explicit language acquisition'. *Studies in Second Language Acquisition* 24: 143–88.

Ellis, N. 2005. 'At the interface: dynamic interactions of explicit and implicit knowledge'. *Studies in Second Language Acquisition* 27: 305–52.

Ellis, N. 2006. 'Selective attention and transfer phenomena in SLA: contingency, cuecompetition, salience, interference, overshadowing, blocking and perceptual learning'. *Applied Linguistics* 27: 164–94.

Ellis, N. 2007. 'The weak interface, consciousness, and form-focused instruction: mind the doors' in Fotos, S. and H. Hossein (eds.): *Form-Focused Instruction and Teacher Education: Studies in Honour of Rod Ellis.* Oxford: Oxford University Press.

Ellis, R. 1984. *Classroom Second Language Development.* Oxford: Pergamon.

Ellis, R. 1985. 'Sources of variability in interlanguage'. *Applied Linguistics* 6: 118–31.

Ellis, R. 1988. 'The effects of linguistic environment on the second language acquisition of grammatical rules'. *Applied Linguistics* 9: 257–74.

Ellis, R. 1991. 'Grammar teaching—practice or consciousness-raising' in Ellis, R. (ed.): *Second Language Acquisition and Second Language Pedagogy.* Clevedon: Multilingual Matters.

Ellis, R. 1992. 'Learning to communicate in the classroom'. *Studies in Second Language Acquisition* 14: 1–23.

Ellis, R. 1993. 'Second language acquisition and the structural syllabus'. *TESOL Quarterly* 27: 91–113.

Ellis, R. 1994. 'A theory of instructed second language acquisition' in Ellis, N. (ed.): *Implicit and Explicit Learning of Languages*. San Diego: Academic Press.

Ellis, R. 1999. 'Item versus system learning: explaining free variation'. *Applied Linguistics* 20: 460–80.

Ellis, R. 2002a. 'Methodological options in grammar teaching materials' in Hinkel, E. and S. Fotos (eds.): *New Perspectives on Grammar Teaching in Second Language Classrooms*. Mahwah, NJ: Lawrence Erlbaum.

Ellis, R. 2002b. 'Does form-focused instruction affect the acquisition of implicit knowledge? A review of the research'. *Studies in Second Language Acquisition* 24: 223–36.

Ellis, R. 2003. *Task-based Language Learning and Teaching*. Oxford: Oxford University Press.

Ellis, R. (ed.) 2005a. *Planning and Task-Performance in a Second Language*. Amsterdam: John Benjamins.

Ellis, R. 2005b. 'Planning and task-based research: theory and research' in Ellis, R. (ed.): *Planning and Task-Performance in a Second Language*. Amsterdam: John Benjamins.

Ellis, R. 2005c. 'Measuring implicit and explicit knowledge of a second language: a psychometric study'. *Studies in Second Language Acquisition* 27: 141–72.

Ellis, R. 2006. 'Researching the effects of form-focused instruction on L2 acquisition'. *AILA Review* 19: 18–41.

Ellis, R. 2008. *The Study of Second Language Acquisition*. (2nd edn.) Oxford: Oxford University Press.

Ellis, R. 2009. 'The differential effects of three types of task planning on fluency, complexity, and accuracy in L2 oral production'. *Applied Linguistics* 30: 474–509.

Ellis, R. 2010. 'Theoretical pluralism in SLA: is there a way forward', in Seedhouse, P., S. Walsh, and C. Jenks (eds.): *Conceptualising 'Learning' in Applied Linguistics*. Basingstoke: Palgrave MacMillan.

Ellis, R. 2012. *Language Teaching Research and Language Pedagogy*. Malden, MA: Wiley-Blackwell.

Ellis, R. 2015. 'Researching acquisition sequences: Idealisation and de-idealisation in SLA'. *Language Learning*: Special issue.

Ellis, R. and G. Barkhuizen. 2005. *Analysing Learner Language*. Oxford: Oxford University Press.

Ellis, R., H. Basturkmen, and S. Loewen. 2001. 'Learner uptake in communicative ESL lessons'. *Language Learning* 51: 281–318.

Ellis, R. and X. He. 1999. 'The roles of modified input and output in the incidental acquisition of word meanings'. *Studies in Second Language Acquisition* 21: 319–33.

Ellis, R. and R. Heimbach. 1997. 'Bugs and birds: children's acquisition of second language vocabulary through interaction'. *System* 25: 247–59.

Ellis, R., S. Loewen, and R. Erlam. 2006. 'Implicit and explicit corrective feedback and the acquisition of L2 grammar'. *Studies in Second Language Acquisition* 28: 339–68.

Ellis, R. and N. Shintani. 2013. *Exploring Language Pedagogy through Second Language Acquisition Research*. London: Routledge.

Ellis, R., Y. Tanaka, and A. Yamazaki. 1994. 'Classroom interaction, comprehension and the acquisition of word meanings'. *Language Learning* 44: 449–91.

Erlam, R. 2005. 'Language aptitude and its relationship to instructional effectiveness in second language acquisition'. *Language Teaching Research* 9: 147–72.

Eskildsen, S. 2012. 'L2 negation constructions at work'. *Language Learning* 62: 335–72.

Eysenck, M. 2001. *Principles of Cognitive Psychology*. (2nd edn.) Hove: Psychology Press.

Ferguson, C. 1975. 'Towards a characterization of English foreigner talk'. *Anthropological Linguistics* 17: 1–14.

Fernández, C. 2008. 'Reexamining the role of explicit information in processing instruction'. *Studies in Second Language Acquisition* 30: 277–305.

Firth, A. and J. Wagner. 1997. 'On discourse, communication, and (some) fundamental concepts in SLA'. *Modern Language Journal* 81: 285–300.

Firth, A. and J. Wagner. 2007. 'Second/foreign language learning as a social accomplishment: elaborations on a reconceptualized SLA'. *Modern Language Journal* 91: 800–19.

Flege, J. 1987. 'The production of "new" and "similar" phonemes in a foreign language: evidence for the effect of equivalence classification'. *Journal of Phonetics* 15: 47–65.

Foster, P. and P. Skehan. 1996. 'The influence of planning on performance in task-based learning'. *Studies in Second Language Acquisition* 18: 299–324.

Foster, P. and P. Skehan. 1999. 'The influence of source of planning and focus of planning on task-based performance'. *Language Teaching Research* 3: 215–47.

Foster, P. and P. Skehan. 2013. 'Anticipating a post-task activity: the effects on accuracy, complexity and fluency of L2 language performance'. *Canadian Modern Language Review* 69: 249–73.

Fotos, S. 1993. 'Consciousness-raising and noticing through focus-on-form: grammar task performance vs. formal instruction'. *Applied Linguistics* 14: 385–407.

Frawley, W. and J. Lantolf. 1985. 'Second language discourse: a Vygostkyan perspective'. *Applied Linguistics* 6: 19–44.

Gal'perin, P. 1989. 'Organization of mental activity and the effetiveness of learning'. *Soviet Psychology* 27: 65–82.

Gardner, H. 1993. *Multiple Intelligences: The Theory in Practice*. New York: Basic Books.

Gardner, R. 1979. 'Social psychological aspects of second language acquisition' in Giles, H. and R. Clair (eds.): *Language and Social Psychology*. Oxford: Blackwell.

Gardner, R. 1985. *Social Psychology and Second Language Learning: The Role of Attitude and Motivation*. London: Edward Arnold.

Gardner, R. 2001. 'Integrative motivation and second language acquisition' in Dörnyei, Z. and R. Schmidt (eds.): *Motivation and Second Language Learning*. Honolulu: University of Hawai'i Press.

Gardner, R. 2005. 'Motivation and attitudes in second language learning'. *Encyclopedia of Language and Linguistics* (2nd edn.) Oxford: Elsevier.

Gardner, R. and W. Lambert. 1972. *Attitudes and Motivation in Second Language Learning*. Rowley, MA: Newbury House.

Gardner, R. and P. MacIntyre. 1992. 'A student's contributions to second language learning. Part 1: cognitive variables'. *Language Teaching* 25: 211–20.

Gass, S. 1997. *Input, Interaction and the Second Language Learner*. Mahwah, NJ: Lawrence Erlbaum.

Gass, S. 1998. 'Apples and oranges: or why apples are not oranges and don't need to be. A response to Firth and Wagner'. *Modern Language Journal* 82: 83–90.

Gass, S. and A. Mackey. 2007. 'Input, interactions, and output in second language acquisition' in VanPatten, B. and J. Williams (eds.): *Theories in Second Language Acquisition: An Introduction*. Mahwah, NJ: Lawrence Erlbaum.

Gatbonton, E. 1978. 'Patterned phonetic variability in second language speech: a gradual diffusion model'. *Canadian Modern Language Review* 34: 335–47.

Giles, H. 1971. 'Our reactions to accent'. *New Society* 14 October: 713–5.

Giles, H. and N. Coupland. 1991. *Language: Contexts and Consequences*. Milton Keynes: Open University Press.

Goldschneider, J. and R. DeKeyser. 2001. 'Explaining the "natural order of L2 morpheme acquisition" in English: a meta-analysis of multiple determinants'. *Language Learning* 51: 1–50.

Goo, J. and A. Mackey. 2013. 'The case against the case against recasts'. *Studies in Second Language Acquisition* 35: 127–65.

Granena, G. and M. Long. 2012. 'Age of onset, length of residence, language aptitude and ultimate L2 attainment in three linguistic domains'. *Second Language Research* 29: 311–43.

Granena, G. and **Long, M.** 2013. 'Introduction and overview' in Granena, S. and M. Long (eds.): *Sensitive periods, language aptitude, and ultimate attainment (pp. ix–xiii)*. Amsterdam: John Benjamins.

Grigorenko, E., R. Sternberg, and **M. Ehrman.** 2000. 'A theory-based approach to the measurement of foreign language learning ability: the Canal-F theory and test'. *The Modern Language Journal* 84: 390–405.

Guion, S., J. Flege, S. Lieu, and **G. Yeni-Komshian.** 2000. 'Age of learning effects on theduration of sentences produced in a second language'. *Applied Psycholinguistics* 21: 205–28.

Hakuta, K. 1976. 'A case study of a Japanese child learning English as a second language'. *Language Learning* 26: 321–51.

Hall, J., J. Hellermann and S. Pekarek Doehler. (eds.). 2011. *The Development of Interactional Competence*. Bristol: Multilingual Matters.

Han, Z., E. Park, and **C. Combs.** 2008. 'Textual enhancement of input: issues and possibilities'. *Applied Linguistics* 19: 597–618.

Hansen-Edwards, J. 2011. 'Deletion of /t, d/ and the acquisition of linguistic variation by second language learners of English'. *Language Learning* 61: 1256–1301.

Harley, B. 1986. *Age in Second Language Acquisition*. Clevedon: Multilingual Matters.

Harley, B. 1989. 'Functional grammar in French immersion: a classroom experiment'. *Applied Linguistics* 19: 331–59.

Harley, B. and **D. Hart.** 1997. 'Language aptitude and second language proficiency in classroom learners of different starting ages'. *Studies in Second Language Acquisition* 19: 379–400.

Harrington, M. 1987. 'Processing transfer: language-specific processing strategies as a source of interlanguage variation'. *Applied Psycholinguistics* 8: 351–77.

Hassan, X., E. Macaro, D. Mason, G. Nye, P. Smith, and **R. Vanderplank.** 2005. 'Strategy training in language learning—a systematic review of available research' in *Research Evidence in Education Library*. London: EPPI-Centre, Social Science Research Unit, Institute of Education, University of London.

Hatch, E. (ed.). 1978. *Second Language Acquisition*. Rowley, MA: Newbury House.

Hatch, E. 1978. 'Discourse analysis and second language acquisition' in Hatch, E. (ed.): *Second Language Acquisition*. Rowley, MA: Newbury House.

Hatch, E. 1983. 'Simplified input and second language acquisition' in Andersen, R. (ed.): *Pidginization and Creolization as Language Acquisition*. Rowley, MA: Newbury House.

Hawkins, R. 2001. 'The theoretical significance of Universal Grammar in second language acquisition'. *Second Language Research* 17: 345–67.

Hayes-Harb, R. and **K. Matsuda.** 2008. 'Development of the ability to lexically encode novel second language phonemic contrasts'. *Second Language Research* 24: 5–33.

Hedge, T. 2000. *Teaching and Learning in the Language Classroom*. Oxford: Oxford University Press.

Henry, N., H. Culman, and **B. VanPatten.** 2009. 'More of the effects of explicit information in instructed SLA: a partial replication and a response to Fernandez (2008)'. *Studies in Second Language Acquisition* 31: 559–75.

Henshaw, F. 2012. 'How effective are affective activities? Relative benefits of two types of structured input activities as part of a computer-delivered lesson on the Spanish subjunctive'. *Language Teaching Research* 16: 393–414.

Henzl, V. 1979. 'Foreigner talk in the classroom'. *International Review of Applied Linguistics* 17: 159–65.

Horwitz, E. 2001. 'Language anxiety and achievement'. *Annual Review of Applied Linguistics* 21: 112–26.

Horwitz, E., M. Horwitz, and **J. Cope.** 1986. 'Foreign language classroom anxiety'. *The Modern Language Journal* 70: 125–32.

Housen, A. and **M. Pierrard.** 2005. 'Investigating instructed second language acquisition' in Housen, A. and M. Pierrard (eds.): *Investigations in Instructed Second Language Acquisition*. Berlin: Mouton de Gruyter.

Housen, A., F. Kuiken, and I. Vedder. 2012. 'Complexity, accuracy and fluency: definitions, measurement and research' in Housen, A., F. Kuiken and I. Vedder (eds.): *Dimensions of L2 Performance and Proficiency. Investigating Complexity, Accuracy and Fluency in SLA.* Amsterdam: John Benjamins.

Housen, A., M. Pierrard, and S. Van Daele. 2005. 'Structure complexity and the efficacy of explicit grammar instruction' in Housen, A. and M. Pierrard (eds.): *Investigations in Instructed Second Language Acquisition.* Berlin: Mouton de Gruyter.

Howard, M. 2004. 'On the interactional effect of linguistic constraints on interlanguage variation: the case of past tense marking'. International Review of Applied Linguistics in Language Teaching 42: 319–34.

Howard, M., R. Mougeon, and J. Dewaele. 2013. 'Sociolinguistics and second language acquisition' in Bayley, R., R. Cameron, and C. Lucas (eds.): *The Oxford Handbook of Sociolinguistics.* New York: Oxford University Press.

Huebner, T. 1979. 'Order-of-acquisition vs. dynamic paradigm: a comparison of method in interlanguage research'. *TESOL Quarterly* 13: 21–8.

Huebner, T. 1983. *A Longitudinal Analysis of the Acquisition of English.* Ann Arbor: Karoma Publishers.

Hulstijn, J. 2002. 'Towards a unified account of the representation, processing and acquisition of second language knowledge'. *Second Language Research* 18: 193–223.

Hutchby, I. and R. Wooffit. 1998. *Conversation Analysis: Principle, Practice and Applications.* Cambridge: Polity Press.

Hyltenstam, K. 1984. 'The use of typological markedness conditions as predictors in second language acquisition: the case of pronominal copies in relative clauses' in Andersen, R. (ed.): *Second Languages: A Crosslinguistic Perspective.* Rowley, MA: Newbury House.

Hyltenstam, K. and N. Abrahamsson. 2003. 'Maturational constraints in SLA' in Doughty, C. and M. Long (eds.): *The Handbook of Second Language Acquisition.* Malden, MA: Blackwell.

Ioup, G., E. Boustagui, M. El Tigi, and M. Moselle. 1994. 'Reexamining the critical period hypothesis: the influence of maturational state on the acquisition of English as a second language'. *Studies in Second Language Acquisition* 16: 73–98.

Izumi, S. 2002. 'Output, input enhancement, and the noticing hypothesis: an experimental study of ESL relativization'. *Studies in Second Language Acquisition* 24: 541–77.

Jackson, D. and S. Seuthanpronkul. 2013. 'The Cognition Hypothesis: a synthesis and meta-analysis of research on second language task complexity'. *Language Learning* 63: 330–67.

Jarvis, S. and A. Pavlenko. 2008. *Crosslinguistic Influence in Language and Cognition.* New York: Routledge.

Jeon, E. and T. Kaya. 2006. 'Effects of L2 instruction on interlanguage pragmatic development: a meta-analysis' in Norris, J. and L. Ortega (eds.): *Synthesizing Research on Language Teaching and Learning.* Amsterdam: John Benjamins.

Jia, G. and A. Fuse. 2007. 'Acquisition of English grammatical morphology by native mandarin-speaking children and adolescents: age-related differences'. *Journal of Speech, Language and Hearing Research* 50: 1280–99.

Jiang, N. 2000. 'Lexical representation and development in a second language'. *Applied Linguistics* 21: 47–77.

Jiang, N., E. Novokshanova, K. Masuda, and X. Wang. 2011. 'Morphological congruency and the acquisition of L2 morphemes'. *Language Learning* 61: 940–67.

Johnson, J. and E. Newport. 1989. 'Critical period effects in second language learning: the influence of maturational state on the acquisition of English as a second language'. *Cognitive Psychology* 21: 60–99.

Johnson, M. 2004. *A Philosophy of Second Language Acquisition.* New Haven, CT: Yale University Press.

Johnston, M. and M. Pienemann. 1986. *Second Language Acquisition: A Classroom Perspective.* New South Wales Migrant Education Service.

Kasper, G. 1992. 'Pragmatic transfer'. *Second Language Research* 8: 203–31.

Kasper, G. 2006. 'Beyond repair: conversation analysis as an approach to SLA'. *AILA Review* 19: 83–99.

Kasper, G. and C. Roever. 2005. 'Pragmatics in second language learning' in Hinkel, E. (ed.): *Handbook of Research in Second Language Learning and Teaching*. Mahwah, NJ: Erlbaum.

Kasper, G. and K. Rose. 2002. *Pragmatic Development in a Second Language*. Language Learning Monograph Series. Oxford: Blackwell.

Kasper, G. and J. Wagner. 2011. 'A conversation-analytic approach to second language acquisition' in Atkinson, D. (ed.): *Alternative Approaches to Second Language Acquisition*. New York: Taylor & Francis.

Kato, T. 2006. 'Acquisition of Japanese vocabulary by Chinese background learners: the roles of transfer in the productive and receptive acquisition of cognates and polysemy'. PhD Thesis, University of New South Wales, Australia.

Keck, C., G. Iberri-Shea, N. Tracy-Ventura, and S. Wa-Mbaleka. 2006. 'Investigating the empirical link between task-based interaction and acquisition: a meta-analysis' in Norris, J. M. and L. Ortega (eds.): *Synthesizing Research on Language Learning and Teaching*. Philadelphia, PA: John Benjamins.

Kellerman, E. 1978. 'Giving learners a break: native language intuitions as a source of predictions about transferability'. *Working Papers on Bilingualism* 15: 59–92.

Kellerman, E. 1979. 'Transfer and non-transfer: where are we now?' *Studies in Second Language Acquisition* 2: 37–57.

Kellerman, E. 1983. 'Now you see it, now you don't' in Gass, S. and L. Selinker (eds.): *Language Transfer in Language Learning*. Rowley, MA: Newbury House.

Kellerman, E. 1989. 'The imperfect conditional' in Hyltenstam, K. and L. Obler (eds.): *Bilingualism Across the Lifespan: Aspects of Acquisition, Maturity and Loss*. Cambridge University Press.

Kellerman, E. 1995. 'Crosslinguistic influence: transfer to nowhere?' *Annual Review of Applied Linguistics* 15: 125–50.

Kempe, V., P. Brooks, and A. Kharkhurin. 2010. 'Cognitive predictors of generalization of Russian grammatical gender categories'. *Language Learning* 60: 127–153.

Kiss, C. and M. Nikolov. 2005. 'Developing, piloting, and validating an instrument to measure young learners' aptitude'. *Language Learning* 55: 99–150.

Klein, W. 1998. 'The contribution of second language acquisition research'. *Language Learning* 48: 527–50.

Klein, W. and C. Perdue. 1997. 'The basic variety (or: Couldn't natural languages be much simpler?)'. *Second Language Research* 13: 301–48.

Klima, E. and V. Bellugi. 1966. 'Syntactic regularities in the speech of children' in Lyons, J. and R. Wales (eds.): *Psycholinguistic Papers*. Edinburgh: Edinburgh University Press.

Kormos, J. 2013. 'New conceptualizations of language aptitude in second language attainment' in Granena, G. and M. Long (eds.): *Sensitive Periods, Language Aptitude, and Ultimate L2 Attainment*. Amsterdam: John Benjamins.

Kormos, J. and K. Csizér. 2008. 'Age-related differences in the motivation of learning English as a foreign language: attitudes, selves, and motivated learning behavior'. *Language Learning* 58: 327–55.

Kormos, J. and K. Csizér. 2014. 'The interaction of motivation, self-regulatory strategies, and autonomous learning behaviour in different learner groups'. *TESOL Quarterly* 48: 275–299.

Kormos, J. and A. Sáfár. 2006. 'The role of working memory in intensive language learning' in Nikolov, M. and J. Horváth (eds.): *UPRT 2006: Empirical studies in English Applied Linguistics*. Pécs: Lingua Franca Csoport.

Kramsch, C. 2009. *The Multilingual Subject: What Foreign Language Learners Say about their Experience and Why it Matters*. Oxford: Oxford University Press.

Krashen, S. 1981. *Second Language Acquisition and Second Language Learning*. Oxford: Pergamon.

Krashen, S. 1982. *Principles and Practice in Second Language Acquisition*. Oxford: Pergamon.

Krashen, S. 1985. *The Input Hypothesis: Issues and Implications*. London: Longman.

Krashen, S. and R. Scarcella. 1978. 'On routines and patterns in second language acquisition and performance'. *Language Learning* 28: 283–300.

Krashen, S. and T. Terrell. 1983. *The Natural Approach: Language Acquisition in the Classroom*. Oxford: Pergamon.

Krishnan, A. 2009. *What are Academic Disciplines? Some Observations on the Disciplinarity Versus Interdisciplinarity Debate*. University of Southampton: National Centre for Research Methods.

Kuhn, T. 1962. *The Structure of Scientific Revolutions*. Chicago, IL: University of Chicago Press.

Labov, W. 1970. 'The study of language in its social context'. *Studium Generale* 23: 30–87.

Lado, R. 1957. *Linguistics Across Cultures: Applied Linguistics for Language Teachers*. Ann Arbor, MI: University of Michigan.

Lamb, M. 2012. 'A self-system perspective on young adolescents' motivation to learn English in urban and rural settings'. *Language Learning* 62: 997–1023.

Lantolf, J. 1996. 'Second language theory building: letting all the flowers bloom!' *Language Learning* 46: 713–49.

Lantolf, J. 2000. 'Introducing sociocultural theory' in Lantolf, J. (ed.): *Sociocultural Theory and Second Language Learning*. Oxford: Oxford University Press.

Lantolf, J. 2005. 'Sociocultural and second language learning research: an exegesis' in Hinkel, E. (ed.): *Handbook of Research on Second Language Teaching and Learning*. Mahway, NJ: Lawrence Erlbaum.

Lantolf, J. 2006. 'Sociocultural theory and L2'. *Studies in Second Language Acquisition* 28: 67–109.

Lantolf, J. 2007. 'Conceptual knowledge and instructed second language learning: a sociocultural perspective' in Fotos, S. and H. Nassaji (eds.): *Form-Focused Instruction and Teacher Education: Studies in Honour of Rod Ellis*. Oxford: Oxford University Press.

Lantolf, J. 2011. 'The sociocultural approach to second language acquisition' in Atkinson, D. (ed.): *Alternative Approaches to Second Language Acquisition*. New York: Routledge.

Lantolf, J. and S. Thorne. 2006. *Sociocultural Theory and the Genesis of Second Language Development*. Oxford: Oxford University Press.

Lardiere, D. 2007. *Ultimate Attainment in Second Language Acquisition: A Case Study*. Mahwah, NJ: Lawrence Erlbaum.

Larsen-Freeman, D. 1976. 'An explanation for the morpheme acquisition order of second language learners'. *Language Learning* 26: 125–34.

Larsen-Freeman, D. 1997. 'Chaos/complexity science and second language acquisition'. *Applied Linguistics* 18: 141–65.

Larsen-Freeman, D. 2006. 'The emergence of complexity, fluency, and accuracy in the oral and written production of five Chinese learners of English'. *Applied Linguistics* 27: 590–619.

Larsen-Freeman, D. 2007. 'Reflecting on the cognitive-social debate in second language acquisition'. *Modern Language Journal* 93: 773–87.

Larsen-Freeman, D. 2010. 'Not so fast: a discussion of L2 morpheme processing and acquisition'. *Language Learning* 60: 221–30.

Larsen-Freeman, D. 2011. 'A complexity approach to second language development/acquisition' in Atkinson, D. (ed.): *Alternative Approaches to Second Language Acquisition*. Abingdon: Routledge.

Larsen-Freeman, D. and L. Cameron. 2008. *Complex Systems and Applied Linguistics*. Oxford: Oxford University Press.

Larsen-Freeman, D. and M. Long. 1991. *An Introduction to Second Language Acquisition Research*. London: Longman.

Larson-Hall, J. 2008. 'Weighing the benefits of studying a foreign language at a younger starting age in a minimal input situation'. *Language Teaching Research* 24: 35–63.

Laufer, B. 1998. 'The development of passive and active vocabulary in a second language: same or different?' *Applied Linguistics* 19: 255–71.

Lave, J. and E. Wenger. 1991. *Situated Learning: Legitimate Peripheral Participation*. Cambridge: Cambridge University Press.

Lee, S. and H. Huang. 2008. 'Visual input enhancement and grammar learning. A meta-analytic review'. *Studies in Second Language Acquisition* 30: 307–31.

Lee, N., L. Mikesell, A. Joaquin, A. Mates, and J. Schumann. 2009. *The Interactional Instinct: The Evolution and Acquisition of Language*. Oxford: Oxford University Press.

Lee, J. and B. VanPatten. 2003. *Making Communicative Language Teaching Happen*. New York: McGraw-Hill.

Leeman, J. 2003. 'Recasts and L2 development: beyond negative evidence'. *Studies in Second Language Acquisition* 25: 37–63.

Lenneberg, E. 1967. *Biological Foundations of Language*. New York: Wiley and Son.

Leow, R. and M. Hama. 2013. 'Implicit learning in SLA and the issue of internal validity: a response to Leung and Williams's (2011) "The implicit learning of mappings between forms and contextually derived meanings"'. *Studies in Second Language Acquisition* 35: 545–57.

Leung, J. and J. Williams. 2011. 'The implicit learning of mappings between forms and contextually derived meanings'. *Studies in Second language Acquisition* 33: 33–5.

Levelt, W. 1989. *Speaking: From Intention to Articulation*. Cambridge: Cambridge University Press.

Levin, L. 1972. 'Comparative studies in foreign-language teaching'. *Goteborg Studies in Educational Sciences* 9.

Li, S. 2010. 'The effectiveness of corrective feedback in SLA: a meta-analysis'. *Language Learning* 60: 309–65.

Li, W. and Z. Hua. 2013. 'Translanguaging identities and ideologies: creating transnational space through flexible multilingual practices among Chinese students in the UK'. *Applied Linguistics* 34: 516–35.

Liceras, J. 1985. 'The role of intake in the determination of learners' competence' in Gassand, S. and C. Madden (eds.): *Input in Second Language Acquisition*. Rowley, MA: Newbury House.

Lightbown, P. 1983. 'Exploring relationships between developmental and instructional sequences in L2 acquisition' in Seliger, H. and M. Long (eds.): *Classroom-Oriented Research in Second Language Acquisition*. Rowley, MA: Newbury House.

Lightbown, P. 2000. 'Anniversary article: classroom SLA research and language teaching'. *Applied Linguistics* 21: 431–62.

Lightbown, P. 2008. 'Transfer appropriate processing as a model for classroom second language acquisition' in Han, Z. (ed): *Understanding Second Language Process*. Clevedon: Multilingual Matters.

Lin, P. 2012. 'Sound evidence: the missing piece of the jigsaw in formulaic language research'. *Applied Linguistics* 33: 342–47.

Loewen, S. and J. Philp. 2006. 'Recasts in adults English L2 classrooms: characteristics, explicitness, and effectiveness'. *Modern Language Journal*, 90: 536–56.

Loewen, S., R. Erlam, and R. Ellis. 2009. 'The incidental acquisition of 3rd person-s as implicit and explicit knowledge' in Ellis, R., S. Loewen, C. Elder, R. Erlam, J. Philp, and H. Reinders (eds.): *Implicit and Explicit Knowledge in Second Language Learning, Testing and Teaching*. Bristol: Multilingual Matters.

Long, M. 1981. 'Input, interaction and second language acquisition' in Winitz, H. (ed.): *Native Language and Foreign Language Acquisition*. Annals of the New York Academy of Sciences 379.

Long, M. 1983a. 'Does second language instruction make a difference? A review of the research'. *TESOL Quarterly* 17: 359–82.

Long, M. 1983b. 'Native speaker/non-native speaker conversation in the second language classroom' in Clarke, M. and J. Handscombe (eds.): *On TESOL '82*. Washington, DC: TESOL.

Long, M. 1990. 'Second language classroom research and teacher education' in Brumfit, C. and R. Mitchell (eds.): *Research in the Language Classroom*. ELT Documents 133. Modern English Publications.

Long, M. 1991. 'Focus on form: a design feature in language teaching methodology' in de Bot, K., R. Ginsberg, and C. Kramsch (eds.): *Foreign Language Research in Cross-cultural Perspective*. Amsterdam: John Benjamins.

Long, M. 1996. 'The role of the linguistic environment in second language acquisition' in Ritchie, W. and T. Bhatia (eds.): *Handbook of Second Language Acquisition*. San Diego: Academic Press.

Long, M. 1997. 'Construct validity in SLA research: a response to Firth and Wagner'. *Modern Language Journal* 81: 318–23.

Long, M. 1998. 'SLA breaking the siege'. *University of Hawai'i Working Papers in ESL* 17: 79–129.

Long, M. 2006. *Problems in SLA*. Mahwah, NJ: Lawrence Erlbaum.

Long, M. 2013. 'Maturational constraints on child and adult SLA' in Granena, S. and M. Long (eds.): *Sensitive Periods, Language Aptitude, and Ultimate Attainment* (pp. 3–41). Amsterdam: John Benjamins.

Long, M. and G. Crookes. 1987. 'Intervention points in second language classroom processes' in Das, B. (ed.): *Patterns of Classroom Interaction*. Singapore: SEAMEO Regional Language Centre.

Long, M. and C. Doughty. 2003. 'SLA and cognitive science' in Doughty, C. and M. Long (eds.): *Handbook of Second Language Acquisition Research*. Malden, MA: Blackwell.

Long, M. and S. Ross. 1993. 'Modifications that preserve language and content' in Tickoo, M. (ed.): *Simplification: Theory and Application*. Singapore: SEAMEO Regional Language Centre.

Loschky, L. 1994. 'Comprehensible input and second language acquisition: what is the relationship?' *Studies in Second Language Acquisition* 16: 303–23.

Loschky, L. and R. Bley-Vroman. 1993. 'Grammar and task-based methodology' in Crookes, G. and S. Gass (eds.): *Tasks and Language Learning: Integrating Theory and Practice*. Clevedon: Multilingual Matters.

Lyddon, P. 2011. 'The efficacy of corrective feedback and textual enhancement in promoting the acquisition of grammatical redundancies'. *Modern Language Journal* 95: Supplementary issue 104–129.

Lyster, R. 1994. 'The effect of functional-analytic teaching on aspects of French immersion students' sociolinguistic competence'. *Applied Linguistics* 15: 263–87.

Lyster, R. 2004. 'Differential effects of prompts and recasts in form-focused instruction'. *Studies in Second Language Acquisition* 26: 399–432.

Lyster, R. and H. Mori. 2006. 'Interactional feedback and instructional counterbalance'. *Studies in Second Language Acquisition* 28: 269–300.

Lyster, R. and L. Ranta. 1997. 'Corrective feedback and learner uptake: negotiation of form in communicative classrooms'. *Studies in Second Language Acquisition* 19: 37–66.

Lyster, R. and L. Ranta. 2013. 'Counterpoint piece: the case for variety in corrective feedback research'. *Studies in Second Language Acquisition* 34: 167–84.

Lyster, R. and K. Saito. 2010. 'Oral feedback in classroom SLA'. *Studies in Second Language Acquisition* 32, Special Issue 2: 265–302.

Macaro, E. 2006. 'Strategies for language learning and for language use: revising the theoretical framework'. *Modern Language Journal* 90: 320–37.

MacIntyre, P. and R. Gardner. 1991a. 'Methods and results in the study of foreign language anxiety: a review of the literature'. *Language Learning* 41: 25–57.

MacIntyre, P. and R. Gardner. 1991b. 'Language anxiety: its relationship to other anxieties and to processing in native and second languages'. *Language Learning* 41: 513–34.

MacIntyre, P., S. Baker, R. Clement, and S. Conrad. 2001. 'Willingness to communicate, social support, and language learning orientations of immersion students'. *Studies in Second Language Acquisition* 23: 369–88.

Mackey, A. 1999. 'Input, interaction and second language development: an empirical study of question formation in ESL'. *Studies in Second Language Acquisition* 21: 557–87.

Mackey, A. 2006. 'Feedback, noticing and instructed second language learning'. *Applied Linguistics* 27: 405–30.

Mackey, A. 2007. 'Introduction' in Mackey, A (ed.): *Conversational Interaction in Second Language Acquisition: A Collection of Empirical Studies*. Oxford: Oxford University Press.

Mackey, A. and J. Goo. 2007. 'Interaction research in SLA: a meta-analysis and research synthesis' in Mackey, A. (ed.): *Conversational Interaction in Second Language Acquisition: A Collection of Empirical Studies*. Oxford: Oxford University Press.

Mackey, A., J. Philp, T. Egi, A. Fujii, and T. Tatsumi. 2002. 'Individual differences in working memory, noticing of interactional feedback and L2 development' in Robinson, P. (ed.): *Individual Differences in L2 Learning*. Amsterdam: John Benjamins.

MacWhinney, B. 2001. 'The competition model: the input, the context' in Robinson, P. (ed.): *Cognition and Second Language Instruction*. Cambridge: Cambridge University Press.

Major, R. and E. Kim. 1996. 'The similarity differential rate hypothesis'. *Language Learning* 46: 465–96.

Markee, N. 2000. *Conversation Analysis*. Mahwah, NJ: Lawrence Erlbaum.

Markee, N. 2005. 'Conversation analysis for second language acquisition' in Hinkel, E. (ed.): *Handbook of Research in Second Language Teaching and Learning*. Mahwah, NJ: Lawrence Erlbaum.

Markee, N. 2008. 'Toward a learning behavior tracking methodology for CA-for-SLA'. *Applied Linguistics* 29: 404–27.

Marsden, E. 2006. 'Exploring input processing in the classroom: an experimental comparison of processing instruction and enriched input'. *Language Learning* 56: 507–66.

Masgoret, A. and R. Gardner. 2003. 'Attitudes, motivation, and second language learning: a meta-analysis of studies conducted by Gardner and associates'. *Language Learning* 53: 123–63.

Matsumura, S. 2003. 'Modelling the relationships among interlanguage, pragmatic development, L2 proficiency and exposure to L2'. *Applied Linguistics* 24: 465–91.

McDonough, K. 2007. 'Interactional feedback and the emergence of simple past activityverbs in L2 English' in Mackey, A. (ed.): *Conversational Interaction in Second Language Acquisition: A Collection of Empirical Studies*. Oxford: Oxford University Press.

McDonough, K. and A. Mackey. 2000. 'Form and meaning: Designing communicative tasks to target grammar in Thai classrooms'. *Foreign Language Annals* 33: 82–92.

McDonough, K. and A. Mackey. 2006. 'Responses to recasts: repetitions, primed production, and linguistic development'. *Language Learning* 56: 693–720.

McKay, S. and S. Wong. 1996. 'Multiple discourses, multiple identities: investment and agency in second language learning among Chinese adolescent immigrant students'. *Harvard Educational Review* 3: 577–608.

McLaughlin, B. and R. Heredia. 1996. 'Information processing approaches to research on second language acquisition and use' in Ritchie, R. and T. Bhatia (eds.): *Handbook of Second Language Acquisition*. San Diego: Academic Press.

McNamara, J. 1973. 'Nurseries, streets and classrooms: some comparisons and deductions'. *Modern Language Journal* 57: 250–55.

Meara, P. 2009. *Connected Words*. Amsterdam: John Benjamins.

Meisel, J., H. Clahsen, and M. Pienemann. 1981. 'On determining developmental stages in natural second language acquisition'. *Studies in Second Language Acquisition* 3: 109–35.

Mellow, J. 2006. 'The emergence of second language syntax: a case study of the acquisition of relative clauses'. *Applied Linguistics* 27: 645–70.

Miller, E. and R. Kubota. 2013. 'Second language identity construction' in Herschensohn, J. and M. Young-Scholten (eds.): *The Cambridge Handbook of Second Language Acquisition*. Cambridge: Cambridge University Press.

Muñoz, C. 2006. 'The effects of age on foreign language learning: the BAF project' in Muñoz, C. (ed.): *Age and the Rate of Foreign Language Learning*. Clevedon: Multilingual Matters.

Myles, F. 2004. 'From data to theory: the over-representation of linguistic knowledge in SLA'. *Transactions of the Philological Society* 102: 139–68.

Myles, F., J. Hooper, and R. Mitchell. 1998. 'Rote or rule? Exploring the role of formulaic language in classroom foreign language learning'. *Language Learning* 48: 323–63.

Naiman, N., M. Fröhlich, H. H. Stern, and A. Todesco. 1978. *The Good Language Learner.* Research in Education Series No 7. Toronto: The Ontario Institute for Studies in Education. Reprinted in 1995 by *Multilingual Matters.*

Nation, P. 2001. *Learning Vocabulary in Another Language.* Cambridge: Cambridge University Press.

Nation, R. and B. McLaughlin. 1986. 'Experts and novices: an information-processing approach to the "good language learner" problem'. *Applied Psycholinguistics* 7: 41–56.

Neguerela, E. and J. Lantolf. 2006. 'Concept-based instruction and the acquisition of L2 Spanish' in Salaberry, R. and B. Lafford (eds.): *The Art of Teaching Spanish: Second Language Acquisition from Research to Praxis.* Washington, DC: Georgetown University Press.

Nelson, R. 2013. 'Expanding the role of connectionism in SLA theory'. *Language Learning* 63: 1–33.

Newman, F. and L. Holzman. 1997. *The End of Knowing: A New Developmental Way of Learning.* London: Routledge.

Nobuyoshi, J. and R. Ellis. 1993. 'Focused communication tasks'. *ELT Journal* 47: 203–10.

Noels, K., L. Pelletier, R. Clement, and R. Vallerand. 2000. 'Why are you learning a second language? Motivational orientations and self-determination theory'. *Language Learning* 50: 57–85.

Norris, J. and L. Ortega. 2000. 'Effectiveness of L2 instruction: a research synthesis and quantitative meta-analysis'. *Language Learning* 50: 417–528.

Norris, J. and L. Ortega (eds.). 2006. *Synthesizing Research on Language Teaching and Learning.* Amsterdam: John Benjamins.

Norton, B. 1997. 'Language, identity, and the ownership of English'. *TESOL Quarterly* 31: 409–29.

Norton, B. 2000. *Identity and Language Learning: Gender, Ethnicity and Educational Change.* Harlow: Longman.

Norton Peirce, B. 1995. 'Social identity, investment and language learning'. *TESOL Quarterly* 29: 9–31.

Norton, B. and C. McKinney. 2011. 'An identity approach to second language acquisition' in Atkinson, D. (ed.): *Alternative Approaches to Second Language Acquisition* (pp. 73–94). Oxford: Routledge.

O'Malley, J. and A. Chamot. 1990. *Learning Strategies in Second Language Acquisition.* Cambridge: Cambridge University Press.

Odlin, T. 1989. *Language Transfer.* Cambridge: Cambridge University Press.

Ohta, A. 2001. *Second Language Acquisition Processes in the Classroom: Learning Japanese.* Mahwah, NJ: Lawrence Erlbaum.

Oller, J., L. Baca, and A. Vigil. 1977. 'Attitudes and attained proficiency in ESL: a sociolinguistic study of Mexican Americans in the Southwest'. *TESOL Quarterly* 11: 173–83.

Olshtain, E. 1983. 'Sociocultural competence and language transfer: the case of apologies' in Gass, S. and L. Selinker (eds.): *Language Transfer in Language Learning* (pp. 232–249). Rowley, MA: Newbury House.

Onwuegbuzie, A., P. Bailey, and C. Daley. 1999. 'Factors associated with foreign language anxiety'. *Applied Psycholinguistics* 20: 217–39.

Ortega, L. 2009. *Understanding Second Language Acquisition.* London: Hodder Education.

Ortega, L. 2011. 'SLA after the social turn' in Atkinson, D. (ed.): *Alternative Approaches to Second Language Acquisition* (pp. 167–180). London: Routledge.

Ortega, L. 2012. 'SLA for the 21ˢᵗ century: disciplinary progress, transdisciplinary relevance and the bi/multicultural turn'. *Language Learning* 63: 1–24.

Oxford, R. 1989. 'Use of language learning strategies: a synthesis of studies with implications for teacher training'. *System* 17: 235–47.

Oxford, R. 1990. *Language Learning Strategies: What Every Teacher Should Know.* Rowley, MA: Newbury House.

Oyama, S. 1976. 'A sensitive period in the acquisition of a non-native phonological system'. *Journal of Psycholinguistic Research* 5: 261–85.

Palmberg, R. 1987. 'Patterns of vocabulary development in foreign-language learners'. *Studies in Second Language Acquisition* 9: 201–20.

Pang, F. and P. Skehan. 2014. 'Self-reported planning behaviour and second language performance' in Skehan, P. (ed.): *Processing Perspective on Task Performance*. Amsterdam: John Benjamins.

Paradis, M. 2004. *A Neurolinguistic Theory of Bilingualism*. Amsterdam: John Benjamins.

Paradis, M. 2009. *Declarative and Procedural Determinants of Second Languages*. Amsterdam: John Benjamins.

Patkowski, M. 1980. 'The sensitive period for the acquisition of syntax in a second language'. *Language Learning* 30: 449–72.

Pavlenko, A. 2002. 'Poststructuralist approaches to the study of social factors in second language learning and use' in Cook, V. (ed.): *Portraits of the L2 User*. Clevedon: Multilingual Matters.

Pawley, A. and F. Syder. 1983. 'Two puzzles for linguistic theory: nativelike selection and nativelike fluency' in Richards, J. and R. Schmidt (eds.): *Language and Communication*. London: Longman.

Peck, S. 1978. 'Child-child discourse in second language acquisition' in Hatch, E. (ed.): *Second Language Acquisition*. Rowley, MA: Newbury House.

Penfield, W. and L. Roberts. 1959. *Speech and Brain Mechanisms*. New York: Atheneum Press.

Philp, J. 2009. 'Pathways to proficiency: learning experience and attainment in implicit and explicit knowledge of English as a second language' in Ellis, R., S. Loewen, C. Elder, R. Erlam, J. Philp, and H. Reinders (eds.): *Implicit and Explicit Knowledge in Second Language Learning, Testing and Teaching*. Bristol: Multilingual Matters.

Piaget, J. 1973. *Memory and Intelligence*. New York: Basic Books.

Pica, T. 1983. 'Adult acquisition of English as a second language under different conditions of exposure'. *Language Learning* 33: 465–97.

Pica, T. 1992. 'The textual outcomes of native speaker–non-native speaker negotiation: what do they reveal about second language learning' in Kramsch, C. and S. McConnell-Ginet (eds.): *Text and Context: Cross-disciplinary Perspectives on Language Study*. Lexington, MA: D.C. Heath and Company.

Pica, T. 2002. 'Subject-matter content: how does it assist the interactional and linguistic needs of classroom language learners?' *The Modern Language Journal* 86: 1–19.

Pica, T., R. Kanagy, and J. Falodun. 1993. 'Choosing and using communication tasks for second language research and instruction' in Crookes, G. and S. Gass (eds.): *Task-based Learning in a Second Language*. Clevedon: Multilingual Matters.

Pica, T., R. Young, and C. Doughty. 1987. 'The impact of interaction on comprehension'. *TESOL Quarterly* 21: 737–58.

Pienemann, M. 1984. 'Psychological constraints on the teachability of languages'. *Studies in Second Language Acquisition* 6: 186–214.

Pienemann, M. 1985. 'Learnability and syllabus construction' in Hyltenstam, K. and M. Pienemann (eds.): *Modelling and Assessing Second Language Acquisition*. Clevedon: Multilingual Matters.

Pienemann, M. 1998. *Language Processing and Second Language Development: Processability Theory*. Amsterdam: John Benjamins.

Pienemann, M. 2005. 'An introduction to processability theory' in Pienemann, M. (ed.): *Cross-linguistic Aspects of Processability Theory*. Amsterdam: John Benjamins.

Pienemann, M. 2011. 'Developmental schedules' in Pienemann, M. and J. Kessler (eds.): *Studying Processability Theory*. Amsterdam: John Benjamins.

Pienemann, M., M. Johnston, and G. Brindley. 1988. 'An acquisition-based procedure for second language assessment'. *Studies in Second Language Acquisition* 10: 217–43.

Pienemann, M. and J. Kessler. (eds.) 2011. *Studying Processability Theory*. Amsterdam: John Benjamins.

Pimsleur, P. 1966. *Pimsleur Language Aptitude Battery (PLAB)*. New York: Harcourt Brace Jovanovich.

Pinker, S. 1999. *Words and Rules*. New York: Basic Books.

Plonsky, L. 2011. 'The effectiveness of second language strategy instruction: a meta-analysis'. *Language Learning* 61: 993–1038.

Poehner, M. 2008. *Dynamic Assessment: A Vygotskian Approach to Understanding and Promoting Second Language Development*. Berlin: Springer.

Poehner, M. and J. Lantolf. 2005. 'Dynamic assessment in the language classroom'. *Language Teaching Research* 9: 233–65.

Prabhu, N. S. 1987. *Second Language Pedagogy*. Oxford: Oxford University Press.

Preston, D. 1996. 'Variationist perspectives on second language acquisition' in Bayley, R. and D. Preston (eds.): *Second Language Acquisition and Linguistic Variation*. Amsterdam: John Benjamins.

Preston, D. 2002. 'A variationist perspective on second language acquisition' in Kaplan, R. (ed.): *The Oxford Handbook of Applied Linguistics*. New York: Oxford University Press.

Purpura, J. 1999. *Learner Strategy Use and Performance on Language Tests: A Structural Equation Modelling Approach*. Cambridge: Cambridge University Press.

Ramage, K. 1990. 'Motivational factors and persistence in foreign language study'. *Language Learning* 40: 189–219.

Rampton, B. 1995. *Crossing: Language and Ethnicity among Adolescents*. London: Longman.

Rampton, B. 1998. 'Second language research in late modernity: a response to Firth and Wagner'. *Modern Language Journal* 81: 329–33.

Ravem, R. 1968. 'Language acquisition in a second language environment'. *International Review of Applied Linguistics* 6: 165–85.

Reber, A. 1976. 'Implicit learning of synthetic learners: the role of instructional set'. *Journal of Experimental Psychology, Human Learning and Memory* 2: 88–94.

Reber, A., F. Walkenfeld, and R. Hernstadt. 1991. 'Implicit and explicit learning: individual differences and IQ'. *Journal of Experimental Psychology: Learning Memory and Cognition* 11: 888–96.

Rebuschat, P. 2013. 'Measuring implicit and explicit knowledge in second language research'. *Language Learning* 63: 595–626.

Regan, V. 1996. 'Variation in French interlanguage: a longitudinal study of sociolinguistic competence' in Bayley, R. and D. Preston (eds.): *Second Language Acquisition and Linguistic Variation*. Amsterdam: John Benjamins.

Révész, A. 2012. 'Working memory and the observed effectiveness of recasts on different L2 outcome measures'. *Language Learning* 62: 93–132.

Révész, A. 2014. 'Towards a fuller assessment of cognitive models of task-based learning: investigating task-generated cognitive demands and processes'. *Applied Linguistics* 35: 87–92.

Richards, K. 2006. 'Being a teacher': identity and classroom conversation'. *Applied Linguistics* 27: 51–77.

Ringbom, H. 1978. 'The influence of the mother tongue on the translation of lexical items'. *Inter language studies bulletin* 3: 80–101.

Ringbom, H. 1987. *The Role of the First Language in Foreign Language Learning*. Clevedon: Multilingual Matters.

Ringbom, H. 1992. 'On L1 transfer in L2 comprehension and L2 production'. *Language Learning* 42: 85–112.

Robinson, P. 1996. 'Learning simple and complex rules under implicit, incidental rule-search conditions, and instructed conditions'. *Studies in Second Language Acquisition* 18: 27–67.

Robinson, P. 2001. 'Individual differences, cognitive abilities, aptitude complexes and learning conditions in second language acquisition'. *Second Language Research* 17: 368–92.

Robinson, P. 2002. 'Learning conditions, aptitude complexes and SLA: a framework for research and pedagogy' in Robinson, P. (ed.): *Individual Differences and Instructed Language Learning*. Amsterdam: John Benjamins.

Robinson, P. 2003. 'Attention and memory during SLA' in Doughty, C. and M. Long (eds.): *Handbook of Second Language Acquisition*. Malden, MA: Blackwell.

Robinson, P. 2007. 'Aptitudes, abilities, contexts and practice' in DeKeyser, R. (ed.): *Practice in Second Language Learning: Perspectives from Applied Linguistics and Cognitive Psychology*. New York: Cambridge University Press.

Robinson, P. 2011. 'Task-based language learning: a review of the issues'. *Language Learning* 61: 1–36.

Rodrigo, V., S. Krashen, and B. Gibbons. 2004. 'The effectiveness of two comprehensible-input approaches to foreign language instruction at the intermediate level'. *System* 32: 53–60.

Romaine, S. 2003. 'Variation' in Doughty, C. and M. Long (eds.): *The Handbook of Second Language Acquisition*. Malden, MA: Blackwell.

Rymer, R. 1993. *Genie: An Abused Child's Flight from Silence*. New York: Harper Collins.

Sahlström, F. 2011. 'Learning as social action' in Hall, J., J. Hellermann, and S. Pekarek Doehler (eds): *The Development of Interactional Competence*. Bristol: Multilingual Matters.

Saito, K. 2012. 'Effects of instruction on L2 pronunciation development: a synthesis of 15 quasi–experimental intervention studies'. *TESOL Quarterly* 46: 842–54.

Saito, K. and Lyster, R. 2012. 'Effects of form-focused instruction and corrective feedback on L2 pronunciation development of /r/ by Japanese learners of English'. *Language Learning* 62: 595–633.

Samuda, V. 2001. 'Guiding relationships between form and meaning during task performance: the role of the teacher' in Bygate, M., P. Skehan, and M. Swain (eds.): *Researching Pedagogic Tasks, Second Language Learning, Teaching and Testing*. Harlow: Longman.

Samuda, V. and M. Bygate. 2008. *Tasks in Second Language Learning*. New York: Palgrave Macmillan.

Sanz, C. and K. Morgan-Short. 2004. 'Positive evidence versus explicit rule presentation and negative feedback: a computer-assisted study'. *Language Learning* 54: 35–78.

Sasaki, M. 1996. *Second Language Proficiency, Foreign Language Aptitude, and Intelligence*. New York: Lang.

Sato, C. 1985. 'Task variation in interlanguage phonology' in Gass, S. and C. Madden (eds.): *Input in Second Language Acquisition*. Rowley, MA: Newbury House.

Saville-Troike, M. 1988. '"Private speech": evidence for second language learning strategies during the "silent period"'. *Journal of Child Language* 15: 567–90.

Schachter, J. 1974. 'An error in error analysis'. *Language Learning* 27: 205–14.

Schachter, J. 1986. 'In search of systematicity in interlanguage production'. *Studies in Second Language Acquisition* 8: 119–34.

Schegloff, E., G. Jefferson, and H. Sacks. 1977. 'The preference for self-correction in the organisation of repair in conversation'. *Language* 53: 361–82.

Schieffelin, B. and E. Ochs. 1986. 'Language socialization'. *Annual Review of Anthropology* 15: 163–91.

Schmidt, R. 1983. 'Interaction, acculturation and the acquisition of communication competence' in Wolfson, M. and E. Judd (eds.): *Sociolinguistics and Second Language Acquisition*. Rowley, MA: Newbury House.

Schmidt, R. 1994. 'Deconstructing consciousness in search of useful definitions for applied linguistics'. *AILA Review* 11: 11–26.

Schmidt, R. 2001. 'Attention' in Robinson, P. (ed.): *Cognition and Second Language Instruction*. Cambridge: Cambridge University Press.

Schmidt, R. 2010. 'Attention, awareness, and individual differences in language learning' in Chan, W., S. Chi, K. Cin, J. Istanto, M. Nagami, J. Sew, T. Suthiwan, and I. Walker (eds.): *Proceedings of CLASIC 2010*. Singapore: National University of Singapore, Centre for Language Studies.

Schmidt, R. and S. Frota. 1986. 'Developing basic conversational ability in a second language: a case-study of an adult learner' in Day, R. (ed.): *Talking to Learn: Conversation in Second Language Acquisition*. Rowley, MA: Newbury House.

Schmitt, N. 1998. 'Tracking the incremental acquisition of second language vocabulary: a longitudinal study'. *Language Learning* 48: 281–317.

Schmitt, N. 2008. 'Review article: instructed second language vocabulary learning'. *Language Teaching Research* 12: 329–63.

Schumann, J. 1978a. 'The acculturation model for second language acquisition' in Gingras, R. (ed.): *Second Language Acquisition and Foreign Language Teaching*. Arlington, VA: Center for Applied Linguistics.

Schumann, J. 1978b. *The Pidginization Process: a Model for Second Language Acquisition*. Rowley, MA: Newbury House.

Schumann, J. 1980. 'The acquisition of English relative clauses by second language learners' in Scarcella, R. and S. Krashen (eds.): *Research in Second Language Acquisition*. Rowley, MA: Newbury House.

Schumann, J. 1986a. 'Locative and directional expressions in basilang speech'. *Language Learning* 36: 277–94.

Schumann, J. 1986b. 'Research on the acculturation model for second language acquisition'. *Journal of Multilingual and Multicultural Development* 7: 379–92.

Schumann, J. 1997. *The Neurobiology of Affect in Language*. Malden, MA: Blackwell.

Schumann, J. 2004a. 'Introduction' in Schumann, J. et al. (eds.): *The Neurobiology of Learning: Perspectives from Second Language Acquisition*. Mahwah, NJ: Lawrence Erlbaum.

Schumann, J. 2004b. 'Preface' in Schumann, J. et al. (eds.): *The Neurobiology of Learning: Perspectives from Second Language Acquisition*. Mahwah, NJ: Lawrence Erlbaum.

Scrivener, J. 2005. *Learning Teaching: A Guidebook for English Language Teachers*. Oxford: MacMillan Education.

Seedhouse, P. 2004. *The Interactional Architecture of the Language Classroom: A Conversation Analysis Perspective*. Malden, MA: Blackwell.

Seedhouse, P. 2005. '"Task" as research construct'. *Language Learning* 55: 533–70.

Seidlhofer, B. 2001. 'Closing a conceptual gap: the case for a description of English as a lingua franca'. *International Journal of Applied Linguistics* 11: 133–58.

Selinker, L. 1972. 'Interlanguage'. *International Review of Applied Linguistics* 10: 209–31.

Sfard, A. 1998. 'On two metaphors for learning and the dangers of choosing just one'. *Educational Researchers* 27: 4–13.

Shanks, D. 2003. 'Attention and awareness in "implicit" sequence learning' in Jimenez, L. (ed.): *Attention and Implicit Learning*. Amsterdam: John Benjamins.

Sharwood Smith, M. 1986. 'Comprehension vs. acquisition: two ways of processing input'. *Applied Linguistics* 7: 239–56.

Sharwood Smith, M. and E. Kellerman. 1986. 'Crosslinguistic influence in second language acquisition: an introduction' in Kellerman, E. and M. Sharwood Smith (eds.): *Cross-linguistic Influence in Second Language Acquisition*. Oxford: Pergamon.

Sheen, Y. 2008. 'Recasts, language anxiety, modified output and L2 learning'. *Language Learning* 58: 835–874.

Sheldon, A. and W. Strange. 1982. 'The acquisition of /r/ and /l/ by Japanese learners of English: evidence that speech production can precede speech perception'. *Applied Psycholinguistics* 3: 243–61.

Shin, S. and L. Milroy. 1999. 'Bilingual acquisition by Korean schoolchildren in New York City'. *Bilingualism: Language and Cognition* 2: 147–67.

Shintani, N. 2011. 'A comparative study of the effects of input-based and production-based instruction on vocabulary acquisition by young EFL learners'. *Language Teaching Research* 15: 137–58.

Shintani, N. 2012. 'Repeating tasks with young beginner learners'. *RELC Journal* 43: 39–51.

Shintani, N. 2015a. 'The effectiveness of processing instruction and production-based instruction on L2 grammar acquisition: A meta-analysis'. *Applied Linguistics* 36(3).

Shintani, N. 2015b. 'The incidental grammar acquisition in focus on form and focus on forms instruction for young, beginner learners'. *TESOL Quarterly* 49(1).

Shintani, N., S. Li, and R. Ellis. 2013. 'Comprehension-based versus production-based instruction: a meta-analysis of comparative studies'. *Language Learning* 63: 296–329.

Shintani, N. and R. Ellis. 2010. 'The incidental acquisition of English plural -*s* by Japanese children in comprehension-based lessons: a process-product study'. *Studies in Second Language Acquisition* 32: 607–37.

Shook, D. 1999. 'What foreign language reading recalls reveal about the input-to-intake phenomenon'. *Applied Language Learning* 10: 39–76.

Siegel, J. 2003. 'Social context' in Doughty, C. and M. Long (eds.): *The Handbook of Second Language Acquisition*. Malden, MA: Blackwell.

Singleton, D. 1987. 'Mother and other tongue influence on learner French: a case study'. *Studies in Second Language Acquisition* 9: 327–45.

Singleton, D. 1989. *Language Acquisition: The Age Factor*. Clevedon: Multilingual Matters.

Singleton, D. 1999. *Exploring the Second Language Lexicon*. Cambridge: Cambridge University Press.

Singleton, D. 2003. 'Critical period of general age factor(s)?' in García Mayo, M. and M.García Lecumberri (eds.): *Age and the Acquisition of English as a Foreign Language*. Clevedon: Multilingual Matters.

Singleton, D. 2005. 'The critical period hypothesis: a coat of many colours'. *International Review of Applied Linguistics* 10: 209–31.

Sjöholm, K. 1976. 'A comparison of the test results in grammar and vocabulary between Finnish- and Swedish-speaking applicants for English' in Ringbom, H. and R. Palmberg (eds.): *Errors Made by Finns and Swedish-speaking Finns in the Learning of English*. Abo, Finland: Department of English, Åbo Akademi. ERIC Report ED 122628.

Skehan, P. 1986. 'Cluster analysis and the identification of learner types' in Cook, V. (ed.): *Experimental Approaches to Second Language Acquisition*. Oxford: Pergamon.

Skehan, P. 1998. *A Cognitive Approach to Language Learning*. Oxford: Oxford University Press.

Skehan, P. 2002. 'Theorising and updating aptitude' in Robinson, P. (ed.): *Individual Differences and Instructed Language Learning*. Amsterdam: John Benjamins.

Skehan, P. 2009. 'Modelling second language performance: integrating, complexity, accuracy, fluency and lexis'. *Applied Linguistics* 30: 510–32.

Skehan, P. 2011. *Researching Tasks: Performance, Assessment, Pedagogy*. Shanghai: Shanghai Foreign Language Education Press.

Skehan, P. (ed.). 2014a. *Processing Perspective on Task Performance*. Amsterdam: John Benjamins.

Skehan, P. 2014b. 'The context for researching a processing perspective on task performance' in Skehan, P. (ed.): *Processing Perspective on Task Performance*. Amsterdam: John Benjamins.

Skehan, P. and P. Foster. 1999. 'The influence of task structure and processing conditions on narrative retellings'. *Language Learning* 49: 93–120.

Skilton-Sylvester, E. 2002. 'Should I stay or should I go? Investigating Cambodian women's participation and investment in adult ESL programs'. *Adult Education Quarterly* 53: 251–86.

Skinner, B. 1957. *Verbal Behaviour*. New York: Appleton Century Crofts.

Snow, C. and M. Hoefnagel-Höhle. 1978. 'The critical age for language acquisition: evidence from second language learning'. *Child Development* 49: 1114–28.

Spada, N. 1986. 'The interaction between type of content and type of instruction: some effects on the L2 proficiency of adult learners'. *Studies in Second Language Acquisition* 8: 181–99.

Spada, N., L. Jessop, W. Suzuki, Y. Tomita, and A. Valeo. 2014. 'Isolated and integrated form-focused instruction: effects on different types of L2 knowledge'. *Language Teaching Research* 18(4).

Spada, N. and P. Lightbown. 1993. 'Instruction and the development of questions in L2 classrooms'. *Studies in Second Language Acquisition* 15: 205–224.

Spada, N. and P. Lightbown. 1999. 'First language influence and developmental readiness in second language acquisition'. *The Modern Language Journal* 83: 1–21.

Spada, N. and Y. Tomita. 2010. 'Interactions between type of instruction and type of language feature: A meta-analysis'. *Language Learning* 60: 263–308.

Sparks, R., L. Ganschow, and J. Javorsky. 2000. 'Déjà vu all over again: a response to Saito, Horwitz, and Garza'. *The Modern Language Journal* 84: 251–9.

Sparks, R., J. Patton, L. Ganschow, and N. Humbach. 2009. 'Long-term crosslinguistic transfer of skills from L1 to L2'. *Language Learning* 59: 203–43.

Sridhar, S. and K. Sridhar. 1986. 'Bridging the paradigm gap: second language acquisition theory and indigenized varieties of English'. *World Englishes* 5: 3–14.

Stockwell, R. and J. Bowen. 1965. *The Sounds of English and Spanish*. Chicago: Chicago University Press.

Stockwell, R., J. Bowen, and J. Martin. 1965. *The Grammatical Structures of English and Spanish*. Chicago: Chicago University Press.

Suchert, A. 2004. 'The neurobiology of attention' in Schumann, J., S. Crowell, N. Jones, N. Lee, S. Shuchert, and L. Wood (eds.): *The Neurobiology of Learning: Perspectives from Second Language Acquisition*. Mahwah, NJ: Lawrence Erlbaum.

Swain, M. 1985. 'Communicative competence: some roles of comprehensible input and comprehensible output in its development' in Gass, S. and C. Madden (eds.): *Input in Second Language Acquisition*. Rowley, MA: Newbury House.

Swain, M. 1995. 'Three functions of output in second language learning' in Cook, G. and B. Seidlhofer (eds.): *Principle and Practice in Applied Linguistics: Studies in Honour of H. G. Widdowson*. Oxford: Oxford University Press.

Swain, M. 1998. 'Focus on form through conscious reflection' in Doughty, C. and J. Williams (eds.): *Focus-on-form in Classroom Second Language Acquisition*. Cambridge: Cambridge University Press.

Swain, M. 2000. 'The output hypothesis and beyond: mediating acquisition through collaborative dialogue' in Lantolf, J. (ed.): *Sociocultural Theory and Second Language Learning*. Oxford: Oxford University Press.

Swain, M. 2006. 'Languaging, agency and collaboration in advanced second language learning' in Byrnes, H. (ed.): *Advanced Language Learning: The Contributions of Halliday and Vygotsky*. London: Continuum.

Swain, M. and S. Lapkin. 1995. 'Problems in output and the cognitive processes they generate: a step towards second language learning'. *Applied Linguistics* 16: 371–91.

Swain, M. and S. Lapkin. 2002. 'Talking it through: two French immersion learners' response to reformulation'. *International Journal of Educational Research* 37: 285–304.

Swain, M., and S. Lapkin. 2007. 'The distributed nature of second language learning: a case study' in Fotos, S. and H. Nassaji (eds.): *Focus on Form and Teacher Education: Studies in Honour of Rod Ellis*. Oxford University Press.

Swan, M. 1994. 'Design criteria for pedagogic language rules' in Bygate, M., A. Tonkyn and E. Williams (eds.): *Grammar and the Language Teacher*. New York: Prentice Hall.

Swan, M. 2005. 'Legislating by hypothesis: the case of task-based instruction'. *Applied Linguistics* 26: 376–401.

Takahashi, S. 1996. 'Pragmatic transferability'. *Studies in Second Language Acquisition* 18: 189–223.

Tarone, E. 1982. 'Systematicity and attention in interlanguage'. *Language Learning* 32: 69–82.

Tarone, E. 1983. 'On the variability of interlanguage systems'. *Applied Linguistics* 4: 143–63.

Tarone, E. 1985. 'Variability in interlanguage use: a study of style-shifting in morphology and syntax'. *Language Learning* 35: 373–403.

Tarone, E. 1988. *Variation in Interlanguage*. London: Edward Arnold.

Tarone, E. and G. Liu. 1995. 'Situational context, variation, and second language acquisition theory' in Cook, G. and B. Seidlhofer (eds.): *Principle and Practice in Applied Linguistics: Studies in Honour of H. G. Widdowson*. Oxford: Oxford University Press.

Tarone, E. and B. Parrish. 1988. 'Task-related variation in interlanguage: the case of articles'. *Language Learning* 38: 21–44.

Tavakoli, P. and P. Foster. 2011. 'Task design and second language performance: the effect of narrative type on learner output'. *Language Learning* 61: 37–72.

Taylor, B. 1975. 'The use of overgeneralization and transfer learning strategies by elementary and intermediate students of ESL'. *Language Learning* 25: 73–107.

Thomas, J. 1983. 'Cross-cultural pragmatic failure'. *Applied Linguistics* 4: 91–112.

Tomasello, M. and C. Herron. 1988. 'Down the garden path: inducing and correcting overgeneralization errors in the foreign language classroom'. *Applied Psycholinguistics* 9: 237–46.

Tomlin, R. and V. Villa. 1994. 'Attention in cognitive science and second language acquisition'. *Studies in Second Language Acquisition* 16: 183–203.

Toth, P. 2006. 'Processing instruction and a role for output in second language acquisition'. *Language Learning* 56: 319–85.

Towell, R., R. Hawkins, and N. Bazergui. 1996. 'The development of fluency in advanced learners of French'. *Applied Linguistics* 17: 84–119.

Trahey, M. and L. White. 1993. 'Positive evidence and preemption in the second language classroom'. *Studies in Second Language Acquisition* 15: 181–204.

Tran-Chi-Chau. 1975. 'Error analysis, contrastive analysis and students' perceptions: a study of difficulty in second language learning'. *International Review of Applied Linguistics* 13: 119–43.

Trofimovich, P., A. Ammar, and E. Gatbonton. 2007. 'How effective are recasts? The role of attention, memory, and analytical ability' in Mackey, A. (ed.): *Conversational Interaction in Second Language Acquisition*. Oxford: Oxford University Press.

Trofimovich, P., E. Gatbonton, and N. Segalowitz. 2007. 'A dynamic look at L2 phonological learning: seeking processing explanations for implicational phenomena'. *Studies in Second Language Acquisition* 29: 407–48.

Trude, A. and N. Tokowicz. 2011. 'Negative transfer from Spanish and English to Portuguese pronunciation: the roles of inhibition and working memory'. *Language Learning* 61: 259–80.

Truscott, J. and M. Sharwood-Smith. 2011. 'Input, intake, and consciousness'. *Studies in Second Language Acquisition* 33: 497–528.

Tseng, W., Z. Dörnyei, and N. Schmitt. 2006. 'A new approach to assessing strategic learning: the case for self-regulation in vocabulary acquisition'. *Applied Linguistics* 27: 78–102.

Tseng, W. and N. Schmitt. 2008. 'Toward a model of motivated vocabulary learning: a structural equation modelling approach'. *Language Learning* 58: 357–400.

Tudor, I. 2001. *The Dynamics of the Language Classroom*. Cambridge: Cambridge University Press.

Ullman, M. 2001. 'The declarative/procedural model of lexicon and grammar'. *Journal of Psycholinguistic Research* 30: 37–69.

Ur, P. 1996. *A Course in Language Teaching: Practice and Theory*. Cambridge: Cambridge University Press.

Ushioda, E. 2001. 'Language learning at university. Exploring the role of motivational thinking' in Dörnyei, Z. and R. Schmidt (eds.): *Motivation and Second Language Acquisition*. Honolulu, HI: University of Hawai'i Press.

Ushioda, E. 2009. 'A person-in-context relational view of emergent motivation, self and identity' in Dörnyei, Z. and E. Ushioda (eds.): *Motivation, Language Identity and the L2 Self*. Bristol: Multilingual Matters.

VanPatten, B. 1990. 'Attending to form and content in the input'. *Studies in Second Language Acquisition* 12: 287–301.

VanPatten, B. 1996. *Input Processing and Grammar Instruction in Second Language Acquisition*. Norwood, NJ: Ablex.

VanPatten, B. 2004a. 'Input-processing in second language acquisition' in VanPatten, B. (ed.): *Processing Instruction: Theory, Research, and Commentary*. Mahwah, NJ: Lawrence Erlbaum.

VanPatten, B. 2004b. *Processing Instruction: Theory, Research, and Commentary*. Mahwah, NJ: Lawrence Erlbaum.

VanPatten, B. 2007. 'Input processing in adult second language acquisition' in VanPatten, B. and J. Williams (eds.): *Theories in Second Language Acquisition: An Introduction*. Mahwah, NJ: Lawrence Erlbaum.

VanPatten, B. and T. Cadierno. 1993. 'SLA as input processing: a role for instruction'. *Studies in Second Language Acquisition* 15: 225–43.

VanPatten, B. and S. Oikennon. 1996. 'Explanation vs. structured input in processing instruction'. *Studies in Second Language Acquisition* 18: 495–510.

VanPatten, B. and J. Williams. (eds.). 2007. 'Introduction' in *Theories in Second Language Acquisition*. Mahwah, NJ: Lawrence Erlbaum.

Varonis, E. and S. Gass. 1985. 'Non-native/non-native conversations: a model for negotiation of meaning'. *Applied Linguistics* 6: 71–90.

Vásquez, C. and J. Harvey. 2010. 'Raising teachers' awareness about corrective feedback through research replication'. *Language Teaching Research* 14: 421–443.

Veronique, G. 2013. 'Socialization' in Herschensohn, J. and M. Young-Scholten (eds.): *The Cambridge Handbook of Second Language Acquisition*. Cambridge: Cambridge University Press.

Verspoor, M., K. de Bot, and W. Lowie. 2011 (eds.). *A Dynamic Approach to Second Language Development*. Amsterdam: John Benjamins.

Vygotsky, L. 1978. *Mind in Society*. Cambridge, MA: MIT Press.

Vygotsky, L. 1986. *Thought and Language* (Newly revised and edited by Kozulin, A.). Cambridge, MA: MIT Press.

Wang, Z. 2014. 'Online time pressure manipulations' in Skehan, P. (ed.): *Processing Perspective on Task Performance*. Amsterdam: John Benjamins.

Wardhaugh, R. 1970. 'The contrastive analysis hypothesis'. *TESOL Quarterly* 4: 123–30.

Weiner, B. 1992. *Human Motivation: Metaphors, Theories and Research*. Newbury Park, CA: Sage.

Wenger, E. 1998. *Communities of Practice: Learning, Meaning, and Identity*. Cambridge: Cambridge University Press.

Wesche, M. 1981. 'Language aptitude measures in streaming, matching students with methods, and diagnosis of learning problems' in Diller, K. (ed.): *Individual Differences and Universals in Language Learning Aptitude*. Rowley, MA: Newbury House.

Wharton, G. 2000. 'Language learning strategy use of bilingual foreign language learners in Singapore'. *Language Learning* 50: 203–43.

White, L. 1987. 'Markedness and second language acquisition: the question of transfer'. *Studies in Second Language Acquisition* 9: 261–86.

White, L. 1991. 'Adverb placement in second language acquisition: some effects of positive and negative evidence in the classroom'. *Second Language Research* 7: 133–61.

White, L. 2003. *Second Language Acquisition and Universal Grammar*. Cambridge: Cambridge University Press.

Widdowson, H. G. 1979. 'The significance of simplification' in Widdowson, H. G. *Explorations in Applied Linguistics*. Oxford: Oxford University Press. Previously published in *Studies in Second Language Acquisition* 1.

Williams, J. 2005. 'Learning with awareness'. *Studies in Second Language Acquisition* 27: 269–304.

Williams, M. and R. Burden. 1997. *Psychology for Language Teachers*. Cambridge: Cambridge University Press.

Williams, M. and R. Burden. 1999. 'Students developing conceptions of themselves as language learners'. *System* 83: 193–201.

Willing, K. 1987. *Learning Styles and Adult Migrant Education*. Adelaide: National Curriculum Resource Centre.

Willis, D. and J. Willis. 2007. *Doing Task-based Teaching*. Oxford: Oxford University Press.

Winitz, H. 1981. *The Comprehension Approach to Foreign Language Instruction*. New York: Newbury House.

Winke, P. 2013. 'The effects of input enhancement on grammar learning and comprehension: a modified replication of Lee (2007) with eye-movement data'. *Studies in Second language Acquisition* 35: 323–52.

Winke, P., A. Godfried, and S. Gass. 2013. 'Introduction to the special issue: eye-movement recordings in second language acquisition research'. *Studies in Second Language Acquisition* 35: 205–12.

Wode, H. 1976. 'Developmental sequences in naturalistic L2 acquisition'. *Working Papers on Bilingualism* 11: 1–13.

Wode, H. 1977. 'The L2 acquisition of /r/'. *Phonetica* 34: 200–17.

Wode, H. 1981. *Learning a Second Language: An Integrated View of Language Acquisition*. Tübingen: Gunter Narr.

Wode, H., A. Rohde, F. Gassen, B. Weiss, M. Jekat, and P. Jung. 1992. 'L1, L2, L3: continuity vs. discontinuity in lexical acquisition' in Arnaud, P. and H. Bejoint (eds.): *Vocabulary and Applied Linguistics*. Basingstoke: Macmillan.

Wong Fillmore, L. 1976. 'The second time around: cognitive and social strategies in second language acquisition'. Unpublished PhD dissertation, Stanford University.

Wray, A. 2000. 'Formulaic sequences in second language teaching: principle and practice'. *Applied Linguistics* 21: 463–89.

Yashima, T. 2002. 'Willingness to communicate in a second language: the Japanese EFL context'. *Modern Language Journal* 86: 54–66.

Yilmaz, Y. 2012. 'The effects of explicit correction and recasts on two target structures via two communication modes'. *Language Learning* 62: 1134–69.

Yoshida, M. 1978. 'The acquisition of English vocabulary by a Japanese-speaking child' in Hatch, E. (ed.): *Second Language Acquisition*. Rowley, MA: Newbury House.

Young, R. 1988. 'Variation and the interlanguage hypothesis'. *Studies in Second Language Acquisition* 10: 281–302.

Young, R. and R. Bayley. 1996. 'VARBUL analysis for second language acquisition research' in Bayley, R. and D. Preston (eds.): *Second Language Acquisition and Linguistic Variation*. Amsterdam: John Benjamins.

Young, R. and C. Doughty. 1987. 'Negotiation in context: a review of research' in Lantolf, J. and A. Labarca (eds.): *Research in Second Language Learning: Focus on the Classroom*. Norwood, NJ: Ablex.

Young, R. and E. Miller. 2004. 'Learning as changing participation: discourse roles in ESL writing conferences'. *Modern Language Journal* 88: 519–35.

Yuan, F. and R. Ellis. 2003. 'The effects of pre-task and online planning on fluency, complexity and accuracy in L2 monologic oral production'. *Applied Linguistics* 24: 1–27.

Zhang, X. and J. Lantolf. 2014. 'Natural or artificial: is the route of L2 development teachable'. *Language Learning*: Special Issue 1.

Ziegler, N. 2015. 'Synchronous computer-mediated communication and interaction'. Ms. under review.

Zuengler, J. and K. Cole. 2005. 'Language socialization and second language learning' in Hinkel, E. (ed.): *Handbook of Second Language Teaching and Learning*. Mahwah, NJ: Lawrence Erlbaum.

# Index